Understanding English as a Lingu

CW00821813

Published in this series

Understanding English as a Lingua Franca

BARBARA SEIDLHOFER

OXFORD
UNIVERSITY PRESS

OXFORD
UNIVERSITY PRESS

Great Clarendon Street, Oxford OX2 6DP, United Kingdom

Oxford University Press is a department of the University of Oxford.
It furthers the University's objective of excellence in research, scholarship,
and education by publishing worldwide. Oxford is a registered trade
mark of Oxford University Press in the UK and in certain other countries

ISBN: 978 0 19 437500 9

Printed in Great Britain by Ashford Colour Press Ltd.
This book is printed on paper from certified and well-managed sources

For Henry Widdowson, sine qua non

Acknowledgements

Over the years of writing this book, I have been fortunate in receiving help and encouragement from many friends and colleagues.

When I first put the idea for this book to Cristina Whitecross a decade ago, she saw the point immediately and she has given the project continuous support ever since. I have also greatly benefited from her expert editorial advice in getting this book into shape for publication. My thanks, too, to the OUP team, particularly Julia Bell and Ann Hunter, who sensitively shepherded the book through its last phase of copy-editing and production, and to Nora Dorn, who perceptively prepared the index.

Several readers have given me valuable feedback on the whole manuscript or parts of it and so helped me to improve the text. I would like to thank Janina Brutt-Griffler, Sandy McKay, Anne Burns, as well as an anonymous reviewer for their time and expertise. Jennifer Jenkins not only generously commented on the manuscript in its original and revised versions but has also been an ever-dependable source of information and encouragement, and a partner in spirited debates over many years. It has been a great pleasure to see Jennifer's and my own research students getting to know each other; together with those of Anna Mauranen. A new generation of scholars including Martin Dewey, Alessia Cogo, Elina Ranta, Susanne Ehrenreich, Beyza Björkman, Jagdish Kaur, and several others are demonstrating that the study of ELF continues to thrive and to attract sharp and inquisitive minds.

Among the researchers who have made a particularly significant contribution to ELF studies are my colleagues here in Vienna, where they provide a highly inspiring and mutually supportive environment. Marie-Luise Pitzl, Angelika Breiteneder, and Stefan Majewski were in at the very beginning of the VOICE project, and they and the other 'Voices'—Theresa Klimpfinger, Ruth Osimk, and Michael Radeka—have been a pleasure to work with, both individually as researchers and as an incredible team, helped by a number of able assistants. Most of them have also given me constructive feedback on different chapters. Cornelia Hülmbauer, my co-researcher on the DYLAN project, as well as Kathrin Kordon, Julia Lichtkoppler, Heike Böhringer, Anita Wolfartsberger, and Claudio Schekulin have all given me their support, too, as have several other doctoral and MA students, through the expertise and enthusiasm with which they also conduct their own research on ELF.

Further afield, several researchers who have shared an interest in ELF for quite some time have, of course, contributed to my thinking, in particular Juliane House, Karlfried Knapp, Kurt Kohn, Andy Kirkpatrick, Robin

Walker, Maria Grazia Guido, Alan Firth, Christiane Meierkord, and the late Werner Hüllen. Other colleagues have supported me by their openness and willingness to engage with ELF issues from the perspective of their own complementary areas of interest and expertise. These include Ulrich Ammon, Suresh Canagarajah, Ron Carter, Guy Cook, Jim Cummins, Zoltan Dörnyei, Gibson Ferguson, Susan Gal, Saran Kaur Gill, Claus Gnutzmann, David Graddol, Matthias Hüning, Ken Hyland, Frauke Intemann, Friederike Klippel, Claire Kramsch, Diane Larsen-Freeman, Georges Lüdi, Tim McNamara, Marko Modiano, Lorenza Mondada, Kumiko Murata, Daniel Perrin, Edgar Schneider, Barbara Soukup, Arturo Tosi, Sue Wright, Yasu Yano, my colleagues in all the DYLAN teams—and two outstanding scholars, no longer with us and much missed: Christopher Brumfit and Willis Edmondson.

I have also benefited from discussions, in conference rooms and around dinner tables, about various aspects of and perspectives on ELF with several colleagues and friends who tend to take a more sceptical view of ELF, especially Peter Trudgill, Michael Swan, and Robert Phillipson. The views of Braj Kachru and Randolph Quirk have been a stimulating challenge and have helped me to clarify my own understanding of ELF.

I would also like to thank Guy Aston, Vicki Hollett, and Leo van Lier for advice on specific issues, and Moira Runcie and Barnaby Newbolt for their trust in offering additional financial support through OUP for the VOICE project.

By far the greatest debt I owe is to the person to whom this book is dedicated— and who will be as happy as I am that it is finally going into print!

In various parts of this book, I have drawn on papers in which I discussed ideas I also deal with here, mainly Seidlhofer 2001, 2002, 2003a, 2005, 2007, 2009a, 2009c, Seidlhofer and Widdowson 2009, and Widdowson and Seidlhofer 2003.

Preface: why, what, what not, who for?

...we should STRIVE to reach the: (.) english? as the native speaker(s) does. it's the AIM. or maybe it's impossible

...i i think that the MOST important thing is to have a ce:rtain level of understanding. since we understand us who cares about the rules.

Two extracts from *VOICE, the Vienna-Oxford International Corpus of English*

It is now accepted as a fact that English, as a cause and consequence of globalization, currently serves as the most widespread means of international and intercultural communication that the world has ever seen. But this does not mean it is uncontroversial. People are uncertain about what kind of English this is, who it 'belongs' to, and how they should react to it. Even those who use English as a lingua franca (ELF) on a daily basis differ markedly in their attitudes to it, as the above extracts show. These extracts come from a workshop discussion at an international student conference and are just two examples of the kind of usage that now occurs in so many interactions in the world. This phenomenon is so widespread and so crucial for international communication that it has become imperative to take it seriously and try to find out how and why ELF functions as it does. This is what this book sets out to do: to arrive at 'a certain level of understanding' of ELF by both seeking to explain the concept as such and describing how ELF users interact amongst themselves, how they understand each others' ELF. Understanding ELF in both these senses is not an easy task to tackle in one book, and so while this is not a bulky volume it has been long in the making, as the years spent writing it were also the years in which ELF research gathered considerable pace and momentum. Although discussion about the 'ownership' of English has been going on for quite some time, this issue and its implications, so central to an understanding of ELF, still stand in need of conceptual clarification. This has become more pressing as the number of ELF users continues to increase with accelerating globalization.

Nobody is likely to deny that English has, in one way or another, in some shape or form, become a global lingua franca in the contemporary world. But acknowledging the existence of ELF is, of course, not the same as approving of it, and two kinds of disapproval have been widely expressed, both related to this question of ownership. The first concerns the way in which English is perceived as an alien invasive force, occupying the space of other languages and so threatening linguistic and cultural diversity. The second kind of disapproval concerns the form, or forms, that English takes in its international uses, perceived as its various 'deviations' from the established standard of 'proper' English, which are seen to undermine the very integrity and intelligibility of the language itself.

These reactions are oddly contradictory. The first assumes that English is being transferred essentially intact into various contexts of use, carrying with it the sociocultural and political values that are encoded in it. In this view, the very use of the language involves complicity in its hegemonic influence, whether intended or not. The second reaction assumes that, far from remaining intact, the language is dispersing and deteriorating into reduced and deviant versions of the original. According to one reaction, it is English that threatens its non-native users, and according to the other it is the non-native users who threaten English. Though contradictory, what both reactions have in common is a refusal to accept that English, like any natural language, is dynamic and variable and could not otherwise function as a means of communication at all.

It is surely strange that in the face of the obvious spread of ELF, the view still widely persists that the only English that should be given recognition for international use is the standard language as defined by its native speakers. One explanation may be the inertia of norms, combined with vested interests. But I think the most significant factor that has prevented real progress towards a fresh conceptualization of English is the surprising disinclination of sociolinguists to engage seriously with the naturally adaptive process of language variation that ELF represents. From other perspectives, the critical discussion of ELF has received important impulses from thinking in many fields that are not so much concerned with the linguistics of English, but more with sociopolitical and cultural issues, including globalization, multilingualism, cultural and postcolonial studies, often in conjunction with the advocacy of linguistic diversity and human rights. But what has been conspicuously lacking is a serious consideration of the significance of ELF from within the communities of academics and practitioners concerned with English who are—or should be—most directly affected by it: descriptive linguists in various areas of expertise such as lexicogrammar, historical linguistics or sociolinguistics, and applied linguists and practitioners concerned with areas such as language education policy, language pedagogy, assessment, or interpreting. Whatever the explanation for this relative neglect, the consequence is that debates on the meta-level about the pros and cons of ELF have only created an illusion that we are facing up to the issues, while really allowing things to stay as they are. As long as the language itself remains untouched, and untouchable, this is unlikely to change.

What I shall argue in this book is that English as a lingua franca needs to be understood as an entirely 'ordinary' and unsurprising, sociolinguistic phenomenon. There is, as I have indicated, a good deal of resistance to understanding it as such, and indeed reluctance to try to understand it at all. The reasons for these reactions can be traced to deep-rooted attitudes to English that go back a long way. So although the global spread of English as a lingua franca belongs very much to the present, it needs to be put in perspective by reference to the past. This is why I have dedicated a good deal of space in this book to a discussion of how ELF relates to, and challenges, established ideas about what English is and how one might go about describing it.

As far as questions of teaching and learning are concerned, it is an obvious fact that ELF users, though instructed to learn and use the standard language at school very often do not do so but make use of English in other ways for one reason or another. But for what reason? One might argue that it is because teachers have failed to get them to learn the language properly and that they are therefore sent out into the world with a linguistic deficiency. This argument would lead us to suppose that, in spite of a long history of such failure, an approach to teaching (hitherto undiscovered) might be devised one day that does get learners to conform to the standard language. It also assumes as self-evident that conforming to the standard language is what users of English need to do in order to be communicatively competent. The use of ELF, however, provides abundant evidence that the 'deficient' English that learners acquire can be put to efficient use as a communicative resource.

Such evidence has generally been regarded as inadmissible in the teaching of English as a foreign or other language. It has usually been taken as axiomatic that the only kind of communication that can be sanctioned is that which conforms to norms of linguistic correctness. This in turn is based on the assumption that the main reason for learning English, as with any other foreign language, is to communicate with its native speakers (or rather a subset of them whose English corresponds to the approved norms of usage). But this ignores the fact that English is unlike other languages: as is now well attested, most of its users do not mainly, or even at all, engage with native speakers, and so these norms are no longer communicatively appropriate. Nor does the assumption hold that there are inextricable links between 'a language' and 'a culture'. This is not to deny that English does carry associations of a colonial past and a capitalist present, for instance when Australian, British, or North American television series are broadcast the world over. But looking closely at how people now use ELF we can see how they generally do this without becoming 'anglicized'—if anything, they are 'de-anglicizing' their English.

So understanding the nature and implications of ELF involves taking account of a range of issues about language ownership, variation, and pedagogy. But not only is it, as I have indicated, relevant to such areas as sociolinguistic research and language teaching but also to a whole spectrum of practical and theoretical issues both within and beyond academia concerning, for example, language assessment, translation and interpreting, language and education policy, international research and development, professional communication, and diplomatic mediation and peace-keeping. Of course, each of these areas of activity has its own concerns and priorities and, as I have frequently experienced at conferences, these will usually give rise to different reactions to ELF, often mutually contradictory. It would be surprising if this book did not meet with the same diversity of reactions.

While I obviously will not be able to satisfy all expectations a book on this topic may raise, I can make it as clear as possible what my intention was in writing it. To begin with, the book focuses on spoken ELF, as it is by studying the spoken language that emergent processes of variation and change can be most readily observed. Once these processes are understood, more work will have to be done on how they are relevant to various kinds of written communication. Of course, the book does not aim to offer a comprehensive description of spoken ELF usage as such. Its perspective is conceptual rather than descriptive and although a good deal of description appears, this is meant to exemplify various phenomena and processes, and especially, to show that none of these are actually unique to ELF. It was tempting to provide more description of data in VOICE, the Vienna-Oxford International Corpus of English, which has been developed alongside the writing of this book over recent years. But this would not have been appropriate to my main purpose, and anyway more and more description is now becoming available in individual studies. My primary concern is to present a clear argument for a well founded conceptualization of ELF, and I have homed in on the issues that seem most important for this purpose. There was much more that I would have liked to include, but then left out so as not to distract from the main line of argument—not only more description but more theoretical discussion—and more controversy. So any readers with a special interest in one particular area, be it sociolinguistics, language variation and change, language learning and teaching, social psychology, anthropology, sociology, or any other area are likely to feel that their interests have not been adequately represented, that the book is either 'too linguistic' or 'not linguistic enough'. But I would hope that it nevertheless gives some indication of how an understanding of ELF is relevant to their concerns.

I mentioned earlier that this book has been long in the making. When I first announced my intention to compile a corpus of ELF interactions at an English studies conference in 2000, many found this a strange idea. A decade on, ELF research has really taken off: with the corpora VOICE (now accessible online) and ELFA, the corpus of English as a Lingua Franca in Academic Settings, more and more descriptive work being published and studies undertaken for PhD theses and MA dissertations becoming available, a series of annual international conferences, and a newly founded international journal, the *Journal of English as a Lingua Franca*, the field of ELF study is thriving. As is of course the phenomenon that is being studied as ELF continues to spread. Most of its users are not much concerned about the controversial issues their activities give rise to: they just get on with using ELF in their daily personal and professional lives as the most effective, and often only, means of communication available to them.

The primary purpose of this book is to raise awareness in (mainly applied) linguists and language teaching practitioners about the significance of ELF.

I do not claim that this is the first or only attempt at doing this. There have been a number of articles and book chapters dealing with conceptual questions regarding ELF, and there are now a few excellent sources that provide insights into recent empirical ELF research to date, and these have obviously informed my own thinking. In writing this book, I have also drawn and expanded on earlier work I have published myself in articles and book chapters (listed in the Acknowledgements section) and integrated them into the discussion. This procedure has enabled me to connect up-to-date studies with ELF work as it has evolved over recent years and to make connections with areas of research outside ELF, but relevant to it, such as second language acquisition, socio-linguistic variation, World Englishes, and earlier conceptual and empirical approaches to English for international communication.

ELF is a controversial topic. Both as a phenomenon and as an area of study it has aroused a good deal of animated debate and animosity. It has been said that the study of ELF is ideologically motivated, and if this means that ELF researchers have particular ways of thinking about the way the world is and about desirable goals and actions, then of course it is. But so is every other way of thinking about 'English'. Ideologies can either be aimed at change in society, or at adherence to conformity. Of course, change is more notice-able than continuity or stagnation, and this is what defenders of the general validity of Standard English tend to overlook. Whether one believes in the need for change in established ways of thinking, or for preserving the status quo, there is some obligation, I would think, to make explicit the grounds for the belief through argument and empirical evidence. This is what I have tried to do in this book in putting forward a case for change. But it is not a propaganda exercise to promote the study of ELF as a new 'paradigm', or a new 'ELF model' for teaching. And it certainly does not have the agenda of furthering the global dominance of English at the expense of other languages. Its purpose, as its title indicates, is to try to get at a fuller understanding of this global phenomenon and to consider what implications this understand-ing might have for our thinking about the role of English alongside other languages and the most appropriate approach to teaching and learning it.

Vienna
April 2011   Barbara Seidlhofer

Contents

I

What is this thing called English?

...the English language no longer belongs numerically to speakers
of English as a mother tongue, or first language. The ownership
(by which I mean the power to adapt and change) of any language
in effect rests with the people who use it, whoever they are,
however multilingual they are, however monolingual they are.

C. J. BRUMFIT: *Individual Freedom in Language Teaching: Helping
Learners to Develop a Dialect of Their Own*

1.1 English as an international language (EIL)

This book is about English as an international language. This, of course,
is a topic that has been extensively discussed elsewhere, and I take as
my starting point comments made by David Graddol in his wide-ranging study *English Next* (Graddol 2006). In his introduction to the book,
Graddol summarizes the main findings of his earlier treatment of the topic
(Graddol 1997) in a list of bullet points. The first of these is that 'the future
development of English as a global language might be less straightforward
than had been assumed'. He then comments as follows:

It is difficult to recapture the sense of complacency evident amongst some native
English speakers in the mid-1990s for whom even the first of these points provided
a challenge. The global 'triumph' of English was understood as a done deal. And,
given the widespread recent discussion in the west about the global impact of China,
it is equally difficult to appreciate the general lack of awareness, little more than five
years ago, of the rapid transformation already then taking place in East Asia. But the
world has been changing so fast that it scarcely seems to be the same place as that of
the 1990s[1]...
(Graddol 2006: 10)

What has not changed, Graddol observes, is the enormous global demand for
learning English, with learners becoming ever more numerous, and beginning

at an ever earlier age. The popularity of English has become a fact so familiar that it is hardly newsworthy any more. However, he continues:

> But at what point do we pause, take a fresh look at what is happening and decide that what is going on now is not just 'more of the same'. After scrutinising current trends, including those which have not yet reached the statistical yearbooks, I conclude that *there has been a significant—even dramatic—qualitative change: one that may be taking the language in a very new direction.*
> (Graddol 2006: 10f., emphasis added)

It is precisely this 'very new direction' that the present book sets out to explore. Its basic message is that the dramatic 'qualitative change' Graddol is referring to is due to the role that English now plays as a global lingua franca, and that this must have significant consequences for the language itself and the way we conceive of it.

Of course nobody would dispute the fact that English has spread all over the globe to become the predominant international language. This, after all, is the principal reason why it figures as the primary foreign or other language in school curricula all over the world. In the early 21st century, English is not only an international language, but *the* international language.

It is impossible to give exact figures for 'speakers of English', not least because just how you define who qualifies as a speaker is bound to be arbitrary.[2] So while estimates of speakers are bound to be vague, the orders of magnitude seem to be fairly clear. Here are some figures, which taken together certainly amount to the conclusion that 'native speakers' of English are clearly outnumbered by 'non-native speakers': Crystal (2003b: 69) gives the following estimates for speakers of English in terms of Kachru's model of 'concentric circles' (Kachru 1992): 'Inner Circle', i.e. first language in, for example, UK, USA: 320–380 million; 'Outer Circle', i.e. additional language, in India, Nigeria: 300–500 million; 'Expanding Circle', i.e. foreign language, in China, Russia: 500–1000 million.[3] This means that 'one in four of the world's population are now capable of communicating to a useful level in English' (Crystal 2006a: 425) and in turn, that roughly only one out of every four users of English in the world is a 'native speaker' of the language. While this insight should not lead us to ignore the fact that about three quarters of the world's population are left without such command of English and often without even any prospect of gaining access to it, it does not alter the fact that the spread of English, geographically but also in terms of social strata and domains of use, is on a scale that no other language has ever reached in the history of the planet. The German author Beneke (1991: 54) adds another way of looking at this when he estimates that 80 per cent of all communication involving the use of English as a second or foreign language does not involve any 'native speakers' of English. This was as long ago as 1991, and bearing in mind the growing figures for speakers in the 'Outer' and 'Expanding Circles', the percentage Beneke quotes is likely to be even higher now.

The global spread of English is unprecedented and unparalleled, and comparisons that are often made between the role of English in today's world and the role of Latin, French, Arabic, and other lingua francas in earlier times simply do not hold. No other language called 'world language' has ever had both the global expansion and the penetration of social strata and domains of use that English now has. This fact may sometimes irk speakers of other 'big' languages, such as those of French in the European Union, but even they cannot but reluctantly acknowledge it. The reluctance in part at least would seem to stem from the view that the reasons for the rapid ongoing growth of English lie in the economic and political power, past and present, of English speaking nations, especially the United States, and so to concede the international role of the language is, to a degree, to succumb to this power. The view that the spread of English is necessarily a function of linguistic imperialism is one that I shall return to in a later chapter. For the moment, we need to note that the international significance of the language cannot be explained in such simple and seemingly straightforward terms.

The term 'English as an international language' (EIL) is usually understood as covering uses of English within and across Kachru's 'Circles', for intranational as well as international communication. But English is international in two very different ways: it has been 'exported' to many regions of the world by its 'native' speakers, primarily through colonization, and so has invaded these places. It has, however, to an even larger extent been 'imported' by people all over the world who decided to learn it as a useful language in addition to their first language(s).

In the first case, generally as a consequence of colonial rule, English has been taken up in various places in the world and institutionalized as a *local* means of *intra-national* communication in countries in what Kachru (1992) refers to as the 'Outer Circle': we might call these manifestations of *localized EIL*. It is now generally acknowledged that the variations in usage that have naturally developed endonormatively in the communities of this 'Outer Circle' have their own legitimacy, and are, in effect, different Englishes in their own right; and a good deal of work has been devoted to recording and codifying their distinctive character. Schneider's 2007 book *Postcolonial English* conveys this sense of the local, and locale, very clearly. In discussing the perspectives of the settlers and the indigenous populations in (former) colonies, he explains that:

> [...] the essential point [...] is that both groups who share a piece of land increasingly share a common language experience and communication ethnography, and thus the forces of accommodation are effective in both directions and in both communities, and result in dialect convergence and increasingly large shared sets of linguistic features and conventions.
> (Schneider 2007: 32)

These 'shared sets of linguistic features and conventions' then serve to define essentially nation-based local linguacultural norms as the basis for delimiting distinct post-colonial varieties with their independent identities. This is how 'English' becomes (World) 'Englishes', with countable distinct entities. Thus it is now established as entirely appropriate to speak of Indian English, Nigerian English, or Singapore English, for example.[4]

But apart from this pluralized, localized EIL, English has also become international as a, indeed *the*, common *global* means for *inter-national* communication. This then is not localized but globalized EIL, which is characterized by continuously negotiated, hybrid ways of speaking. Other than members of 'Outer Circle' varieties, speakers do not orient to their local speech communities but are involved in de-territorialized speech events, so that establishing common linguacultural ground, what Schegloff (1972) calls 'formulating place', becomes an intrinsic part of every encounter. Globalized EIL, as a variable way of using English can be observed, for example, in business meetings, tourist encounters, diplomatic negotiations, conference discussions, and so on.

This distinction between localized EIL and globalized EIL is one that Kachru's model does not capture, for the use of globalized EIL is something that people engage in across all three 'concentric circles': from the 'Inner Circle', where English is the majority first language (for example, the UK, USA), from the 'Outer Circle', where English is an additional language (India, Nigeria, Singapore) and—as the largest group—from the 'Expanding Circle', where English is taught and learnt as a foreign language (from Afghanistan, Bolivia, China, Denmark, Ethiopia, . . . to Yemen). In these contexts, English is used as a convenient common means of communication among people with different native languages. It is the massive and increasing extent of these uses, stimulated by developments in electronic communication and enhanced mobility, that has been primarily responsible for establishing English globally as the predominant international language—English as a Lingua Franca.

1.2 What's in a name? A note about terminology

A cautionary note about terminology is called for here. There is always the problem that in discussing any phenomenon one needs to use terms, at least to start with, that are in common currency and will be recognized. This however does not necessarily imply an acceptance of the concepts the labels express, nor does it indicate a lack of awareness of their complexity and their shortcomings. And of course, any categorization, and the terms that result from it, has to be based on a process of abstracting from the details of 'reality', of homing in on those qualities and distinctions that seem relevant for the matter under consideration while ignoring others.

Thus in the above pages, I make use of the well known terminological distinction that Kachru makes between English speakers in the 'Inner', 'Outer', and 'Expanding Circles'. I do so because the study of World Englishes has been a vigorous field of research for a long time and it can therefore be expected that most readers will be familiar with the Kachruvian circles model. What is often called the 'World Englishes paradigm' thus offers a framework of thinking about the role, and especially the history, of English in the world that many can relate to, a convenient way of referring to a very rough distinction between English used as a native language (ENL), English used as a additional/second language in post-colonial settings, where English has a special and often official role (ESL),[5] and English being learnt and used elsewhere as a foreign language (EFL). As we shall see later, however, the three circles model, which Kachru himself only put forward as a tentative suggestion, is conceptually problematic and open to criticism. Despite this, however, no alternative models and terms that have been put forward have gained widespread acceptance and currency in the literature. So far, the Kachruvian terms have remained well established, even in the writings of those that have voiced incisive criticism of them.[6] Indeed, it seems more constructive to discuss the shortcomings of existing and familiar terminology than simply to invent new labels and so leave untouched the issues thrown up by the existing terminology. It should be noted therefore that my use of these terms at the moment is only a starting point and a provisional convenience so that readers can connect with something familiar: hence the use of quotation marks up to this point to indicate these are taken to be useful labels rather than valid concepts. Having briefly explained my reasons for using these terms despite their shortcomings, I shall dispense with quotation marks from now on for better readability. The problems connected with these terms will, of course, be discussed in more detail in subsequent chapters.

Other terms I have used that call for comment are 'native speaker' and 'non-native speaker'. Here too I added quotation marks to indicate that these terms are also provisional and conceptually problematic. The problems, as with Kachru's circles, are of course not only to do with the definitional, semantic meaning, with what the terms actually denote, but with the connotations that they have come to carry, and with the considerable ideological baggage they have accumulated over a long time. The term 'native speaker' is notoriously elusive of definition and, rather like the term 'Inner Circle' connotes evaluative associations that it is difficult to avoid. This is perhaps even more the case with the term 'non-native': a definition by negation that is often felt to suggest some sort of deficit. But these connotations have little to do with what the terms themselves mean. Obviously enough, a negation only indicates a deficit if what it negates is regarded as desirable or necessary. Surely very few people will regard the negative prefix in words such as *non-violent, non-sectarian, non-predatory, non-toxic*, etc. as indicating a deficit. *Domestic*, or *combustible*, or *existent* denote neither 'positive' nor 'negative' qualities, and the same is true of their opposites, *non-domestic, non-combustible, non-existent*. How these adjectives are seen will depend entirely on the specific context. And I would argue that the same holds, in principle, for *native* and *non-native* premodifying the noun *speaker*: whether these adjectives indicate an advantage or a disadvantage will also depend on the context. One of the main objectives of this book is to explore just how the contexts and purposes of the use of English, and the numbers and kinds of its speakers, have changed so dramatically over recent decades that the connotations of the terms *native speaker* and *non-native speaker* are bound to change too. As we shall see, when we consider the important roles English has come to play in people's lives all over the world outside 'native speaker' communities, being a 'native speaker' ceases to be an asset.

There is much published criticism of the terms 'native' and 'non-native', which I do not need to repeat here. The issues involved are discussed from the perspective of English as a lingua franca, and alternative labels offered, in Jenkins 2000: 6ff. While I fully endorse Jenkins' reasoning, I do not generally adopt alternative labels at this point, one reason being that this would result in a confusing mixture of terminology, particularly because I often quote from secondary literature that uses the traditional labels. The main reason though is that I have come to the conclusion that it is not even necessary to use quotation marks when I employ the terms myself. This is because I take them to mean very simply what they actually denote (rather than what they have come to connote for many): a native-speaker of English is somebody whose L1 is English, and a non-native speaker of English is somebody who has an L1, or L1s, other than English. One thing we know about the non-native speakers (but not about native speakers) is that they are at least bilingual.

I am convinced that the connotations of the terms 'native' and 'non-native' will change, and are already changing. Until a couple of decades ago, in a world and mindset that basically only had room for the two categories indicated by the labels, 'native' tended to have mainly positive associations, suggesting speakers' property rights and superior competence, while the negative particle in 'non-native' pointed to the absence of these desirable assets. However, precisely due to the unprecedented global spread of English, in so many functions and guises, a much more differentiated view of 'speakers' has been evolving. The phenomenon of English as the first truly global language, and globalization with its consequences for how we now live and communicate, is bound to lead to such a shake-up of our traditional ideas of what constitutes 'a language' and 'legitimate speakers' that the terms themselves will simply become obsolete. So my own feeling is that, after so much agonizing about the terms 'native' and 'non-native', the problem will actually resolve itself in that new and appropriate words will emerge. It may well be that in the not too distant future we will be wondering why we ever thought that we needed these terms at all.

These issues will be taken up in subsequent chapters. For the time being, it is worth noting that there is a lexical gap where a word for 'non-native' speaker is needed, just as there is—as will be discussed in section 1.5 below—a conceptual gap where there should be a concept for 'non-English-as-a-native-language' ('non-ENL'). An important 'test' as to whether this book fulfils its purpose will be whether readers who came to it with very categorical ideas about the impermeability of Kachru's circles and the advantages of native speakers of English feel the need not just to question the validity of these categories but to perform a much more radical shift of orientation commensurate with new perspectives—and new problems, inevitably—that the globalized world presents us with.

1.3 English as a lingua franca (ELF)

The term 'lingua franca' is usually taken to mean 'any lingual medium of communication between people of different mother tongues, for whom it is a second language' (Samarin 1987: 371).[7] Note though that this definition applies to local/regional lingua francas[8] as they exist in many parts of the world, usually serving speakers of particular, fairly stable combinations of first languages rather than the truly global phenomenon of English as a lingua franca (ELF). These lingua francas often have no native speakers, and this notion is carried over into some definitions of English as a lingua franca, as in the following two examples:

[ELF is] a 'contact language' between persons who share neither a common native tongue nor a common (national) culture, and for whom English is the chosen foreign language of communication.
(Firth 1996: 240)

ELF interactions are defined as interactions between members of two or more different linguacultures in English, for none of whom English is the mother tongue.
(House 1999: 74)

While these definitions could be said to highlight a particularly striking feature of ELF, namely that the majority of its users are not native speakers of English, it has to be remembered that of course ELF interactions include interlocutors from the Inner and Outer Circles, and take place in these contexts too, such as meetings at the United Nations headquarters in New York, tourist cruises around Sydney harbour, or academic conferences in Hyderabad. I therefore prefer to think of ELF as *any use of English among speakers of different first languages for whom English is the communicative medium of choice, and often the only option.* Due to the numbers of speakers involved worldwide, this means that ENL speakers will generally be in a minority, and their English will therefore be less and less likely to constitute the linguistic reference norm. But it is important to note that this conceptualization of ELF is a functional and not a formal one (and the relationship between functions and forms will be a prominent theme of this book as a whole).

Whatever the setting that ELF is used in, we find ourselves in an unprecedented linguistic situation. For the first time in history, a language has reached truly global dimensions, across continents, domains, and social strata, and as a consequence, it is being shaped, in its international uses, at least as much by its non-native speakers as its native speakers. This process has obviously been accelerated by the dramatic expansion of electronic communication through the internet, which has so far enhanced the social prestige attributed to typical global users of English—global players, indeed—although there are already indications that English may well not retain the status of the primary internet language (Crystal 2006b; Graddol 2006: 44). For the time being, though, the role of English as a global lingua franca is growing. Brumfit describes how ELF users:

are an increasing significant group who operate in an increasingly global economy which has an impact on the economy in all countries [... and] the internet, mobile phones and other technology increasingly establishes the potential for use of English which is quite independent of the controls offered by traditional educational systems, publishing outlets and radio/television.
(Brumfit 2002: 5)

In other words, 'in the world out there', ELF has taken on a life of its own, in principle independent to a considerable degree of the norms established by its native users, and that is what needs to be recognized. ELF would appear to be the preferred term for this phenomenon as it makes a link with the first, 'original' lingua franca spoken as a kind of trade language in the Mediterranean region between the 15th and 19th centuries. This was 'a pidgin, probably based on some Italian dialects in its earliest history, and included elements from Spanish, French, Portuguese, Arabic, Turkish, Greek and Persian' (Knapp and Meierkord 2002: 9). As Jenkins (2007: 1) points out, this 'plurilinguistic composition, then, clearly exemplifies an intrinsic and key feature of lingua francas: their hybrid nature'. Contemporary ELF, with the majority of its speakers coming from first-language (L1) backgrounds other than English, is also bound to be particularly hybrid due to the large numbers of first languages of its users. Thus obviously the most powerful group in the sense of 'agents of language change' (Brutt-Griffler 1998: 387) in the development of ELF is that constituted by the non-native speakers of English.

In the quotation given at the beginning of the chapter Brumfit explains that, in the light of what we know about sociolinguistics, this is an incontrovertible fact:

... the English language no longer belongs numerically to speakers of English as a mother tongue, or first language. The ownership (by which I mean the power to adapt and change) of any language in effect rests with the people who use it, whoever they are, however multilingual they are, however monolingual they are. The major advances in sociolinguistic research over the past half century indicate clearly the extent to which languages are shaped by their use. ... Statistically, native speakers [of English] are in a minority for language use, and thus in practice for language change, for language maintenance, and for the ideologies and beliefs associated with the language—at least in so far as non-native speakers use the language for a wide range of public and personal needs.
(Brumfit 2001: 116)

That 'non-native speakers use the language for a wide range of public and personal needs' is well documented (see Crystal 2003b, 2004; Graddol 1997, 2006; Jenkins 2009; Kachru *et al.* 2006; Kirkpatrick 2010b; Melchers and Shaw 2003; Mesthrie and Bhatt 2008), so it would seem reasonable and uncontroversial that they should be accorded the right to take an active role in the development of the language, and to be taken seriously as legitimate users, not just learners or speakers of an interlanguage in need of improvement towards the norms of a standard native variety. However, while the international nature of English in the first sense as locally diverse forms in Outer Circle settings (localized EIL) has been the subject of mainstream linguistic enquiry for some time now, the same cannot be said of the global spread of the language in the second sense (globalized EIL, i.e. ELF).

There has, of course, been a general awareness of ELF as part of the more general recognition that the international role of English calls for a re-thinking of its established status. It has taken quite some time, but fundamental concerns to do with the global spread and use of English have eventually become an important focus of research in applied linguistics. The debate has been conducted particularly vigorously over the last two decades, variously highlighting cultural, ecological, socio-political, educational, and psychological issues. The recognition that a huge portion of uses of English occurs in contexts where it serves as a lingua franca, far removed from its native speakers' linguacultural norms and identities, has been an important leitmotif in this discussion. And yet, the implications of these insights have not been followed through. This becomes most evident when we consider how knowledge of and about the language is conceived of, reproduced, passed on to future users, in various contexts in which English is taught. While the global role of English is now increasingly being referred to in teacher education curricula, in ELT conferences, and in teaching materials, this special status of English has had virtually no effect (so far) on how the language is formulated as a subject in syllabuses and teaching materials. This is true despite that fact that there is applied linguistics writing specifically dealing with ELT that has argued for quite a while now that fresh thinking about the subject 'English' is called for—see in particular Widdowson 2003. But the daily practices of most of the millions of teachers of English worldwide seem to have largely remained untouched by the developments outlined above: very few teachers 'on the ground' take part in this meta-level discussion, and most classroom language teaching per se has changed remarkably little considering how much the discourse *about* it has. This is to say that for teachers of English across the globe, the main knowledge-base and point of reference has not moved with the tide of applied linguistics research: the language as used by Inner Circle speakers and codified in grammars, dictionaries, and textbooks remains, by and large, unquestioned as the only legitimate object of study and target of learning, certainly in regions where English is taught as a foreign language (i.e. in Kachru's Expanding Circle).[9] This state of affairs has resulted in an incongruity in the discourse of ELT which, although it is giving rise to some misgivings and unease, is hardly addressed directly and proactively. The problem, then, is a mismatch between what has happened to the role of English in the world on the one hand and how it is thought of as 'a language' and a language subject on the other. It is the overarching argument of this book that this incongruity can only be remedied by creating and accepting a new concept of ELF in its own right.

1.4   Towards a reconceptualization of English

The ground for this reconceptualization has been prepared in many areas of applied linguistics. In the discourse of language planning and education policy, monoculturalism, monolingualism, monomodels, and monocentrism have yielded to multiculturalism, multilingualism, polymodels, and pluricentrism (cf. Auer and Wei 2009; Bamgbose, Banjo, and Thomas 1995; Bhatia and Ritchie 2006; Blackledge 2005; Ferguson 2006; Heller 2007; Kachru 1992; Kirkpatrick 2010a; McArthur 1998; Smith and Forman 1997; Wright 2004). Journals and handbooks on multilingualism and multiculturalism are booming. European sociolinguists have expressed their concern about 'English only? in Europe' (Ammon *et al.* 1994), and a lively debate has been gathering momentum about the place of English compared to other languages in foreign language education, particularly as to whether English poses a threat to the European ideals of individual plurilingualism and societal multilingualism (Ammon 2006; Anderman and Rogers 2005; House 2003; Phillipson 2003a; Seidlhofer 2003a; Tosi 2005; van Els 2005). In 2006, the European Commission gave substantial funding to two large research projects on multilingualism: DYLAN (Dynamics of Languages and Management of Diversity) and LINEE (Languages In a Network of European Excellence) (see Böhringer, Hülmbauer, and Vetter 2010). In a plenary talk of a LINEE conference, Susan Gal (2010) argues that 'there is today a transformation in the sociolinguistic regime of Europe: from coercive monolingualism to coercive multilingualism', resulting in a regime of 'superdiversity'.[10] All this would seem to indicate, then, that we must have come a long way from a 'Western world' mindset which constrained us to think of a language as typically instantiated in its standard form and by monolingual native speakers within national borders. But have we?

A useful area to consult with regard to this question, and one closely related to language teaching, is second language acquisition (SLA) research. Changes have certainly been happening in this field of study. As long ago as 1997, 'mainstream' SLA was criticized for adopting:

a skewed perspective on discourse and communication, which conceives of the foreign language speaker as a deficient communicator struggling to overcome an underdeveloped L2 competence, striving to reach the 'target' competence of an idealized native speaker.
(Firth and Wagner 1997: 285)

Since then, important arguments have been put forward for going 'beyond the native speaker' (Cook 1999), and for addressing the monolingual bias of traditional SLA work: albeit still a minority research agenda in SLA, the insight is gradually taking hold that the minds of (monolingual) L1 users are different from those of L2 users, who by definition are at least bilingual—and of course multilinguals outnumber monolinguals in the world at large. It follows that automatically expecting non-native speakers of a language to strive to get as close as possible to the linguistic competence of the native speakers is a non-starter, especially in the case of English, which is spoken by more non-native than native speakers, and whose native speakers are often monolingual and thus not the best models. Instead, what needs to be understood is the phenomenon of multicompetence (Cook 2002). Indeed, since the late 20th century, a very considerable diversification of SLA study has taken hold (as discussed in Firth and Wagner 2007; Swain and Deters 2007; Zuengler and Miller 2006) based on research in sociocultural theory and situated learning (Lantolf and Thorne 2006; Pavlenko and Lantolf 2000; Sfard 2008), social identity (Norton 2000) and multicompetence/L2 user theory (Cook 2002, 2003; Herdina and Jessner 2002; Jessner 2006; Kecskes and Papp 2000; Todeva and Cenoz 2009). However, despite the momentous changes that globalization and technology have brought about in the linguistic make-up of the world, the target competence implicit in the multifarious approaches to SLA research has hardly been debated, and therefore is, by and large, still assumed to be some notion of 'native speaker'. As Jenkins puts it:

...the main focus of enquiry for the majority of SLA researchers is, nevertheless, on finding ways of facilitating the acquisition of as near native-like competence as required by the learner, teacher, or 'system'...
(Jenkins 2006a: 139)

While 'native' competence (whatever that may mean, for it has never been satisfactorily defined) may be an appropriate target for ESL contexts and for foreign languages, it clearly is not in the case of lingua francas, of which ELF currently is the prime example. Far more people learning English today will be using it in international contexts rather than in just English-speaking ones. Therefore, taking account of this difference between second language/foreign language and lingua franca would be crucial in the formulation of relevant target competences, and should thus have considerable consequences for SLA theorizing in general. However, the sociolinguistic reality of ELF has not, it would seem, impacted on mainstream SLA (see, for example, the 2009 special issue of *Applied Linguistics* devoted to 'Complexity, Accuracy, and Fluency (CAF) in Second Language Acquisition Research' (Volume 30, Number 4). Ironically, English is the language most studied in SLA research—but in the guise of ESL/EFL, not ELF. It is as if it did not matter which 'E' is studied: English is English is English. This means that there is a blatant mismatch between the purpose for which English is most learnt in the world, namely ELF use, and what is focused on in SLA, namely ESL/EFL. What makes things worse is that there is then a kind of backwash effect in that the insights gained from studying the learning of English as a second or foreign language are assumed to be relevant for *all* language teaching, including that of future ELF users, thus giving rise to recommendations for pedagogy which are, at best, anachronistic.

Turning now to the literature about the teaching of English and teacher education, it is true of course that this has undergone major changes over recent decades. Whereas language teachers used to be mainly educated about and preoccupied with various approaches to the description and instruction of the target language, we now find a much wider variety of concerns with the kind of socio-political and other issues referred to above demanding at least as much attention as the language proper. This has led to a broader conception of the profession, and to a discourse of ELT in which notions of 'correctness', 'norms', 'standards', 'mistakes', and 'authority' seem to have given way to a preoccupation with more educational/pedagogic concerns characterized by terms such as 'learner-centredness' (Tudor 1996), 'learner autonomy' (Dam 2001), 'teacher cognition' (Borg 2003; Breen *et al.* 2001), '(self-) reflection/ reflective practice' (Pennycook 1999a; Schön 1983; Atkinson and Claxton 2000), 'action research' (Burns 2007), 'exploratory practice' (Allwright and Hanks 2008), and 'critical, transformative, and listening critical pedagogy through English' (Pennycook 1994: 326).

The most important consequence of the global spread of English for the teaching of English has been the questioning of the native speakers' 'owner-ship of English', referred to in the Brumfit quotation at the beginning of this chapter, and pursued in Widdowson (1994, 2003). A discussion has gathered momentum which highlights the potential special expertise non-native teachers have because they know the target language as a foreign language, share with their students the experience of what it is like to try and make it their own, often through the same first language/culture 'filter', and can represent relevant role models for learners (see Braine 1999; Brutt-Griffler and Samimy 1999; Kamhi-Stein 2004; Kramsch 1998; Llurda 2005; McKay 2002; Medgyes 1994/1999; Rampton 1990; Seidlhofer 1999; Sifakis 2007).[11]

Changes in the perception of the role of English in the world have significantly influenced thinking about approaches to teaching (if not necessarily the teaching itself) and led to an increased socio-political and intercultural awareness. There is a myriad of books and articles on 'English as an international language' and 'intercultural communication' going back over a quarter of a century (see, for example, Abbott and Wingard 1981; Brumfit 1982, 2001; Byram and Fleming 1998; Canagarajah 1999, 2005; Gnutzmann 1999; Holliday 1994; Kramsch 1993; Kramsch and Sullivan 1996; McKay 2002; Quirk and Widdowson 1985; Smith 1981; Strevens 1980). As far as linguistic models as targets for learning are concerned, these have now at least begun to figure as a concern and matter for reflection on the meta-level, and some important writings have appeared on this theme over recent years, including Block and Cameron 2002; Canagarajah (2007b); Dewey and Cogo (2007); Ferguson (2009); Gnutzmann and Intemann (2008); Jenkins (2000, 2006b, 2007); Holliday (2005); Kirkpatrick (2007a and b); McKay and Bokhorst-Heng (2008); Rubdy and Saraceni (2006); Saxena and Omoniyi 2010;

Seidlhofer (2003a, 2004); Sifakis (2007); Widdowson (2003). Although this is an impressive list of books and articles whose titles promise to make a difference to the field, these publications differ considerably in the extent to which they actually tackle the issue of the language content as such. Specific proposals addressing the question as to just what might constitute learning goals instead of the increasingly questioned native-speaker model are scarce indeed. And when we look at curricula, textbooks, and reference materials to draw conclusions as to what constitutes actual course content, we see that native-speaker models remain firmly entrenched.

The situation briefly sketched here regarding approaches to teaching and teaching content could thus be summarized by saying that the discourse about English teaching has changed, but the actual content of courses has not: the discourse makes little effective contact with the realities of practical pedagogy. This leaves English as a subject in a kind of limbo, caught between innovations in the discourse about the teaching of the language and a lack of innovation in terms of the actual language content. This state of affairs allows the symbolic power of 'native-speaker English' to assert itself beyond its historical relevance, and to be reproduced (in the sense of Bourdieu and Passeron 1970) throughout ELT institutions and practices worldwide.

Closely connected with issues of ownership, because of its gate-keeping function, is the question of language testing. When native-speaker models are recognized as having limited relevance in the light of the global role of English, this is bound to raise questions about the linguistic norms for testing. A lively debate about precisely this issue has only just now begun in applied linguistics: these are, then, 'testing times for testers'—the title of Jenkins' first paper in the 'Point and counterpoint' exchange with Lynda Taylor in *ELT Journal* (Jenkins 2006c, 2006d; Taylor 2006). This intensive discussion encapsulates all the difficult issues that the emergence of ELF has set in train—for testing research as well as the testing industry.[12] Here we come to a point which will be discussed in more detail below, namely that there is an urgent need for much more descriptive work on how ELF is successfully used in different contexts. This is bound to affect in very significant ways just *what* is, or can be, tested. In recent years, the field of language testing, just like the other areas we have been looking at, has also widened considerably. So apart from the question of linguistic norms for testing, there is now a great deal of work being undertaken on the broader social dimension of language testing. This constitutes a relatively new research focus concerned with the societal 'surveillance' functions of tests, in particular the impact these have as instruments for the creation and maintenance of boundaries and the construction of identities (McNamara and Roever 2006; Shohamy 2001). However, even the most critical voices in language testing, such as those represented in Section 3 of the *International Handbook of English Language Teaching* (Cummins and Davison 2007) entitled 'Assessment and Evaluation in ELF: Shifting Paradigms and Practices' do not call into question the actual linguistic target models that underlie the tests which they examine and find problematic. Shohamy (2007) concludes her contribution thus:

Despite the power of tests, English language teachers can adopt more resistant roles in their own English language teaching context, demanding greater participation and representations in the decision making process, decisions not only about what is tested, but how and why.

(Shohamy 2007: 529)

The question I would want to raise is how far English language teachers do have a say in 'what is tested'. They may have on a fairly trivial level, such as which items taught in the course feature in a test. But the big *what* in terms of *whose* English is being tested in settings all over the world, no matter whether in the Inner, Outer, or Expanding Circles, has hardly been challenged.

1.5   A conceptual gap

This brief account of recent developments relevant for the teaching of English in a globalized world demonstrates that a fundamental re-orientation in the teaching of English ought surely to have been under way for a while now: from correctness to appropriateness, from parochial domesticity and exclusive native-speaker norms to global inclusiveness and egalitarian licence to speak in ways that meet diverse local and situational needs. But, as we have seen, this has not happened. While pedagogic ideas about teaching, learning, and testing on the one hand and sociolinguistic ideas about the independence and prestige of indigenized varieties of English on the other may have undergone quite dramatic changes, while the empire has been writing back and non-native teachers have been developing and asserting an enhanced sense of their professional identities, assumptions about the 'E' itself in ELT/TEFL/TESOL have remained curiously unaffected by these momentous developments. In the teaching of English worldwide, what constitutes a valid target is still determined with virtually exclusive reference to native-speaker norms. True, at least the perception of what constitutes 'native speakers' has been widening with reference to the Outer Circle. But the question in most urgent need of exploration has hardly been addressed, namely just what the 'English' is that is being taught and learnt in this emerging global era, how it squares with the socio-political and socio-economic concerns discussed in the profession, and what its relevance is for the subject taught in classrooms all over the world. In short, English as a lingua franca has not really entered people's consciousness as a new and alternative concept of 'English'. What we are faced with instead is a conceptual gap.

It seems to me that this insistence on target language models may have to do with a process that Breen (2007) explores in a paper about teacher development entitled 'Appropriating Uncertainty'.[13] On the one hand, it is obvious that the major geopolitical, technological, and social changes that are making themselves felt so acutely will necessarily entail changes in ELT as well. On the other hand, this requirement for change may be perceived as too overwhelming, particularly when it affects the very core of the subject that English teachers teach, the language itself. So paradoxically, the fact that the reality of 'English' has been changing so rapidly and radically under the influence of globalization may be the reason why prescriptive models of the target language are particularly resistant to change. It is as if the teaching profession, seeing that changes are unavoidable, reacts not by rethinking the *what*, but rather the *how*, the latter being relatively more manageable, more subject to local control, and providing some measure of continuity. By addressing questions of the 'how', professionals can be 'seen to be doing things':

> The concept of performativity has been proposed by Lyotard (1984) in his analysis of significant changes in contemporary society. He argues that the metanarratives guiding education until recently have been criteria related to truth and justice. His analysis reveals that both have been replaced by a preoccupation with action: with how things are done. ... *Performativity entails that personal and professional worth is reduced to what individuals can be seen to do and to assessable criteria of how competent they are in doing it.*[14]
> (Breen 2007: 1071, emphasis added)

However, 'doing things' is not enough, it is also high time that major conceptual adjustments are made. This can perhaps best be illustrated with a couple of examples. The way 'English' is typically talked about in the relevant literature, even in writings about such central issues as non-native teachers and English as a global language, bears out the fact that the *what* is not being called into question: English as a native language (ENL) has remained the default referent, implicitly or explicitly. Here are two examples from well known books:

> ... we suffer from an inferiority complex caused by glaring defects in our knowledge of *English*. We are in constant distress as we realize how little we know about *the language* we are supposed to teach.
> (Medgyes 1994: 40, emphases added)

> I believe in the fundamental value of a common language, as an amazing world resource which presents us with unprecedented possibilities for mutual understanding, and thus enables us to find fresh opportunities for international cooperation. In my ideal world, everyone would have fluent command of a single world language. I am already in the fortunate position of being a fluent user of *the language* which is most in contention for this role, and have cause to reflect every day on the benefits of having it at my disposal.
> (Crystal 2003b: viii, emphasis added)

Consider what Medgyes and Crystal[15] mean by 'English' and 'the language'. Clearly this will depend to some degree on what they regard as 'a language', and there is, of course, no definitive answer to this question (see Makoni and Pennycook 2007), especially in the case of 'English' in all its guises all over the globe. What constitutes a language, and in particular 'English as a global language', is necessarily a discursive construct in need of deconstruction, and we shall go into this question in later chapters. The point I wish to make here about the above two extracts is that 'English' simply is not problematized in them, and this has the effect of throwing readers back on the implicit, default referent, whether this is the one intended by the authors or not: one particular kind of English, namely that used by educated native speakers like Crystal himself. What he is 'a fluent speaker' of is ENL (English as a native language), and this English is then bound to be understood to be 'the language in most contention' for the role of 'a single world language', thus assuming that the 'E' is the same in ENL and ELF. But of course they cannot be. ENL is full of conventions and markers of in-group membership such as characteristic pronunciations, specialized vocabulary, idiomatic phraseology, and references and allusions to shared experience and the cultural background of particular native-speaker communities.

And this is precisely the reason why educated non-native speakers of English (such as Medgyes himself) are so resigned and defeatist about the 'glaring defects' in their knowledge of it: they cannot, by definition, be members of that NS community, no matter how hard they try, no matter how long they study. But the crucial thing is that for most contexts in which English is used around the world, the native-speaker community is irrelevant anyway. If non-native speakers using English as an international language (i.e. the vast majority) could bring themselves to embrace the much more relevant model of a competent ELF speaker, their supposed disadvantage would become an advantage enjoyed by bi- or multilingual speakers as the far better adapted communicators in intercultural interactions. They would benefit from what Kramsch (1997) calls the 'privilege of the non-native speaker'.

It seems clear, then, that every time we talk and write about 'English as a global language' we quite inevitably bring into play some rather fundamental issues. But the fact that they are fundamental has, so far at least, not meant that they get addressed explicitly. On the contrary, the general picture is one of lack of awareness: we are faced here with a conceptual mismatch between outdated ideas about native-speaker privilege and the overdue acknowledgement of the reality of ELF: that, as pointed out by House (1999: 74), ELF is successfully used by countless non-native speakers in 'influential frameworks', i.e. 'global business, politics, science, technology and media discourse' and as Brumfit (above) indicates '[t]he ownership (by which I mean the power to adapt and change) of any language in effect rests with the people who use it'. Yet, entrenched attitudes and established traditional views of native-speaker authority are still asserted and accepted very widely.

It is important to note that what I am arguing for here is the need to be aware of, and conceptually clear about, different concepts of 'English' in accordance with what has already been happening in the development of the language—something that some linguistic lay people in areas such as business seem to find much easier than linguists and language teachers (see Ehrenreich 2009). I do not wish to be misunderstood to be making recommendations for any particular alternative linguistic forms, or for immediate drastic changes in ELT for all learning purposes. However, it is high time for applied linguists and (English) language teachers to develop fresh ways of thinking critically about what 'English' is, given its changed role and status in the world.

1.6 English: foreign language versus lingua franca

The crucial task, then, is to introduce conceptual clarity into what is at times a somewhat confused and emotional debate about the implications, linguistic and otherwise, of the global spread of English. One way of doing this is to keep apart the notions of 'English as a foreign language' (EFL) and 'English as a lingua franca' (ELF). The acronyms are treacherously similar, but the concepts are quite different.

EFL first. In settings where English is conceived of as a foreign language, much like Italian as a foreign language or Japanese as a foreign language, the focus is very much on where the language comes from, who its native speakers are, and what cultural associations are bound up with it. For most languages, this is the predominant or even only option: the more limited the use of a language is outside the areas where it is spoken natively, the more relevant the FL orientation will be—for instance, in the cases of Albanian, Basque, Czech, or Thai. But also when you learn and use English as a foreign language, you are encouraged to strive to do 'as the natives do', you accept their authority as distributors of their language, on which they have a sort of franchise, with institutions such as the British Council, the Fulbright Program, and publishers based in English-speaking countries acting as the main 'distributing agents'. Conceiving of 'English' in this way is the obvious option for learners and users of English who have a particular interest in (one of the) English-speaking cultures, and wish to identify with the community that speaks it, for instance because they love the literature, have friends there, or because they want to study in or emigrate to a country where English is a dominant/majority/official language. In this case, the linguacultural norms of (the respective) native speakers of English may indeed be the relevant model. Here it is to be expected that NNSs (learners and teachers) will defer to NS norms of using the language—not only in terms of what is grammatically correct, but also of what is situationally appropriate and typical, with all the fine nuances, resonances, and allusions embedded in shared knowledge and experience acting as 'membershipping devices'. It follows that if, as a 'non-native' speaker, you make a bid for membership of this NS community, you strive to abide by these norms and are judged by your success in doing so—and you expect to be praised or criticized, accepted or rejected by native speakers of English.

ELF, English as a lingua franca, is guided by quite different needs and wants. It is spreading in various and varied manifestations and adapted to the needs of intercultural communication, in settings such as a business meeting in São Paolo with participants from Brazil, China, Germany, and the USA, or a press conference with participants with over 20 different first languages at the EU Commission in Brussels, perhaps with speakers switching to and fro between English and French. The main objective here is to make use of the (only) language shared by all interactants, the lingua franca, in order to achieve the fullest communication possible. In such situations, as happens all across the globe in millions of interactions every day, it is usually taken for granted that speakers will have a command of English that varies along a continuum from minimal to expert, but that they regard themselves as capable of accomplishing the task at hand. One could say that speakers have decided for themselves that they can meet the requirements of participation in a particular speech event. What then happens is that the participants gauge a level of language at which they can operate, and settle on ad hoc, pro tem norms that are adequate to the task and commensurate to the command of the linguistic resources they have in common. The crucial point in all this is that these norms are tacitly understood to be established during the interaction, within the current possibilities, and that they are primarily regulated by interactional exigencies, rather than by what native speakers would say, or would find correct, or 'normal', or appropriate. In such ELF interactions, participants are typically focused on co-constructing a viable modus operandi to achieve a communicative goal, whether that is negotiating a business contract, hammering out a political compromise, arguing about scientific experiments, or having a good time with a group of tourists in a seaside taverna. In such situations, it would be interactionally counter-productive, even patently absurd in most cases, for speakers to (strive to) adhere to ENL linguacultural norms when no ENL speakers may even be present. It thus follows that if, when interacting with other ELF users, you nevertheless make a bid for membership of a different, irrelevant community of ENL speakers and strive to abide by their norms, for instance by using highly idiomatic language full of (ENL) cultural allusions, this is actually likely to be perceived as a failure to adapt to the ELF situation.

In summary, we can align ways of approaching these concepts as follows:

	Foreign language (EFL)	Lingua franca (ELF)
Linguacultural norms	pre-existing, re-affirmed	ad hoc, negotiated
Objectives	integration, membership in NS community	intelligibility, communication in a NNS or mixed NNS–NS interaction
Processes	imitation, adoption	accommodation, adaptation

Table 1.1 Conceptual differences between EFL and ELF

Like any schematic representation, this table idealizes and simplifies the distinction—its purpose is to bring out the main differences more clearly in order to make them an object of reflection, not to claim that these are totally disparate, 'either-or' phenomena devoid of any elasticity or overlap. Its purpose here is to represent a conceptual framework for more detailed discussion in subsequent chapters of this book.

For the moment, the point to be made is that in order to capture the nature of English we need to acknowledge the vital role and authority of ELF users as active contributors to the development of the language by appropriating the language in a process Brutt-Griffler (2002) has termed macroacquisition, 'second language acquisition by speech communities,[16] that links language change to its spread' (ibid.: xi). Brutt-Griffler's main interest is in post-colonial settings, so she does not discuss English as a lingua franca as such. However, at a time when in many parts of the world some knowledge of English has come to be taken for granted as a kind of basic skill, it seems to be reasonable to extend the notion of macroacquisition to contexts where English is a pervasive element in the education as well as in the working lives of a large portion of the population.

But whereas there is now a vast literature not only about Inner Circle but also about Outer Circle Englishes (Platt, Weber, and Ho 1984; Kachru *et al.* 2006; Schneider 2007), larger-scale, systematic efforts to record what happens linguistically in the Expanding Circle and *across* all circles, i.e. in ELF, are only at their beginning (see below). The discrepancy is stark when we compare research into ENL with research into ELF: the general picture we get here is that there is an established English being described more and more precisely in terms of native-speaker behaviour, and then distributed. This not only does not recognize diversity but acts against it. This increasing precision in description, made possible through sophisticated technology and large corpora, is said to get closer and closer to the reality of native-speaker language use. But it is important to realize that native-speaker language use is just *one* kind of reality, and one of very doubtful relevance for lingua franca contexts.

1.7 The need for description

As long as all the descriptive effort is geared to capturing native and nativized language use, the profession's attention is deflected from the increasingly urgent issues concerning the use of English as a lingua franca. Now that the right to descriptions in their own terms has finally been recognized for nativized varieties of English in Outer Circle communities, it is high time that we granted the same right to ELF as used across all circles, including the Expanding Circle, especially in areas where the use of ELF is a fact of everyday life for large parts of the population. My contention, then, is that we must overcome the (explicit or implicit) assumption that ELF could possibly be a globally distributed, franchised copy of ENL, and take on board the notion that it is being spread, developed independently, with a great deal of variation but enough self-regulating stability to be viable for lingua franca communication. This assumption is of course one that has to be investigated empirically, but the point I wish to make here is that the need to do so has hardly been acknowledged, and accordingly efforts in this direction have been few and far between. And they have, due to the conceptual gap discussed earlier in this chapter, evoked a wide range of reactions. These will be considered at various points in this book. They include outright rejection and emotional attacks, sober acknowledgement that something long overdue is happening, great enthusiasm, and unwarranted, premature extrapolations from very limited preliminary findings to questions of pedagogy.

Talking about traditional TEFL aiming at distributing English in its established and encoded ENL forms is not to say, of course, that the description of 'E' in TEFL has not moved in the last decade or two—it has moved considerably, but in the other direction as it were, closer and closer to the home base: linguistic descriptions proper have been focusing on English as it is spoken and written as a first language.[17] Technological developments have made it possible to sharpen that focus, so that we can say with precision which features of spoken English characterize casual conversations among friends and acquaintances in specific parts of the UK (Carter and McCarthy 1997), not to mention the precision with which written and spoken genres can now be profiled by reference to the British National Corpus (BNC), the Collins COBUILD Bank of English, and the Longman-Lancaster Corpus. Such corpora make it possible to conduct extremely revealing, fine-grained analyses of native-speaker usage and are a very impressive descriptive achievement. But of course they also have the effect of further enhancing the prestige and authority of English as a native language (see also Chapters 2 and 3).

The last quarter of the 20th century saw momentous developments and indeed a great enrichment of the study of L1 English, but also of Outer Circle varieties. The sheer scale and sophistication of corpus-based descriptions have revolutionized our thinking about what constitutes legitimate descriptions of any language. In terms of products for the general public, we now have entirely empirically-based reference works such as the *Longman Grammar of Spoken and Written English,* promoted as 'Grammar for the 21st century' (Biber *et al.* 1999), the *Cambridge Grammar of the English Language* (Huddleston and Pullum 2002) and the similarly titled *Cambridge Grammar of English* (Carter and McCarthy 2006). These grammars are not all the same (see Huddleston 2008) but they are alike in that what they describe is *the* English language, and its properties are essentially the property of native speakers. The same is true of dictionaries. On the Collins Website (http://www.collins.co.uk/books. aspx?group=57) we are told: 'When you use a Collins Dictionary, you are one of the best-informed language users in the world'. But it is a very specific kind of English that the dictionary informs its users about, and one that is a far cry from the global reality of English. This limitation was also what occasioned Kachru's criticism of the *Cambridge International Dictionary of English* for using the term 'international' for referring to 'America, Britain and Australia' (Kachru 1997: 70f.)

The scope of descriptions of 'the English language' has actually widened dramatically in the last two decades, and now includes younger ENL varieties such as New Zealand and Australian English: the Australian *Macquarie Dictionary* went from its first edition in 1981 (Delbridge *et al.* 1981) to its fifth in 2009 (Butler 2009). 2008 saw the founding and the inaugural conference of the International Society for the Linguistics of English in Freiburg, Germany. The conference theme was 'The Linguistics of English: Setting the Agenda', and the programme of papers, workshops, and posters demonstrated the enormous width of that agenda, with English being examined both dia-chronically and synchronically, with both Inner and Outer Circle varieties (but not ELF) figuring prominently. While until not so long ago the only well documented varieties of English were British and North American, the International Corpus of English (ICE), founded in 1990, now includes 20 varieties of nations or regions where English is either an official language or a majority first language (http://ice-corpora.net/ice/index.htm). As Green-baum points out:

Its [ICE's] principal aim is to provide the resources for comparative studies of the English used in countries where it is either a majority first language...or an official additional language. In both language situations, English serves as a means of communication between those who live in these countries.
(Greenbaum 1996: 3, 4)

Greenbaum adds, however:

Excluded from ICE is the English used in countries where it is not a medium for communication between natives of the country.
(ibid.)

So ELF *across* Inner, Outer, and Expanding Circles (and within the Expanding Circle) is again left out of account. That this is still the way the international corpus project conceives of 'English' is confirmed by a message to prospective contributors:

We always welcome new research teams onto the ICE project, and hope that the number of teams will increase in the coming years.

...

Please bear in mind too that the ICE project collects data from countries in which English is the first language or a second official language. If this is not the case in your country, you might be interested in joining the International Corpus of Learner English (ICLE) project instead.
(Joining the ICE Project, http://ice-corpora.net/ice/joinice.htm)

While these criteria obviously make sense with regard to the design of ICE, looked at from an ELF perspective they confirm with particular force the con-ceptual gap that I have been discussing in this chapter: if it isn't either native or nativized English it must be learner English.[18]

So although 'English' is international and indeed global, the term 'inter-national English' is usually not taken to include ELF (cf. Todd and Hancock 1986; Trudgill and Hannah 2008). This means that the use of the language by the majority of its speakers, those with other first languages who use English as a lingua franca for communicating with other lingua franca speakers, is excluded from all these important descriptive programmes.

The situation that presents itself, then, is oddly contradictory and paradoxical: on the one hand, we have a very lively and prolific field of research on how 'English'—depending on the specific researcher's domain of interest and ideological orientation—is being variously spread, used, forced upon, or withheld from the world at large, coupled with assertions of local values and the importance of intercultural communication in pedagogy. On the other hand, the rapid development in computer technology that has opened up hitherto undreamt-of possibilities in language description ignores the English that is actually taken up and used locally and interculturally across the world.

What is more, these two contrary developments are interdependent and even reinforce one another: the more global the use of 'English' becomes, the greater the motivation, and of course the market, for descriptions of it. The more such products are on offer, the more these are regarded, quite rightly, as promoting the dominance of (L1) English, and thus the more forceful the attempts in (or on behalf of) the 'non-native' speaker communities to resist this imposition (cf. Canagarajah 1999 and 2005; Pennycook 1994; Phillipson 1992 and 2009; Holliday 2005).

The intellectual battles which are being fought over issues rooted in ideological positions, commercial interests, ecological concerns, and social identities go largely unnoticed by the largest group of users of English: those to whom English serves on a daily basis as a lingua franca for conducting their affairs, often entirely among so-called non-native speakers of the language, with no native speakers present at all. These are people who have learnt English as an additional language, and to whom it serves as the most useful instrument for communication that cannot be conducted in their first language, be it in business, casual conversation, science, or politics—in conversation, in print, on television, or on the internet. Wherever such interactions take place and whatever the specific motivations and uses of English as an international lingua franca, the mismatch sketched in the last two paragraphs is quite striking: ELF speakers themselves are usually not particularly preoccupied with the two prevailing research foci described above, which could be glossed 'corpus-based description of native English' and 'resisting linguistic imperialism'. They are not primarily concerned with emulating the way native speakers use their mother tongue within their own communities, nor with socio-psychological and ideological meta-level discussions. Instead, their central concerns are relevance, efficiency, and personal satisfaction in language learning and language use. As Kachru says, 'the hunger for learning the language—with whatever degree of competence—is simply insatiable' (Kachru 1997: 69). This is one reason why fighting the (ab)use of 'English' for exerting power and domination via mainstream ELT is such an enormous task: people need and want to acquire this instrument whatever the ideological baggage that comes with it—a fact acknowledged, at least implicitly, even when it is deplored, as in Canagarajah's 1999 *Resisting Linguistic Imperialism in English Teaching* (p.180f.). Another reason of course is that it is not in the interest of those who, for want of a feasible alternative, are still widely perceived as the 'source' or 'owners' of the commodity 'English' to encourage a discussion about ethical questions and the suitability of the goods they have to offer. And as long as 'English' is kept in the conceptual straightjacket of ENL, it is difficult to see how change can be proactively brought about.

For a while now, linguists, teacher educators, and teachers have been told, and have generally accepted, that 'real English' is ENL as captured and described in sophisticated analyses of large ENL corpora (see also Chapter 3). But while this English may well be 'real' for (some, certainly not all) native speakers, 'real English' in a global perspective is surely not ENL but ELF. This, then, is why there is an urgent need for rich, empirically well founded descriptions of how ELF speakers use the language in and on their own terms—or to show that this is what they are doing, and that they are communicating effectively in doing so. This is how ELF can be made a linguistic reality for academics and educators who are socialized into paying heed to 'linguistic facts': people believe what they see, so they should be enabled to see ELF in action. Detailed accounts of ELF interactions are necessary to counter the pervasive myth that adherence to ENL norms is necessary for effective intercultural communication. Only descriptions of what non-conventional forms ELF speakers actually use in their interactions can provide the basis for the more interesting and theoretically challenging research into how these forms function pragmatically, and into what is going on when people communicate via ELF across all kinds of linguacultural differences: how do they negotiate what is interactionally relevant, accommodate to each other, make creative use of their diverse linguistic repertoires, and cooperate in the co- or re-construction of the 'English' that they learnt?

The compiling of VOICE, the Vienna-Oxford International Corpus of English (VOICE 2009) was undertaken to provide such a descriptive basis. VOICE is a computer corpus of audio recordings and transcriptions of spoken ELF interactions.

Since the primary interest of ELF research is to further the understanding of how the language develops when used, predominantly but not only, by non-native speakers across the boundaries of primary speech communities, it stands to reason that the first ELF corpora should be focused on capturing how ELF is spoken rather than written. Although the compilation of a corpus of spoken data is incomparably more difficult and time-consuming than of written data, the decision to focus on spoken interactions seemed imperative, as it is in speech that variability in language is most readily discernable. The interactants' negotiation of meaning in real-time, spontaneous talk is relieved of the self-monitoring pressure of writing, and allows us to observe the use of what Labov refers to as the vernacular, where attention is paid to communicative content rather than to linguistic forms themselves (Labov 1984: 29). In addition, when the speech events are highly interactive, researchers can also gain some measure of insight into how mutual understanding among the interlocutors is co-constructed. For these reasons, observations about ELF use made in this book will usually make reference to this kind of spoken ELF.

VOICE comprises over one million words (over 110 hours) of naturally occurring, non-scripted face-to-face interactions via ELF, covering a range of domains (educational, leisure, and professional, with the latter subdivided into business, organizational, and research/science). The 151 interactions recorded in the corpus are complete speech events of various types such as conversation, interview, meeting, panel, press conference, question–answer session, service encounter, and workshop discussion. The speakers come from some 50 different (mainly but not exclusively European) first-language backgrounds, including a minority (7 per cent) of native speakers of English. The transcripts are supplemented by detailed event descriptions giving information about the nature of the speech event and the interaction taking place, as well as about the participants in these ELF interactions. The corpus is freely accessible for research purposes (http://www.univie.ac.at/voice/page/index.php). In addition, 23 recordings of transcribed speech events can also be listened to online. Examples of analyses based on VOICE will be discussed mainly in Chapters 5 and 6.[19]

1.8 Conclusion

This, then, is the challenge of ELF, and it is twofold. First, there is the need to establish it as a viable *concept* in principle: to accept that it is not a kind of fossilized interlanguage used by learners failing to conform to the conventions of Inner Circle native norms but a legitimate use of English in its own right, an inevitable development of the globalization of the language. Second, there is a need for *descriptions* of the functions and forms of ELF (which in turn will support the concept): to apply to it the considerable expertise that has so far largely been devoted to descriptions of Inner Circle English.

This book is an attempt to take up this challenge. It will investigate the conceptual and descriptive issues that I have sought to identify in this first chapter. I begin in the next two chapters with an account of established ideas about English, the conceptual status quo, so to speak. I then go on in subsequent chapters to explore alternative ways of thinking about the language, which I argue are more appropriate to its status as an international lingua franca. I will then provide examples of ELF interactions from a number of sources including VOICE and discuss how these empirical findings of actual usage compare with proposals that have been made for prescribing simplified versions of English as an international language. Finally I will consider what implications ELF might have for how the language is pedagogically designed as a subject.

Notes

1 Since Graddol wrote this, the impact of China and other countries such as India has grown even more rapidly. This state of affairs is perceived as worrying by people/countries for whom the global spread of 'their' language (English)

represents an advantage. This may explain the debates often raging, for example, in Britain (and hardly noticed elsewhere) about 'the state of the language' (see Jones and Bradwell 2007; Ostler 2010).

2   See Crystal 2003a regarding the difficulties involved in counting speakers.

3   It is interesting to compare these figures with the first edition of the book in 1997. Figures have shot up for Outer and Expanding Circle (see review by Leech in *Journal of Pragmatics* 2004: 'The second edition shows a remarkable reversal of the figures for L1 and L2 speakers: in the first edition, native speakers substantially outnumbered L2 speakers [if one regards OC as NN], whereas in the second edition the opposite is true.'). Crystal 2006a offers a very useful comparison and discussion of figures given in different sources.

4   Such a 'World Englishes' view of Outer Circle varieties obscures the fact that English in the usually linguaculturally very diverse post-colonial countries or regions functions as a lingua franca, too.

5   The acronym ESL is itself misleading as it is used differently in different parts of the world, and in different areas of research and education. So while it indicates English as a 'second language' in the sense of an (official) additional language, side by side with local/indigenous languages in post-colonial settings, it can, alternatively, also denote a 'second language' in a sequential sense, in that people of different first languages have learnt, or are learning and using English, especially in ENL settings such as Britain or the USA. In this sequential sense, the acronym ESL can sometimes also merge in meaning with EFL, with both current in language teaching circles, ESL being preferred in the USA and EFL in Britain.

6   See Jenkins 2009, especially Unit A3, for an introductory yet very thorough treatment of this.

7   I discuss the question of the relationship between ELF and the original concept of lingua franca in more detail in Chapter 4. It has been proposed (Canagarajah 2007a) that a better term for what I, and others, call ELF would be LFE—Lingua Franca English. This however, misleadingly suggests that it should be categorized in formal terms as a variety of the language, a kind of World English like Indian or Nigerian English but (to anticipate the discussion later in this book, especially in Chapter 4), ELF as I conceive of it is functionally and not formally defined: it is not a variety of English but a variable way of using it—English that functions *as* a lingua franca.

8   Purists might object to the plural form 'lingua francas', but it is now used so frequently in English, like 'formula(s)' or 'studio(s)', that it seems sensible to treat it as one English (compound) word with a regular(ized) plural –*s* suffix, much like 'chaise longues' in the furniture trade or 'pied-à-terres' in legal and real estate language.

9   Even in the Outer Circle, the acceptability of local norms for assessment has only begun to be discussed (cf. Lowenberg 2002). Note that, ironically, in the widely-used Test of English for International Communication (TOEIC), the 'I' for 'International' is part of the acronym because in the listening section, speakers of English from Australia, Britain, New Zealand, and North America can be heard, rather than exclusively from the USA. But on http://en.wikipedia.org.wiki/TOEIC we are told: 'However all the voice actors for the speaking test have lived in the United States for an extended period.' This url also contains numerous links to regional TOEIC websites.

10 I could not help noticing, by the way, that the abstracts of all five plenary lectures posted on the website of the conference entitled 'New Challenges for Multilingualism in Europe' were in English, indexing ELF as the conference language.

11 For those who find it hard to believe that these developments are indeed quite recent, it might be interesting to have a look at papers which document interactions about the 'native–non-native' question, such as Akoha *et al.* (1991), which clearly show how new and strange challenges to 'native-speakerism' seemed only a couple of decades ago, even to some applied linguists.

12 There are signs of language assessment researchers beginning to take note of ELF research: see McNamara (2011).

13 In his paper, Breen discusses ways of dealing with changes in the Zeitgeist of educational institutions that teachers are grappling with in their professional lives, but it seems to me that the analogy holds for coping with rapid and bewildering changes that affect their understanding of their subject matter, too.

14 Note that Lyotard's notion of performativity is not to be confused with Judith Butler's (see Chapter 5).

15 I hope it is clear that I am trying to make a general point here, not blaming Peter Medgyes and David Crystal in particular: I picked the two quotations from hundreds which would have made exactly the same point. This was because their books are also thematically particularly relevant for my concerns here, and declare it as their aim to contribute to open access and equity in this area. Medgyes' was a very early book on non-native teachers of English and their attitude to the language. I should also add that in recent conversations I have had with David Crystal it was clear that he takes a keen interest in ELF, and this is also borne out in his own publications (Crystal 2004; Facchinetti, Crystal, and Seidlhofer 2010).

16 A simple definition of the term *speech community* is '[t]otal set of speakers of the same (native) language' (Bussmann 1996 s.v. *speech community*). Brutt-Griffler (2002: 141) acknowledges this but goes on to explain why she finds this definition unsatisfactory, since it is not 'flexible enough to recognize levels of speech community affiliation, as well as the potential for multiple affiliations'. She therefore prefers to regard a speech community as a community 'on the basis of shared subjective knowledge' (ibid.: 23, 141ff.). I take up the issue of the definition of the concept of community in Chapter 4.

17 But see below for corpora of Learner English.

18 For the most important corpora of Learner English, see the websites of ICLE, the *International Corpus of Learner English* (http://www.uclouvain.be/en-cecl-icle.html) and LINDSEI, the *Louvain International Database of Spoken English Interlanguage* http://www.uclouvain.be/en-cecl-lindsei.html; Granger (2003); Granger (2008).

19 Another substantial corpus explicitly designed for the investigation of ELF usage is ELFA, the Helsinki-based corpus of *English as a Lingua Franca in Academic Settings* (cf. Mauranen and Ranta 2008). As its name indicates, ELFA comprises speech events of academic ELF. At the time of writing, the corpus itself is not freely accessible over the internet, but the ELFA website can be consulted on <http://www.uta.fi/laitokset/kielet/engf/research/elfa/corpus.htm>.

A more recent development is TELF, the *Tübingen English as a Lingua Franca* corpus, a somewhat smaller collection but with the added advantage of video-recordings and post-recording interviews featuring mixed groups of four to six native and non-native speakers of English from diverse linguacultural back-grounds (but again, at the time of writing the corpus is not freely accessible over the internet; see www.telf.uni-tuebingen.de).

The work of VOICE has been extended in that it has provided the methodologi-cal basis for another, complementary ELF corpus in the 'ASEAN+3' region called ACE (*Asian Corpus of English*) that is being prepared by a project consortium with its centre in Hong Kong (see Kirkpatrick 2010a and <http://www.ied.edu.hk/ rcleams/view.php?secid=227>).

2

Assumptions and presumptions

The true repository of the English language is its native speakers,
and there are so many of them that they can afford to let
non-natives do what they like with it so long as what they do is
confined to a few words here and there.

PETER TRUDGILL: *Sociolinguistic Variation and Change*

2.1 Anglo-Saxon attitudes

The discussion in Chapter 1 has shown that the global spread of English, its
causes and its consequences have long been a focus of critical meta-level discussion. However, this discussion has not on the whole been followed up by a
consideration of what has been, and is, happening to the language as such. In
other words, the realization of the global role of English has not so far led to
any radical reconceptualization of this English. Instead, we find a deep-seated
assumption that the language remains, and indeed should remain, essentially
the same as it has always been: the property and preserve of its native speakers,
irrespective of who uses it and in what contexts. It is the purpose of this chapter
to have a closer look at these assumptions, and to try and identify the reasons
why they are so persistent to this day—as will also be apparent in subsequent
chapters. Since these attitudes still remain an impediment to an understanding
of ELF, they need to be addressed. This is what I propose to do in this chapter
in order to clear the ground for later discussion of the nature of ELF.

As we have seen in Chapter 1, the 1990s and early 2000s saw a spate of
publications that testified to a realization of the rapid global spread of English
and its implications. We find reactions to this reality coming from various
areas of expertise and motivated by very different attitudes to English. So one
can say that these 15 years or so were the time when the debate developed
critical mass and sustained momentum. It therefore seems useful to home
in on this period in order to identify the various positions taken vis à vis the
unprecedented global role of English, and in particular to ask how
representatives of these positions conceptualize the language itself.

Many native speakers of English are, of course, not averse to encouraging the belief that the language is essentially their property—and property,
furthermore, that can be turned to considerable economic advantage. For
example, we find the following in a British Council report:

Britain's real black gold is not North Sea oil but the English language. It has long been at the root of our culture and now is fast becoming the global language of business and information. The challenge facing us is to exploit it to the full.
(*British Council Annual Report* 1987–8)

Ten years later, it would appear that the challenge had been successfully met. Here is an extract from a British Council conference prospectus:

The incredible success of the English language is Britain's greatest asset. It enhances Britain's image as a modern, dynamic country and brings widespread political, economic and cultural advantages, both to Britain and to our partners.
(The British Council, Conference prospectus, ELT conference 1998)

The front page of *The Observer* newspaper revealed, two years later, that:

This week the Government will announce that the number of people with English as a second language has overtaken the number who speak it as their native tongue. …Insiders say the drive to make English the global *lingua franca* comes directly from Tony Blair.[1]
(*The Observer*, 29 October 2000: 1)

In this article, we also learn that [the then British Education and Employment Secretary] 'David Blunkett…will tell a meeting of business leaders on Tuesday to capitalize on their advantage as native speakers'.

Jumping ahead to later in the 2000s, we can see that although at least some institutions seem to have become a little more wary of making triumphalist statements about their ownership of English, the underlying message has not changed. For instance, on the British Council's Education UK website we find the following exhortation:

There are no limits to the range of English language courses offered in the UK. Over 600,000 learners a year come to the UK to achieve their ambitions, to experience modern UK life, and to *use the language in its natural home*. Why not join them?
(http:/www.educationuk.org/GB1262435261080, accessed 6 March 2011, emphasis added)

So here again we have the seemingly unproblematic, self-evident equation between 'English', 'modern UK life', and the 'natural home' of the language. And in a recent *Annual Report* of the British Council, there is a passage which conveys a sense of unease as to how to reconcile the (undeniable) global status of the language with the (understandable) wish to retain 'ownership':

One of the UK's great strengths is its status as the original home of the English language. This is still important even in an age where that language belongs to the whole world. We understand the importance of this, but there are many who underestimate it. Over the coming year we must do what we can to help the authorities to understand the importance of the UK as a student destination, and of the special place and nature of English language learning, so that they take these benefits fully into consideration in the design and implementation of the regulations. (*Accreditation UK Annual Report* 2009/10, British Council in partnership with English UK: p. 5)

So the assumption persists that English is essentially the property of its native speakers and therefore an asset they are uniquely placed to exploit. But this also carries with it the implication that they have the right, and even the responsibility, to protect it. This protective attitude to the language is often voiced with considerable fervour in letters to the editor, usually by linguistic laypersons. To get back to the period focused on in this chapter, here is an extract from an impassioned article entitled 'It just isn't English', which appeared in none other than the quality paper *The Times*. It is however not a letter to the editor from the linguistically naive 'man in the street', but a contribution in a section entitled 'Times 2 Analysis' and written by the senior journalist Derwent May, author of several academic books, whose opinion is likely to carry some weight:[2]

In fact, the Paris health authority has just decreed that English must be the language used in all published reports by its laboratories and hospitals, just as Renault decreed last year that all its internal reports must be in our—*i.e. the world, language.*

English may be used more and more throughout the world—but what kind of English? ... In these new towers of Babel, Poles lift their voices at the end of a sentence, meaning they have finished, while most of their listeners wait politely for them to go on. 'A' and 'the' pile up where they are not needed, or blow away where they are ...

Subtleties such as the use of the perfect tense are crushed out of existence. How to convey to these impatient talkers the way in which that fine and distinctive tense enables us English to look at the past from the point of view of the present: 'I have finished'. As for the pluperfect, enabling us to look at the past from the past ('I had finished'), there was never any hope in Kitzbühel for that. The conversationalists have to manage with 'He have gone there yesterday'. ...

Though English people may well find themselves engaged in these multinational English conversations, there is no evidence yet that they are letting themselves be influenced by the new barbarisms.

Nevertheless, there is something sinister about these pools of corrupt English lying about in the world. They are not just unpleasant for English people to encounter—and indeed for foreigners who care about speaking pure English. One also feels that they could grow and spread and eventually invade good English itself. They are like pools of language disease.

(May in *The Times*, 5 March 2000: 4, emphasis added)

The view we find so passionately argued here, then (if 'argued' is the right word), is that English as an international language must conform to the 'pure' English (supposedly) used by its real 'owners'—who are here, by the way, taken to be English people (not even British people, let alone Americans or Australians). The opinion expressed here with such vehemence is that wherever English is used and whoever uses it, this English language is essentially the language of the English and its integrity as such needs to be protected. Any deviation from 'pure English' constitutes corrupt English and, what is worse, there is a danger that these barbarisms may spread like a disease. We shall come back to the notion of 'spread' in Chapter 4.

For now, it is worth noting that, ironically, from an ELF perspective one could agree with Derwent May's observations, encapsulated in the title of his piece: 'It just isn't English'. By his own logic, if what constitutes 'English' is limited to his idea of 'pure English English', then ELF of course is not that 'English'. So in that respect he is right. It is just unfortunate for him and for those of a like mindset that they feel so strongly about the way 'these impatient talkers' manage their intercultural encounters to their own satisfaction, according to their own ideas of appropriateness, and with their own sense of identity. Unfortunate indeed, because these talkers won't go away, and they will persist in speaking their own English.

It might be objected that newspaper articles are hardly a source of informed scholarly arguments and that if we were to examine what language professionals have to say on the matter, we would not encounter views such as those of May. However, this is not so. In the following quotation, for example, we find much the same Anglo-Saxon attitude, even if expressed in more measured terms, and with a touch of humour:

There are...anglophone people who regard this expansion of English as a danger to the language. One reason is an irrational fear that one just cannot trust foreigners with one's language: who knows what they will get up to with it if native speakers are not at all times totally vigilant? After all, some foreigners seem to think that English is their language: some French and German speakers have invented *English words which do not exist in English*, such as *lifting*, or *wellness*, or *handy*, or *pullunder*. This, however, is not a danger to English. *It is on the contrary quite interesting and amusing, and does not make any difference to anything important.* It is a [sic] even a kind of compliment, perhaps. *The true repository of the English language is its native speakers, and there are so many of them that they can afford to let non-natives do what they like with it so long as what they do is confined to a few words here and there.*
(Trudgill 2002: 150f., emphases added)

As one of those German-speaking 'non-natives' myself, I see several points in this short passage that call for comment.

The observation that 'some French and German speakers have invented English words which do not exist in English' is intriguing. If they are invented, how then can it be said that *lifting*, *wellness*, *handy* (noun: a mobile/cell phone in German), and *pullunder* are English words? Trudgill touches here on something that I find centrally important for thinking about English as a lingua franca, although he approaches the matter from a very different perspective. Though these are *not* English words that are attested in the usage of the English, or other native speakers, they are nevertheless recognizable as being *in* English (and not in Finnish, for instance, or Swahili)—so English in a way. In what way? One can only conclude that these 'foreigners' are using the resources inherent in the English code, but in a way that native speakers do not recognize (in the sense of acknowledge) as theirs. We shall come back to this later (in Chapters 4 and 5). For now, let us look at the rest of the quotation.

Coming from an eminent sociolinguist, and particularly in a volume entitled *Sociolinguistic Variation and Change*, it seems odd to see any naturally occurring, regularly attested forms of language use described as 'interesting and amusing', if they were not intended to be. Most surprising, though, is the categorical statement that 'the true repository of the English language is its native speakers'—this is asserted as an axiom that by definition does not require any substantiation or justification. It is a simple fact that in the unparalleled situation English finds itself in, native speakers have ceased to be the only 'true repository' of the language. If—following Trudgill's own logic—it is the number of speakers that is important, then 'non-natives' might say that numerically, it is they that now are 'the true repository of the English language', and that there are so many of them that they can afford to let 'natives' do what they like with it so long as what they do is confined to their own native-speaker communities.

Academic enquiry is essentially incompatible with dogmatic assertion, but in the 'native-speaker question' there seems to be a convergence of layperson' and linguists' deep-seated belief in something that, elusive as it is of precise definition, cannot be argued but only believed in. In his introduction to the fascinating volume entitled *A Festschrift for Native Speaker*, Florian Coulmas observes that:

> linguists of every conceivable theoretical orientation agree that the concept of the native speaker is of fundamental importance for the field. This is clearly reflected in the literature, where this concept is so often made use of by linguists stating the principles or aims of their analytic work.
> (Coulmas 1981: 1)

Coulmas then offers several extracts from linguistic writing that demonstrate this, and comments:

> These are but a few quotations that bear witness to the significance of this key concept of linguistics. The authors may not always mean the same thing when they use the term 'native speaker'; but despite irreconcilable differences between its more often than not implicit definitions, they obviously find it hard to dispense with it.
> (ibid.: 2)

These observations are then summarized thus:

> ...the nativeness criterion is maintained across theoretical boundaries and contrasts. The quotations...witness significant differences regarding the conceptual status of 'native speaker'...Yet, notwithstanding these fundamental differences, the speaker whom the linguist is concerned about is invariably claimed to be a native speaker. He is the one who can legitimately supply data, and his language is what grammatical analyses are meant to account for. Thus, nativeness is the only universally accepted criterion for authenticity.
> (ibid.: 5)

The reason why Coulmas finds it necessary to emphasize the central role of the native speaker in linguistics in such detail is precisely that it is usually so taken for granted that it is not even noticed; and this has not changed significantly in the decades since 1981. As the theoretical and descriptive linguist Laurie Bauer observes in a summary statement in 2007:

> The native speaker of a language has been given great status by both structuralist and generative linguistics, in both theoretical and applied linguistics. The notion of 'native speaker' is highly problematic, though this has largely gone unnoticed.
> (Bauer 2007: 76)

As regards language teaching, the applied linguist Vivian Cook succinctly adds: 'By default, the only adequate descriptions in education are those of native speakers'. Significantly though, the paragraph where this statement occurs ends like this: 'Descriptions of native speaker English are a temporary measure until proper descriptions of L2 users are made' (Cook 2007: 245).

Reflecting on these statements in a dispassionate way it strikes one as somewhat odd that scholars should maintain such a strong and unconditional belief in something they can neither define nor agree upon. It should therefore not surprise us if it is felt to be unsettling and that defences go up when for the first time ever in the history of a language, the native speakers' monopoly is seriously challenged.

2.2 The assumption of native-speaker authority

What seems to underlie the attitudes discussed above is the supposition that there is such a thing as *the* English language, a stable entity, an established preserve of its native speakers. That even a sociolinguist of the stature of Peter Trudgill should have such a normative attitude is an indication of just how deeply entrenched the assumption is, since it would seem, paradoxically, to be contradictory to his own views on the inevitability, and desirability, of language variation and change.

The same assumption of the stable homogeneity of English also underlies the notion of linguistic imperialism propounded by Robert Phillipson and Tove Skutnabb-Kangas (Phillipson 1992; Phillipson and Skutnabb-Kangas 1999). Their views have been very influential in stimulating debate about issues which are of direct relevance to the concerns of this chapter, and for this reason I shall dwell on them a little, in particular on the points of convergence or divergence of our positions.

The argument that English is intrinsically hegemonic can only hold if one accepts the implicit (counterfactual) assumption that the intrinsic qualities of the language remain unchanged in different communities and contexts of use rather than get adapted to suit the needs of different kinds of speakers in different contexts. In this static view, where such adaptation does occur, it is perceived as a problem. This assumption of stable homogeneity denies the positive realization that the adaptation may be evidence of users actually resisting the hegemony of the language by appropriating it for their own purposes.

And so again, variation from the norm of 'the English language' is denied any real significance. According to this logic, non-native speakers just cannot win: either they subject themselves to native-speaker authority and obediently strive to meet the norms of the hegemonic language, or they try to assert themselves against the hegemony, only to then be told that they got it wrong because they have the misfortune not to be native speakers. So the primacy accorded to NS norms puts the NNS user of English in an inescapable double bind.

How difficult it is to recognize and overcome this normative attitude is perhaps most apparent when we consider the writings of scholars whom we would expect to be particularly sensitive to its pitfalls. In the period this chapter focuses on, for example, Phillipson and Skutnabb-Kangas (1999: 29) put forward various proposals for 'charting and countering Englishization'. They suggested a number of research questions, focusing on the role of English in Denmark, one of which is formulated and commented on like this:

> What is the significance of senior Danish politicians, who *use English with moderate proficiency*, inevitably *creating false and unintended impressions* when talking impromptu to the 'world' press?
>
> As an aside to this latter question, it should be mentioned that the four Danish exceptions to the Maastricht Treaty were hammered out at a summit in Edinburgh in 1991, at the close of which the Danish Foreign Minister referred to the 'so-called Edinburgh agreement', *implying that no real obligation had been entered into*. When Salman Rushdie came to Denmark in 1996 to receive an EU literature prize—an event which was postponed because of a security scare—the Danish Prime Minister was asked by Rushdie whether the death threat was real or hypothetical, to which he replied that he did not have the 'ability' to answer the question. . . . Are both *errors* due to mother-tongue transfer?
>
> (Phillipson and Skutnabb-Kangas 1999: 29f., emphases added)

It is important to note that the contexts described here were very clearly international gatherings, so it is difficult to see why the authors assume that their ENL norm expectations should be relevant. So when they say that Danish politicians 'use English with moderate proficiency', they mean the same native-speaker English that Crystal, May, and Trudgill are referring to in the quotations discussed above, and which is simply assumed to be relevant in the setting described here. My contention would be that it is irrelevant.

To take the example of 'so-called': it is true that ENL corpora and dictionaries based on them usually indicate that the 'sarcastic' use of this premodifier is the more frequently attested one overall (though see below). But what is typical, or expected, in native-speaker language use is not particularly relevant in the situation described here: the Danish Foreign Minister is not a native speaker of English, and he was not speaking on behalf of ENL speakers, nor presumably exclusively to ENL speakers. He was using English as a means for international communication, in the way he no doubt often has occasion to use it, with interlocutors who use it in the same way.

And how are we to know what his intentions were, whether or not he wanted to add a note of sarcasm to his remark? The people present would have had access to other contextual factors (more important than the actual wording) such as co-text, gesture, intonation, voice quality, and background knowledge to guide their interpretation, and it is thus very likely indeed that they would have understood whatever he meant by 'so-called', perhaps 'the agreement called the Edinburgh agreement'. So to my knowledge there is no evidence that what he said 'creat[ed] false and unintended impressions', except perhaps in those intent on judging what he said exclusively by NS norms.

I would also claim that 'ability' in the second example would be perfectly intelligible to listeners attuned to the intercultural encounter, as saying that he could not give a (definitive) answer to the question. It can only be perceived as odd if one insists on judging it entirely from the point of view of ENL expectations and conventions. So to see these two wordings discussed as 'errors' in this context struck me as counterproductive in a paper that argues against 'Englishization'—indeed, the sentiment expressed seems to be that the Danish Prime Minister's English was not English enough. This was a surprising point of view to encounter, coming from authors who are known as committed activists for human language rights. It is an indication that it remains difficult to accept ELF as a use in its own right, and ELF speakers as language users in their own right.

The conceptual problem, perhaps particularly for ENL speakers (and for non-native speakers who have aspired to and achieved a very native-like command of English), lies in the inclination to perceive anything that does not quite meet NS expectations (based on individual intuition) as an 'error'. For some people, such 'errors' can be taken as 'barbarisms' or symptoms of 'language disease' offensive to a native speaker's sense of what is 'right' and 'pure'. Others, as we have seen, express concern that the 'errors' they diagnosed may 'create false and unintended impressions', i.e. that the disadvantaged non-native speakers will not succeed in making themselves understood.

But intelligibility depends on so much more than on linguistic accuracy. Numerous studies in anthropology, sociolinguistics, and social psychology conducted since the mid-20th century have demonstrated how attitudes influence perception and can lead to a different 'reading' of linguistic forms used, depending on who the speakers/writers are thought to be. These show that perceptions of ethnic, racial, and linguacultural differences can lead to expectations of intelligibility problems which are independent of the actual linguistic forms that speakers produce. A study illustrating this particularly graphically is Rubin's experiment (Rubin 1992) carried out via a matched guise procedure (cf. Lambert *et al.* 1960). Rubin used an identical stimulus recording by a US native speaker giving a short lecture, accompanied once by a slide suggesting the lecturer was a Caucasian, and once by a slide suggesting an Asian lecturer, and then compared the effect of the two stimuli on his respondents' (US ENL undergraduates) processing and evaluation of the speech. He discusses his results thus:

...when they [the respondents] were faced with an ethnically Asian instructor, participants responded in the direction one would expect had they been listening to nonstandard speech. Evidence from the discriminant analysis suggests that participants stereotypically attributed accent differences—differences that did not exist in truth—to the instructors' speech. Yet more serious, listening comprehension appeared to be undermined simply by identifying (visually) the instructor as Asian. (Rubin 1992: 519)

Although Rubin's study was conducted at a US university, its implications are clearly relevant to other communicative settings in that they 'provide dramatic evidence' that native-speaker respondents 'are reacting to factors extraneous to just language proficiency' (ibid.: 518). This is a difficulty that ELF users are also up against, even in contexts where native-speaker norms are much less relevant than in Rubin's study. Jenkins (2007: Chapter 3) provides a comprehensive overview of these attitude problems with particular reference to accents.

Earlier analyses of intelligibility involving speakers with different social prestige have explored the phenomenon of non-reciprocal intelligibility (especially the classic study by Wolff 1959), disabusing us of the naive notion that understanding what somebody says depends simply on them getting the code 'right'. The role that relative socioeconomic status and cultural affinities play is at least as important, so that there will be a tendency to understand a speaker 'more easily' when they are perceived as socially superior.[3] Quite often, then, intelligibility is directly related to the (conscious or unconscious) willingness, or unwillingness, to understand. And given the current socioeconomic power of the ENL nations, this, of course, is another challenge that ELF speakers are up against, and one that is intricately connected with the native-speaker ideology I have been discussing.

The non-recognition of the fact that ELF interactions tend to develop their own, locally negotiated norms, rather than follow native-speaker conventions leads to an added difficulty for ELF speakers when they communicate with groups consisting of both native and non-native speakers in that their tendency to defer to NS 'authority' and NSs' often all-too-ready acceptance of the role of arbiters of linguistic correctness or acceptability mutually reinforce each other. This can lead to judgements of 'incorrectness' even when NNSs produce utterances which actually follow a clearly established ENL pattern.

The criticism of the Danish Foreign Minister's use of 'so-called' discussed above can serve as an illustration of this. Even brief consultation of the British National Corpus (BNC) through a couple of queries using the free simple search activity of the whole corpus, each yielding just 50 results of the 2,644 occurrences of 'so-called', shows that there are indeed cases of what I have referred to as the sarcastic meaning of 'so-called'—though I should add that I had to look hard for very clear instances, as in:

AJY 730 I probably quite enjoyed the idea that I was going to prove a lot of so-called experts wrong.
(*The Daily Telegraph*, electronic edition of 11 April 1992)

A pattern that clearly also emerges, however, is that when experts (of the 'real' rather than the 'so-called' kind) refer to or explain a concept or term they assume their audience may not be familiar with, the relevant proper name or technical term is often preceded by 'so-called'. This can serve the purpose of somebody 'in the know' being helpful to somebody less knowledgeable, and possibly of indicating that the speaker/writer acknowledges this uneven distribution of specialist knowledge as normal, a kind of face-saving device out of consideration for the interlocutor/audience. There were many instances of this kind of use, even in the very restricted search I conducted. Here are a few examples, with the relevant parts highlighted in bold:[4]

HLJ 2617 OPEC country representatives met their counterparts from 12 non-OPEC oil producing countries (the **so-called NOPEC group**) on April 23 in Vienna...
(*Keesings Contemporary Archives*. Harlow: Longman Group UK Ltd 1992.)
C9V 761 This is one of the **so-called auto-immune group of diseases** in which the body produces antibodies to its own tissues, and thus begins to destroy them. (Gibson, Robin and Sheila Gibson. 1987. *Homeopathy for Everyone*. London: Penguin Group.)
FYX 142 When we got back from Majorca, I was sent to another school for a year, and then I took the **so-called eleven-plus examination**. (Hawking, Stephen W. 1993. *Black Holes and Baby Universes*. London: Bantam Corgi.)
ABH 1640 In 1989 and early 1990, they worked together through the **so-called Inter-Regional Group of deputies**. (*The Economist*. 1991. London: The Economist Newspaper Ltd.)
H7K 1236 The main orogeny in the north of Europe, coming at the end of the Carboniferous, is defined by the **so-called 'Hercynian front'**. (Ager, Derek V. 1984. *The Nature of the Stratigraphical Record*. Basingstoke: Macmillan Publishers Ltd.)

There are even instances of 'so-called' premodifying 'X agreement', without any obvious trace of sarcasm, such as:

HKP 1882 However, efforts to abolish intra-EC border controls received an early setback with the failure to materialize by January 1990 of the **so-called 'Schengen agreement'** on a scheduled lifting of barriers, and negotiations on the harmonization of indirect taxation had to be shelved in the face of strong opposition from several member states. (*Keesings Contemporary Archives*. 1990. Harlow: Longman Group UK Ltd.)

It may well be, then, that the Danish Foreign Minister, in the extract cited by Phillipson and Skuttnabb-Kangas, is using 'so-called' in very much the same way, as if saying 'OK, this is the name used for this agreement amongst EU politicians/insiders, I don't expect you to know this necessarily, but I'll use the name because that's what it is now called'. This, I would claim, is a finely nuanced use of 'so-called' which might well have been accepted as perfectly 'normal' if the analysts had not been looking for 'problems' and 'errors'. It needs to be emphasized here, of course, that from an ELF point of view, the fact that this utterance can be read as perfectly appropriate in ENL terms is not what is relevant here in itself, but what needs to be noted is how difficult it seems to be to recognize a sophisticated use of language when it is known to have been produced by a non-native speaker.

Again, we are faced here with an incongruity between outdated ideas about native-speaker privilege and the overdue acknowledgement of the reality of ELF: as pointed out by House (see Chapter 1), ELF is successfully used by countless non-native speakers in 'influential frameworks', i.e. global business, politics, science, technology, and media discourse and, as Brumfit (see again Chapter 1) indicates '[t]he ownership (by which I mean the power to adapt and change) of any language in effect rests with the people who use it'. Yet, entrenched attitudes and established traditional views of native-speaker authority keep getting transferred from NS communities to the quite different contexts of ELF users.

2.3 Convictions and contradictions

Phillipson and Skutnabb-Kangas are well known as campaigners against what they see as the hegemonic influence of major linguacultures such as the Anglo-American ones on other less powerful ones. Their commitment to linguistic equity and ecology, however, is at odds with their assumption of the necessary relevance of NS English in all communicative contexts. This illustrates the problem outlined in Chapter 1: the conceptual gap in people's minds where English as a lingua franca should by now have got established as an autonomous concept next to (rather than subordinate to) ENL norms. The problem is further illustrated by the endnote attached to the paragraph cited above:

> The Danes are, of course, not alone in having *problems with English*. In the latest communication, in four languages, from the follow-up group preparing the revision of the Draft Universal Declaration on Language Rights, the Catalan secretariat states that this key document is 'in the way of' being translated (=in the course of) and that the scientific council is 'pretending' to provide a forum for debate (=aiming at). It is unreasonable to expect that Danes, Catalans or other users of English as a second language use *English* supremely well. The dice are loaded against them, the conditions for communication are not symmetrical, and *native speakers often seem to be unaware* of this.
> (op. cit., p. 33 n6, emphases added; glosses in parentheses are the authors')

It is absolutely true that the conditions for communication are not symmetrical, but mere demonstrations of moral support and pleading for equity will not change anything. As long as both conservative and radical commentators alike persist in adhering exclusively to ENL norms, irrespective of the actual settings in which these interactions take place, non-conformity can be used as a weapon against ELF users. As long as ELF interactions are approached with an ENL mindset, 'errors' will be identified where there is no evidence that that non-conformity to NS norms has any detrimental effect on communication.[5]

I raised these issues in a journal article (Seidlhofer 2001), and Robert Phillipson took them up again in his book *English-Only Europe?* published in 2003. I want to emphasize that, again, I found myself in sympathy with much of what he has to say in this book, and welcomed the fact that he continued our exchange about this question. But again I was also made aware that several years on, Phillipson still seemed to be in two minds about English when used in international contexts.

On the one hand, he perceives some ELF issues very clearly, as evidenced in the following quotation:

Native speakers have greater facility in speaking the language, but not necessarily greater sensitivity in using it appropriately. In many international fora, competent speakers of English as a second language are more comprehensible than native speakers, because they can be better at adjusting their language for people from different cultural and linguistic backgrounds.
(Phillipson 2003a: 167)

On the other hand, Phillipson (2003a) concludes his section on 'The diffusion of whose English?' by revisiting the anecdote about Salman Rushdie and the Danish Prime Minister, and he adds a new comment:

At a press conference in Copenhagen, Rushdie asked why it was that the Danes were unable to guarantee his safety for a few hours on the first day. The Danish Prime Minister replied that he did not have the 'ability' to answer the question. If he had stated that he was not 'able', for security reasons, to do so, he would have avoided *casting doubt on his own mental faculties. The tiny shift from adjective to noun makes all the difference.*
(ibid.: 170, emphasis added)

Phillipson immediately follows this paragraph with the following comments:

...the contexts from which I have drawn the anecdotes in this chapter... are formal, with little scope for meaning negotiation. Many people may have a high tolerance threshold for users of ELF, but clearly the conditions for communication in high-level negotiations and in the media are often inequitable (*it is grossly unjust to expect a Danish politician to have native-speaker English:* see Box 5.2. [example of a BBC interview], and *language use is of crucial importance.* We should therefore be concerned with how communication can be made more democratic and effective.
(ibid.: 171, emphases added)

I wholeheartedly agree with the last sentence from this quotation, and also with the observation that 'language use is of crucial importance'—the question is how the two relate. What I find puzzling is how in two consecutive paragraphs, the expression of commitment to 'more democratic' communication can be reconciled with claiming that by using 'ability' instead of 'able', the Danish Prime Minister 'cast [...] doubt on his own mental faculties' and that '[t]he tiny shift from adjective to noun makes all the difference.' All the difference to what? And to whom? To the author, the answers are self-evident: it makes all the difference to how a native speaker, taking himself as representative, necessarily interprets the utterance whatever the context. Is it not he himself who is being 'grossly unjust' by 'expect[ing] a Danish politician to have native-speaker English'?

The work of Phillipson has been notable and highly influential, in that it has instigated an important debate about the implications of the global spread of English, which is why what he has to say needs to be given particular attention, especially in the context of the discussion in the present chapter. His 2009 book *Linguistic Imperialism Continued* in a way continues our dialogue, and it also includes an exchange with several other scholars who have commented on his work from different points of view.

From my own point of view, it is clear that we continue to agree about certain things, but to disagree about the crucial question of how to deal with the changed role of the language. For instance, the book reviews reprinted in Phillipson (2009) include that of Ammon (2001), at the end of which Phillipson criticizes the German sociolinguist for not having edited the book carefully. Some of the examples he quotes may well be in need of correction, but he also takes Ammon to task for 'countless German-influenced forms that disrupt, without impeding, comprehensibility' (p. 250).

The point I am trying to make, then, is that it will not do to discuss these issues and resulting problems of inequity, however critically, while at the same time persisting in passing native-speaker judgements as to what is appropriate usage in predominantly non-native ELF contexts. What ENL speakers find easy to process and comfortable or pleasant to read or listen to is not an a priori consideration for ELF interactions, not one that is more important than the perceptions and communicative preferences of non-native ELF users. The 'problems' which Danish and Catalan politicians, German academics, and others have 'with English' may be problems in the eye of the native-speaker beholder. But these are only problems if we assume the only relevant 'English' to be ENL and expect ELF to conform to conventions that are at home in ENL communities.

Campaigns for linguistic human rights cannot afford to ignore the need to rethink expectations and attitudes towards the forms that the language will take in such contexts. As long as this is not done, a major factor in the disadvantaging of non-ENL speakers will remain in place. Unlike many other injustices in the world, these issues are at least more readily amenable to intervention and resolution, so long as there is a will to take on the conceptual challenge. It needs to be understood that 'English' does not simply transfer intact from one context to another—the 'E' in *English as a Native Language* is bound to be something different in kind from the 'E' in *English as a Lingua*

Franca, and must be acknowledged as such—it is in *this* way that 'language is of crucial importance'. Once this happens, it will be obvious that simply being a native speaker of English is *not* an advantage in ELF interactions—if anything, it is more likely to be a drawback because (as Phillipson also points out) it is non-native ELF speakers who often find it easier to use English appropriately in intercultural settings.[6]

2.4 Conclusion

As is evident from the quotations I have considered and commented on in this chapter, there is a deep-seated assumption shared by both popular and scholarly opinion, across the whole spectrum of linguistic laypersons, linguists, activists, and governmental institutions, that the only proper English is the English of its native speakers (ENL). Though it is acknowledged that variable versions occur, these are seen in terms of deviations from established and supposedly stable norms which alone are regarded as constituting the legitimate language. From this point of view, ENL is assumed to be not only the norm against which any ELF non-conformities are seen as in some way defective, but also represents the model to which all learning of the language should aspire. What arguments are given to support this assumption? This is the question I shall take up in Chapter 3.

Notes

1   The then British Prime Minister.
2   Derwent May was literary editor of *The Listener* and the *Sunday Telegraph*. He is the author of books on Proust and Hannah Arendt, and of *Critical Times: The History of the Times Literary Supplement*. (See: http://www.standpointmag.co.uk/writers/?showid=Derwent%20May, 5 March 2011)
3   In fact, Skutnabb-Kangas (e.g. 1984) herself discusses the intricate nature of intelligibility, so I would have expected to see the same critical stance applied to judgements in the examples cited here.
4   The letter and figure code preceding each example is provided by the BNC and indicates where the extract comes from and where it can be found in the corpus.
5   Such a monolingual ENL mindset could helpfully be counterbalanced by attempts to communicate via 'receptive multilingualism' proposed by e.g. ten Thije and Zeevaert 2007.
6   Similar findings are reported by Charles and Marschan-Piekkari (2002); Jenkins (2007); Sweeney and Zhu (2010); and Wright (2008).

3
Standard English and real English

This is Standard Future: the old measures, or existing grades,
are inadequate, and we will aim at something better. It is a very
interesting use. Instead of referring back to a source of authority,
or taking a current measurable state, a standard is set, projected,
from ideas about conditions which we have not yet realized but
which we think should be realized. There is an active social history
in this development of the phrase.

RAYMOND WILLIAMS: *Keywords. A Vocabulary of Culture and Society*

3.1 Standard English ideology

In Chapter 2, I discussed the persistence of the view, both explicit and
implicit, that the only people who can really claim to speak proper English
are its native speakers. Having looked at this as a well entrenched attitude, we now move on to a consideration of the arguments that have
been put forward in support of such a view. It is only by understanding
the arguments first that we can then attempt to counter those that we
may find untenable when considering the role of English in the contemporary world. The belief that imposed language uniformity is good for
society and that the standard variety is the only legitimate one is referred
to as 'standard language ideology'. This is a phenomenon that has been
an object of sociolinguistic research for quite a long time (cf. for example
Cameron 1995; Milroy 2001) but it has usually been discussed with reference to language variation within particular speech communities, for
example, Standard English versus particular local dialects of English. Due
to the global spread of English and the role the language has come to play
as an international lingua franca across conventional speech communities
it would seem to be obvious that Standard English ideology is a special
case of standard language ideology. For here what we are faced with is the
claim that a national standard language should be valid not only within a
particular country but globally.

What characterizes any standard language ideology is that it tends to have been so internalized by most people who have been socialized in conventional educational settings that it tends to operate at the subconscious level. Another important factor is that at least in 'western', and certainly in Anglo-American linguistics, the big standard languages have been the ones most studied, and the fact that not all cultures are 'standard language cultures' (Milroy 2001) has generally been neglected. It is therefore not surprising that there have been no clear proposals in mainstream linguistics or education for any conceivable (let alone acceptable) alternatives to standard models.[1] Beliefs and attitudes are usually transmitted and reproduced through education without either teachers or learners being aware of them because they have become naturalized in the course of history.

Any attempt to uncover the Standard English ideology so widely held not only by linguistic laypersons but also by linguists and language professionals will therefore have to proceed historically to some degree. The objective here would be to explain how certain ideas about language arose out of particular socio-political and socio-economic conditions and to ask whether and to what extent changes in these conditions brought about a corresponding adaptive change to the ideas.

A consideration of how ideas change, or do not, over time necessarily brings up the tricky question of how to deal with the terminology that is used to express them. It would seem reasonable to mark any change of ideas with a complete change of terms. The disadvantage of this, however, is that it can misrepresent how ideas evolve, how new ones develop from, and are dependent on, those which are familiar, as if the present was not a continuation of but a complete break from the past. In this chapter I shall be examining and challenging established ways of thinking about English and shall first need to use established terms to do so. How far these terms are appropriate to a changed way of thinking arising out of changed circumstances is a matter I shall take up subsequently. This way of proceeding is intended to examine the issues involved without glossing over them by inventing new terms from the start.

Although the standard language ideology that attributes Standard English (henceforth StE) a special and privileged status has a long history, the case for preferring, and promoting StE as the global language has powerful advocates in the contemporary world. We might start by considering the views of scholars whose works have been the staple diet of students and teachers of English in many parts of the world. One of them is Randolph Quirk. An acknowledged authority on English grammar, and an iconic representative figure in the field, Quirk has been a household name among authors on StE for many decades: he founded the Survey of English Usage and drew on the descriptions of educated British English which this database yielded for two celebrated grammars of English (Quirk *et al.* 1972; Quirk 1985). But Quirk has not only described StE as such, he has also long been concerned with the relationship between this variety of the language and global uses and varieties of English. An early example of this work is to be found in a paper he presented at a conference celebrating the fiftieth anniversary of the British Council in 1985 (subsequently published in Quirk and Widdowson 1985) entitled 'The English language in a global context'. In it, he made some widely quoted statements about StE, one of which provides us with a way into the issues that the present chapter will focus on:

> The *relatively narrow range of purposes* for which *the non-native* needs to use English (even in ESL countries) is arguably well catered for by a single *monochrome standard form* that looks as good on paper as it sounds in speech. There are only the most dubious advantages in exposing *the learner* to *a great variety of usage*, no part of which he will have time to master properly, little of which he will be called upon to exercise, all of which is embedded in a *controversial linguistic matrix he cannot be expected to understand*.
> (Quirk 1985: 6, emphases added)

The first problem here is that the 'standard form' of English is actually very difficult to define. As Peter Trudgill puts it:

> there seems to be considerable confusion in the English-speaking world, even amongst linguists, about what *Standard English* is.
> (Trudgill 1999: 117)

In a review article on the book in which Trudgill's paper appeared, Nikolas Coupland comes to the conclusion that:

> ... 'standard English' still seems to me to be a 'confused and confusing' territory for sociolinguistics, and probably much more so than we should be comfortable with. 'Standardness' and 'non-standardness' are too deeply ingrained into sociolinguistic theory and methods for us to dispense with received perspectives and begin again, conceptually.
> (Coupland 2000: 632)

The confusion is even apparent in a recent publication of which Trudgill himself is joint author. At one point we are told:

> ... it is important to stress that the codification and distinctiveness of Standard English do not extend beyond grammar to any other areas of language usage.
> (Trudgill and Hannah 2008: 3)

Later, however, it would seem that the distinctiveness of StE also extends to its vocabulary. Thus, with reference to British English:

> As far as grammar and vocabulary are concerned, this generally means Standard English as it is normally written and spoken by educated speakers in England and, with certain differences, in Wales, Scotland, Northern Ireland, The Republic of Ireland, Australia, New Zealand and South Africa.
> (ibid.: 2008: 5)

We need to note too that allowance is made here for 'certain differences' and these are said to identify varieties of StE, so on this account there is no 'single monochrome standard form', as Quirk puts it.

I shall return to the problem of defining StE later. Meanwhile, there is another matter arising from the above quotation from Quirk that calls for comment. With the global spread of English, the language has now penetrated the daily lives of innumerable people to such an extent that it is not just needed for a 'relatively narrow range of purposes'. The question is therefore whether an extended range of purposes can indeed be catered for 'by a single monochrome standard form', even if such a form exists. As an epiphenomenon accompanying socio-economic and political developments in the world, English is all-pervasive, from casual small talk to corporate business negotiation. As Melchers and Shaw put it, 'wide use of English is a natural consequence of the way the world is now' (2003: 196). The consequence of these developments is that, as we have seen, non-native users of English greatly outnumber native speakers of the language, and this fact should lead to a reconsideration of several other propositions in the above quotation. Thus, referring to a representative of the majority group of speakers as 'the non-native' sounds somewhat outdated to say the least. Due to the lingua franca function of English, there are many people who avail themselves of this convenient means of communication on a daily basis, but they often conceive of themselves as users, not 'learner[s]', and they are quite automatically exposed 'to a great variety of usage', while not feeling any desire to 'master' this range of forms 'properly' themselves. It is, then, indeed a 'controversial linguistic matrix' that lingua franca users of English inhabit. They live in the presence of English (Berns *et al.* 2007) but for this very reason it would seem patronizing now to say that they 'cannot be expected to understand' this situation. While linguistic laypersons may not have an expert understanding of the complex linguistic landscape surrounding them, this does not mean that people have not made conceptual adjustments in their thinking about ways of communicating in today's world.

Quirk's concern for the global status of English did not end in 1985. In 1988, he delivered a lecture to the Japanese Association of Language Teachers that was subsequently published in the journal *English Today*, entitled 'Language varieties and standard language' (Quirk 1990)—so we continue on the theme of the educational and pedagogic significance of StE. This paper was also reprinted in Quirk's 1995 collection *Grammatical and Lexical Variance in English*, so he must have retained his views at least up to that time.[2]

Essentially, the thrust of Quirk's argument in this 1990/1995 paper is that StE should be the only variety taught both in contexts where English is the first language (in British schools) and in those where it is a foreign or an additional official language (in Spain, but also in India). Quirk does not deny the difficulties of defining StE, but, as I shall argue, he does take a rather non-problematic view of its currency in the world at large. Essentially he takes the normative view, discussed in the preceding chapter, that however the language may vary in its usage throughout the world, the norm that should be conformed to is the standard, and that this serves as a corrective to needless complexity and ensures effective communication. But what argument does

Quirk advance in support of this view? And how far is his perspective on StE still valid, some twenty years on, given the global role of English today?

3.2 Setting the standard

The first thing to consider here is the question I touched on earlier about how StE is to be defined. In arguing for the special status of StE, Quirk draws a strict line between native and non-native varieties. The former are then subdivided into institutionalized and non-institutionalized varieties, while non-native varieties are all designated non-institutionalized. By institutionalized varieties Quirk means those which are 'fully described and with defined standards observed by the institutions of state' (1990: 6) and StE is just such an institutionalized variety. It needs to be noted, however, as Quirk recognizes, that StE is only *one* version of English as a native language (ENL). In spite of the frequent practice of referring to the two as if they were synonymous, StE does not refer to the language of all native speakers but only to a relatively small sub-set of them. Most native speakers of English do not, in fact, conform to StE norms, especially in their spoken usage. This is why when people who learnt English in their own countries first travel to Britain, the USA, etc., it often comes as a surprise to them that they very rarely encounter, particularly in spoken interactions, the Standard English they were expecting to hear.

Quirk includes American English and British English, plus 'one or two others with standards rather informally established, notably *Australian English*' (op. cit.). No non-native Englishes are included, and Quirk gives the following reason for this: 'I am not aware of there being any institutionalized non-native varieties' (op. cit.). This categorization results in such long-recognized 'types' belonging to Kachru's Outer Circle as Indian English or Nigerian English being lumped together with what Quirk calls 'performance varieties' such as French English, Japanese English, or Russian English, which would in Kachru's scheme belong to the Expanding Circle.

What this categorization leaves out of account is the sociocultural reality of the role English plays in various settings in particular for the construction of social identities (cf. Schneider 2007). This is a reality which is not sanctioned by institutional norms. Quirk insists on drawing a clear distinction between 'varieties identified on ethnopolitical grounds' and 'those identified on purely linguistic grounds'. But it has long been recognized that such a distinction is untenable, and this raises again the difficulty of defining StE as a distinct variety. There are no exclusively linguistic criteria for the delimitation of varieties. Language is a continuum in time and space, so what linguists can do is indicate variable features, but they cannot, as linguists, identify the boundaries which demarcate one variety from another (see Chambers and Trudgill 1998). What this means is that the identification of any variety as 'the standard' will be a matter of institutional expediency—what Milroy (2001: 531) refers to as 'imposition of uniformity upon a class of objects'. The essential question is what it is that motivates the institutionalization of a particular variety as 'standard', and this inevitably brings in complex ethno-political, socio-economic, and other interests. StE is a linguistic object—something that is described in grammars and dictionaries, but it is also itself an ideological construct. I take up the problematic issue of the demarcation of linguistic boundaries in some detail in Chapter 4.

Varieties, then, are social constructs that exist in and through the perception of speakers. And so it is that if we consult publications on so-called nativized varieties of English from the last two decades, it seems clear that linguists such as Banjo (1997), Bamgbose (1992, 1996, 1998), and Jowitt (1991) researching Nigerian English, for example, would hold that a Standard Nigerian English (which in this case might be Nigerian Pidgin English)[3] is, in principle, just as desirable as a Standard New Zealand English: there is a complex dialectic between ethno-political/sociocultural and linguistic factors in that whether or not an endonormative (linguistic) standard can become a reality depends, more than anything else, on the self-perception of the speakers concerned.[4]

Quirk quotes Kujore (1985) in his support as saying that 'although earlier observers have talked freely of Standard Nigerian English, the fact is "that any such standard is, at best, in process of evolution"'. But it is actually difficult to see what the difference in principle is between a standard that is, in Quirk's own terms, 'in process of evolution' (Nigerian English) and a standard that is 'rather informally established' (Australian English) (Quirk 1990: 6). For the latter, the publication of the *Macquarie Dictionary* in 1981 was an important indication of Australia's endonormative orientation, and as early as 1986, Trudgill noted that Australian English had even developed further to show some regional differentiation too. And Gordon and Deverson make a comment about neighbouring New Zealand that resonates with themes discussed with reference to ELF in the previous chapters:

The word 'antipodean' has come to seem rather outdated...We are where we are, rather than at the other end of the world from somewhere else. We are now evolving our own ways, our own standards, looking less over the shoulder at the example of Mother England.
(Gordon and Deverson 1998: 175)

But just as more and more descriptions of Australian and New Zealand English are becoming available (for example, Burridge and Kortmann 2008; Peters, Collins, and Smith 2009), there are similar efforts being made for Nigerian English (Alo and Mesthrie 2004; Gut 2004; Igboanusi 2002; Jowitt 1991, and the International Corpus of English, with the ICE Nigeria project based at the University of Augsburg; see http://ice-corpora.net/ice/icenige. htm). The complex picture these studies reveal of the sociolinguistic dynamics in Nigeria in particular would seem to make the question whether Nigerian English is 'institutionalized' or not one of rather secondary interest.

It needs to be noted, however, that the pursuit of recognition through codification and institutionalization is driven by essentially the same belief in the necessity to legitimize a variety by establishing standard norms that we have seen in the case of Quirk and StE. Paradoxically, therefore, 'World Englishes' are acknowledged as legitimate (and indeed as distinctive 'Englishes') because they are StE-like in that it can be shown that they vie in status with StE as symbolically representing some kind of national or communal identity. For all their differences, therefore, Kachru and Quirk would seem to think alike in that they both take institutionalization and codification as *the* way in which variations in the use of English can be taken as valid. In both cases it is believed that ways of speaking have to belong to some community or other as a property, and no allowance is made for the encoding potential of English being used variably and *without* institutional sanction across communities and cultures. It is thus mainly because of what they symbolically represent as expressions of independent communal identity that language variation and change in post-colonial settings (in Kachru's Outer Circle) has, on the whole, been given the sociolinguistic seal of approval—and this contrasts with the status of the English used in non-ENL, non-post-colonial settings, which generally is still not granted such attention and recognition.[5]

From Quirk's point of view, such variable manifestations of English are not worthy of attention because no matter how widespread and socioculturally significant they are as a means of communication, they are not institutionally established. For him, speakers in these areas are only capable of what he calls 'performance varieties'. As he puts it:

The problem with varieties in this branch is that they are inherently unstable, ranged along a qualitative cline, with each speaker seeking to move to a point where the varietal characteristics reach vanishing point, and where thus, ironically, each variety is best manifest in those who by commonsense measures speak it worst.
(op. cit.: p. 5f.)

Apart from the fact that all language is 'inherently unstable', whether and to what degree these 'performance varieties' are problematically unstable is surely an empirical question, and one that some efforts have been undertaken to address in the years that have passed since Quirk made this statement. I will discuss this empirical work in more detail in Chapters 5 and 6. For the moment it suffices to say that there is already evidence that this non-native English exhibits regularities (much like any natural language) which contradict the notion that 'performance varieties' are totally arbitrary and erratic. What seems particularly significant in the present context is that there are strong indications in the empirical findings of actual non-native ELF performance that speakers, sensitive to communicative needs, exercise a good deal of control as a function of mutual accommodation, as I shall seek to demonstrate later in this book (see also Seidlhofer 2009a).

Accommodation, of course, is something that happens in flight as it were, as speakers in a given situation, usually unconsciously adjust their speech and their non-verbal behaviour, and fine-tune these to become more accessible and more acceptable to each other. This process has been shown to play a very important role in international intelligibility (see especially Jenkins 2000: Chapter 7), but it is something that is easily overlooked when one assumes that unless there is a norm that controls the way people speak, things fall apart. In this respect, linguists could learn a great deal from anthropology, biology, and social psychology, which demonstrate that people naturally cooperate with each other, basically because it is in their interest to do so (see, for example, Dunbar 1996; Giles and Coupland 1991; Ridley 1996).

We shall be looking in some detail at ways in which ELF users cooperate with each other in Chapters 5 and 6, drawing on data from VOICE (see Chapter 1.7). The interactions recorded in this corpus are predominantly of a consensual kind where it is in the participants' interest to cooperate and where they do so willingly in the co-construction of agreed meanings. It is important to note, however, that there are also occasions where such willingness is absent and where the use of ELF turns out to be conflictual in its consequences. Such occasions are strikingly documented in Guido (2008), which presents an account of the unequal encounters mediated through English between Nigerian asylum seekers and Italian immigration officers. These encounters are unequal in two respects. In the first place, there is an obvious inequality of participant status between the refugees and their interrogators, which makes the latter disinclined to make allowances in the interests of common understanding. But common understanding is inhibited by a second inequality, and this has to do with the kind of English that each side brings to the interaction. The Nigerian English that the asylum seekers will naturally have recourse to tends not to be recognized by the Italian immigration officers as a legitimate 'nativized' variety but as failure to conform to the standard language and is therefore seen as evidence of incompetence. What is likely to make matters worse is that the asylum seekers, naturally *assuming* the effectiveness of their own English, may well find it difficult to adapt it appropriately as a lingua franca.

What comes across very clearly in Guido's research is the need to take into account how ELF interactants perceive of English and of themselves as users of it. Such perceptions will obviously influence the way interactions proceed, and the linguistic forms they exhibit. Throughout this book, I focus on the positive features of ELF, but as Guido's work makes clear, it has its problematic features and here too there is a need for description.

Increasingly, the recognition is taking hold that English as an international language belongs to all who use it, and that people who learn it as an additional language have an active role in the way the language spreads and changes. As mentioned in Chapter 1, Brutt-Griffler's detailed study of 'the post-colonial in the colonial' (Brutt-Griffler 2002: vii) demonstrates the active historical role of non-native users of English as *agents* in the development of English: they are not just at the receiving end, but contribute to the shaping of the language and the functions it fulfils and so, as speech communities, take possession of the language in a process she terms 'macroacquisition'. Since these communities, where English does not have a particular intranational role are, of course, different in kind from post-colonial communities, their uses of the language are not conditioned by the same factors. Hence the problems that Guido (2008) discusses, where Outer Circle and Expanding Circle speakers conflict. This difference in the way English is appropriated is an issue of particular theoretical interest which I shall take up later. For the time being, what needs to be emphasized is that agency with respect to the development of the language in its global use, its spread and change, resides in non-native speakers just as much as with native speakers in principle, and in practice even more so, due to the difference in speaker numbers.

It seems, then, that L2 users of English have come a long way from a mindset in which, as Quirk puts it in the above quotation, 'each speaker seek[s] to move to a point where the varietal characteristics reach vanishing point'. What we already know about ELF communication also challenges Quirk's witty continuation that 'each variety is best manifest in those who by commonsense measures speak it worst'. For non-native ELF speakers, being able to use the language like native speakers and without traces of their L1 is increasingly perceived as unnecessary, unrealistic, and, at least by some, as positively undesirable. Indeed, countless ELF speakers have begun to assert their identities and to operate according to their own 'commonsense' criteria. These relate not to externally defined native-speaker norms but to their emically perceived communicative needs and wants in the situation they find themselves in. In current parlance, this process might be called 'reclaiming the local' (Canagarajah 2005; Rubdy 2009), though perhaps with different (if compatible) priorities compared to Outer-Circle-oriented discussions on this theme. From this perspective, 'each variety is best manifest' in those who manage to make use of ELF as a convenient, mutually negotiated means of communication while at the same time consciously retaining linguistic traits of their distinct identities. In that sense, there may well be cases where those who 'speak it [their variety] worst' by Quirk's standards actually speak it best. This line of thinking thus entails 'transcending the nativeness paradigm' (Brutt-Griffler and Samimy 2001).

3.3 'Nativeness'

It seems clear that, like any other users of natural languages, ELF speakers are capable of regulating their communicative interactions according to their own needs and that the argument that standards of communication in English must necessarily depend on conforming to the norms of StE is not tenable. However, since in Quirk's thinking, StE is, as we shall see below, equated with nativeness the corollary to this is that effective communication can only be achieved by adopting the patterns of behaviour of a particular sociocultural group of educated ENL users of the language. To lend support to his argument that non-native speakers of a language are necessarily communicatively handicapped, Quirk makes reference to a famous psycholinguistic study of the competence differences between native and non-native speakers of French (Coppieters 1987), which in his view 'strikingly underscores the native/non-native distinction' (Quirk 1990: 6) and serves as a corrective to what he calls 'liberation linguistics' which overvalues regional, social, and ethnic varieties to the detriment of StE. Coppieters' study, he reports, found that the 'near-native' non-native speakers performed significantly less well on tests in which they had to judge the (un)acceptability of sentence pairs. Quirk goes on to comment:

The difference in the sets of scores [between NSs and NNSs] was reflected in the comments by the non-natives. Though they always managed to understand and make themselves understood fairly well through the linguistic and situational context, they said repeatedly that they had developed no intuitions about the distinction between the imperfect and the passé composé: and two who said this had worked in important professional positions in France [TL=F] for 15 and 21 years respectively. It would be interesting to see similar controlled experiments for English with such pairs as 'The spacecraft is now 1000 km from [+- the] earth', 'She [+-has] lived there for three years.'
(op. cit.: 6f.)

Again, we are faced with issues of identity here, but of simple logic, too. What Quirk is emphasizing is that individuals who are considered near-native and have lived in a 'target language' environment for a long time do not necessarily 'become' native speakers (see the discussion of this question in Davies 2003). They often (choose to) retain aspects of their L1 identity amidst the new setting into which they have moved. While the evidence in Coppieters' study is of a grammatical nature, the observation has been often made particularly in relation to L2 pronunciation, no matter whether people consider themselves as EFL learners striving for near-nativeness or ELF users not usually pursuing such a goal. As Jenkins (2000) explains:

Learners who in all other respects achieve a very high degree of proficiency in English frequently retain a number of L1 phonological features. Although motor control is likely to be an element in this process, identity is probably the more salient issue. As Dalton and Seidlhofer argue, 'Pronunciation is so much a matter of self-image that students may prefer to keep their accent deliberately, in order to retain their self-respect or to gain the approval of their peers'. Therefore, insisting on learners conforming to target-language pronunciation norms and renouncing those of their mother tongue 'may even be seen as forcing them to reject their own identity' (1994: 7).
(Jenkins 2000: 16)[6]

Leaving aside the possibly considerable effect of Coppieters' experimental design, which meant that respondents were rating decontextualized sentence pairs, I would read the results of this study as corroboration of the overriding significance of identity in the use of language, as evidence of the assertion of speakers' sense of self, which overrides the need or desire to strive to mimic native speakers in the peculiarities of their verbal behaviour. In other words, the distinction between native speakers and non-native speakers can indeed be important but, I would argue, for entirely different reasons from those that Quirk is suggesting. To me, Coppieters' results indicate very clearly that speakers can get by perfectly well in an L2 and that they can be successful in 'important professional positions' *without* developing native-speaker intuitions about every aspect of the language.

In a nutshell, what we are contemplating here is the intrinsic functional redundancy of the grammatical 'shibboleth' L1 features that were the focus of the Coppieters experiment Quirk reports on: they are socio-psychologically important in that they serve the function of signalling membership of a certain native-speaker community and underscore the distinction between 'them' and 'us', but they do not play a communicatively important role and are not crucial for intelligibility. Note too that Quirk is talking about speakers with very considerable experience of using French, and in conditions with incomparably higher intrinsic pressures for conformity than typical international ELF settings have (even if we acknowledge the misplaced persistence of NS mindsets in those contexts also). It is thus surprising indeed that an expert linguist should overlook this crucial difference and generalize from findings on the *local* use of French for the teaching of English for *global* purposes.

The main conclusion I would draw from the local settings of the Coppieters study is that native-speaker intuitions and 'perfect mastery' of French are simply not important to the individuals described, and are irrelevant for their success as full members of the society they live in. Quirk's conclusion, however, is exactly the opposite:

The implications for foreign language teaching are clear: the need for native teacher support and the need for non-native teachers to be in constant touch with the native language.
(Quirk 1990: 7)

Even allowing for the time lag between the publication of the paper under discussion and the accelerated globalization of English at present, this is a surprising assertion. It is first of all pedagogically naive in that there is no simple match between the language offered to learners and what they pick up—between 'input' and 'intake' in SLA terms—if it were that simple, then these very advanced French speakers, being 'in constant touch with the native language' would have picked up those 'shibboleths'—with the important proviso that I called into question above that they perceived these as necessary and desirable.

What seems particularly problematic is Quirk's argumentative 'chain'. According to him, standards of communication in English depend on conforming to StE, which in turn can only be sanctioned and ratified by native speakers of English. This means that the notions of *nativeness* and *standard* are conflated to such an extent that they become mutually dependent, indistinguishable, even identical—whereas of course they are, in principle, independent: there are countless NSs of non-standard English, just as there are countless NNSs of StE. After reading Quirk's paper one is left with the rather defeatist impression that it is only (a subset of) native speakers of English who can be trusted to speak proper English up to the standards that any communication situation might require. But as we shall see later, especially in Chapters 5 and 6, there is now empirical research that shows that there is no generally valid, direct relationship between communicative effectiveness and correctness in terms of the norms of native speakers and/or StE.

The above quotation about the need for native teacher support seems to be expressive of the conservative reflexes of many native speakers of English who effectively take Kachru's term 'Inner Circle' to imply that (quite contrary to what Kachru himself intended) they are at the centre of the universe when it comes to English—no matter who uses it, wherever in the world it is used, and for whatever purposes. This would also explain why Quirk, after deploring the tendency he has observed in various teaching contexts 'to permit learners to settle for lower standards than the best' (op. cit.: 9) concludes his paper thus:

Certainly, if I were a *foreign* student paying good money in Tokyo or Madrid to be taught English, I would feel cheated by such a tolerant pluralism. My goal would be to acquire *English* precisely because of its power *as an instrument of international communication*. I would be annoyed at the equivocation over English since it seemed to be *unparalleled in the teaching of French, German, Russian, or Chinese.*

I would be particularly annoyed at irrelevant emphasis on the different varieties of English when I came to realize they *mattered so little to native speakers of English...*

Of course, it is not easy to eradicate once-fashionable educational theories, but the effort is worthwhile for those of us who believe that the world needs an international language and that *English is the best candidate at present on offer.* Moreover, the need to make the effort is something for which we must bear a certain responsibility—and in which we have a certain interest.

(op. cit.: 10, emphases added)

We have here again the Anglo-Saxon attitude I discussed in Chapter 2: the 'instrument of international communication' is assumed to be StE, equivalently native-speaker English, the Queen's English, Quirk's English, an assumption of the legitimacy of native-speaker centrality which marginalizes other users of the language as 'foreign'. It is as if (particularly privileged) native speakers of English not only carried the legitimate form of the language with them when they go abroad, but also a part of England, so that they themselves come to embody a piece of land as it were, a little England. This attitude is itself, one might argue, encapsulated in the reference made here to 'a foreign student paying good money in Tokyo or Madrid'. For the 'foreign student' is of course not a foreigner in his or her own country, but referred to as such by the native speaker of English talking about the teaching of 'his' language in a country that is foreign to him—a prime example of 'native-centrism' and particularly striking if we remember that the paper is the written record of a lecture delivered in Tokyo, to a predominantly Japanese audience, where very obviously it was the (English native) speaker that was the foreigner.

3.4 'Foreignness'

There are two matters about the 'foreignness' of English arising from these remarks that are of particular significance here. One concerns the status of the language, and the other the status of its non-native users. With regard to the former, we need to note a non-sequitur in Quirk's line of argument: from a study concerned with French, Quirk draws implications about foreign language teaching in general, which he then applies to English, the implication being that all foreign languages are alike. But of course languages are 'foreign' in very different ways. The role of English in the world is unparalleled, and therefore ELF is, by definition, different even from other, regional lingua francas. This is explained particularly clearly by a French scholar of English:

Since the middle of the nineteenth century, the role of English has done nothing but grow. The decline of the British Empire has not entailed a corresponding decline in the language (compare the fate of French)—quite on the contrary. English is not an *international language*, after the fashion of Spanish or Russian, but a *world language*, a consequence of the economic and cultural strength of the Anglo-Saxon world (the United States) and the increasing role of the media.
(Chevillet 1994: 118, translated by and quoted in McArthur 1998: 31)

This is also why, for people who intend to make use of English as a world language,[7] learning goals cannot be of the same kind as for traditional 'foreign languages'. It may be entirely appropriate for foreign language teaching (FLT) concerned with languages other than English to combine the learning of a language with learning about and appreciating the culture associated with them, on the assumption that the primary purpose of learning is to engage with the primary community that speaks that foreign language. But ELF users typically operate in international settings in which native speakers of English may or may not figure, but certainly are not a priori models, as is quite clear from many descriptions of actual ELF interactions, such as those of Firth (1996); House (2002); Meierkord (2002); Pölzl and Seidlhofer (2006); and the studies reported in Seidlhofer, Breiteneder, and Pitzl (2006); Mauranen and Ranta (2009); Björkman (2011); and Archibald, Cogo, and Jenkins (2011). It follows that the 'foreignness' of English is functionally and conceptually different from that of other languages, with native speakers of English having no special status as the yardstick of acceptability, let alone intelligibility in ELF contexts. The English which has such 'power as an instrument of international communication' (Quirk 1990: 10) is predominantly the English spoken by non-native speakers, and therefore has, as Chevillet indicates, a very different status from other languages like French or Russian or Spanish and is simply not the same as the English Quirk is talking about.

The second issue, the status of the 'foreign' user (and therefore, first, learner) of English, underlies the whole argument of the primacy of ENL as *the* English language, and therefore the only acceptable norm for use and model for learning. Apart from the objections already raised against this

Anglo-Saxon attitude (see Chapter 2), there is also a practical side to it. If English is to serve as 'an instrument of international communication', it must obviously be readily available for this purpose, and that means that it must be possible to acquire it with relative ease. But if, as Quirk and others propose, this English must be in conformity with standard NS norms including all the NS 'shibboleths', it becomes difficult to acquire for a number of reasons, and as a result is really only available to its native speakers—or rather that smallish educated sub-set of native speakers whose language is judged to be standard. If we then also accept the first assumption that the status of English is the same as any other foreign language, it would follow that international communication is in effect under the hegemonic control of a select community of English native speakers. And of course if as a user or learner you strive to conform to their norms, you become, wittingly or willingly or not, complicit in their dominance—especially and ironically, of course, because your striving will always be likely to fall short of conformity anyway. This essentially is the argument put forward by Phillipson that was discussed in the previous chapter, and so paradoxically enough endorses the very idea of the unique primacy of native-speaker English that he sets out to challenge.

The advocacy of ENL as an international language inevitably privileges its speakers and disempowers all other users. They will always remain at a disadvantage. We might note that this adherence to the view of NSs as the sole owners of the language is also the core of what is probably the main dilemma of EU language policy—the equation of 'English' with ENL and the view of 'English' being the property of its native speakers is the main obstacle to the official acknowledgment of what is the de facto main lingua franca of the European Union and its institutions: if 'English' in the EU were conceptualized not as ENL and therefore the 'property' of the British and Irish, but as ELF and thus the property of all its users, English native speakers would lose their privilege in ELF communication, and EU citizens would not need to feel that they are disadvantaged by succumbing to the 'owners' of the language, i.e. the British and the Irish (see Seidlhofer 2010; Wright 2009).

Concerns about the dangers of the hegemonic imposition of the language have led to calls for resistance on the part of, or rather on behalf of, teachers. Pennycook, for example, in an article entitled 'Pedagogical implications of different frameworks for understanding the global spread of English' argues as follows:

Drawing on notions of post-colonialism and resistance, it [the post-colonial performative response] suggests that English can be appropriated and used for different ends. But it also suggests that such appropriation is not achieved without considerable struggle. Thus the postcolonial performative position is one that sees English language teaching as part of a battle over forms of culture and knowledge ... *an attempt to challenge central norms of language*, culture and knowledge, and to *seek ways of appropriating English* to serve alternative ends. The challenge to develop new post-colonial pedagogies is, to my mind, one of the crucial challenges facing English language teachers today.
(Pennycook 1999b: 153; emphases added)

Pennycook does not, however, go into details about what these 'central norms of language' might be, let alone how exactly language teachers might go about challenging them or developing 'contextual (i.e. location-specific) post-colonial pedagogies for English'. It is not made clear whether by 'appropriation of the language' Pennycook means the kind of variable use of ELF that I have been discussing, nor how this appropriation is related to the new post-colonial pedagogies he mentions and how it is to be operationalized and made real for teachers and learners. In Holliday's book, which claims to struggle with the problems of teaching English as an international language (Holliday 2005), ELF is only mentioned in passing. While presenting a great deal of data illustrating important issues, there is no sign at all of any struggle to come to terms with the changing role and status of the language itself and its implications for teaching, or any awareness that there is any problem here to struggle with at all.

The calls for resistance to 'central norms of language' (Pennycook), or 'native-speakerism' (Holliday), and for 'relocating English' (Saraceni 2009), and 'reclaiming the local' (Canagarajah) are timely, much-needed challenges to conventional ways of thinking and acting, and they make for inspiring reading for applied linguists. But they do not address the conceptualization of 'English' itself, and so the central question remains what form this resistance should take, what is actually involved in relocating English or reclaiming the local. What action can be taken, for example, by teachers to translate these exhortations into their own reality? A major difficulty for them is that the main professional capital ascribed to them by students, parents, school authorities, etc. is expertise in 'the language' they teach. And here it would seem obvious that these calls for resistance are consistent with, and complementary to, the arguments I am putting forward for understanding ELF. For as long as teachers accept the ownership claims of NSs and do not have a conceptual alternative, exhortations and resolutions to 'challenge central norms of language' will lack a basis for action. If teachers are to meet the challenge to develop new pedagogies for English teaching, they need first to challenge the primacy of ENL and their own reduced status as non-native speakers that they believe this gives rise to. They need to develop a coherent and sustainable alternative conceptualization of what this 'English' is that they should encourage their students to learn, and some awareness of what alternative approach to teaching/learning might be appropriate to this 'relocation' of English, dissociated from the imposition of 'native-speakerism'. Otherwise, what we do is to undermine teachers' beliefs in what they do without offering them any viable substitute, thereby leaving them in the limbo of insecurity.[8] Research on ELF can therefore lend substance to the advocacy of critical resistance. The arguments I present in this book indicate how critical approaches to language can be substantiated by an understanding of how ELF speakers actually *realize* this resistance, how they make it a reality by putting it into words.

The conceptualization and operationalization of such alternatives present formidable challenges. The attitude of NS superiority is, as we have seen, deep-seated. But so is the attitude of deference to it. This finds expression, paradoxically enough, even among those who are themselves recommending the challenge to native-speaker norms. It is evident in the contradictory statements made by, for example, van Els who, in the same paper, convincingly argues on the one hand that the ownership of a lingua franca passes to its non-native speakers and on the other observes that the Dutch should not be complacent about their English because 'only very few are able to achieve a level of proficiency that approximates the native or native-like level' (2000: 29). Similarly, Hoffman (2000: 19) describes the English of European learners as spanning 'the whole range from non-fluent to native-like', as though fluency in English were not a possibility for those whose speech does not mimic that of a native speaker. In other words, non-native speakers should appropriate the English which they speak, but unless it conforms to native speaker norms, it is unacceptable, not good enough. On this account, English as an international language is to be judged as if it were English as a native language—the contradiction is quite apparent but seems to have passed unnoticed.

Hoffmann and van Els are helpful examples for illustrating this conceptual issue precisely because their writings over a long time have shown them to be beyond suspicion of being enthusiasts for Anglo-Saxon attitudes. My interpretation of their infelicitous wordings above is precisely that they show a problem I have been at pains to expose—not only for laypersons but also linguists—namely that notions of competence and fluency and (in Quirk's case, StE) tend to be so intricately tied to the idea of 'the native speaker' that it requires a special effort not to unwittingly perpetuate these assumptions and transfer them to the special case of ELF, where they clearly do not hold.

Pennycook's challenging call for resistance and other proposals for critical pedagogy have contributed to a heightened sense of insecurity and unease among English language teachers at what is for them the most critical level: that of the language which they teach—the main basis of their professional qualification, the hub around which their daily practices revolve. Widespread politically correct rhetoric is no effective antidote for this unsatisfactory situation, and so the familiar disabling inadequacy syndrome among non-native teachers of English persists. In Chapter 1, I quoted an expression of this by Peter Medgyes in his book *The Non-Native Teacher*. It is of interest to cite it again (see page 58), but alongside remarks by another non-native speaker of the language, celebrated for his contribution to post-colonial literature:

The two non-native speakers are different in that Ngugi is talking about people in post-colonial settings and Medgyes sees himself as a representative of English teachers in mainland Europe. But both seem to share the assumption of the uniformity of English and to deny the inherent flexibility of the language, its adaptability to change: for them, English is English is English. It is this way of conceiving of the language that is the root of the problems described here. The distress expressed in Medgyes' book, whose objective after all is to foreground the particular strengths of non-native language

We suffer from an *inferiority complex* caused by *glaring defects* in our knowledge of English. We are in *constant distress* as we realize how little we know about *the language* we are supposed to teach. (Medgyes 1994: 40, emphases added)	The effect of the *cultural bomb* is to annihilate a people's belief in their names, in their languages, in their environment, ... in their capacities and ultimately in themselves. It makes them see their past as one *wasteland of non-achievement* and it makes them want to distance themselves from that wasteland. It makes them want to identify with that which is furthest removed from themselves; for instance, with *other people's languages* rather than their own. (Ngugi wa Thiong'o 1981: 3, emphases added)

Table 3.1 Assumptions about English

teachers, indicates that (in Ngugi's words) these teachers' 'belief ... in themselves' has been 'annihilated', and I think it is not an exaggeration to say that the 'inferiority complex' ascribed to these teachers on the basis of the 'glaring defects' in their 'knowledge of English' causes them to 'see their past as one wasteland of non-achievement'. I would argue that offering teachers rallying cries and inspirational talk about their linguistic human rights is not what is most likely to cut through this negative spiral. Rather, what is required is a reconceptualization, supported by thick descriptions, of how 'the language they are supposed to teach' is used appropriately and effectively in the function it predominantly has in the world at large, namely as English as a lingua franca, not English as a native language.

3.5 'Real English'

Medgyes and Ngugi talk about English as if it were a uniform entity: *the* English language—the definite article signifying an article that is also definite: English as an object or thing. This, as we have noted earlier in this chapter, is equated by Quirk with StE, and this in turn defined by Trudgill and Hannah in terms of grammar, and (perhaps) vocabulary. So the language is conceived of as essentially the linguistic code as institutionally established and recorded in grammars and dictionaries. Over recent years, however, corpus linguistics has been able to reveal details of how native speakers exploit these encoded resources in the language that they actually produce. Based on the analysis of large amounts of behavioural data, accounts can now be given of recurring patterns of language, of typical occurrences and recurrences of words and phrases that constitute idiomatic native-speaker usage. This, it is claimed, unlike abstract descriptions of the language code, is 'real language'. It is this idiomatic usage that is now put forward as the norm for users and the model for learners. For example, textbooks and reference books based on data drawn from the CANCODE[9] corpus of spoken conversations of native speakers are stamped on their cover with a 'real language guarantee'. The products with a 'real language guarantee' are presented on the Cambridge International Corpus Website interestingly called 'international' simply by virtue of containing several corpora of British and North American English and the Cambridge Learner Corpus, which consists of 'exam scripts written by students taking Cambridge ESOL exams'.

In a prestigious journal for teachers of English, Ron Carter writes the following under the sub-heading 'Real English':

> The CANCODE data is, of course, real data. Now 'real' is a word I'd like to dwell on for a moment because it is widely used at present in our cultures, particularly in our ELT culture. ... The word 'real' invariably carries positive associations. People believe they want or are told to want, or, indeed, actually want what is real, authentic, and natural in preference to what is unreal, inauthentic, and unnatural.
> (Carter 1998: 43)[10]

The same view of the necessary pedagogic primacy of native speaker usage leads to the claim that materials based on the COBUILD Bank of English 'help learners with real English'.[11] I will return to corpus descriptions of English usage and their validity for pedagogy later in this book but for the moment we need to note that their appearance on the scene is likely to increase the distress that Medgyes expresses. For knowing the language now not only means knowing what is 'proper' English with reference to its grammar and lexis, but what is 'real' English as exemplified in the idiomatic patterns of actually occurring native-speaker behaviour—and not only knowing the forms of these patterns, but also, of course, knowing in what contextual circumstances they can be appropriately used. This is likely to expose the 'inadequacies' of non-native teachers even more glaringly, and to exacerbate their inferiority complex.

One way of relieving the distress would be for the teacher to avoid sole responsibility for knowing the language and transferring it to the corpus itself. This seems to be what the authors of the *BNC Handbook* have in mind:

> In language teaching increasing access to corpora may modify the traditional role of the teacher as authority about the use of the language to be learned, and reduce the sense of inferiority felt by many non-native speaker teachers. More generally, there is much to be said about the way in which thinking about language, particularly the English language, is politicized, and hence about the political implications of changing the basis on which assessments of correctness or appropriateness of usage are made.
> (Aston and Burnard 1998: 43)

To what extent the shift of pedagogic authority from the teacher to the corpus will alleviate the non-native speaker sense of inferiority must be open to doubt. The assumption, of course, still remains that the NS norm of usage represented by the corpus, and supposedly only inadequately known by the teacher, *is* indeed the only acceptable authority, so when Aston and Burnard refer to 'the political implications of changing the basis on which assessments of correctness or appropriateness of usage are made' what has changed about the 'basis' is how it can be accessed, not how it is conceptualized.[12] There is an alternative—though of course not one available to a corpus called the British National Corpus—and that is to give these non-native speaker teachers access to a corpus capturing the successful use of English among non-native speakers, as a lingua franca, thus offering relevant models for many learners wishing to use the language for similar purposes.[13] I shall be exploring this alternative in Chapters 5 and 6.

I should make it quite clear that I do not at all call into question the value and validity of corpus analysis itself. It is clearly a major innovation in linguistic description. The point I am making here is that in promoting 'real English' as the only valid norm for the language users or model for the language learner, the innovation is being used to sustain the established traditional belief of the primacy of ENL. It is a belief that, in principle, Carter seems to share with Quirk, with 'nativeness' now not only associated with a grammatical code, 'single monochrome' StE, but with patterns of actually occurring idiomatic native-speaker usage.

Innovative techniques of description are one thing. Innovative attitudes to what is described are another. Innovative attitudes, particularly if they call into question established belief, always run the risk of sounding like what Quirk refers to as 'half-baked quackery' (1990: 9, 1995: 30) and clearly, this is a danger one has to guard against. But the situation with regard to the global spread of English is such that some rethinking about what constitutes legitimate usage and appropriate objectives for learning English is urgently needed—and I will be focusing on issues of pedagogy in Chapter 8. What I am arguing for in this chapter is not a rejection of all norms and standards, but a reappraisal of their justification, and of the assumption that one standard suits all purposes. The central issue, then, is whether ELF users should be accorded the right to be 'norm-developing' rather than simply 'norm-dependent' (Kachru 1985: 16f.). Certainly, if one thinks of their sheer numbers (as discussed in Chapter 1), there is a prima facie case for so doing since from a global perspective it is ELF rather then ENL that might be termed 'real English'. At all events, the very scale of ELF as a global phenomenon surely calls for some reconsideration of established assumptions about the necessary primacy of the standard native-speaker language. As I have mentioned, post-colonial versions of the language have already been accorded legitimacy in sociolinguistic enquiry, and indeed identified as World Englishes (WE) in their own right. Empirical evidence (of which more in later chapters) indicates that comparable processes of language spread and variation are at work in the emergence of ELF, albeit with some important differences (see Seidlhofer 2009c).

In this respect, Schneider (2003 and 2007) seems particularly relevant: he describes 'the dynamics of New Englishes' (the first part of his 2003 title) as determined by general sociolinguistic processes. In elaborating his 'Dynamic

Model' of the evolution of New Englishes he pays particular attention to communication, accommodation, and identity formation—all of which also figure prominently in the discussion of this chapter. Schneider believes that his model:

holds promises of an applied nature by repositioning and suggesting a reconsideration of the role and assessment of norms of correctness in the usage of English in different countries.
(Schneider 2003: 273)

Of course, the sociocultural role of the language in the New Englishes that Schneider is referring to is very different from the one it has in ELF contexts, and I go into this difference in Chapter 4. But it is a role that also has significant implications for how the language is used, and this, too, calls for a reconsideration of established ideas.

3.6 Conclusion

In this chapter I have given critical consideration to the argument in support of the assumption exemplified in Chapter 2, that English is essentially the standard language claimed as the property of its native speakers, and that this should be the norm against which all other usage is evaluated. I have argued that given the extent to which the language has been appropriated for use as a global lingua franca, this position is not tenable, and that we are faced with an unprecedented situation which is giving rise to unprecedented ideas as to what it means 'to speak a language' to achieve effective communication, who the legitimate speakers of the language are, and whose language is worthy of description. I have argued that changes in the role of English in the world and its widespread and increasing use as a lingua franca for global communication call for a reconsideration of how the language has traditionally been perceived and taught. With reference to the quotation from Williams' *Keywords* at the beginning of this chapter, I have suggested that '[i]nstead of referring back to a source of authority' or 'old measures', we need to project 'from ideas about conditions which we have not yet realized but which we think should be realized'. And as Williams says, this is indeed a matter of 'active social history'.

Notes

1 This conventional ideology has, however, been questioned (see Grace 1981; Makoni and Pennycook 2007; Mühlhäusler 1996). We shall return to these alternative perspectives later in the book.

2 It is fascinating to read Kingsley Bolton's account of Quirk's change of heart over the years: he started off as a 'linguistic liberal' with his book *The Use of English* in 1962, but a couple of decades later had become a staunch guardian of StE, particularly also for the teaching of English 'overseas' (Bolton 2006: 243f.)

3 Schneider (2007: 312) comments: '...I argue that "indigenized varieties...are as legitimate offspring of English as the varieties said to be "native" and...spoken in

former settlement colonies' (Mufwene 2004: 205). This position is also supported by the realities in many of the countries discussed earlier [in his book], where such distinctions are explicitly blurred. Nigeria is a case in point: "in this country it would be futile to look for a clear boundary between English as an L1, as an L2, and Pidgin English (and also between Pidgin, as a second language, and Creole, when defined as a child's mother tongue or L1, for that matter)." (ibid.)

4   As the prolific research on post-colonial Englishes indicates, the struggle for acknowledgement has been largely successful in many countries (cf. Hoffmann and Siebers 2009; Kachru 1992; Kachru, Y. Kachru, and Nelson 2006; McArthur 2002; Mesthrie and Bhatt 2008; Schneider 1997 and 2007; Smith and Forman 1997). Post-colonial literatures flourish, as does the study of the language used by writers such as Achebe, Okara, Rao, Rushdie, Saro-Wiwa, and many others. For these contexts, the naive notion of a monolithic, uniform, inadaptable linguistic medium owned by its original speakers and forever linked to their rule(s) has been recognized as simply counterfactual, and has therefore given way to the realization that indigenized varieties of English are legitimate Englishes in their own right (cf. Mufwene 2001). In legitimizing these Englishes, codification is regarded as a crucial prerequisite for the emergence of endonormative standards in indigenized varieties (cf. Bamgbose 1998).

5   Note though that Graddol (1997: 11) claims that the all-pervasive use of English in the Expanding Circle, not only in influential and institutional networks such as global business, science, and media discourse but also for many everyday activities, lends the language second-language rather than foreign-language status in some countries in the so-called Expanding Circle.

6   Daniels (1995) expresses the same point in a particularly striking way: 'Remember that the mother tongue is, as the name suggests, for a majority of people, the language of their first tender exchanges. If all the utterances we produce were laid end to end (which they are, in time), they would lead us back to those precious and, for most of us, happy days. Hence L1 discourse is a sort of umbilical cord which ties us to our mother. Whenever we speak an L2 we cut that cord, perhaps unconsciously afraid of not being able to find it and tie it up again when we revert to L1. A possible way of avoiding the cut is to continue using the sounds, the rhythms and the intonation of our mother tongue while pretending to speak L2. In contrast, to speak an L2 like a native is to take a drastic step into the unknown, accompanied by the unconscious fear of no return. In the light of these few arguments, is seems to me to be very likely that an L2 learner who protests his/her wish to pronounce it correctly, is doing just that. He/she is saying "I wish I could allow myself to pronounce it authentically" and not "I want to pronounce it authentically" '.

7   As opposed to those who are aiming to master a particular variety of ENL, perhaps because they wish to blend in with their Australian friends, want to study in Britain, or emigrate to New Zealand.

8   Witness the title and abstract of Alastair Pennycook's plenary talk at the TESOL 2011 Annual Convention:

'Teaching English as Something Other Than Language'.

English is an impossible idea. It is plural, fuzzy, unbounded, mixed, emergent, and indefinable. English can no longer be pinned down; it is a set of ideas, aspirations, desires, hopes, and threats. This plenary asks what it is we are involved in when we teach English.

(http://www.tesol.org/s_tesol/convention2011/plenaryspeakers.asp)

9 CANCODE stands for 'Cambridge-Nottingham Corpus of Discourse in English. See http://www.cambridge.org/at/elt/catalogue/subject/custom/item3637700/ Cambridge-International-Corpus-Cambridge-International-Corpus/

10 Ronald Carter, 'Orders of reality: CANCODE, communication, and culture', *ELT Journal* 52/1: 43–56, 64. Interestingly, three years later an article commenting on the exchange between Carter and Cook was published in the same journal. In this paper, the authors show Carter's claim about the invariably positive connotations of 'real' to be false: Laura Gavioli and Guy Aston, 'Enriching reality: language corpora in language pedagogy'. *ELT Journal* 55/3: 238–46. All these articles are reprinted together in Seidlhofer 2003b.

11 *Cobuild English Language Dictionary* 2nd edn: Helping Learners with Real English (Cobuild Series). http://www.amazon.com/Cobuild-English-Language-Dictionary-2nd/dp/0003750299 (accessed 14/9/09)

12 But see Aston (2008) for a different take more compatible with an ELF perspective.

13 A corpus of transcriptions of spoken ELF interactions that is now freely accessible for research purposes is VOICE, the Vienna-Oxford International Corpus of English (http://www.univie.ac.at/voice/). For examples of analyses based on VOICE see Chapters 5 and 6.

4

Reconceptualizing 'English'

The innovations in paradigms of creativity, the range in types
of English...and the functional allocation of the language
increasingly reflect this crosslinguistic and cross-cultural nature of
its uses and users. The question, then, is: what types of response
does this profile of world Englishes elicit from our profession?

BRAJ B. KACHRU: *The Paradigms of Marginality*

4.1 Appropriation and adaptation

In previous chapters I have discussed the persistent and resistant traditional
belief that there is only one kind of 'real' or 'proper' English and that that
is the language of its Inner Circle native speakers, who are, as Trudgill puts
it, the 'true repository' of the language: English is English is their English.
However, these outdated ideas are now being challenged by the emergence of
ELF. Therefore, several basic concepts require rethinking.

I have argued in Chapters 2 and 3 that in appropriating the language, non-
native users do not simply adopt it, but adapt it to suit their communicative
purposes: *their* English is not the same as that of native speakers. Chinua
Achebe, in an often quoted passage, refers to 'a new English, still in commun-
ion with its ancestral home but altered to suit its new African surroundings'
(Achebe 1975: 62). But as the language has spread as a global lingua franca,
the alteration, or adaptation, will, of course, need to suit a much wider range
of surroundings than the African ones that Achebe has in mind. As Graddol
puts it:

People have wondered for some years whether English had so much got its feet under
the global office desk that even the rise of China—and Mandarin—could ever shift it
from its position of dominance. The answer is that there is already a challenger, one
which has quietly appeared on the scene whilst many native speakers of English were
looking the other way, celebrating the rising hegemony of their language.

...The new language which is rapidly ousting the language of Shakespeare as the
world's lingua franca is English itself—English in its new global form. ...this is not

English as we have known it, and have taught it in the past as a foreign language. It is a new phenomenon, and if it represents any kind of triumph it is probably not a cause of celebration by native speakers.
(Graddol 2006: 11)

It is not native-speaker English that has become dominant by being adopted worldwide, Graddol suggests, but English 'in its new global form'—a language adapted by its lingua franca users to make it their own. How far such users can, or should, assert their independence in this way is a matter of considerable dispute. Some would claim that the independence is in part illusory in that the hegemony of native-speaker English survives however variously it is used. Others, as we have seen, would not recognize the right of such users to be independent anyway. So although the 'new phenomenon' that Graddol mentions may have 'quietly appeared on the scene' now that it has appeared, it has prompted a good deal of animated discussion about 'linguistic imperialism' (Phillipson 1992), 'the politics of English as an international language' (Pennycook 1994), and the 'linguistic human rights' of non-native users of English (Ammon 2000). Especially controversial has been the claim that users of English as an international lingua franca are entitled to appropriate the language and actively contribute to its development.

The issue of ownership is a central one and in this chapter I shall explore it in some detail. The issue was raised particularly provocatively by Widdowson in the early 1990s in a plenary talk at an annual TESOL convention—and thus right in the 'lion's den' so to speak, since TESOL is, after all, the world's largest association of teachers of English, linguaculturally firmly rooted in the USA. In the talk, subsequently published in TESOL Quarterly, Widdowson proposed the following argument:

How English develops *in the world* is no business whatever of native speakers in England, the United States, or anywhere else. They have no say in the matter, no right to intervene or pass judgement. They are irrelevant. The very fact that English is an international language means that no nation can have custody over it. To grant such custody over the language is necessarily to arrest its development and so undermine its international status.
(Widdowson 1994: 385, emphasis added)[1]

What Widdowson is highlighting here is the logical impossibility for native speakers of acknowledging (and even taking pride in) the status of English as a world language on the one hand while on the other hand also insisting on its ownership and on control over its international development: native speakers of English cannot have it both ways. If they are proud of the fact that what used to be 'their' language has now become the world's language, then they must also grant it the freedom to develop 'in the world' as a global lingua franca. So with reference to Graddol, it is not just that this development is 'probably not a cause for celebration by native speakers', it logically *cannot* be.

To me, this seems such a sound (even obvious) argument that it is difficult to believe that anybody should deny its validity. However, there is a significant difference between accepting logical arguments and following through their implications, a difference brought about by such factors as the inertia of tradition and 'real world' pressures such as vested interests in power and economic control. This may be the main reason why, many years on, the language is still, generally speaking, perceived to be in native-speaker custody. What may be regarded as an indication that things are beginning to change, however, is that now that we are well into the 21st century, there are also non-native speakers of English who feel that there is a need, and indeed that they have the right, to question the dominance of native speakers of English when it comes to using the language as the world's major lingua franca. Here, for example, is what a German scholar writes in the introduction to a book he has edited:

A number of contributions to the present volume point out real advantages of the English-speaking world, or its scientists, and disadvantages of the other language communities and their scientists. Here the question of dominance in the literal sense arises, namely dominance of the native speakers of the world lingua franca by means of their language over the non-native speakers, let alone the non-speakers.

... In order to raise awareness of these problems I have postulated, in my contribution to this volume as well as elsewhere (Ammon 2000), the 'non-native speakers' right to linguistic peculiarities'. It may appear a rather hopeless postulate considering the well-founded linguistic veneration of the native speaker, but I believe it deserves close examination, also re the possibilities of a political campaign to gather support similar to that for female linguistic rights. The feminist campaign too was far from being taken seriously at the beginning but has certainly had considerable success meanwhile. I am aware that the postulate of equity for non-native speakers of English, to put it in another way, faces far more formidable obstacles than did, or does, linguistic gender neutrality. It needs, first of all, adequate specification before it can be taken seriously. (Ammon 2001: viif.)

Here we are presented with very strong and persuasive arguments for the linguistic 'emancipation' of non-native speakers of English, and by a German sociolinguist who is a highly experienced user of English as a lingua franca, both as a speaker at international conferences and as a prominent author and editor of internationally published scholarly work. Ammon is asserting his right, and that of his fellow non-native English speaking scholars, to their own English.

But it is not a matter of native speakers generously conceding the right of non-native speakers to use and adapt the language as they think fit. Adaptation naturally happens as a consequence of the very process of appropriation. So English could not actually function as an international language at all if it were simply adopted rather than adapted.

It is a commonplace to say that language variation and change are inevitable processes intrinsic to the very use of any living language. Given the fact that English is undoubtedly a living language, and given the fact that its global spread is happening, and indeed gathering pace at a quite unprecedented rate, it is quite obvious that it will vary and change. To put it simply, language variation and change will happen wherever a language is used, and since English is used globally, it is also developing globally rather than only within native-speaker communities. However, this seemingly uncontroversial fact seems to be denied by those who adhere to what Widdowson (1997a, 2003) has termed a 'distribution' view quite prevalent among many commentators on English as a global language. If you take such a distribution view, Widdowson says:

...you can think of English as an adopted international language, and then you will conceive of it as a stabilized and standardized code leased out on a global scale, and controlled by the inventors, not entirely unlike the franchise for Pizza Hut and Kentucky Fried Chicken. Distribution of essentially the same produce for consumers worldwide: English not so much a lingua franca, but rather a franchise language. There are no doubt people who think in these conveniently commercial terms, and if English as an international language were indeed like this, there would be cause for concern.
(Widdowson 2003: 50f.)

In this distribution view, the native speakers retain the language as their property and lease it out to other users who, not being owners, have no right to make any alterations to it. As we have already noted, however, this 'adoption view' in the terminology of the present chapter, contradicts everything we know about language variation and change, and is therefore untenable. It would seem to follow, then, that the only viable alternative is what can be called the 'adaptation view': one that acknowledges the realities of language spread. Widdowson summarizes the differences between these two views and points out their incompatibility:

...we might think of English as an international language not in terms of the distribution of a stable and unitary set of encoded forms, but as the spread of a virtual language which is exploited in different ways for different purposes.
...When we talk about the spread of English, then, it is not that the conventionally coded forms and meanings are transmitted into different environments and different surroundings, and taken up and used by different groups of people. It is not a matter of the actual language being distributed but of the virtual language being spread and in the process being variously actualized. The *distribution* of the actual language implies *adoption and conformity*. The *spread* of the virtual language implies *adaptation and nonconformity. The two processes are quite different.*
(Widdowson 2003: 50, emphases added)

The idea of the 'virtual language' is an important one that we shall come back to in Chapter 5. For now, what matters is that language spread (as opposed to distribution) inevitably involves a transfer of ownership and with it the natural consequence of variable adaptation.

It is important to emphasize, however, that claiming the right to own English does not at all mean that its users must relinquish ownership of other languages. English in its adapted form co-exists as a linguistic resource alongside others, drawn upon as appropriate to particular domains and contexts of use. This is what Brutt-Griffler (2002: 110) refers to as 'stabilization of bilingualism through the coexistence of world language with other languages in bilingual/multilingual contexts'. Such a perspective has very considerable implications for language policy in contexts where the spread of English is claimed to constitute a general threat to linguistic diversity, and an unfair advantage for ENL speakers. There has been much controversial debate about this issue as it relates to different parts of the world (see, for example, Skutnabb-Kangas 2000; Phillipson 2003b; Brutt-Griffler 2004; Brutt-Griffler 2009; Ferguson 2006). There is no doubt that in some parts of the world, there are very real fears for the survival of local and regional languages as people (particularly the young) increasingly turn away from their L1 and towards English, which they perceive as useful and 'cool'. But this state of affairs does not automatically validate the claim that English is necessarily and generally a threat to other languages. This idea seems to be based on the assumption that languages are complete and functionally comprehensive entities and that they are bound to compete with each other for the same communicative space and cannot peacefully co-exist as parts of a more general linguistic repertoire to be exploited as appropriate in different domains of use. When this assumption is compounded by the belief that different languages necessarily belong to different nation states and represent their values and interests, it is not surprising that the *dominance* of English is taken to imply *domination* by its native speakers. But once one denies this right of exclusive ownership and dissociates the language from its native speakers and recognizes it as a partial and expedient resource that anyone can make use of—in other words, once one thinks of English as ELF, then the language obviously no longer poses the same threat of domination.

Certainly, as I perceive the context I am most familiar with, Europe, linguistic diversity is more likely to be protected by a new conceptualization of English as ELF rather than by political rhetoric and linguistically and educationally naive exhortations to European citizens to learn languages other than English—by which is meant languages other than ENL, of course (cf. House 2003; Seidlhofer 2003a). In contrast to a clinging to this outdated view of languages harking back to 19th century nation states, a forward-looking approach to questions of 'European multilingualism' requires the acceptance of a new concept of English, as ELF: appropriated and adapted to serve communal and communicative needs. ELF is bound to co-exist with other languages; it forms part of individuals' bi- or multilingual repertoires, and these repertoires can but represent a reconciliation of two or more languages, each with its own functional domains. As a consequence, the total encoding possibilities of each language are only partially exploited, and this raises a more general question about what the 'linguae' in multilingualism actually consist of, what we mean when we talk about 'a language' and what constitutes competence in it. I shall return to these questions presently. For the moment, the point to be made is that once English is conceived of as common property and thus freed from the ties that bind it to its native speakers and their national interests and becomes altered by its new owners to suit their needs and purposes, it becomes available as an additional resource to be drawn upon as and when functionally required.

4.2 The sociolinguistics of ELF

Although the widespread occurrence of this appropriation and adaptation of English as a lingua franca is an established fact, its recognition as an entirely natural, and indeed inevitable, sociolinguistic process has been consistently withheld. And here we come again to the conceptual gap referred to in Chapter 1: an awareness of the existence of ELF on the one hand, and a denial of its legitimacy as a use of language and therefore as a worthy object of linguistic study on the other hand. Trudgill, for example, seems to be in no doubt about the importance of ELF as a unique linguistic phenomenon:

> There are many languages which have played important roles as institutionalised lingua francas: Latin was the lingua franca of the Roman Empire, and continued to play an important role in European learning until quite recently. But the extent to which English is employed like this is without parallel. Never before has a language been used as a lingua franca by so many people in so many parts of the world. English is also remarkable in having more non-native than native speakers...
> (Trudgill 2002: 150)

Oddly enough, this acknowledgement of the importance of ELF does not prevent Trudgill, on the very same page from trivializing ELF usage as 'quite interesting and amusing' and as not making 'any difference to anything important'.

One might have supposed that the fact that the situation of English in today's world is without parallel should make for an exciting time for linguists, since it is to be expected that some of the theoretical/conceptual and descriptive linguistic research on the language is likely to be without parallel, too. At the most general level, one could say that what we are witnessing in the case of the extensive use of English as a lingua franca that Trudgill acknowledges, is an accelerated language spread due to a new globalized world, and with it, inevitably, accelerated processes of language variation and, ultimately, change.

There is, of course, plenty of excitement in the sociolinguistic community about language variation and change as manifested in other areas of English usage. The clearest evidence of this is the impressive volume of publications on various aspects of this phenomenon. For instance, in the book series *Varieties of English Around the World*, Manfred Görlach has been offering descriptions and overviews as well as annotated bibliographies in volumes entitled *Englishes* (1991), *More Englishes* (1995), *Even More Englishes* (1998), and *Still More Englishes* (2002). In addition, journals such as *English World-Wide* and *World Englishes* are going strong. The latter journal's founding co-editor, Braj Kachru, pioneered the description of the developmental processes and manifestations of non-native Englishes and campaigned successfully for the sociolinguistic recognition of these (post-colonial) varieties in what he terms the Outer Circle.

In these times of heightened migration and crosscultural contacts, the literature on their linguistic consequences has proliferated. We have extensive and authoritative work on language variation and change (for example, Chambers *et al.* 2002; Trudgill 2002; and the journal *Language Variation and Change*); on language contact/contact linguistics (for example, Goebl *et al.* 1996; Myers-Scotton 2002; Hickey 2010, and the series *Cambridge Approaches to Language Contact*); on bi- and multilingualism; on second language acquisition (for example, Brutt-Griffler 2002; Cook 2002); and New Englishes (for example, Platt *et al.* 1984; Kachru 1992; Schneider 2003 and 2007; Kortmann and Schneider 2008; Mesthrie and Bhatt 2008). Such work has given rise to new descriptive insights as well as to intriguing new theoretical perspectives. All this, then, is testimony to the fascination exerted by the richness of functions and forms of the English language in the world.

In the world? Not quite. For, oddly enough, English as a lingua franca as used across all of Kachru's circles is excluded in practically all of the fascinating current research and discussion in sociolinguistics and descriptive linguistics in general. This is very strange since ELF is an entirely natural language development: it exemplifies perfectly how language varies and changes in reaction to circumstances and conditions of use, and as such is entirely comparable to what is going on in the Inner and Outer Circles. The unprecedented and accelerated spread of English and the resulting variation and change would seem to be precisely the kind of phenomenon that should interest (socio)linguists. But perversely, ELF is left out of account.[2]

This refusal to take ELF and ELF speakers seriously is all the more perverse since it flies in the face of everything that sociolinguists have held dear all along: interest in the intricate relationship between linguistic variation, contexts of use and expressions of identity, insistence on the intrinsic variability of all language, and the natural virtues of linguistic diversity. How then can this denial of ELF be explained?

4.3　Established concepts and convenient fictions

The explanation, I suggest, lies in the disinclination to question received wisdom, to subject taken-for-granted ideas to critical scrutiny in the light of changed circumstances. It is perhaps only natural for linguists, like everybody else, to avoid uncertainty by looking for security in established concepts and values—to subscribe to what Kuhn (1962) refers to as 'normal science'. So this reluctance to adapt to changed circumstances should not surprise us. Interesting parallels with earlier attitudes are as easy to find as they are instructive. Denial is exactly what has often been a first reaction in history at times of swift and unsettling change. Widdowson (2003) cites one particularly striking example that bears directly on the issue of acceptable variation that we are concerned with. The first issue of the British Council-sponsored journal *English Language Teaching* in 1946 carried a feature that gave advice about correct usage. In response to a query from a reader about the expressions 'fry-pan' and 'frying pan', we find the following:

'Fry-pan' is not accepted as standard English and is considered incorrect by most grammarians. It is probably an American form.
(Widdowson 2003: 33)

That was a long time ago ago, and it is, of course, unlikely that any linguist nowadays would have the temerity to make such a pronouncement. The criteria for deciding on what is accepted as Standard English and what is not have of course been expediently adjusted over the years. But just what these criteria are, what actually constitutes StE, remains elusive of definition. I return here to issues touched on in the previous chapter. For it is this very elusiveness, I believe, that is indicative of a conceptual confusion that prevents an understanding of ELF and calls for the kind of reconceptualization that is the central concern of this present chapter.

Standard English is said to be a variety, and the criterion for defining it that is usually offered is that it is the language of educated native speakers but without any explicit indication as to what it means to be 'educated'. After all, everybody who has been to school has been educated up to a point, so at what point are they educated enough to count as standard speakers? According to Trudgill, Standard English is a dialect but 'unlike other dialects, Standard English is a purely social dialect' (Trudgill 1999: 122). The social class that is taken to be the community of its users is the middle-class, so by 'educated' is presumably meant the degree of education typically achieved by this particular social group. But then, of course, we need to know on what basis this group is to be defined, and again there are no clear criteria for this. Standard English turns out to be a very vague notion indeed. And yet it is routinely invoked as a well defined concept.

More generally the notion of variety itself proves to be difficult to define. As Trudgill himself recognizes:

How we divide these continua up is also most often linguistically arbitrary, although we do of course find it convenient normally to make such divisions and use names for dialects that we happen to want to talk about for a particular purpose *as if* they were discrete varieties.
(Trudgill 1999: 122)

As we have seen in the last chapter, the particular purpose for talking about Standard English *as if* it were a discrete variety would seem to be to set it up as the norm or model against which all other usage is measured and found wanting. But if our particular purpose is not to measure conformity but to explore the continuum of use, then the making of such discrete divisions obviously becomes very *in*convenient.

The important point that Trudgill is making is that discrete varieties are a convenient methodological fiction. The very fact that any natural language is of its nature unstable, always in flux and variable, means that any definition of a variety, or code, or established norm is an idealized construct. Sociolinguists have often taken Chomsky to task for assuming an ideal speaker–listener in a homogeneous speech community, but their identification of varieties is also inevitably based to some extent on idealization and the assumption of homogeneity. There are no varieties until linguists circumscribe them as ideal stable entities. There is only the continuum, the continual process of variation.

This convenient fiction divides up the language continuum and reifies languages and language varieties as separate entities or bounded units. But then what has been arbitrarily constructed as a methodological expediency takes on a life of its own. Languages are taken to exist as a matter of fact, as distinct and separate things: *the* Arabic language, *the* English language, *the* French language: definite codes, clearly demarcated as distinct. The view that generally still predominates is that if you are bilingual, you are in possession of two of these entities, and if multilingual, more than two, each a separate compartment of competence. And these entities are presented as complete and self-enclosed so that if you are to legitimately claim to possess them, you have to possess them in their entirety. Otherwise you have only an imperfect and inadequate command of them, a restricted competence, and little if any credit is allowed to a partial but adequate proficiency which may be perfectly well suited to your needs.

If our purpose is to account for the way language actually functions in use, this way of thinking becomes problematic. As an illustration, consider the case of code-switching and style-shifting. These phenomena are functionally alike in that both involve the use of alternative expressions available in the user's linguistic repertoire. They are, however, generally seen as distinct in that in code-switching the alternates come from two different languages, and in style-shifting they come from just one (see, for example, Saville-Troike 2003). In practice, however, this distinction is difficult to make. Take the following (invented) expressions:

1 The problems that were caused by this disagreement...
2 The problems that emanated from this dispute...
3 The problems attendant on this contretemps...

One might suggest that we can identify a style shift between examples 1 and 2 in that both expressions draw on the lexical and grammatical encodings available in English, whereas in 3 we see a code-switch in that use is made of a lexical item from another language, namely French. One difficulty about this, however, is that the word *contretemps* is included in the *Oxford English Dictionary*, and its occurrence in actual native speaker English usage attested in the *British National Corpus* (it occurs 11 times). On this evidence, we might say that the word has now become naturalized and nativized as English, so that 3 is just as much an example of style-shifting as the other two expressions. But this is not evidence of how things are from a user perspective. For the question obviously arises as to which native speakers would have this word in their vocabulary. Many would find it entirely foreign and so for them would constitute a code-switch. But then the same might well apply to the word 'emanated'. This might well be as foreign (and as incomprehensible) for some users as 'contretemps' even though its status as an English lexical item would be confirmed by reference to a dictionary, and by its conformity here to English morphological rule. So what for some language users would be a style-shift, would for others be a code-switch, and vice versa.

The point that I am making here is that the distinction between code-switching and style-shifting is based entirely on the demarcations that are imposed by linguistic description and do not necessarily represent the reality of user experience. For the English that its individual native speakers know and put to use is not at all the same as the language that linguists describe in its entirety in grammars and dictionaries or record comprehensively as usage. The English language that is documented and presented as reference bears little resemblance to the actual language that individuals experience as use. No matter how expert a user of English might be, their expertise is confined to only a fraction of the recorded language. ELF is often said to be deficient, as we have seen, in that it is incomplete and restricted. But all English *as actually used* is similarly, and necessarily, incomplete and restricted, its acquisition and use bounded by functional need. Nobody knows the language, the whole language, and nothing but the language. And this is, of course, as true of other languages as it is of English. Bilinguals and multilinguals do not know two, or more, languages in their entirety but only partially, each complementing the others. It is not a quantitative matter of the cumulative collection of different codes, but of knowing how to use their partial knowledge strategically and appropriately as a composite linguistic resource. And this, of course, is just what ELF users do. A major reason, I believe, for the conceptual gap I have been referring to, is the assumption that the use of language has to be the use of a particular recognized language which is in effect based on the persistent methodological fiction that represents languages and language varieties as discrete entities which can be circumscribed and described in their entirety. The gap, I believe, can only be closed if we take a quite different perspective and think not of varieties but of *variation*, not of how far forms of language conform to *codified norms*, but how they *function* as the exploitation of linguistic resources for making meaning.

This view is consistent with a postmodern *Weltanschauung* (to make use of my own multilingual resource) that seeks to take account of the radical changes brought about by globalization. As Rampton puts it:

> [...] in the discourses that one can call 'postmodern', there is now much more of a preoccupation with fragmentation, contingency, marginality, transition, indeterminacy, ambivalence, and hybridity.
> (Rampton 1997: 330)

As we have seen, there are many aspects of ELF that can be said to characterize it as a postmodern phenomenon: it can be described as a hybrid, fragmented, contingent, marginal, indeterminate use of language. As such, rather than simply excluding it from serious enquiry on the grounds that it cannot be conveniently accommodated within established conceptual frameworks, it is high time, as I have suggested, to consider how these old frameworks can be revised or replaced to account for new realities.

4.4   ELF, 'World Englishes', and the concept of 'variety'

I have argued that in ELF we see the same process of natural appropriation and adaptation that occurs in post-colonial settings. In these settings, the process results in 'World Englishes' and is assigned legitimacy. In the case of ELF, legitimacy is usually withheld. It is relevant to ask why this should be so.

In the quotation cited at the beginning of this chapter, Kachru points to the need to take into account new linguistic realities—what he calls 'innovations in paradigms of creativity'—and asks what response they elicit from the linguistics profession. He provides his own reply as follows:

There are essentially two types of response. One is to view this overwhelming linguistic phenomenon as an age-old process of language dynamics accentuated by the complex culturally and linguistically pluralistic contexts of language acquisition, language function, language contact, and language creativity. This response demands questioning the earlier paradigms, asking new probing questions, and looking for fresh theoretical and methodological answers. The second response, from a number of active scholars, is to marginalize any questions—theoretical, methodological, and ideological—which challenge the earlier paradigms or seek answers appropriate to new global functions of English.
(Kachru 1996b: 242)

The language dynamics that Kachru has in mind is that which relates to the use of English of his Outer Circle, but his remarks, I would argue, are just as relevant to ELF as it occurs elsewhere in the world *across* all three Circles. Here too, the same kind of factors affecting variable usage come into play. So the same welcoming of new challenges that Kachru demands regarding developments in the Outer Circle should now also be expected when dealing with ELF. But no such welcome has so far been forthcoming.

One way of denying legitimacy to ELF and reducing its status as 'an overwhelming linguistic phenomenon' is to associate it with earlier phenomena that went under the name 'lingua franca'. For Kachru himself, it seems the term is inextricably bound up with its original, very limited meanings, above all in the sense of:

an intermediary contact language (*Vermittlungssprache*), used primarily by the Arabs, and later, also the Turks, with travellers from Western Europe, by prisoners of war, and by the Crusaders.
(Kachru 1996a: 906)

Kachru (2005) also approvingly quotes McArthur (2001):

...the current condition of the English language worldwide is both straightforward and convoluted. It is straightforward in that English is now widely agreed to be the global lingua franca; it is convoluted in that the term lingua franca has traditionally

referred to low-level makeshift languages, whereas English is a vast complex whose 'innumerable clearly distinguishable varieties' [Burchfield 1986] range from high social and scientific registers through to some of the most maligned basilects on earth. What then does 'lingua franca' mean when used by such commentators with regard to English?
(McArthur 2001: 1)

It may be that the term *lingua franca* triggers, for some people, an association with a 'low-level makeshift' language, and that historically some such usages were pejoratively designated by that name. But this does not mean that the term must be restricted to refer just to these particular manifestations and cannot apply to the general phenomenon of cross-linguacultural mediation. Lingua franca usage is not 'low-level' and makeshift *by definition*. One might mention in passing that Isaac Newton's account of gravity and the laws of motion in his *Principia Mathematica* and Francis Bacon's utopian novel *Nova Atlantis* were written in a lingua franca, and there is not much that is low-level and makeshift about those.

What seems to be suggested by these remarks by Kachru and McArthur is that when English is used as an international language it can *either* be a lingua franca, which is by definition low-level and makeshift *or* a clearly distinguishable variety, and only such varieties would qualify as a legitimate use of language worthy of study. It is they alone that represent 'the global functions of English'. So the identification of 'World Englishes' rests on the methodological fiction discussed earlier that varieties can be defined as discrete entities. In this respect, a key concept of the earlier paradigm, far from being questioned or challenged, is simply taken as self-evidently valid. Indeed, the notions of geographically defined speech communities and linguistic varieties are so deep-rooted that they survive even in critical discussions of Kachru's model in the 2000s. For instance, Bruthiaux (2003) points out that:

we need to acknowledge that while the Three Circles model has provided us with a convenient shorthand for labeling contexts of English worldwide, the categories that the model created have also had the unfortunate side-effects of reifying the content of these categories and of encouraging the notion that Englishes are Englishes, regardless of circle.
(Bruthiaux 2003: 174)

This observation is entirely compatible with the line of argument taken in this book. However, Bruthiaux himself seems much preoccupied with who should be 'in' and who should not, what should count as a variety and what should not:

for a variety to emerge, local practices must surely gain norm value through recurring, spontaneous use across a range of communicative functions as well as in emblematic domains such as the media, artistic creation, and popular culture.
(ibid.: 168)

This insistence on 'variety-creating conditions' (ibid.) is surprising as it amounts to a (albeit well founded) redrawing of circle boundaries rather than an abolishment, and it actually sits uncomfortably with Bruthiaux' strong arguments and his statement towards the end of his paper—which I would wholeheartedly endorse—that:

...much is to be gained by focusing less on where speakers of English come from and more on what they do—or don't do—with the language...
(ibid.: 175).

If this is recognized, so too will be the fact that for much English use as a lingua franca in the world, questions of variety status are simply irrelevant—these are questions that may still exercise (some) linguists, while the actual speakers have moved on. And linguistics needs to move on accordingly.[3]

Getting away from anachronistic and irrelevant discussions of variety status when thinking about ELF is an important step. And obviously enough, it is one that is easier to take for postmodern scholars than for traditional sociolinguists in university English departments—and for English teachers educated in these departments. As we have seen in this chapter and in the previous ones, academics in various branches of English studies have been socialized into thinking about English as manifested in different varieties located in space and time, social strata, and domains of use, with the concomitant belief that recognizing 'more varieties' as independent entities amounts to progress in that it acknowledges and values diversity rather than ignoring or suppressing it. To illustrate this point, I remember an animated discussion following a talk at the 13th IAWE conference in Regensburg in October 2007 that can be seen as representative of many similar debates. This was about the different meanings carried by the terms *English in Ghana* as opposed to *Ghanaian English*, and about the sensibilities involved in deciding for one rather than the other: the speaker, Jemima Asabea Anderson, had presented a host of formal features that she regarded as 'strong indicators that warrant the postulation of a variety of English called 'Ghanaian English' that still lacks codification' (Anderson 2009: 27). She then explained that in Ghana, 'the label "Ghanaian English" is still associated with imperfect usage or error varieties that are used among Ghanaians' (op. cit.: 28f.). This view contrasted with that of Anderson's audience in Regensburg, where the label 'Ghanaian English' was favoured by the sociolinguists present as expressing the claim to, and recognition of, Ghanaian English as a legitimate and distinct national variety. What this example makes clear is that in mainstream sociolinguistics, putting the modifier (in this case *Ghanaian*) in front of *English* is generally seen as an expression of recognition of a distinct variety based on the description of specific features of the language used in a particular territory.

(Presumably) in the same vein, the term *English as a lingua franca* (ELF) is now sometimes replaced by *Lingua Franca English* (LFE) (see Chapter 1, endnote 2), as in Canagarajah 2007b (but not 2006a and b). Since I could not find an explicit rationale for this in this paper itself, I quote Pennycook's explanation:

Canagarajah makes a related point in his discussion of lingua franca English (LFE). This distinction between English as a lingua franca and lingua franca English is important since the former tends towards an understanding of a pre-given language that is then used by different speakers, while the latter suggests that LFE emerges from its contexts of use. According to Canagarajah, 'LFE does not exist as a system out there. It is constantly brought into being in each context of communication' (2007a: 91). (Pennycook 2009: 202f.)

As I see it, this is an unhelpful proposal, albeit for the right reasons. While I fully agree with a view of ELF under constant negotiation and can thus see the danger of any formulation 'English as a ...' suggesting a pre-given entity, I would claim that simply renaming ELF as LFE is not at all helpful but on the contrary is actually misleading: the analogy in form between the term *Lingua Franca English* and the terms *Ghanaian English, Indian English, Nigerian English*, and *Singapore English* would in fact suggest that 'LFE' should be categorized in formal terms as a distinct variety of the language in the World Englishes paradigm. This would thus reaffirm a way of thinking about ELF in terms of 'variety counting', as belonging to the same kind of (national/territorial) Englishes that are now finally recognized, on the basis of descriptions of particular linguistic features, as the distinct and rightful 'property' of various groups of speakers with a shared sociocultural background.[4] But ELF as I conceive of it is different in kind, functionally and not formally defined; it is not a variety of English but a variable way of using it: English that functions *as* a lingua franca. The absolutely crucial question, of course, remains how the 'English' that functions as a lingua franca is conceptualized and how it functions (i.e. how it can be described), and this is what we shall focus on in the next chapters.

Of course, as Trudgill (quoted in 4.3. above) points out, describing varieties *as if* they were discrete entities may be justified on the grounds that it is convenient to do so 'for a particular purpose'. After all, any systematic enquiry, no matter how closely it claims to represent reality, necessarily depends on some degree of idealization in the conversion of data into evidence. So the relevant issue is what particular purpose justifies this idealization and how it relates to the questions—theoretical, methodological, and ideological—that Kachru says must be probed and not marginalized.

The first point that needs to be made here is that although I have said that the conceptualization of languages or varieties as bounded units is a convenient fiction for the purposes of linguistic analysis, it is important to recognize that language users themselves will tend to think of the language they use in a similar way. Motivated by socio-political and other considerations, they mark out linguistic boundaries to define the communal space in which they can invest their group identity and in which they can feel socially secure. So in this case the representation of languages and varieties as bounded entities is not an expedient fiction for linguistic analysis but something experienced as a matter of social fact. As Blackledge and Creese (2008) put it:

If languages are invented, and languages and identities are socially constructed, we nevertheless need to account for the fact that at least some language users, at least

some of the time, hold passionate beliefs about the importance and significance of a particular language to their sense of 'identity'.
(Blackledge and Creese 2008: 535)

To think in terms of discrete linguistic units therefore is consistent with established folk-linguistic notions about the close correspondence between language and community. And here we return to issues touched on in Chapter 3 about the underlying motivation for identifying the variations in Outer Circle or post-colonial settings as constituting distinct 'World Englishes'.

The language variations that represent the World Englishes that Kachru and his associates have been concerned with are closely tied to, and indeed the means of expression of, a shared social and cultural history, a shared physical space, and thus a vast store of shared knowledge and experience that makes for a sense of community—a *speech community* indeed. Such communities constitute a relatively stable space in which local cultures can thrive and find expression. Seen in this light, it is easy to see why the notion of *variety*, and for the World Englishes paradigm the notion of *indigenized/nativized varieties* such as Indian English, Nigerian English, Singapore English, etc. is so crucial. It asserts the right of the speakers in these ex-colonial territories to their own endonormative Englishes, independent of the language of the former colonizers. To these speakers, the suggestion that their English is 'just' a lingua franca ('low-level' and 'makeshift' that is) would, of course, be anathema. Although English does fulfil the function of a vehicular language in these territories as well, the language has also become appropriated as a means of expression of particular local bi- or multilingual identities. As Thumboo puts it in his chapter 'Literary Creativity in World Englishes':

Th[e] internationalization of languages, as illustrated by English, occurs in a variety of contexts generated between the impact of colonialism on the one hand, and the response of the colonized cultures on the other. There are two facets to this, far less interlinked than such terms as 'post-colonial' would suggest. For reasons of expediency and good management, colonial powers sought to maintain the same policies for all colonies. There was, in this sense, a kind of colonial homogeneity that contributed to its hegemony and identity. It is remarkable to see the extent to which the same texts, songs, educational methods were practised in every part of the British Empire. On the other hand, the politics and subsequent history of former colonies tend to break away from that homogenized hegemony in an attempt to recover national shape, rhythm, and identity, the uniqueness of the pre-colonial—and in some cases colonial—inheritance. While it anticipates what is to follow, this accounts for the various Englishes that have emerged in Asia.
(Thumboo 2006: 406)

And under the subsection heading 'Impulses behind the New English Writing', Thumboo comments:

In these literatures there is an attempt to restore dignity, to re-establish the self, and to compensate for deprivation and depersonalization.
(ibid.: 410)

It is understandable, then, that the appropriation of English and the naming of distinct African and Asian varieties with their own literatures play a very important specific role in post-colonial contexts. Intranational/intracultural functions of the language assume particular significance for the expression of local identities, and the focus is on efforts to 'recover... the uniqueness of the pre-colonial', as Thumboo puts it in the above extract.

Here, I think, we find an explanation for why variation in Outer Circle English is described in terms of discrete varieties. Such description is in effect a declaration of independence with each separate variety representing a separate communal identity. Each is recognized as an English in its own right, distinct from and independent of the Inner Circle language, though still bearing its prestigious name as a guarantee of equality—hence the insistence on Englishes in the plural.[5] Hence too the primary importance that is attached to the need for codification and the establishment of non-native norms. They serve to consolidate the claim to independence, as Kachru points out quite explicitly:

The ideological and cultural hegemony of English has, to some extent, been counteracted by the use of English in the Outer Circle as a tool for national and regional cultural identity of its users. This identity is unrelated to the Judeo-Christian and Western ethos and its canons. In this sense, then, English has successfully worked as a language for inculcating nationalism and cultural renaissance in, for example, South Asia, West Africa, and East Africa. It was through English that ethnic, linguistic, religious, and regional barriers were crossed to mobilize the educated class about the pan-regional political, social, educational issues.
(Kachru 1996a: 911)[6]

While the function of what Kachru describes in the last sentence is clearly that of ELF, for him the premium is on what is culturally and linguistically distinct about each variety rather than on commonalities that could facilitate global international/intercultural communication.[7]

So, to return to Trudgill's remarks, one can see why it is not only convenient but appropriate to assume the distinctiveness of varieties for the particular purpose of accounting for the socio-political realities of English in the post-colonial contexts of the Outer Circle.

But the situation in non-post-colonial contexts is very different. Where languages and national societies have not been imposed upon by colonizing forces but buttressed (perhaps rather too well) by local governments and education systems, different sentiments prevail. It would be unwise to generalize too widely here, since the situation in different parts of the world, from Japan to Portugal, China to Iran, and Argentina to Norway is bound to vary greatly (as discussed in detail in Bruthiaux 2003). But what can be seen in all these Expanding Circle settings is a fairly strong reliance on national lingua-cultures coupled with efforts to participate in the 'international community'. In Europe in particular, the dominant discourse is one of overcoming the linguistic monocultural mindset associated with 19th century nation states.

National histories and cultures are taken for granted and the topical debates revolve around the tricky issue of how the protection of minorities and the celebration of (linguistic and cultural) diversity can be reconciled with the need for a common means of communication (Seidlhofer 2010; Wright 2009). In certain cases, the function of the latter is served by regional languages, but for the whole of Europe the de facto lingua franca is now English.[8]

And so it is that we get two very different 'images' or interpretations of the term *lingua franca*, perceived as predominantly undesirable in the one and predominantly desirable in the other. It seems that especially in post-colonial settings, the term *lingua franca* is still primarily associated with the original, traditional meaning of linguaculturally reduced, even impoverished, 'low-level makeshift languages'.[9] These connotations appear to suggest that calling global English a lingua franca is seen as a step backwards in the struggle for the recognition of distinct cultural identities, maybe even a sign of 'deprivation and depersonalization' (see Thumboo above). But the term 'lingua franca' does not have to carry these negative connotations. It can refer to a mode of language use which is, on the contrary, both liberating and effective for personal expression.

My experience, especially but by no means only in Europe, is that in international encounters the fluidity and flexibility highlighted in descriptive ELF research as a quality that strengthens the communicative robustness of intercultural interactions, with norms negotiated ad hoc depending on specific participants' repertoires and purposes, is clearly seen as an asset—a further language existing side by side with the pretty much taken-for-granted national languages. 'Lingua franca' thus conveys a sense of a liberating additional means of communication, increasing the repertoire of languages that speakers rely on to function effectively in all areas of their professional and private lives.

Again, we need to be cautious about assuming that concepts appropriate to one kind of situation are transferable to others. As Kachru himself has repeatedly said, 'the spread of English and the number of its non-native users is a unique linguistic phenomenon' (Kachru 1996a: 908), and at the beginning of an article actually entitled 'English as a lingua franca', he emphasizes again that:

[t]he unprecedented functional range and social penetration globally acquired by English demands fresh theoretical and descriptive perspectives...

The global uses of English...do not accord with the original connotations of lingua franca: The current profile of English demands a redefinition of the term, its uses, and its implications.

(ibid.: 906f.)

What is most important to realize is that English as a lingua franca is a concept that we need to include in our theoretical repertoire for the 'unique linguistic phenomenon' Kachru describes above, not as a replacement of but as an addition to other Englishes, whether native or nativized, whether ENL, ESL, or EFL, whether global(ized) or local(ized). There is a need for all Englishes as resources for speakers to draw on variously in different contexts and for different purposes. Accomplished communicators regularly modify their language in different settings in order to accommodate to their interlocutors and to facilitate intelligibility. In ELF situations, speakers of any kind of English, from EFL, ENL, and ESL contexts, need to adjust to the requirements of intercultural communication. But speakers from the Inner and Outer Circles, who are accustomed to using English as a language that is perfectly adequate for local domestic purposes, may not recognize the need to make such modifications and here difficulties often arise (Guido 2008; Wright 2009). In this respect, people from the Expanding Circle, for whom the language is not so intricately bound up with communal significance, usually find it easier to employ it as a lingua franca resource. Again, it becomes clear why an understanding of ELF calls for a reconsideration of our established ideas and why adhering to the delimitations of the three-circle model is counter-productive for ELF interaction. The point to be stressed is that ELF cannot be primarily identified with any of the Kachruvian Circles but is a function of the transcultural exploitation of the *communicative resources of all three*. ELF thus needs to be added as an option to be made use of when appropriate, and as a conceptual innovation reflecting the realities of globalized communication in the 21st century.

To a European like myself, the term *lingua franca* has positive connotations not least because it also triggers associations with what was *the* universal language of learning over many centuries, Latin. And the term itself (though opinions on this vary)[10] has Latin roots which developed in the Romance languages. Thus 'frank' comes from Old French 'franc' meaning 'free', and lives on in Italian 'franco', as does Italian 'lingua', that is 'tongue, language'. It is thus not simply fanciful to think of 'lingua franca' as 'free language'. This is also acknowledged in a recent authoritative source, the *International Handbook of the Science of Language and Society* (Ammon *et al.* 2004):

An alternative theory is that franca is understood in the sense of 'free', i.e. free of connections with particular countries and ethnicities. (Vikør 2004: 329)

It is in this alternative sense, then, that I understand *English as a lingua franca*: as a means of intercultural communication not tied to particular countries and ethnicities, a linguistic resource that is not contained in, or constrained by, traditional (and notoriously tendentious) ideas of what constitutes 'a language'.

4.5 Rethinking the concept of community

Of course, the freeing of 'a language' from particular territories and groups of people is precisely one of the conceptual challenges that we are faced with in the age of globalization. In the *Oxford Companion to Politics of the World*, Held and McGrew define globalization as:

a process (or set of processes) which embodies a transformation in the *spatial* organization of social relations and transactions, expressed in transcontinental or interregional flows and networks of activity, interaction and power. ... it can be linked to a *speeding up* of global interactions and processes, as the development of worldwide systems of transport and communication increases the *velocity* of the diffusion of ideas, goods, information, capital and people.
(Held and McGrew 2001: 324)

Particularly relevant to our purposes here is Held and McGrew's observation that globalization has brought with it quite radical changes to how political (and other) communities function:

Political communities are in the process of being transformed. ... Political communities today are no longer discrete worlds. Growing enmeshment in regional and global orders and the proliferation of transborder problems has created a plurality of diverse and overlapping collectivities which span borders binding together directly and indirectly the fate of communities in different locations and regions of the globe.
(ibid.: 327)

The authors call these newly emerging collectivities 'global, regional, and transnational communities of fate, identity, association, and solidarity' (ibid.). What interests us here is the very substantial role of English in the 'transcontinental or interregional flows and networks of activity, interaction, and power'. Whichever approach to understanding globalization we take, *transformation* is always salient as a key word in trying to capture what is going on. And transformation is, therefore, also affecting English itself. In this respect, again, it is not usually difficult for people to accept this fact at the level of principle—there is, in talk about globalization, broad agreement that we are living in an age of rapid change, mostly due to the ever-increasing pace of technological developments. What also happens, however, particularly at times of rapid change, is that people like to hold on to some certainties, to keep some facets of their lives in place as they are, to react against forces that threaten elements in which their very identities are invested (see also Joseph 2004; Pavlenko and Blackledge 2004; Riley 2007).

The problem is that transformation and identity are sometimes difficult to reconcile: while transformation calls for the ability to let go and adapt to radically altered conditions, identity may want to be confirmed, acknowledged, accepted, preserved. Change and preservation are thus in constant tension, and it is a human instinct to perceive what is new in terms of what is familiar. As a consequence, it is natural for a time-lag to develop between realizing that change has happened and actually making the necessary conceptual adjustments.

This is how I would explain the conceptual gap among both linguists and lay persons discussed at length in earlier chapters—that recognizing that the world has changed does not necessarily lead people to rethink the old concepts of languages and dialects, which in turn results in a failure to confront the question of how and to what extent old concepts of language varieties, and in particular of English, can co-exist with new ones. It may, as I have argued earlier in this chapter, be appropriate to adopt old concepts in some situations and in so doing lend them a new significance. Thus the application of the established sociolinguistic concept of variety has the effect of representing the English used in the Outer Circle as not only on a par with ENL dialects, but since they are demographically dispersed, with the status of separate languages—not just different uses of English but different World Englishes.

But these World Englishes are only one manifestation of English in the world and it is becoming increasingly obvious that new concepts are required to account for other uses of the language in very different social contexts and networks of communication. The 'organization of social relations and transactions' and 'networks of activity, interaction, and power' are of course aspects of everyday life in ENL communities, and how they relate to the variable uses of language has been extensively documented in sociolinguistic research. With globalization, however, these relations, transactions, and networks have of course become much more extensive and cut across conventional communal boundaries, transforming the very concept of community in the process: it is not only political communities but also speech communities that 'are no longer discrete worlds' (cf. Dewey 2007a; Seidlhofer 2007). And English, as both a result and a reinforcement of this process, naturally gets transformed accordingly.[11]

The tradition of thinking of 'a language' as an autonomous and reified object at home in a particular territory is the principal reason for the difficulty people experience with the notion of ELF when considering it from either an ENL, ESL, or EFL perspective. For unlike the speakers of Inner Circle and nativized Outer Circle Englishes, ELF speakers usually do not live in immediate physical proximity with each other and do not constitute a speech community in this sense. The social conditions and relationships between language and society out of which the notions of *community* and *variety* developed have undergone radical change in recent decades. They are themselves, therefore, in need of quite radical reconsideration.

The convenient concept of variety has generally been applied to language variants which are used, extensively and consistently by a community of speakers with their own sociocultural identity, primarily in regular face-to-face contact (cf. Schneider 2003). This, as we have seen, has, over the last couple of decades, been the basis for recognizing indigenized varieties of English, typically in post-colonial contexts. In sociolinguistic thinking, variety status has much less to do with objectively identifiable linguistic features than with identification with a particular, fairly stable community; especially if the community itself thinks they speak a particular variety of their own. So variety is in this sense more of a social than a linguistic construct, and, as I noted earlier, it is this that justifies assigning variety status to the Englishes of the Outer Circle.

But just what is a *community*? This surely is the crucial question here on which everything depends. Again traditionally, a community has been understood in a predominantly physical, local sense. The *Compact Oxford Dictionary*'s definition is 'a group of people living together in one place', with the expression 'the international community' as a kind of metaphorical extension of this sense. In addition to this association with physical proximity and shared territory, the word *community* has traditionally also carried with it an expectation of some degree of social cohesion, whereby one learns to belong to a particular community by being socialized into its values and beliefs, its 'heritage' if you will. This again made for some measure of stability and thus permanence.

From an ethnographic perspective, Hymes describes a community as 'a local unit, characterized for its members by common locality and primary interaction' (Hymes 1962: 30). The idea of a speech community, according to Fishman (1971: 232) 'probably translated from the German *Sprachgemeinschaft*', builds on this traditional sense of *community* in its simplest definition as the '[t]otal set of speakers of the same (native) language' (Bussmann 1996. s.v. *speech community*).

It is this primary interaction, i.e. frequent face-to-face contact that brings about the conditions for the recognition of distinct varieties of a language. A good illustration of the interdependence of *community* and *variety* with reference to the Outer Circle touched upon above is Schneider's 'Dynamic model of the evolution of postcolonial Englishes' (mentioned in Chapter 1), which clearly conveys the very physical/geographical groundedness of these concepts: 'the essential point of [this] model', he says, is that both settlers and the indigenous people 'who share a piece of land increasingly share a common language experience', resulting in 'shared sets of linguistic features and conventions' (Schneider 2007:32).

As opposed to the evolution of post-colonial Englishes, the evolution of English as a lingua franca has not been tied to interactions among people who 'share a piece of land': ELF is, for the present and mid-term future, the main means of wider communication for conducting transactions and interactions outside people's primary social spaces and speech communities, for enabling 'transcultural flows' (Pennycook 2007).

The traditional concept of *community* is also problematic when applied to diaspora communities: groups of people originally sharing the same ethnic or cultural space but who have been geographically dispersed. Diaspora, understood etymologically as dispersal or scatter, is generally thought of in terms of distribution rather than spread, to refer again to Widdowson's distinction discussed earlier, with the dispersed groups retaining, for a while at least, their linguistic and cultural identity more or less intact, carrying it with them along with their other possessions. As Canagarajah points out, such thinking:

...is informed by traditional assumptions of community, identity, and nationhood. It is based on essences, grounded in territorialist features, and informed by bounded modes of wholeness.

(Canagarajah 2006a: 211)

What is now needed, he goes on to say, is the entirely different postmodern definition that recognizes that diasporas are 'evolving, incomplete, and proliferating' and he quotes Stuart Hall as proposing the kind of definition that is called for:

The diaspora experience as I intend here is defined not by essence or purity, but by the recognition of a necessary heterogeneity and diversity; by a concept of identity that lives with and through, not despite difference; by hybridity. Diaspora identities are those which are constantly producing and reproducing themselves anew, through transformation and difference.
(Hall 1990: 235)

Language is of course crucially implicated in the diaspora experience and the expression of identities. It has been described as 'the focal centre of our acts of identity' as it has 'the extra dimension in that we can symbolize in a coded way all the other concepts which we use to define ourselves and our society' (Le Page and Tabouret-Keller 1985: 247). So it is not surprising that this postmodern view, as I indicated earlier when citing Rampton's description of it, applies as much to the concept of linguistic as it does to sociocultural variation. Transformation is a key process in the globalization of English, and what Hall has to say here would apply to the heterogeneity and diversity of ELF as it functions in the transformation and renewal of identities in general and not only those associated with particular diasporas. Hall's quotation corresponds closely with that of Achebe cited earlier in this chapter: it is by diversifying and transforming English that Achebe alters the language 'to suit its new African surroundings' (Achebe 1975: 62).

The main point to be made, then, is that the situation regarding communities has changed radically in recent times, particularly over the past few decades. While previously it might have been reasonable to think of varieties as dialects which have to do with the *primary socialization*, of upbringing, and with most interactions happening within a relatively close-knit and enclosed *primary community*, in the postmodern world the metaphor of international, or global, community and of diaspora has turned into an everyday reality in a different literal sense. Countless interaction networks are independent of physical proximity and are instantiated through interaction over vast distances, often without the participants ever meeting 'in the flesh'. This means that *virtual communities* have achieved considerable significance in the sum of global interactions, giving rise to a very different meaning of *community*. Jacquemet (2005) describes examples of 'mobile media practices and transnational people' and comments:

In this encounter, a new, deterritorialized social identity takes shape, light-years away from the corporate logic of the nation-state. This new identity coagulates around a sentiment of belonging that can no longer be identified with a purely territorial dimension, and finds its expression in the creolized, mixed idioms of polyglottism.
(Jacquemet 2005: 262f.)

So with the current proliferation of possibilities created by electronic means and easy global mobility, changes in *communications* have accelerated and forced changes in the nature of *communication*: the *media* now available have changed the *modes* of use. And in all this, English is in a pivotal position: already established as a widespread language, it is particularly well placed to play a crucial role in these changed conditions, where communities can no longer be defined mainly in terms of face-to-face contact, and certainly not by a common native language. It is now commonplace, and indeed necessary, for people who want 'to get on in the world', to use a means of communication that takes them beyond traditional community boundaries. Wider networking needs a lingua franca.

What is important here of course is that English as a lingua franca is a language of *secondary socialization*, a means of wider communication to conduct transactions outside one's primary social space and speech community. So instead of varieties in the sense of *dialects* as used in different kinds of primary *community*, in the case of ELF we are looking at variable usage more in terms of *registers* as used in different kinds of *communication*. The distinction introduced by Halliday (Halliday 1978; Halliday, McIntosh, and Strevens 1964) between dialect as a variety with reference to *user*, and register as a variety with reference to *use* captures just this difference. It is likely that at the time when this distinction was proposed, the notion of 'dialect' was considered primary, and dialectology as the study of varieties in particular locations has, after all, always been a staple area of enquiry in sociolinguistics.[12]

But such disjunctive categories do not work for ELF. Dialect maps with their isoglosses that demarcate local usages obviously serve some purposes, but they need now to be complemented with accounts that capture heterogeneity and diversity, the evolving processes of ongoing global change in English. What we are witnessing in worldwide communication, mostly via ELF, is an exponential increase in 'dislocated' interactions driven by needs and wants in specific domains of use, thus foregrounding and upgrading the significance of 'registers' as experientially equally salient. Successful professionals are expected to feel at home in international networks. High-level knowledge and expertise, and certainly anything that makes serious profit (and serious losses), ignores national boundaries and is global of its very nature. Large research projects without an international dimension stand no chance of being funded. But it is not just about money. Many young people communicate happily in chat rooms populated by interactants from all over the world and say that the communities they are part of there are as real to them as their classroom ones. To mention just one anecdote in passing, the other day I heard a report on the radio about an Austrian 'gamer' who has stopped talking to his family because he never leaves his computer; but he 'got married' in cyberspace, and 30,000 other gamers 'came' to his wedding—how's that for a strong sense of community?

At a time when many of us, and particularly those who are regular users of ELF, tend to spend more time communicating with people via email and Skype than in direct conversations with participants in the same physical space, the old notion of community based purely on frequent local, non-mediated contact among people living in close proximity to each other clearly cannot be upheld any more. In contrast with local speech communities, such global communities tend to be referred to as *discourse communities* with a common communicative purpose (Swales 1990). A more recent relevant notion is that of *communities of practice*, i.e. in Eckert and McConnell-Ginet's definition, 'aggregate[s] of people who come together around mutual engagement in an endeavour' (1992: 464). For Wenger (1998: 72ff.), the community of practice is defined by a process of social learning where three basic criteria hold:

1 mutual engagement in shared practices
2 taking part in some jointly negotiated enterprise, and
3 making use of members' shared repertoire.

This repertoire consists of linguistic and other resources which are the agreed result of internal negotiations which can also be used for international/ intercultural communication (Seidlhofer 2007). Even from such a short characterization it should be obvious that describing the dynamics of language use in such communities poses quite different questions from those involved in the description of dialects as reified entities—a far cry from speech communities defined 'by the same (native) language'. Indeed, what may well characterize communities of practice on a global scale is that they do *not* have the same native language.

But as Dewey points out, the concept of 'community of practice' cannot be too restrictively defined if it is to account for ELF communication:

By associating the concepts of 'community' and 'practice', Wenger (1998) points out that it is possible to characterize both of these in more manageable, and potentially more flexible terms. ... Wenger's notion is arguably a more conservative one than is required here, especially given the protean nature of ELF communities. To better reflect this characteristic, we can envisage a still more fluid concept of community of practice, where the practice itself is modified as it is enacted. Nevertheless, by borrowing this term, and perhaps only slightly modifying its earlier definitions, we are able to detach descriptions of language variation and change from geographically defined locations. And, again as Seidlhofer argues, we can move forward still further from a characterization of sociolinguistic work as 'the description of dialects as reified entities' (2007: 314), and can thus better describe current changes in discourse and communication, especially in the use of English as the lingua franca of wider, globally diffuse interactions.
(Dewey 2009: 77f.)

A thorough and thoughtful evaluation of the applicability of the Communities-of-Practice (CofP) approach to understanding how various ELF groups operate is provided by Ehrenreich (2009). Taking a sociolinguistic perspective, she warns against an all-too-ready, superficial adoption of Wenger's framework, indicating that applying it to ELF speakers in general would obviously be stretching the concept so far as to render it meaningless, especially when it comes to groups of ELF speakers that have formed in an ad hoc way, something that happens very frequently. Instead, she suggests that:

a profession, e.g. ELF professionals or linguists, do not constitute one unified CofP, but should rather be conceptualized as 'constellations of interconnected practices' (Wenger 1998: 127).
  ...with the CofP being considerably smaller in scope than, for example, the notion of speech community, there is a clear need to distinguish between different ELF-using CofPs, in which, consequently, linguistic issues may play fundamentally different roles.
(Ehrenreich 2009: 134)

If we accept that the notion of local speech communities has all but lost its relevance for the way people communicate via ELF across physical and linguistic boundaries, then it follows that the often-raised question as to whether ELF 'constitutes a variety' is neither meaningful nor relevant. It belongs to one of the earlier paradigms Kachru mentions as needing to be challenged. We return to the issues raised earlier in this chapter about the applicability of old concepts to new phenomena. We surely cannot simply close our eyes to the contemporary reality of English as a lingua franca just because we cannot neatly slot it into familiar categories of 'variety' and do not wish to call its users a 'community'.

The main argument I am attempting to outline here is, then, that with radical technology-driven changes in society, inevitably our sense of what constitutes a *community* and a *linguistic variety*, and the very status of these concepts as convenient methodological constructs, have to change, too. Alongside local speech communities sharing a dialect, we are witnessing the increased emergence of global discourse communities, or communities of practice, or other groupings sharing their particular modes of communication, with English being the most widely used code. This development has a momentum of its own, and is happening at a pace that gives us little time to adjust our conceptual categories.

But adjust them we must. That is the challenge that Kachru refers to. What we see in ELF is indeed the process of language dynamics whereby the language is adapted and altered to suit the changed circumstances of its use; understanding this inevitably undermines established ideas about community and variety. The appropriation of the language as a lingua franca necessarily focuses attention not on what is proper English in reference to standard or native-speaker norms, but what is appropriate English for new and different communicative and communal purposes.

4.6 Rethinking the concept of competence

If we accept this, then *community* and *variety* are not the only notions in need of reconceptualization. Considering the dynamism of ELF use forces us to question the validity of objectifying and tying languages to particular territories but it also leads us to question the very concept of languages as discrete units. I return here to the earlier discussion in 4.3. about the way languages are conceived as complete and self-enclosed entities. As I pointed out then, one can concede that it may be convenient, and entirely legitimate, to adopt this idealization for a particular theoretical or descriptive purpose. But, as we have seen, if purposes change, then these idealizations lose their validity and become an obstacle to understanding. Nowhere is this more clearly illustrated than in the changing fortunes of the concept of competence.

It was of course Chomsky who brought the concept into prominence, and with him competence is explicitly an idealized construct. It is defined (to cite again the all too familiar passage) as the linguistic knowledge of 'an ideal speaker–listener in a completely homogeneous speech community, who knows his language perfectly . . .' (Chomsky 1965: 3). Critics of Chomsky's linguistics have been quick to point out that there is no such thing as a homogeneous speech community and to conclude that this invalidates his enquiry. But Chomsky is not saying that there is such a thing: it simply suits his purpose to think of communities *as if* they were homogeneous, just as sociolinguists like Trudgill think of varieties *as if* they were discrete. Furthermore, the equally idealized and counterfactual idea that speaker–listeners know their language perfectly has not been challenged but on the contrary is generally assumed to be self-evidently the case. As I noted earlier in this chapter, it is commonly supposed that there is such a thing as a language, complete and self-enclosed, which its native speakers know in its entirety—that there is, in short, a well defined, or at least a definable, competence in the language.

Thus, much research in the field of second language acquisition (SLA) is based on the notion of interlanguage, a transitional continuum of acquisition between two fixed points: the L1 on the one hand and the L2 on the other, and stages in this interlanguage are identified in reference to the terminal point of native-speaker competence.[13] Similarly, virtually all measures of learner achievement are made with reference to this competence, in terms of how far it falls short of native-speaker norms of correctness. But in reality there is no such competence and there are no such norms, although of course it may be convenient to suppose that there are. It may be accepted that a language is intrinsically variable, that its communities of speakers are far from homogeneous, but somehow the contradictory notion survives, and thrives, that its speakers nevertheless all have basically the same unitary competence. It seems obvious that in heterogeneous communities, linguistic knowledge will also vary: people will know their language more or less, in different domains, and their competence will always be partial and incomplete.

The concept of native-speaker competence is taken on trust as self-evident, it is constantly evoked, but never defined. There are volumes of grammars and dictionaries that describe different languages—Arabic, English, German, Russian, and so on—but they do not represent their speakers' competence in those languages. They are essentially an abstraction, a composite account of the ideal speaker–listener. As I said earlier, the language of linguistic description and the language of user experience are quite different phenomena, and the more comprehensive the description, the less it will represent the actual knowledge and ability of its particular native speakers.

All this seems obvious. And yet the myths of complete languages and competence in them persist, even where one might expect them to be challenged. The well known account by Hymes of communicative competence is a case in point (Hymes 1972). Hymes argues that Chomsky's concept of competence needs to be revised to take into account what people know of their language beyond the formal rules of its grammar. There are, he says, four kinds of judgement that somebody competent in a language is capable of making, and only one of these concerns what is grammatically possible. The other three judgements are:

> Whether (and to what degree) something is *feasible* in virtue of the means of implementation available;
> Whether (and to what degree) something is *appropriate* (adequate, happy, successful) in relation to a context in which it is used and evaluated;
> Whether (and to what degree) something is in fact done, actually *performed*, and what its doing entails.
> (Hymes 1972: 281)

The question is, how does one judge the relative possibility, feasibility, appropriateness, and attestedness of some linguistic expression? Relative to what? Clearly such judgements can only be made in reference to some established norm or other. And the norm that Hymes has in mind is that which has warrant in a native-speaker community:

> There is an important sense in which a normal member of a community has knowledge with respect to all these aspects of the communicative systems available to him.
> (ibid.: 282)

But as I have been arguing, there is, of course, an important sense in which there is no 'normal member of a community'. Speakers of a language are notoriously unreliable in their judgements as to whether an expression 'in their language' is possible (i.e. grammatically correct or not) or, given the immense variety of contexts in which the language can be used, whether and to what degree it is appropriate. This 'normal' member of a community is in effect Chomsky's ideal speaker–listener in a completely homogeneous speech community, who knows his language perfectly, or who at least knows what is normal and normally used in the language.

I do not intend by these comments to undervalue the significance of what Hymes has to say. His paper has been of genuinely seminal importance in widening the scope of linguistic enquiry, and his account of communicative competence has been immensely influential, especially in foreign language pedagogy. But although the concept of competence is broadened, it is still implicitly based on the same kind of idealization of language and community that Chomsky makes explicit (see also Leung 2005).

But these four aspects of language and use do not have to be uniquely linked to this concept of native speaker competence. It has generally been assumed, as Hymes himself implied in his formulation, that these judgements have to be made by native-speaking communities, that what is appropriate, for example, must be in relation to *their* contexts of use, and that what is performed must be in relation to what *they* perform. But we can uncouple these aspects from these primary social native-speaking communities and relate them to other kinds of community—communities of practice, for example, which cut across the native/non-native distinctions and where quite different judgements are likely to be made about what is feasible, appropriate to context, and so on.[14] More generally, it is easy to see that these aspects can apply, and I would argue need to apply, to ELF in general. And indeed here one has to accept that it is likely to be appropriate in many, if not most contexts in which English is currently used, *not* to fully conform to native-speaker conventions. This is because these native-speaker conventions derive from quite different local communities of users and are replete with in-group markers of shared sociocultural identity, conditions that just do not obtain in the same way in ELF situations.

A study of what is 'in fact done, actually performed' in the use of English as a lingua franca, can, as we shall see in subsequent chapters, reveal how its users exploit what is possible in order to negotiate feasibility and make their language appropriate to the contexts in which they use it to achieve their purposes. In short, these aspects of language that Hymes identifies can be related not to the definition of some fixed communicative competence, but to the ways language functions in the communication process itself.

4.7 Conclusion

English has spread because it has been appropriated to serve the social and communicative needs and purposes of communities of users beyond those residing within the Inner or even the Outer Circle. And as the language has been appropriated, so it has been adapted, since the norms of use that, to use Achebe's words, 'suit the surroundings' of these Circles are no longer appropriate. The emergence of ELF as a global phenomenon is a linguistic development without precedence, and one, therefore, that calls for a reconsideration of established concepts and assumptions, especially those that relate to variety, community, and competence.

It may be convenient to think of languages or language varieties as self-contained and stable entities for the purpose of linguistic analysis, and this way of thinking may indeed correspond with how the language users themselves conceive of 'their' language as something that defines their particular community. But the concept of community itself as a relatively self-enclosed network of social interaction calls for radical revision in the contemporary world of increased mobility and the unbounded extension of interaction over the internet. What it means to be communicatively competent in English can no longer be described with reference to norms of linguistic knowledge and behaviour that are relevant only to particular native-speaker communities. Conformity to these norms is neither necessary nor sufficient to meet the international demands for the effective use of English as a lingua franca.

What is unprecedented and new about ELF is the extent of its use as both the cause and consequence of the unprecedented and new socio-economic, political, and technological developments in the world that go under the name of globalization. But the kind of linguistic adaptation that it represents is not unprecedented and new at all, but, on the contrary, is a striking example of what Kachru in the quotation cited earlier calls 'an age-old process of language dynamics'. How ELF actually exemplifies this process will be the concern of the next two chapters.

Notes

1 I added the emphasis to 'in the world' because this adverbial has repeatedly been overlooked by some commentators, leading them to misunderstand Widdowson's point to include ENL, and to thus misread the passage as claiming that native speakers are irrelevant for the development of English *tout court*, i.e. irrelevant for ENL. But Widdowson is referring to English as an international language here. For a restatement of the arguments expressed in this article in a wider pedagogical context see Chapter 4 of Widdowson 2003.

2 A case in point is the *Handbook of Language Contact* (Hickey 2010), Part IV of which consists of 'Case Studies of Contact'. In this Part, English gets treated in the following chapters:

21 Contact and the Early History of English
22 Contact and the Development of American English
23 Contact Englishes and Creoles in the Caribbean
24 Contact and Asian Varieties of English
25 Contact and African Englishes

It is striking that there is no explicit mention, let alone detailed treatment, of ELF, which is surely a hugely important language contact phenomenon with reference to English, and one of global relevance.

3 For criticism of Kachru's Three Circles model from the perspective of Bourdieu's notion of linguistic markets see Park and Wee 2009. For a concise discussion of models of the spread of English, see Jenkins 2009 and Kachru 2005 for a response to criticism of his model.

4 This is what Bruthiaux (2003: 168) refers to as ' "me-too" calls [being] heard periodically for additional varieties to be admitted to the ever-expanding family of new Englishes'.

5 For a recent comprehensive source, see Kirkpatrick (2010b).

6 But this, again, is only part of the story; see Tupas 2006: 169, who notes that 'the power to (re)create English ascribed to the Outer Circle is mainly reserved only to those who have been invested with such power in the first place (the educated/the rich/the creative writers, etc.)'.

7 This is not to say of course that linguists do not recognize similarities in developmental patterns across different Englishes—see Schneider (2010) for a succinct survey of these.

8 Of course the distinction between post-colonial and non-post-colonial settings is not as clear-cut as sketched here briefly. Above all, certain globalization forces favouring uniformity are also making themselves felt in the former, particularly in more affluent countries—another reason for questioning any clear demarcation between English use in the Outer Circle and the Expanding Circle.

9 But also in other regions—for instance, some German scholars have expressed the view that a lingua franca has severe limitations in conducting science and research (e.g. Ehlich and Meyer 2011).

10 Different explanations and etymologies can be found in the literature, the details of which are not relevant here. To give just one example, Kachru (1996: 906) explains that '[t]he term *lingua franca*, from Arabic *lisan-al farang*, originally meant the Italian language'. For a recent treatment see Vikør 2004.

11 For a recent collection of papers on globalization and the role of Englishes, see Saxena and Omoniyi (2010); see also the (unsurprisingly) large proportion of space dedicated to English(es) in Coupland (2010).

12 See also James (2000), building on Widdowson (1997), on the distinction between variety and register with reference to ELF.

13 See also the discussion of SLA research in Chapter 1, and Lourdes Ortega's plenary address at the 2010 conference of the American Association of Applied Linguistics: 'The bilingual turn in SLA' (downloadable from her homepage: http://www.2.hawaii.edu/~lortega/).

14 See Jenkins (2000: 73ff.) for a discussion of (lack of) shared sociocultural knowledge and intelligibility in multilingual classroom contexts.

5

The dynamics of ELF usage

I shall also call the whole, consisting of language and actions into which it is woven, the 'language-game' ...

One learns the game by watching how others play. But we say that it is played according to such-and-such rules because an observer can read these rules off from the practice of the game—like a natural law governing the play. But how does the observer distinguish in this case between players' mistakes and correct play?

LUDWIG WITTGENSTEIN: *Philosophical Investigations*

5.1 Variety and variation: state and process

Like any other language, English is a dynamic process, and naturally varies and changes as it spreads into different domains of use and communities of users. As was pointed out in the preceding chapters, the extent of the spread of English now is unlike that of any other language, but in principle there is nothing at all unusual about the processes of variation and change that are activated by it. What is of such sociolinguistic significance about ELF is that, due to its extremely widespread and frequent use by speakers from a vast number of first language backgrounds, it affords us the opportunity of observing these processes happening in an intensified, accelerated fashion, right before our eyes.

As we have seen in previous chapters, ELF is often characterized negatively in terms of its non-conformity to the established norms of grammar (and perhaps lexis) that are said to define the standard variety. Allowance is made for non-conformities in native and nativized versions of English on the grounds that these can be identified as consistent enough to constitute different dialect-like varieties with their own endonormative norms and be identified with particular communities. So it is considered legitimate to recognize, say, Norfolk, or Texan dialect varieties, and nativized varieties like Indian or Nigerian English—in the latter two cases, notwithstanding the extreme degree of idealization required to imagine such homogenized monoliths. Be that as it may, legitimacy tends not to be accorded to ELF because its speakers do not belong to particular primary communities, and its non-conformities are assumed to be too irregular, i.e. not systematic enough to make for variety status. They are therefore only seen exonormatively as deficiencies, as errors (cf. Mollin 2006).

But as was pointed out in the last chapter, the norm against which ELF is measured is itself indeterminate since it is based on such notions as *variety*, *community*, and *competence* which are elusive of clear definition. They are essentially arbitrary constructs designed for convenience and, as we have seen, for some people it is convenient to use them to dismiss ELF as deviant. The reason why these constructs are arbitrary is that they represent a dynamic process as a fixed state of affairs. But language is, of course, not fixed but continually in flux, always variable.[1] If one thinks of a variety as a set of formal features, and privileges one set of formal features as the (all-purpose) standard, then of course ELF looks deviant from such a perspective, formally deviant. But the forms of languages, as Halliday has insistently pointed out, reflect the functions they are designed to serve. So the really interesting question about ELF is not whether it can be designated a *variety* or not, which, as was argued in the last chapter, is always going to be an arbitrary matter of convenience anyway, but what motivates the use of its non-conformist *variations*, how ELF users exploit the resources of the language to communicative effect. In short, how do the language dynamics of ELF (or any other lingua franca for that matter) actually work?

To ask this question is to go beyond the description of formal linguistic properties. Bamgbose, writing about Outer Circle English, suggests that there are norms of three different types, *code norm*, *feature norm*, and *behavioural norm*,[2] and comments:

[o]f these three norm types, the one frequently appealed to is the feature norm, and this is largely because nativization is often narrowly construed as predominantly linguistic. The fact, however, is that linguistic nativization is only one of the processes of indigenizing a non-native variety of English. Equally important are *pragmatic* and *creative* nativization both of which fall largely within the scope of *behavioral norms*. (Bamgbose 1998: 2, emphases added)

Although Bamgbose refers here specifically to norms which will define indigenized non-native English(es) as distinct varieties, the different processes he identifies are apparent in all variable usage and apply to ELF as well. For the understanding of ELF as a natural language process involves going beyond the identification of particular linguistic features to take a much more communicative view whereby linguistic features are investigated not for their own sake but as indications of the various functions ELF fulfils in the interactions it makes possible. So the crucial challenge is to move from the surface description of particular features, however interesting they may be in themselves, to an explanation of the underlying significance of the forms, to ask what work they do, what functions they are symptomatic of. And the research that has been done to date (of which more below) has shown that the explanations that are found when analysing the accomplished interactional work that speakers undertake via ELF very often have to do with pragmatic and creative processes. These processes can lead to innovation on various levels, and for various interconnected reasons, such as maximizing explicitness and thus clarity/intelligibility, exploiting redundancy and thus minimizing effort. When people use ELF, they find ways of exploiting and exploring the meaning potential of the language as a communicative resource and realize (in both senses of the word) the significance of the forms they use, their relative functional usefulness. In other words, form and function can be clearly seen as operating interdependently.

It seems to me that for ELF speakers, the process of nativization as described in the above quotation from Bamgbose can be understood as having new scope and meaning: rather than denoting the formation of varieties of local communities in particular places, nativization can also be understood as the appropriation of the language by individual speakers, who make it their own for particular purposes and conditions of use so that they are 'at home' in it. This idea of seeing ELF also as something that individuals take hold of and variously mould to their needs is not in contradiction but complementary to the process of macroacquisition as described by Brutt-Griffler (2002) (see Chapters 1 and 4). Accomplished ELF speakers, who know on the basis of their (often considerable) experience that they can rely on their 'ways of speaking' (Hymes 1989) for fulfilling whatever communicative needs they have, are likely to develop both a sense that the language is theirs to use and a heightened capability to accommodate to their interlocutors. What Bamgbose describes as 'creative nativization' emphasizes the active, shaping role of speakers, which seems compatible with Pennycook's way of using the notion of performativity for exploring new ways of thinking about language and identity in relation to *Global Englishes and Transcultural Flows* (the title of his 2007 book). In a wide-ranging discussion starting with J. L. Austin's (1962) *How to Do Things With Words* and spanning various philosophers up to Judith Butler's (1997) *Excitable Speech: A Politics of the Performative*, Pennycook observes that the notion of performativity:

provides a way of thinking about relationships between language and identity that emphasize the productive force of language in constituting identity rather than identity being a pregiven construct that is reflected in language use.
(Pennycook 2007: 70f.)

Pennycook is concerned with 'taking the vernacular voices of the popular seriously' (ibid.: 78ff.), and in particular with hip-hop. But what he says about performativity resonates with recent thinking about ELF in general—and it would be surprising if it did not, since though Pennycook does not mention ELF as such, global transcultural flows are obviously effected through ELF as conceptualized in this book. Pennycook argues for 'considering languages themselves from an anti-foundationalist perspective, whereby language use is an act of identity which calls that language into being'(ibid.: 77).

The characterization of language use as acts of identity does not, of course, originate with Pennycook but dates back some twenty years earlier (Le Page and Tabouret-Keller 1985). Here too the point is made that identity is not (to repeat Pennycook's words) 'a pregiven construct that is reflected in language use' but is enacted in the process of performance. We need to be cautious, however, not to be too carried away with the notions of performativity and creativity. It is obvious that when we perform, although we may not follow a pregiven script, we are prompted by some established framework of expectation, or otherwise the performance would be meaningless. Similarly, creativity presupposes the existence of conventional norms against which its non-conformity can be realized. As Pennycook puts it:

> In order to have a usable notion of performativity...we need, on the one hand, to avoid the pull towards performance as open-ended free display (we perform whatever identities we want to) and, on the other, the pull towards oversedimentation (we can only perform what has been prescripted): to some extent, the performative is always along lines that have already been laid down, and yet performativity can also be about refashioning futures. What both concepts have in common is a sense of the present, the real, the everyday...
> (ibid.)

Pennycook is, of course, stating here what has long been accepted—that socially shared frameworks of meaning as culturally identified schemata will always allow for individual room for manoeuvre—there would otherwise be no distinction between semantic and pragmatic meaning, and no possibility of language variation and change. But it would seem that Pennycook conceives of creativity and conformity as in conflict, 'pulls' in opposite directions that are to be avoided. My point would be that they cannot be avoided since they are conceptually interdependent—you cannot have one without the other. So the central (and unavoidable) issue is how they are reconciled in actual performance. As far as ELF is concerned, the crucial question is what aspects of English, what norms or rules of the language, are exploited as a performative resource.

5.2 Performativity and creativity in ELF

In the hundreds of ELF speech events in various domains that we have closely observed in the VOICE project over recent years there is a real sense of speakers performing their own ELF, shaping both the language and their identities in the process. Empirical ELF studies gradually becoming available (see Mauranen and Ranta 2009 and Archibald, Cogo, and Jenkins 2011, for the first substantial collections)[3] allow insights into how speakers constitute and assert their multilingual identities and their joint ownership of the lingua franca they are using—and shaping and developing them in the process.

Observing a multitude of ELF interactions in different settings and with speakers from a great variety of linguacultural backgrounds, we see again and again how people use the language to negotiate meanings with each other in communicative contexts, and do on-line interactional work. This performing process highlights the agency of speakers and so calls to mind the notion of *languaging* as it has been used in sociocultural theory (Swain 2006) and described by Becker as 'an endless social process of orienting and reorienting ourselves to [the] environment' (Becker 2000: 288, quoted in Argaman 2008: 483). Jørgensen (2008: 169) observes that people 'language with all their skills and knowledge' and 'employ whatever linguistic features are at their disposal with the intention of achieving their communicative aims'. Phipps, albeit from a somewhat different point of view,[4] explains that the notion of languaging emphasizes 'full, embodied and engaged interaction with the world' (Phipps 2006) realized through the emergent on-line exploitation of linguistic resources to achieve communicative ends. She describes 'languagers' as people who:

engage with the world-in-action, who move in the world in a way that allows the risk of stepping out of one's habitual ways of speaking and attempt to develop different, more relational ways of interacting with the people and phenomena that one encounters in everyday life. 'Languagers' use the ways in which they perceive the world to develop new dispositions for poetic action in another language and they are engaged in developing these dispositions so that they become habitual, durable. Languaging, then, is an act of dwelling.
(Phipps 2006: 12)

All this resonates with both the remarks about performativity above and with what can be observed in empirical ELF studies: ELF users too are seen to be languagers. They exploit the potential of the language, they are fully involved in the interactions, whether for work or for play. They are focused on the interactional and transactional purposes of the talk and on their interlocutors as people rather than on the linguistic code itself. We can observe ELF users absorbed in the ad hoc, situated negotiation of meaning—an entirely pragmatic undertaking in that the focus is on establishing the indexical link between the code and the context, and a creative process in that the code is treated as malleable and adjustable to the requirements of the moment. These requirements have to do with the message speakers want to convey as well as a host of other factors impinging on the accessibility and acceptability of what is said in terms of clarity, time constraints, and on-line processability, memory, available repertoires, social relationships, and shared knowledge.

In many ways, ELF communication works in much the same fashion as communication among speakers of any language in that meaning is negotiated and co-constructed and, of course, as in any use of natural language, occasional communicative dysfunction does occur. What is particularly noteworthy in the present context though is how ELF speakers can be observed—usually quite unselfconsciously—pushing the frontiers of Standard English when the occasion, or the need, arises. They draw on ELF as a complex adaptive system that, in the words of Cameron and Larsen-Freeman (2007), is 'continually transformed by use'. In this sense, ELF like any natural language:

at any point in time is the way it is because of the way it has been used, and any use of language changes it. Thus, if language is viewed as an open, continually evolving system rather than a closed one, then concepts such as 'end-state' grammars become anomalous.
(Cameron and Larsen-Freeman 2007: 230)[5]

ELF users thus 'act upon, and sometimes against, norms and standards' (Jørgensen 2008: 164) and develop, as Phipps puts it in the above quotation, 'new dispositions for poetic action'.

To start with the obvious, when people choose to communicate via a lingua franca and settle for the means of communication that excludes as few of the participants as possible (cf. van Parijs 2004), they are usually conscious of having to make a certain effort to ensure mutual intelligibility and communicative efficiency (cf. for example, Ehrenreich 2009). There is thus a premium on maximizing pragmatic *clarity* (Kecskes 2007). This goal can be pursued through various means, all interconnected and overlapping. We need to note, though, that communicative efficiency and grammatical correctness are not taken as being in a straightforward relationship whereby the former can be guaranteed through the latter (Hülmbauer 2007, 2009). Clarity can be enhanced by giving prominence to important elements, redundancy added or exploited, explicitness can be increased by making patterns more regular, word classes or semantic relations generally can be made more explicit.

One obvious way of making what one says more accessible is to repeat, or to paraphrase, or a combination of the two. Cogo (2007, 2009) shows other-repetition and code-switching to be important accommodation strategies in ELF talk, and she demonstrates that 'successful ELF communication relies on crucial adaptive accommodation skills along with appreciation and acceptance of diversity' (Cogo 2009: 270). Dewey discusses repetition, synonymy, and rephrasing, remarking that these seem to be perceived as 'important for effectiveness and reliability of communication' among ELF speakers (Dewey 2007b: 342). In a detailed study of forms and functions of repetition in (dyadic) ELF interactions, Lichtkoppler provides the following example:

S1 [Greek]:   okay. (1) (AND) i: don't want my room for june.
S2 [German]: mhm (.) i see. but then you <1> have to </1> move er you have
              to move out (.)
S1:   <1> yeah </1>
S1:   m<2>hm </2>
S2:   <2> to</2>tally you have to (.)

S1:   yeah
S2:   take <3> your </3> **things out of your room.**
S1:   <3> yo- </3>
(Lichtkoppler 2007: 54, also VOICE 2009: PBsve437)

Repetition and paraphrase serve the purpose of clarity and emphasis here, with reformulations getting more and more explicit: *you have to move, you have to move out totally, you have to take your things out of your room.* It seems that S2 wants to make absolutely sure that her message comes across. While the above example illustrates self-repetition/paraphrasing, other-repetition is also well attested in ELF research. A gambit, or conversational move, described by House (2002, 2003) is what she calls a 'Represent', which involves repetition of what an interlocutor has just said:

BRIT: And if erm things like Nigerian English, Indian English which is a sort of variety in itself [it **should be respected**]
MAURI: [**Should be respected**]
(House 2002: 254, emphasis added)

Commenting further on Represents in her 2003 article, House assigns several functions to this gambit, including the signalling of uptake, aiding working memory and requesting confirmation (House 2003 p. 568). Again, the primary concern for speakers seems to be for *convergence* of intended and received message. We often find such repetitions skilfully woven into the flow of the conversation, with interactants deciding in a split second on the function of the repetition and therefore the appropriate response. Pitzl (2010) discusses an example from a business meeting that illustrates this particularly clearly:

S4 [L1=ger-AT]:   <L1ger>na ja {well} </L1ger> if (.) if i m- may erm (.) make a comment there
S2 [L1=kor-KR]:   mhm (1)
S4:   the (.) **impulse channel** (.) erm
S1 [L1=kor-KR]:   **impulse** chann<5>el?</5>
S4:   <5>the </5> **impulse channel or the** <spel> CVS </spel><8> er cha</8>nnel (.)
S2:   <8>mhm </8>
S4:   is very much er (.) LICENCE-driven. (.) meaning (1) if it's (.) in the **impulse channel** (1) the LICENCE is very important. [...]
(VOICE 2009: PBmtg3)[6]

Pitzl comments that S1's reprise may be a request for clarification of the meaning of the term *impulse channel*, and that S4's response:

not only features a repetition of the term *impulse channel*, but also an explanation of it, namely *or the C-V-S eh channel.* As the term *C-V-S* (an acronym for 'convenience store') has been used very frequently in the portion of the meeting preceding this extract, the use of this alternative term would certainly have cleared up any semantic non-understanding that might have existed.
(Pitzl 2010: 78)

Of course, convergence can also be understood in social–psychological terms as a strategy of *accommodation* 'whereby individuals adapt to each other's communicative behaviors in terms of a wide range of linguistic/prosodic/non-vocal features' (Giles and Coupland 1991: 63) to make them more alike, in order to communicate efficiently and in order to gain their interlocutors' approval.[7] In that sense, verbatim other-repetition as in the example above could be seen as ultimate convergence and thus ultimate accommodation. The role of accommodation in ELF talk was first treated in detail and its special significance forcefully argued in Jenkins' work on ELF phonology (Jenkins 2000: Chapter 7). Cogo and Dewey (2006), Cogo (2009), and Seidlhofer (2009a) also discuss the significance of accommodation and offer further examples and analyses, complementing Jenkins' work by looking at ELF speakers' lexico-grammar in particular. It will be rewarding to conduct further studies drawing on Communication Accommodation Theory (Giles, Coupland, and Coupland 1991) to account for ELF speakers' interpretability strategies, which:

can be used to *modify the complexity of speech* (for example, by decreasing diversity of vocabulary, or simplifying syntax), *increase clarity* (by changing pitch, loudness, tempo by incorporating repetition, clarification checks, explicit boundarying devices and so on)...
(Giles and Coupland 1991: 88, emphases added).

Staying on the theme of increasing clarity, there is an abundance of processes that ELF speakers rely on, of which those that result in innovations on any level of language (phonology, lexis, morphology, syntax) obviously are the most noticeable. Perceptually perhaps the most salient are processes of lexical innovation that result in words that are not attested in ENL. We can refer back to the quotation from Trudgill in Chapter 2, in which he commented that 'some French and German speakers have invented English words which do not exist in English, such as *lifting*, or *wellness*, or *handy*, or *pullunder*' (Trudgill 2002: 151).

Of course, new words always arise in any natural language, mostly when expressions are needed for new phenomena. This is why new editions of dictionaries usually draw attention to words that have been recently attested as occurring in native speaker usage, such as *botox, docusoap, ecocide,* and *landline* in the seventh edition of the *Oxford Advanced Learner's Dictionary (2005).* The book *Twentieth Century Words* (Ayto 1999) documents innovations of English vocabulary from 1900 onwards; it is a fascinating collection which drives home the enormous dynamism of lexis and reminds us that, for instance, nobody talked about *Aids, cyber-space,* or *yuppies* before 1982, *spam* was only a brand-name for tinned meat until 1994, and before the inter-ethnic war in former Yugoslavia in the early 1990s the Serbo-Croatian word for *ethnic cleansing* had not been translated into English. The activity of, and thus the word for, *googling* somebody or something is so new that it is not recorded in Ayto (1999).

All these 'new words' were adopted by the ENL speech community, while *wellness, handy,* etc. were not. But they have been adopted by various other groupings, and the processes in ENL and ELF are, in principle, the same—the possibilities the language offers in principle are flexibly exploited when a communicative need arises, whether or not this results in codified and accepted words/forms.

The process is nicely illustrated in the fictional world of J. K. Rowling. The magical community to which Harry Potter belongs naturally needs to exploit English to express a reality unknown to ordinary people—the Muggles. Thus wizards and witches have the ability to 'apparate' or 'disapparate' and they can 'obliviate' memories.[8] We can find a great deal of lexical innovation in ELF similarly motivated by communicative need, often serving the purpose of clarity and accessibility.

Morphology is a particularly striking case. For example, knowing how to parse an utterance one hears (or indeed produces) that is, being able to unambiguously assign word class is an important factor in intelligibility—to know what is a verb and what is a noun, etc. But the morphology of English verbs, for example, is not very regular. Thus while there are quite regular forms among verbs of Romance origin such as *communicate, educate, investigate, negotiate,* others follow a different pattern: *conspire, examine, finance, pronounce.* In the VOICE corpus, however, we find verb forms that have been 'regularized' by applying a regular morphological convention in unconventional ways to produce *conspirate, examinate, financiate,* and *pronunciate*:

S3 [L1=nor-NO]   and then i was sitting e:r later i was sitting at this schizophrenic e:r woman's apartment (.) listening to her talking about the war (.) that was going on outside and all the people that were e:r con-<2> <pvc> **conspirating** {conspiring} </pvc> </2>
(VOICE 2009: LEcon560)

S11 [L1=dan-DK]:   of of (.) for instance erm (.) [org1] gets eventually five different (.) formats (.) and <3> perhaps this </3> task force <4> then (.) </4>
SX-1:   <3><sniffs><sniffs></3>
SX-1:   <4>mhm </4>
S11:   <pvc> **examinates** {examines} </pvc> them (.) examines them (.) and sort of conclude perhaps (.) er
(VOICE 2009: POwgd14)

S14 [L1=fin-FI]:   <slow>that </slow> will be then set up <4> for different disciplines </4>
S12 [L1=ger-AT]:   <4>yes and also </4> <pvc> **financiated** {financed} </pvc>
(VOICE 2009: POwgd325)

S5 [L1=por-PT]:   <1>it's </1> completely different <2> and </2> people can't even <pvc> **pronunciate** {pronounce} </pvc> it
(VOICE 2009: POmtg439)

S2 [L1=pa-ES] :　　　<2>yeah </2> i like celtic music (.) i m-i must say i like celtic music.
　　　　　　　　　　(1) i like celtic music like for example [first name7] [last name7]
　　　　　　　　　　[last name7] [last name7] (.) you know i can't <pvc>**pronunciate**
　　　　　　　　　　{pronounce} </pvc> well in er er right well spanish though. (.)
　　　　　　　　　　[first name7] [last name7] is a: person who plays the: (.) plays
　　　　　　　　　　this istru- instrument so: famous in IREland
(VOICE 2009: LEcon229)

It would seem that what we are witnessing here is a well attested process
of English word-formation, suffixation, resulting in overt/emphatic word-
class marking, in the examples above by the suffix *-ate* for marking verbs.
Formal and functional aspects of such processes of lexical innovation as evidenced in VOICE are discussed in detail in Pitzl, Breiteneder, and Klimpfinger
(2008). Staying with the example of suffixation for word-class marking, this
also occurs with nouns. In StE the word *increase* can, if we disregard word
stress,[9] be either a verb or a noun. Thus we can observe that coining the word
increasement results in unambiguous marking for 'noun-ness':

S1 [L1=ger-DE]:　you get (.) EACH YEAR (1) an <pvc> **increasement** {increase}
　　　　　　　　　</pvc> of your salaries. (.) which is paid by the company. (.)
(VOICE 2009: PBmtg27)

While this lexical innovation comes from a speaker whose L1 is German, an
L1 speaker of Spanish utilizes another suffix to produce an adjective:

S5 [L1=spa-ES]:　which for the time being is not big issue? (.) so (.) <fast> i don't
　　　　　　　　　know what you want to try to develop afterwards </fast> you
　　　　　　　　　gonna be <pvc> **increasive** </pvc> by a hundred per cent or two
　　　　　　　　　hundred per cent
(VOICE 2009: PBmtg27]

A further coinage, by L1 speakers of Polish, Finnish, and, below, Portuguese,
in three different speech events, is *approvement*:

S7 [L1 =por-PT]:　... they will NEVER (.) well they will listen but they'll never (abide)
　　　　　　　　　(.) so er before they be able to approve the budget in the parliament
　　　　　　　　　(.) they must FIRST have the <pvc> **approvement** {approval}
　　　　　　　　　</pvc> at at this level at at the administration level
(VOICE 2009: POwgd510)

These few examples only allow a very brief glimpse at the creative processes
that ELF speakers make use of when engaged in intercultural communication. Readers are referred to Pitzl, Breiteneder, and Klimpfinger (2008) for
many rich and revealing insights into the fascinating wealth of lexical innovations attested in ELF interactions. While it does seem to me that enhanced
clarity and explicitness is a useful pay-off in the above instances, this is of
course an indirect claim to make, as there is no evidence in the data itself as
to speaker intention beyond the impression one gets as observer. It is interesting though to see how many lexical innovations result in patterns that have

greater regularity than the corresponding ENL forms. What we note here is the complementary relationship between creativity and conformity with ELF users exploiting the alternative encoding possibilities inherent in the language. I shall return to this a little later in this chapter.

ELF speakers' creativity, supported by the interactional context, comes across particularly clearly in processes of lexical innovation that serve to fill a lexical gap in the language, where speakers create a new word that they feel a need for. For example, the word *forbiddenness* (VOICE 2009: PRpan13):

is coined to express the notion of "the state of being forbidden". The ELF speaker thus expands the language and fills a "permanent gap" by coining a new word for a particular occasion.
(Pitzl, Breiteneder, and Klimpfinger (2008: 43))

And there are many analogous word formations in VOICE such as *bigness, clearness, mutualness, unitedness, non-compactness,* which may be due either to a temporary or a (perceived) permanent lexical gap in the language. An innovation that is perhaps somewhat less transparent is one in the last line of the following extract:

S1 [L1=ger-DE]   = with champagne glasses standing there not SPEAKing because
                    there was hh (.) VERY loud techno music <ono> ə tʃə tʃ tʃ dətʃə
                    </ono>
S2 [L1=ita-IT]:   @ @@@@@ <9> @@ </9>
S1:   <9>and you </9> couldn't communicate? (.) @@
S2:   so they were just standing a<7>round in front of </7>
S1:   <7>no JUST STANDING </7> there. yeah
S2:   hh <@> people.</@> (.) uhu:. (.)
S1:   it was like a surreal <pvc> **inscenation** </pvc> or something
(VOICE 2009: LEcon573)

Pitzl, Breiteneder, and Klimpfinger (2008: 35) discuss this coinage, suggesting that it is probably a borrowing from German *Inszenierung,* which (it seems to me) conveys a dramatic quality that the common English words *scene, staging,* or *production* do not express so well.[10]

Coinages which reflect the influence of the L1 are also interesting indications of how ELF users draw on their repertoire of linguistic knowledge as a composite resource and illustrate the point made in the previous chapter that the distinction between code switching and style shifting has questionable functional validity (see also Cogo 2009 for a discussion of this issue). Thus, though the word *inscenation* might be seen in some respects to be a switch into German, it nevertheless takes the morphological form of an English word and as such can be seen as a shift in style appropriate to the user's purpose. Drawing on shared non-ENL speaker backgrounds is also one of the 'canny moves' Hülmbauer (2007) discusses and illustrates with a number of examples including the following, in which S1 (L1=Spanish) and S2 (L1=German) are talking about the history of Spain:

S2:   =yeah because we have had a \<pvc\> **dictature** \</pvc\>
      for (.) forty years and (.) you know how the dicta- dictators transformed reality
      and (.) the \<un\> xxx \</un\>
S1:   okay (.) it's it's a: \<pvc\> **relict** \</pvc\> from the (.) er from the past?
S2:   yeah
(Hülmbauer 2007: 10)

S2's *dictature* and S1's *relict* can easily be related to ENL *dictatorship* and *relic* respectively. But, probably due to what she later calls the 'situationality factor' in ELF (Hülmbauer 2009), for the speakers involved here, their coinages may well work better than the conventionally encoded lexical items. As Hülmbauer comments:

Comparing the three languages involved in this speaker constellation, Spanish and German as L1s and English as the common language, it becomes obvious that the two mother tongue forms, *dictadura* and *Diktatur,* are more similar to each other than to the English form. It could thus be argued that the use of the coinage *dictature* may even bring about faster understanding on S1's part than *dictatorship* would do. The passage shows how parallel structures of the individual L1s can be exploited to create novel mutually intelligible expressions.[11]
(Hülmbauer 2007: 25)

There are other occasions when the words of the L1 are incorporated intact into ELF usage, and where code mixing/switching, therefore, can be definitely identified in terms of linguistic forms (see, for example, Cogo 2010; Klimpfinger 2009). But even so, they function as integral elements in the ELF interactions in which they occur, as Klimpfinger illustrates. She comments:

ELF speakers resort to more than two languages in a most creative way to fulfil different discourse functions, to apply certain communication strategies, and to communicate their multilingual identity, which calls for a view that code-switching constitutes an integral part of the discourse practices of ELF conversations.
(Klimpfinger 2009: 367)

Although Klimpfinger uses the conventional term 'code-switching', the non-English elements are integrated and so mesh into the identifiably English elements. It does not seem that ELF speakers switch from one separate code to another, but rather draw on the composite linguistic resource at their disposal, in a process that Jørgensen (2008) terms 'polylingual languaging'.

While so far we have been looking at enhancing clarity and accessibility in terms of processability for listeners, regularization processes can also be regarded as contributing to *economy* of expression for speakers.[12] The example that springs to mind most readily here is the exploitation of redundancy evidenced by ELF speakers' use of zero (rather than –*s*) morpheme for present simple verbs in third person singular. This is discussed in detail in Breiteneder (2005, 2009a, 2009b), Cogo and Dewey (2006), and Dewey (2007b). Standard ENL third person –*s* has, of course, long been recognized as a 'typological oddity' (Trudgill 2002: 98), and so it is not surprising to find that the realization by zero morpheme is widespread not just in ELF but also in native and nativized Englishes; this argument is put forward and demonstrated particularly clearly in Breiteneder (2009a), who emphasizes that:

While the sociolinguistic circumstances of ELF in Europe are certainly different from those of native English dialects and postcolonial Englishes, all the varieties discussed are characterized by multilingual settings, which necessarily create contact situations between various different languages and linguacultures.

When speakers who belong to different linguacultures enter into these intercultural communication situations, it seems that their focus often shifts to communicative effectiveness and economy instead of markers of prestige and social status. This can very clearly be observed in the data recorded where the ELF speakers focus on their joint communicative enterprises and use ELF as a successful means for the exchange of information.

(Breiteneder 2009a: 263)

Cogo and Dewey discuss –*s* and zero as 'competing variants in ELF communication' and comment that it 'appears from the[ir] data that the third person zero is the variant that is winning this competition' (Cogo and Dewey 2006: 77). This is certainly a possibility, and it is fascinating to speculate what will have happened to this grammatical idiosyncrasy of StE in 50 years' time. As Chambers (2002) points out:

Before a change takes hold, there is a gradual, almost imperceptible, rise in frequency until the new form attains some kind of critical mass. At the earliest stage, the change apparently affects too small a population to serve as a model, but at some point it becomes perceptible, though usually beneath consciousness, and spreads through the community. No one has been able to establish the point of critical mass as an absolute value, and it appears to be different for each change, subject, as are all social developments, to countless possible influences.

(Chambers 2002: 361)

And of course, there is never an end-point reached, language change is never completed but always ongoing. So what we currently see in a lot of ELF talk is a 'peaceful co-existence' of morphologically marked and unmarked forms, uttered next to each other by the same speaker. Breiteneder (2009a: 260) discusses the following extract from VOICE, in which –*s* (note, in the fairly prefabricated expression *that means*) alternates with zero:

S8 [L1=cze-CZ]:   …that means (.) if he (.) e:rm m- make disser- dissertation work in er french
S1 [L1=nor-NO]:   hm
S8:   he get the <L1cze> diplom {diploma} </L1cze> of [name1] university
(VOICE 2009: POwgd325)

Economy of processing effort is also achieved by treating the relative pronouns *who* and *which* as interchangeable rather than sticking to the distribution required by ENL norms, i.e. *who* + person and *which* + non-person:

S1 [L1=ger-DE]:   ...we have er i think a good good team there and we can cover france easily (.) i spoke to some german stations and erm (.) yeah there is ONE branch who HAS (1) two or three (.) **people which** i also would trust in
(VOICE 2009: PBmtg27)

S8 [L1=spa-ES]:   hh the **people which** are booking with you huh?
(VOICE 2009: PBmtg300)

S3 [L1=lav-LV]:   and they told something about the laws too that e:r (.) the only **language who** are allowed are english and so o:n so (.) hh it's erm (.) okay it's not so (1) erm: aggressive but e:r still (.) when you have law (.) that you (.) can't do that or that (.) so it's s:ome <6> kind of: er </6> erm (4)
S4 [L1=ita-IT]:   <6>kind of loss of freedom </6>

(VOICE 2009: EDwgd241)

It is interesting to note that in the above extracts (and there are many more examples to be found in VOICE) the speakers would also have had the option of simply using *that* instead of *which* or *who*. One explanation for the choices they made might be that they 'instinctively' preferred the clearly marked relative *wh*-pronouns to *that*, which is more ambiguous in terms of word class. This could be seen as speakers putting clarity and explicitness for their interlocutors over their option of minimizing effort by using the invariable relative pronoun *that*.[13] As with the case of third person –s versus zero marking, we can observe an interesting tension between exploiting redundancy (in the speaker's interest) and adding redundancy (in the listener's interest).[14]

5.3 Exploiting linguistic resources

What I have been doing in these pages is illustrating how ELF users exploit linguistic resources to communicative effect, suggesting how different non-conformist forms in ELF are functionally motivated. I have done this by drawing on examples from the VOICE corpus. In so doing I have interpreted these formal features as evidence of pragmatic function and I recognize that this, of course, is always a difficult thing to do since pragmatic function depends on contextual factors. Empirical work with a corpus is always by definition removed from the context in which the talk happened. The very nature of the VOICE corpus, however, is an advantage here since it offers transcriptions of complete speech events and abundant contextual information. This enables researchers to appreciate who the interlocutors are, why they meet, what they are talking about, and so on, and this makes it possible to a certain degree at least to look at the interactions from the participants' perspective. This in turn makes it easier to go beyond the description of the forms themselves to develop some understanding of what may have motivated speakers to use particular forms in the creative processes of communication. Even the brief extracts above illustrate that the speakers in these ELF interactions are not just calling up elements of a foreign language as they were learnt at school and pressing them into service as 'correctly' as possible in a quasi-display of successful, 'error-free' 'learner language' (Ranta 2009). Rather, the interactants are making use of their multi-faceted multilingual repertoires in a fashion motivated by the communicative purpose and the interpersonal dynamics of the interaction. In many speech events, boundaries between languages also seem to be perceived as fluid or irrelevant, as if speakers were 'disinventing and reconstituting' their languages (Makoni and Pennycook 2007; see also Mühlhäusler 2000; ten Thije and Zeevaert 2007; Böhringer and Hülmbauer 2010; Hülmbauer and Seidlhofer 2011). Seen in this light, the study of ELF is likely to raise further questions about the denomination 'Englishes' and 'World Englishes', i.e. countable (proper) nouns implying separate bounded entities and ties in with work focusing on speakers' plurilingual repertoires rather than parallel monolingualisms (see, for example, Lüdi and Py 2009: Mondada 2004). This perspective is compatible with Mühlhäusler's 'integrationist and ecological' one, in which the focus shifts 'from the consideration of countable languages to that of human communication' (Mühlhäusler 1996: 8f.).

There is one crucial further point to make that the above examples illustrate. It seems that, although empirical ELF research has only started gathering significant momentum, we can say with confidence that the bulk of innovations we observe ELF speakers introducing—be it a certain pronunciation, a morphological variation, a newly coined word, an aspect of syntax, or a discourse feature—is not a matter of arbitrarily replacing a StE pattern with 'just anything'. Rather, what we observe is the unfolding of familiar processes of language variation in language use, but extended in non-canonical, creative ways. Thus when a speaker coins the verb *examinate*, we can discern an underlying analogy pattern, for example, *communication: communicate* is like *examination: examinate*. The new verbs in –*ate* illustrated above (and there are many more in VOICE) then display a range of forms such as endings in –*ed* and –*ing*. The same holds for *increasement*, following the pattern *assess—assessment,* hence *increase—increasement,* and *approve—approvement* (analogous to *improve—improvement*).

Similarly, when speakers employ third person singular present zero, they exploit the redundancy inherent in the language, in this case in the same way that speakers of various native and nativized varieties of English do, extending the use of the otherwise regular present tense form to third person singular. Distinguishing between different relative pronouns, *which* and *who*, is equally redundant and therefore not always felt to be needed as long as the pronoun used is recognizable as a relative one—and indeed there are many other languages that only have one invariant relative pronoun for persons and non-persons alike. The lexical innovations *bigness/clearness/mutualness/forbiddenness/unitedness*, are outcomes of the familiar word formation processes of combining an adjective or past participle with the suffix –*ness*, resulting in a noun and in the case of *non-compactness* we even have multiple affixation.

We can observe that while all these innovations are not attested in StE, they are 'legal' in terms of the English phonological/phonotactic, morphological, and syntactic systems, and these provide speakers with a set of basic bearings that they exploit to communicative effect. The same holds for the words that have been said not to exist in English: *lifting, wellness, handy, pullunder* (see p. 101 above). Why, in principle, if you can have an *uprising*, should you not have a *lifting*? And if we can have the nouns *sickness, weekly, turnover*, why not the nouns *wellness, handy, pullunder*? When creating these words, speakers also made use of the underlying rules in a way that suited the occasion and their communicative needs. What current empirical ELF studies have in common is that they document ELF users' degree of independence of ENL norms. They reveal ELF as far from being an 'impoverished', purely expedient and makeshift code used for lack of something better, but a vibrant, powerful, and versatile shared resource that enables communication across linguacultural and geographic boundaries. Empirical research into such complex and sophisticated interactions further confirms the need to question the received wisdom concerning the terms *community* and *variety* (see Chapter 4) and to reject the idea that there is such a well defined thing as competence in a language that you either acquire and possess or you don't. ELF speakers can clearly be communicatively competent in English without conforming to norms of ENL competence. What we find instead is a process of engaging in appropriate ways of speaking (Hymes 1989), of performing acts of identity (Le Page and Tabouret-Keller 1985; see 5.1. above) by using the underlying resources of the language, not just the conventional ENL encodings, and adjusting and calibrating their own language use for their interlocutors' benefit. The question arises as to how these underlying resources might be defined.

5.4 The virtual language

In the earlier discussion of performativity in Section 5.1 of this chapter, I made the obvious point that creativity is a function of non-conformity, which therefore presupposes the existence of norms of one kind or another. The examples cited in this chapter make it clear that people can perform competently in English without adhering to ENL specifications of competence. But this does not mean that we can dispense with the notion of competence altogether.[15] Pennycook makes the observation that 'performance in language is not the end-point of competence, but rather language is the by-product of performance'. (Pennycook 2007: 60) and quotes Hopper as saying that learning a language is:

not a question of acquiring grammatical structure but of *expanding a repertoire of communicative contexts*. Consequently, there is no date or age at which the learning of a language can be said to be complete. New contexts, and new occasions of negotiation of meaning, occur constantly. A language is not a circumscribed object but a loose confederation of available and overlapping social experiences.
(Hopper 1998: 171)

One can readily agree (and it has now become widely accepted) that learning and using a language is not simply a matter of conforming to its encoded features. But nor is it simply a reactive by-product of performance. It is not a matter of *either* acquiring grammatical structure *or* negotiating meaning in new contexts. It is both: linguistic forms get acquired, adjusted, re-aligned as motivated by functional need. As I suggested earlier, performing and conforming are necessarily interdependent, and 'expanding a repertoire of communicative contexts' will usually be accompanied by expanding lexical and grammatical repertoires as well. When people perform in response to contextual need they do so with reference to some framework of knowledge, some competence or other—but not necessarily that which is sanctioned as the NS standard. The essential point is that competence serves as a prompt that inspires or gives rise to an expression, not as a script to be adhered to in every particular. Whatever pragmatic meaning is performed, it derives from a semantic resource, and when variable pragmatic use gets conventionalized, it then serves as a semantic prompt for further pragmatic use. So the question is, what is the nature of the semantic resource that is drawn upon in ELF?

The examples of ELF we have been considering in this chapter do not conform to norms of native StE. Hence some would dismiss them as not English, or not real English at any rate. But they are recognizably *in* English (rather than in Chinese or German). So what is it that is recognizably English about them? I would argue that they are realizations of a potential that Widdowson refers to as the *virtual language* (Widdowson 1997a, 2003). What emerges from these examples of actually occurring usage is that ELF is not a variety of English with clearly demarcated formal linguistic properties to be set against some institutionalized norm of the so-called standard language, but as the variable exploitation of linguistic resources. The very fact that language varies, that its users, whoever they are, are not bound by established rules and conventions, implies that it must constitute a resource, a potential for making meaning that is not, and cannot be, exhausted by the realizations that are already attested as actual ENL usage. Variation means that there is some virtual *capacity* for exploitation, inherent in the encoded language itself. It is this which constitutes the basis of its creativity. How then can this virtual capacity be characterized?

It seems to me that this question is absolutely crucial for the conceptualization of ELF. As I have argued in earlier chapters, the English used as an international means of communication cannot simply be seen as a replication of ENL, transplanted more or less intact to different places. The development of English in its lingua franca function is largely determined by its (majority) non-native speakers, who are all at least bilingual, and who use English to get a job done, to foster interpersonal relations and express identity, with a focus on communication, intelligibility, and efficiency rather than on correctness and idiomaticity in ENL terms. What ELF research is increasingly yielding insights into is precisely the hybridity and dynamism, fluidity, and flexibility of ELF interactions as manifestations of 'transcultural flows' with heightened variability and a premium on mutual accommodation (see also Firth 2009 about the '*lingua franca* factor'). We observe the use of other languages as a resource or as enrichment (cf. the lexical innovations discussed above). Much of ELF is negotiated ad hoc, dependent on context, purpose, and constellation of speakers and their own linguacultural backgrounds (in terms of discourse conventions, interactional styles, etc.). ELF discourses are creative local realizations, or performances, of a global resource that continually gets appropriated and re-fashioned by its speakers.

But how do we conceptualize this common global resource? English as a global language does not, in Widdowson's terms, get distributed but it spreads: it is not *adopted* but *adapted* (see Chapter 4). But what exactly is it that gets adapted? We can identify variations in the form that ELF takes by reference to the norms of other, familiar Englishes, in particular ENL. But this is a way of describing ELF, not experiencing it as a user. ELF users may or may not know these norms, and so it cannot be said that they are adapting *them*. Obviously, then, ELF cannot just be the adaptation of ENL. So what is it an adaptation of?

With ELF, we are confronted with an English that has taken on a life of its own, and that in many ways is different in kind from ENL, not a version of ENL but an alternative realization of some common linguistic resource. So we need to be able to refer to a construct that can accommodate the dynamic and fluid character of ELF while also accounting for what its realizations across the globe, despite all their diversity, have in common: the underlying encoding possibilities that speakers make use of. It is these possibilities that we can (speculatively) call the virtual language.

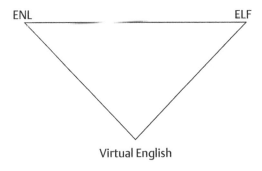

Figure 5.1 *A schematic representation of 'virtual' English*

The idea this very simple diagram is meant to represent is that the virtual language is there as a third point of reference for ELF and ENL speakers alike—as well as for any other Englishes—a kind of *tertium comparationis*, 'the factor which links or is the common ground between two elements in comparison' (OED Online). It is with reference to this virtual English that new words such as the ones discussed above are coined in both ENL and ELF, and, more generally, that speakers can be said to be 'using English', whether the forms they produce conform to attested ones or not.

But this virtual English is, of course, not the only linguistic resource that the majority of ELF users (non-ENL speakers, but also ENL speakers who speak other languages) draw on. As at least bilinguals, they have the resources of other languages available to them as well, and as we have seen in the lexical innovations already illustrated in this chapter, make use of them as active elements in their linguistic repertoire. ELF is in this sense a hybrid, a composite kind of English, a consequence, one might say, of language contact. But the term *language contact* is misleading on two counts.[16] In the first place, languages do not come into contact on their own accord but only through their users, and then they do not only come into contact but converge and merge.

When this happens in ELF, elements of the other language(s) are adjusted to suit the virtual encoding rules of English, as we saw earlier with 'foreign' words being adjusted to conform to English morphology. Unless there is some conformity to such virtual rules, there are, of course, no grounds for calling ELF English at all.

This is not to say that there is an absolute sense in which a particular expression can be said to be within or outside the boundaries of virtual English, particularly because these boundaries will themselves change to a certain degree over time, notably through contact with other languages. And when languages converge and merge, the virtual underlying systems of all languages involved come into play, and will take on more or less prominent roles depending on the specific situation. This we can see most clearly, of course, in varieties of English that have become indigenized through internal use within particular communities, where speakers can reliably draw on the shared resources of more than one language.[17]

So the very hybrid nature of ELF, the traces of so-called language contact are evidence of the existence of some underlying abstract set of rules that, following Widdowson, I have called the virtual language. I have given some indication of what these rules are and how they operate, but given the importance I attach to them, I will try to provide further clarification in the section that follows.[18]

5.5 Constitutive rules and regulative conventions

The concept of virtual language helps to clarify an ambiguity in the very term 'English'—an ambiguity that I have already commented on in Chapters 1 and 3. As already noted in the last chapter, linguists have a way of referring to *the* English language as if it were some definite entity. But, as was also pointed out, this entity is conceived of in two very different ways: as abstract code on the one hand, and as actual usage on the other. Thus, the main tradition in formal linguistics is to focus attention on grammar, as an underlying system of rules which have to be inferred in some way from the data of performance, and these are first person data drawn from the linguist's own introspection as a representative native speaker of the language. With corpus linguists, on the other hand, *the* language (the 'real' language) consists of actual usage which is described by direct third person observation of performance data. We thus have two quite distinct ways of specifying the norm of ENL: as proper encoded 'Standard English' on the one hand and as actually attested real English usage on the other.

It is, of course, the second conception of the language as usage that is currently in favour, and it has become customary to criticize sentence grammars of the traditional kind as reductionist, arid abstractions that do not account for language in performance, the actual language. But then they were never designed to do so. And we need to note that descriptions of actual language based on corpus data are also reductionist in that they fail to account for the potential inherent in the virtual language. The 'real' language of actual performance is only the language that happens to have realized this potential, what has in fact been said and written. What other realizations are possible obviously do not figure as data (cf. Aston 1995; Widdowson 2003).

Both sentence grammarians of the language code and corpus linguists concerned with the description of usage identify patterns of occurrence from which they can infer generalities. But these patterns, and so the generalities that can be inferred from them, are of essentially different kinds. As suggested in Seidlhofer and Widdowson (2009), this difference can perhaps be clarified by invoking another and not dissimilar distinction, that which Searle proposes between *constitutive* and *regulative* rules (Searle 1969, 1995). Thus the rules of a particular game, for example, define the game in the abstract and set limits on what counts as playing it and what does not. Searle takes the example of chess:

…the rules of chess create the very possibility of playing chess. The rules are *constitutive* of chess in the sense that playing chess is constituted in part by acting in accord with the rules. If you don't follow at least a large subset of the rules, you are not playing chess.
(Searle 1995: 28)

But players of the game, of course, realize these rules in various ways in actual performance. If you were to record a range of different performances, you would be able to infer certain rules of an invariant categorical kind that constrain the movement of the different pieces. These are the *constitutive rules* of the game, the code of the game, so to speak, and if you do not conform to them you are not playing chess. But you might also discern a pattern of regularities in the recurrence of certain moves and move sequences: the so-called Queen's gambit, for example, or the Baltic defence. These are features of performance that Searle refers to as regulative rules, and no matter how frequently they occur they do not constitute the game itself but only characterize different ways of playing it. They are, in effect, local usage conventions for acting on the rules of the game and so I shall subsequently use the term *regulative conventions* to refer to them.

If you know nothing of chess, and only have the observed data of actual game playing to rely on, you could probably work out which moves count as categorical and so constitutive and which count as variable and so regulative. And of course, it is entirely possible that certain patterns of regulative behaviour, through repetition, become so established over time that they become ratified as constitutive rules of the game. With chess, as with language, variation then gets categorized as change. As Gleick (1987: 24) has put it 'the act of playing the game has a way of changing the rules'.[19]

I want to suggest that this distinction between rules and conventions of games can be applied to language as well. I am, of course, in distinguished company in likening language to a game, as I acknowledge by quoting Wittgenstein at the head of this chapter. There are indications in this quotation, and elsewhere in the *Philosophical Investigations*, that Wittgenstein recognizes the distinction between what is constitutive of a language and what is regulative in its use—though with Wittgenstein one can never be entirely sure. At all events, the distinction between what is constitutive and what is regulative, obvious enough in principle, is rather easier to apply to games than it is to language. What constitutes a game is usually specified explicitly in a set of prescribed and pre-ordained rules which determine the limits of realization. What constitutes a language, what Chomsky calls the underlying system of rules, is, of course, not pre-determined in this way. It can only be indirectly inferred as a set of encoding properties abstracted from the regulative actualities of performance, what I assume Pennycook refers to as 'sedimented products of repeated acts of identity' (Pennycook 2007: 73). It is these encoding properties that I refer to as the virtual language.[20]

To return now to the question of linguistic norms, it seems clear that to represent actual, attested native-speaker usage as the real language and any non-conformity as some kind of aberration is to elevate a particular set of regulative conventions to the status of constitutive rules. The underlying assumption is not only that the native-speaker way of playing the English game is the best way, whatever the conditions or circumstances, but that it is really the *only* way. If you don't conform to these regulative conventions, you are just not performing English at all. This, of course, is the ownership claim to the language that I have already dealt with in earlier chapters of this book and requires no further discussion here.

But to return to the ambiguity in the term 'English', used as it is to refer both to norms of the abstract code and those of actual usage, where does standard grammar come in? Since this has to do with the abstract code, it would surely seem reasonable to claim that StE does indeed represent the constitutive rules of the language. In which case, it would be a norm that has to be conformed to, whatever variation in regulative conventions there might be in actual performance. This would allow for the possibility that you can play the English language game in all kinds of ways, so long as you keep to the standard rules, and would, of course, correspond with the normative view of StE that I criticized in Chapter 3. So is this a valid view after all? Let us consider the question.

For Chomsky, these virtual properties are essentially rules for sentence generation that will allow for an infinite number of realizations, and these will be subject to all manner of regulative conditions as performance in actual use. And, of course, it is only as performance in use that language is actually experienced. Hence the often cited Hymes dictum 'There are rules of use without which the rules of grammar would be useless' (Hymes 1972: 278)—that is to say, there are regulative rules (or rather, conventions) without which the constitutive rules of grammar could not be realized as use. In his well known model of communicative competence, discussed in the last chapter, Hymes associates such constitutive rules with knowing what is 'possible' in a language and follows Chomsky in thinking of this in terms of grammaticality. But the constitutive rules of the virtual language are far more comprehensive than that and are not restricted to the generation of sentences. As we shall see, they allow for regulative exploitation that would generally be characterized negatively as 'deviant' or positively as 'creative'.

The essential point to be made here is that what is formally possible in a language relates to *all* levels of encoding, and not only to grammar (see Widdowson 2009). Thus the phonotactic rules of a language will determine which sounds and which combinations of sounds are recognized as possible and which are not. So at the phonological level, the rules constitute a virtual resource which can be exploited to make new words at the lexical level. The words *clide* and *gimble*, for example are not actual lexical encodings in English, and so might be described as deviations. But they are virtually possible in that they conform to the constitutive rules of English phonology in just the same way as do actually attested lexical items like *glide* and *bride*, *gimlet*, and *gamble*. Similarly, at the morphological level, the virtual language imposes encoding constraints on word formation, so that words like **lesscare* or **easyun*, though they are *in* English in the sense that they conform to phonological rule and so are not deviant at this level, are (unlike *careless* and *uneasy*) impossible at the morphological encoding level. Again, however, the virtual resource is available at this level to make words which are entirely in accord with encoding rules like *beautiless* (cf. *beautiful*) and *unsad* (cf. *unhappy*)—these are morphologically 'possible' but not codified as normal usage in ENL. And we do find formations like these in VOICE, such as *sugarless* (VOICE 2009: PBmtg414) and *unformal* (VOICE 2009: POwgd37). The coinage *inscenation* discussed above is also perfectly 'possible' phonotactically and morphologically. Also new portmanteau words, or blends, in ELF follow phonotactic and morphological rules: I recently heard an Austrian ELF speaker say 'I am so squirmish!', which may be a—very expressive—blend of the attested lexical items *squirm* and *squeamish*. Obviously, when new words are coined within ENL communities, they also follow these rules, such as the recent noun and verb *blog*. By the same token, at the sentence level, any lexical item that is structured in accordance with these rules can manifest the encoding rules of syntax. In Chomsky's famous illustration of this—*Colourless green ideas sleep furiously*—all of the lexical items are actual words of English, but they do not have to be. They are not, for example, in *the gostak distims the doshes* (quoted in Ogden and Richards 1923: 46) or in the nonsense verse of Lewis Carroll: *the slithy toves/did gyre and gimble in the wabe*, which also illustrate conformity to the constitutive rules of the virtual language at the level of phonology and syntax (for further discussion, see Seidlhofer and Widdowson 2009).

Chomsky's use of actual rather than virtual words to demonstrate the operation of syntactic rules (*colourless*, for example, rather than, say, *beautiless*, or *hueless*) can be assumed to reflect his concern for underlying encoding rules that constitute grammaticality. Such rules are virtual in that, as he says, they can generate an infinite number of sentences, including sentences that have never been actually produced and those that may never be. The point that I would want to make is that the same generative principle applies to the other levels of encoding as well, so that a linguistic expression may be non-conformist at one level but entirely conformist at another. It follows that an infinite number of words can be coined that are morphologically 'possible' but not attested in ENL, including words which have been drawn from other languages and have become Englishized so to speak by adaptation. We have already seen several examples of such ELF coinages in this chapter.

In ELF interactions, we can see speakers utilizing the whole spectrum of Englishization on the one hand and expressing their own identity through use of expressions in their L1, often within one short part of a conversation (see Klimpfinger 2009 for many 'non-Englishized' instances of so-called code-switching attested in VOICE). Here is an extract from Cogo's data which, though short, illustrates many of the processes I have been discussing, as does Cogo (2009). In the following example, friends (with L1 French, German, and Italian respectively) are commenting on a website displaying honeymoon pictures:

18 JEAN: no it's nice yeah … yeah they have picture of them
19 KAREN: =eh?
20 JEAN: =they have pictures of them you know … in
21   Australia, [in Kathmandu, in Tibet, like
22 KAREN: [(laughing)
23 ANNA: they sent pictures … [on the internet/
24 JEAN: [it's nice but it's **a bit**
25 ANNA: =**too much** eh?
26 JEAN: =**cheesy**
27 KAREN: [YE::AH
28 ANNA: [YE::AH
29 KAREN: yeah **a bit too much** I think (laughing)
30 JEAN: so … **blue flower** ↑ we say, … **fleur bleue**/
31 ANNA: why … [to say that it's cheesy?
32 JEAN: [fleur-yeah … fleur bleue means … you
33   know when you have these pictures with little

```
34              angels of
35 KAREN:       a:::h [yeah
36 ANNA:              [yeah
37 JEAN:        fleur bleue
38 KAREN:       kitsch- [kitschig
39 JEAN:               [kitschig yeah (laughter)...
```
(Cogo and Dewey 2006: 67)

As discussed in Cogo and Dewey (2006: 66ff.), this is a particularly striking example of speakers co-constructing meaning by exploiting their linguistic resources and actively accommodating to each other, involving at times the direct use of their own or their interlocutors' L1, as well as paraphrasing, elaborating, and translating.

It is easy to see how the encoding possibilities virtual in the language provide a resource for innovation in ELF. The standard language and 'mono-codal' use of English is just one realization of this potential at the grammatical level which has been established, or 'institutionalized' and so, in effect a reflection of regulative convention. It represents what has been encoded, but not what *can* be. The novel encodings in ELF that result from this exploitation of the virtual code are, of course, unconventional forms when measured against the standard norm. But if we accept, in accordance with the Halliday view, that these standard encodings have been functionally motivated, then there is no reason why innovations should be measured with reference to ENL contexts and functions. These innovations have their own functions to serve, in their own contexts.

The interesting question, then, is what motivates the way ELF users make creative use of the possibilities inherent in the virtual language. To refer again to the passage quoted in 5.1, Bamgbose talks about the need to consider the creative and pragmatic and not just the linguistic features of what might be called non-conformist variants of English. He is referring to the nativization of post-colonial varieties. The same applies to the dynamics of ELF variation as well.

5.6 Conformity and creativity

Generative rules, according to Chomsky, provide for linguistic creativity, and here we encounter an apparent paradox. Creativity would usually be understood as involving some kind of rule violation, but as conceived by Chomsky it would seem on the contrary to be the function of conformity to rule. The paradox is, however, only apparent. For although, by definition, the generated sentences all conform to sets of underlying grammatical rules of the virtual language, these rules can be realized in an infinite number of ways as actual sentences. And, as we have seen, the same applies to other levels of encoding: the virtual rules that constitute the language at the phonological and morphological levels are also generative in the same sense and they too, therefore, can be exploited as a creative resource to produce a variety of combinations,

including those that have never been actually produced and those that may
never be. The essential point to be made is that conformity to virtual rule does
not preclude creativity but actually provides the necessary condition for its
occurrence: the very identification of what is creative obviously depends on
the reference to some norm or other that it does not conform to (for further
discussion see Widdowson 2008). The point is, however, that these norms are
inherent in the virtual language at different levels. They are not those which
have been grammatically fixed as the standard language of ENL, and they are
available for exploitation in ELF.

One can then, it seems to me, accept Chomsky's claim that a generative
grammar 'accommodates the creative aspect of language use' (Chomsky
1965: 6), but with the important proviso that this generative potential of the
virtual language is not only present at the grammatical but at all levels of language. This claim is, however, contested in other views of creativity. Carter,
for example, takes a very different line:

...his [i.e. Chomsky's] view is limited by restricting language use to well formed,
usually invented, sentences rather than stretches of text or naturally occurring,
contextually variable sequences of speaking turns in which creative patterns can form
and re-form dynamically and organically over stretches of discourse, and emerge
co-creatively between speakers. Chomsky's notion of creativity here is not a statement
about the capacity of the individual to produce strikingly innovative language or to
co-create meanings in everyday conversational exchanges involving more than one
speaker, but rather a statement about a genetically endowed capacity to exploit an
underlying system.
(Carter 2004: 78)

In the light of the claims for the virtual language that I have been making,
I cannot agree with Carter here because he does not distinguish between code
and usage: it is not that Chomsky 'restrict[s] language use to well formed,
usually invented, sentences' but that language use is not his concern at all.
What Carter refers to as 'stretches of text or naturally occurring, contextually
variable sequences' (or synonymously as 'stretches of discourse') are samples of
actual language in performance, which Chomsky quite explicitly excludes from
consideration. His concern is with the 'underlying system', the virtual language
that gets variably actualized, and it is this that provides the creative potential.
Carter sets up an opposition between creative and generative capacities, but no
such opposition is called for. The point is that in Chomsky's conception, 'the
capacity to exploit an underlying system' and 'the capacity...to produce strikingly innovative language' are one and the same thing. Where else, one has to
ask, could innovative language come from if not from such exploitation?

Carter observes that 'creative patterns can form and re-form dynamically
and organically', and 'emerge co-creatively', and his book provides a wealth
of examples of the outcomes of this creative process. The question that interests us here, however, is how these creative patterns emerge, and what *from*.
Creativity cannot be conjured out of nothing, by a process of independent
self-generation. As I have noted, there must be some presupposed set of rules

or norms for otherwise a use of language cannot be identified as creative at all.[21] The argument of Carter's book is, as he says himself, predicated on the proposition that 'linguistic creativity is not simply a property of exceptional people, but an exceptional property of all people' (Carter 2004: 13). I agree that, in principle, all people have this exceptional property, but exceptionality is always relative to a norm of one kind or another. If something is a property of all people, then creativity simply is a design feature of human language in general, the regulative exploitation of the norms that constitute the virtual language. It seems to me, therefore, that what is called for is an extension of Carter's treatment of creativity to include the creativity of ELF speakers and non-native Englishes in general.

All uses of language, I have suggested, are actual realizations of the virtual language—exploitations of the underlying system. These realizations can be directly recorded, and records in abundance are now available in corpora of ENL usage. Studies based on these corpora reveal that these realizations conform to certain regulative conventions—patterns of lexico-grammatical co-occurrence that are sufficiently frequent to represent a performance norm, and, as has already been discussed in Chapter 3 (though not in these terms) these regulative patterns have been taken by some corpus linguists as constitutive, which has given rise to the dogma that the only real language is the actual language and hence the only real English is that which is attested as ENL.

But ENL is only *one* way, not the only way, of playing the English language game—and considering the development of English in the world, it is actually becoming a minority way. It does not exhaust the creative potential of the virtual language. The examples of ELF that were discussed earlier in this chapter provide convincing evidence, I would argue, of such exploitation of the creative possibilities inherent in the virtual language. The requirement to play the game in conformity with the regulative conventions of ENL, on the other hand, would necessarily preclude any exploitation of this potential. The curious thing is, however, that the current orthodoxy of the 'authentic' requires EFL learners to be non-creative, to conform to these regulative patterns and replicate the idiomatic usage of native-speaker performance as closely as possible. These patterns are the result of some creative pragmatic process in the past, but the assumption seems to be that this process is the prerogative of native speakers and once it has produced its patterns of usage, what non-natives have to do is to reproduce them. Exceptional language not in conformity with these regulative norms is not considered to be creative in this case, but only evidence of failure. It would seem then on this account that as far as English is concerned, 'linguistic creativity is…an exceptional property of all people', but with the exception, it would seem, of all those who are not approved native speakers, that is to say, the majority of its users in the world today.

In this restrictive view, then, the rules of the English language game are a particular set of regulative conventions customarily followed by native speakers. It is assumed that you can only play the game, or at least play it properly, if you copy the moves that have been made by a particular group of players. No allowance would seem to be made for any possible independent access to constitutive rules that would enable you to realize the virtual language in alternative ways, and ways that also draw on other linguistic resources. As I indicated earlier, it is not only that a certain set of regulative conventions are privileged and preferred but that conventions are taken as constitutive of *the* language and that therefore any usage not in accordance with them, far from being creative, is regarded as not really English, not real English at all.

The examples of ELF considered earlier, like so much of the English that is actually produced across the globe, do not conform to these conventions, so if this is not real English, what is it? My argument is that it is no less real than that which has been performed in accordance with the set of regulative conventions sanctioned as the 'proper' grammar or usage. It is a different but not a deficient way of realizing the virtual language, of playing the English language game. Language performance gets regulated to suit different socio-cultural conditions and communicative purposes, but as these conditions and purposes change, so do the regulative conventions. There is no reason to suppose that ENL, the English that is performed by its native-speaking communities is appropriate to other users—in fact, it is likely that it is not. Other users have to perform in other conditions, have other purposes to meet, have other linguistic resources at their disposal, and so naturally will actualize the language in other ways. When people talk about 'real English', they assign absolute reality to one kind of realization. When they talk about 'proper English', they assign absolute value to one way of being appropriate.

5.7 Conclusion

ELF users exploit the possibilities of the virtual language to their own ends, appropriate it for their own purposes. ELF users thereby produce actual language that is exceptional to the extent that it does not fully conform to the regulative conventions that define ENL grammar and usage. This is what makes these users creative. Of course their language is bound to correspond with such usage in some respects, and for obvious reasons. Since the virtual language is an abstraction, a mental construct, it can only be made a reality when acted upon, performed, when it is made actual, and ELF users will naturally make use of actualizations in English they have been exposed to, and instructed in. Where the creativity lies is in the manner in which they draw on the abstract virtual rules underlying these actualizations to regulate their performance in real time, actualizations that often go well beyond what they have been presented with as the English that they should emulate. Essentially what we see in ELF usage is the exploitation of encoding possibilities to produce linguistic forms that are functionally appropriate and effective. What is significant about ELF is not its formal properties as such, but how they function to communicative effect, and this I explore in more detail in the next chapter.

Notes

1 This also becomes apparent, of course, when considering how some widely used non-standard ENL forms gain acceptance over time (sometimes in a relatively short period) and cease to be stigmatized. A next step may well be that they become accepted as StE. Current candidates include the third person plural pronouns *they/their* for gender-neutral reference in the singular, as in *How can you expect a person to remember what they were doing five years ago?* (Carter and McCarthy 2006: 198d); and even the reflexive pronoun *themself* is encountered in free variation with *themselves* in spoken language: *That's from doctors. Doctors themselves saying that. On what the Labour Party have claimed for <u>themself</u> as being their issue. Now that would worry me. That would worry me if I was a Labour Party Member because...* (BNC **JJD** 264–265: from a Bradford Metropolitan Council debate) and even in writing: *You won't be the first or last man or woman who gets <u>themself</u> involved in a holiday romance* (BNC **K4D** 386). Another example is the widespread use of *amount of* and *less* with countable nouns, as in *a large amount of students*, *less students*. For research on and discussions of such ongoing language change, see Bauer 1994, Mair 2006.

2 He defines these types thus:

   (i) Code norm: A standard variety of a language or a language selected from a group of languages and allocated for official or national purposes.

   (ii) Feature norm: Any typical property of spoken or written language at whatever level (phonetic, phonological, morphological, syntactic, orthographic, and so on) and the rules that go with its production or use.

   (iii) Behavioural norm: The set of conventions that go with speaking, including expected patterns of behaviour while interacting with others, the mode of interpreting what is said and attitudes in general to others' manner of speaking. (Bamgbose 1998: 2)

3 A new dedicated journal, the *Journal of English as a Lingua Franca*, will be launched in 2011 and published by de Gruyter Mouton from 2012.

4 Phipps is concerned with the learning of modern foreign languages, mostly in the UK.

5 For a more detailed treatment of their approach, see Larsen-Freeman and Cameron 2008.

6 Examples from VOICE 2009, i.e. from VOICE Online 1.0. appear as they do in the corpus (output style: voice), with three modifications: the speaker's L1 is given in square brackets, three dots (...) indicate where part of an utterance is left out to keep quotations short, and the speech event ID (for example, PBmtg3) is indicated at the end of each example.

7 We should note, of course, that there will be occasions of unequal encounter where conditions for accommodation will not be favourable, as in the case of the Nigerian asylum seekers and Italian immigration officers referred to in Chapter 3 (see again Guido 2008). Nor is business communication via ELF always harmonious and free of friction and misunderstanding, but here again ELF talk is like talk in any natural language. Interestingly, ELF business partners have also been shown to make skilful use of 'strategic miscommunication' (see House 1999; Pitzl 2010; and Kaur 2009 on pre-empting problems of understanding).

8 Thanks to Cristina Whitecross for drawing my attention to these 'magic' word formations.

9   On the (relatively limited) role of word stress as such for international intelligibil-ity, see Jenkins 2000: 150f.

10 I asked several educated ENL speakers, and all of them said they did not regard *inscenation* as an English word. However, it is actually attested in ENL (though not listed in the *Oxford Advanced Learner's Dictionary* (the reference dictionary for VOICE), but in the *Oxford English Dictionary*, and glossed: 'Theatrical repre-sentation, *mise en scène*', with four quotations given from 1900, 1963, 1971, and 1997 (OED Online). This illustrates very clearly how coinages can happen more than once, as obviously speakers 'of the same language' do not all share the same repertory, not just diachronically but also synchronically.

11 The same point can be made about *relict*, though the relationship is more direct with German, which has *Relikt*, than with Spanish. In fact, Hülmbauer wrote her article about two years before the finalization and release of VOICE Online 1.0, in which the word in question is now treated as a switch into German:

LEcon229:243S1:   <12>okay </12> okay (.) it's it's a:<LIger> relikt {relic} </LIger> from the (.) er from the past?

12 Of course, economy of effort is a general criterion at work in all language use, so ELF can be seen to be like any other natural language in this respect, except that as has already been stated, processes of variation seem to unfold in an accelerated fashion in ELF.

13 Further work on the relative frequency of the different relative pronouns would of course have to be undertaken to investigate this hunch empirically.

14 For more on the exploitation of redundancy see Chapter 6.4 below.

15 The idea that language is simply a by-product of performance could be seen as an over-reaction to the equally simplistic idea that language is essentially abstract code. Note that in Speech Act theory, Austin's (1962) performativity has to be sup-plemented by Searle's (1969) identification of felicity conditions that have to be met. To suggest that people can just perform, intransitively so to speak, is similar to the idea of 'pure' observation discredited by Popper (1959), i.e. the idea that people can just observe without some preconception of what they are supposed to be observing.

16 And for this reason, the wealth of research on language contact/dialect contact (Trudgill 1986), on 'linguistic outcomes of language contact' (Sankoff 2002), 'koi-neization and accommodation' (Kerswill 2002) and 'space and spatial diffusion' (Britain 2002) makes for fascinating reading from an ELF perspective as it is out-lined in this chapter: while the descriptions of many processes and categories are clearly relevant for ELF, others do not fit at all and call for a rethinking of familiar concepts. There is a great deal of interesting work lying ahead for sociolinguists at the interface of 'traditional' research into language variation and ELF.

17 A particularly striking case is the mingling of both virtual English and virtual Japa-nese in what Honna (2008) calls 'English in Japanese', resulting in expressions that Japanese people use both when they speak Japanese and when they speak English—and it is not always clear which 'language' they are in. For instance, in a section entitled 'Japanese Phrasing of English', Honna discusses the 'remark-able prefix coming from English to Japanese…*my*, as in *my-car, my-home*…Less proficient Japanese speakers of English might use the phraseology in an English sentence. English speakers new from abroad are often baffled to be asked by Japa-nese: 'Did you come here in *my car*?' (meaning 'Did you come here in your own

car?') Or, 'Do you have *my home*?' ('Do you have your own house?') (Honna 2008: 96). An example encountered in Japanese contexts is '*Lovely My Town* on a real-estate billboard. It is not intended to be English ad copy, although it is composed of three English words [but a] representation of the loan-word collocation constructed on the basis of the Japanese phrasing of English … where *My-Town* is a noun made of two English loans' (ibid.: 108).

Honna makes the intriguing comment that 'Japanese has two specific ways of writing foreign words, and choosing one over the other involves a decision, the socio-psychological nature of which is too complicated to dwell upon here. But the fact should be mentioned that what is written in the Roman alphabet is not (at least theoretically) supposed to be an English phrase, but a Japanese one, however English it may look like' (ibid.) Under the heading 'English or Japanese?', Honna comments: 'Since those English-originated words and phrases that we have been discussing are used in Japanese linguistic and cultural contexts, it seems most proper that they be treated as new constituents of Japanese language. Actually, however, they are almost always considered as English, not Japanese. … What is happening in the language contact situation in Japan is not the contamination of Japanese by English, but amalgamation of English words into Japanese lexicon by means of a set of indigenization processes … No matter what linguistic purists may wish to see, no language stands alone. Languages get affected by others when they become in contact with one another under multilingual social circumstances.' (ibid.: 114f.)

18 The notion of the virtual language has, of course, various theoretical implications which, however, cannot all be discussed within the scope of this book. For instance, it would be interesting to follow through what the significance of the virtual language is in addressing the issues that Schneider discusses: '[H]ow can differences or similarities between World Englishes be accounted for by their developmental patterns?' (Schneider 2010: 372). Similarly, it might be rewarding to examine the possibility of invoking the virtual language as a more general point of reference for the elements within Jenkins' (2000) Lingua Franca Core. These and similar questions will, I hope, keep ELF researchers busy in the years to come.

19 Thanks to Jennifer Jenkins for pointing this quotation out to me.

20 An area of sociolinguistic research with clear relevance and intriguing implications for ELF and the notion of the virtual language in particular is that of vernacular universals (see Chambers 2004; Filppula *et al.* 2009) and vernacular angloversals (Mair 2003; Sand 2008) about which there has been a great deal of lively debate (see Kortmann 2010 for a succinct summary and further references).

21 For a detailed treatment of (linguistic) creativity in general see Pitzl 2011, Chapter 3, and with reference to ELF, her Chapters 4–8.

6

Form and function in ELF

The internal organization of natural language can best be explained
in the light of the social functions which language has evolved to
serve. Language is as it is because of what it has to do.

M. A. K. HALLIDAY: *On Language and Linguistics*

6.1 The function of non-conformity

As I have argued in the last chapter, simply to home in on the formal
properties of ELF and their lack of conformity to the norms of ENL is
to fail to understand how ELF functions as an entirely natural linguistic
phenomenon. Like any other use of language, formal properties of ELF
are functionally motivated, and since the functions they are required to
serve differ from those served by the forms of native speaker usage, their
non-conformity is a natural consequence of appropriate communicative
adaptation. Total conformity with ENL conventions would in effect be
*dys*functional. In this chapter, I want to continue on the theme of ELF
usage exemplifying the kind of creative dynamism that is intrinsic to the
working of any natural language.

Creativity I have argued is not, as Carter describes it, an exceptional property, but a natural process of performance. To be creative is to exploit the
constitutive rules of the virtual language but to do so without fully adhering
to established regulative conventions, quite simply because these conventions
are not necessarily appropriate to communicative purpose. The language
game is played differently. But there are, nevertheless, certain basic social
functions that the language game has to fulfil, however it is played. One of
these is a conceptualizing function, language as the means for referring to
things and events out there and so of relating the first person, the 'I', to the
third person environment. Another is a communicating function, language as
the means of engaging with other people, of relating the first person to the
'you', the second person other. Halliday argues that these functions, which he
calls ideational and interpersonal respectively, are semantically embodied in

the formal features of the language code, and his systemic/functional grammar (Halliday and Matthiessen 2004) provides a detailed description of how they inform the internal organization of Standard English:

All languages are organized around two main kinds of meaning, the 'ideational' or reflective, and the 'interpersonal' or active. These components, called 'metafunctions' in the terminology of the present theory, are the manifestations in the linguistic system of the two very general purposes which underlie all uses of language: (i) to understand the environment (ideational), and (ii) to act on the others in it (interpersonal). (Halliday 1994: xiii)

To refer to the quotation from Halliday at the head of his chapter, since ELF is a natural language, it also is as it is because of what it has to do. So the question arises as to how these functions get realized in the unconventional forms that occur in ELF usage.

Let us consider first an example of how ELF fulfils a conceptualizing function, how it is used to make reference to the third person world. Increasingly over recent years, key events that have required widespread communication in ELF have been global health scares, such as the outbreak of the novel H1N1 flu (commonly called swine flu) in Mexico and the concern that it might spread to become a pandemic in 2009. In that year, the Secretary General of the United Nations, Ban Ki-moon, addressed a conference of members of the pharmaceutical industry to urge them to make a vaccine against the virus more readily available. Interviewed by CNN, Ban Ki-moon subsequently made reference to the importance of taking note of 'scientific research and its evidences'. If we consider this expression from the perspective of what would be typically expected in ENL usage, it is unusual. According to the codification found in corpus-based grammars and dictionaries, it deviates from the norm both in regard to the rules of the standard code and to the conventions of idiomatic usage. The word *evidence* is usually classed as an uncountable noun that cannot be pluralized.[1] Thus Carter and McCarthy (2006) include the word *evidence* in a list of some forty 'examples of singular non-count nouns [which] are count nouns in many other languages' (section 177c) and they mark this list with the 'error warning' symbol (cf. section 3i) used throughout the *Cambridge Grammar of English*. Ban Ki-moon in this ELF situation is making it into a count noun that can be pluralized. With regard to conventions of ENL usage, even a brief perusal of the BNC and the Corpus of Contemporary American English indicates that 'and its evidences' is an unusual phrase, and that the preferred ENL collocate of *scientific research* tends to be *findings* rather than evidence—and certainly not *evidences*. So measured against native speaker norms, Ban Ki-moon is here producing 'defective' English on two counts. And of course this is not a momentary lapse, an isolated occurrence of abnormality, but only one instance of a more general non-conformity that characterizes his use of the language. And not only *his* use of the language: pluralizations such as *informations, advices, knowledges, mobilities*, etc. are also attested in VOICE.

Here is an example from a discussion at a student conference, with partici-
pants from Albania, Croatia, the Czech Republic, Estonia, France, Italy, the
Netherlands, Norway, Russia, Slovakia, Sweden, and Switzerland. S11 and
S1 both use the plural *advices*:

S11 [L1=fre-CH]: …they said okay we are on the project but our communication
is not good. (.) come on listen to us and tell us what could we
do. what we can do. and we went we went like e:r two days er
we register exactly like this {S11 points at person recording} we
listened we analyzed and we said okay your communication is
not absolutely perfect? (.) and maybe you could do this or try this
or (1) become aware that (.) communication is not exactly what
you thought? and language is not always so. we gave some <pvc>
advices. </pvc> and it was for free (.) and for free now two person
have found the possibility to GO on acting like this doing e:rm
repres- e:r <@> linguistic genre </@> and get some money. (1)
they did it for FREE (.) TWO. days (.) it took three days with the
analysis that's all.

S1 [L1= fre-FR]: erm (.) h- how did it happen. (.) i mean HOW did you know that
they needed the: kind of <pvc> **ad<6>vices</6>** </pvc>

(VOICE 2009: EDwsd499)

From a normative perspective, then, we might conclude that these students
and Ban Ki-moon have failed to learn proper English. But such supposed
failure does not seem to have prevented Ban Ki-moon from discharging his
duties as the Secretary General of the United Nations, duties which require
a particularly high degree of communicative effectiveness—an observation I also made in Chapter 3 (section 3.3) regarding the significance Quirk
attributes to competence differences between native and non-native speakers,
and the fact that the respondents in Coppieters' experiment had not developed 'native' grammatical intuitions, yet had been successful in important
professional positions for many years.

Let us first note that the form that Ban Ki-moon produces here can be
described as another example of the exploitation of the creative possibilities in
the virtual language that was discussed in some detail in the last chapter. His
unconventional pluralization of *evidence* can be seen as the exploitation of the
morphosyntactic potential inherent in the code that has been realized in innumerable other cases which have become established as normal—*conveniences*,
for example, *accommodations,* and so on. These forms have evolved to meet
some functional need. It happens that the need to pluralize *evidence* has not,
or not yet at least, arisen in approved NS circles, but there is nothing in the
language itself that precludes its production should an occasion arise which
makes it conceptually appropriate. And one might indeed argue that here we
have just such an occasion in that the plural *evidences* is more specific in reference than either the singular form *evidence* (which indicates generality rather
than particular instances) or the more conventional plural noun *findings*
(which indicates results which do not necessarily constitute evidence).

The main point to be made is that non-conformity of form does not at all preclude functional effectiveness but on the contrary can enhance it. It can be seen here, as in innumerable other examples of ELF usage, as the exploitation of the virtual resources of the language for making appropriate reference to things.[2] The Secretary General of the United Nations does not play the English language game entirely according to the regulative conventions of native speakers like the President of the United States, for example, or the British Prime Minister. But then why should he, unless his way proves to be dysfunctional in the complex ELF negotiations he is involved in? As far as I know, there is no evidence (or are no evidences) of occasions where this is the case.

Many further examples from ELF usage that illustrate the same point have already been discussed in the literature, and in Chapter 5 above.[3] A particularly interesting and salient one closely connected to our consideration of count versus non-count nouns is the use of articles by ELF speakers, where a preference for zero article has been observed where ENL article use is idiomatic, as well as a preference for the use of the definite article to lend extra emphasis to a referent that is conceptually important in the discourse. ELF article use has been shown to be highly systematic in its pragmatic functioning.[4] Dewey (2007a and 2007b) as well as Cogo and Dewey (2006) provide a rich discussion of ELF article use. Dewey describes very clear findings in his corpus with many cases:

> ... where a speaker elects to use the zero article in contexts where the preferred English as a native language (ENL) pattern would involve the definite article. This is often the case where an ENL norm for definite article use involves a degree of idiomaticity and/ or redundancy, such as ordinals (*the first, the second*, etc.) or superlative adjectives (*the best, the most*) where the definite article is communicatively redundant due to the semantic value of words like *first* and *best*, which inherently express uniqueness. ...
>
> If an item is deemed particularly important it is often preceded by the definite article, while if the item is relatively unimportant the zero article is often used. Therefore, a primary function of *the* is to provide additional emphasis and signify increased importance relative to the discourse. This suggests that patterns of article use in ELF are more context dependent and meaning driven than they are in ENL. In particular, the formal rules handed down through idiomatic use in ENL have little or no value in lingua franca settings. It is simply not the case in ELF that the selection of an article will depend on the nature of a noun in terms of any inherent qualities, such as level of specificity, uniqueness and so on. It is instead a resource which is variably used as a means of giving additional prominence to a referent.
>
> (Dewey 2007a: 341)

Similar observations can be made not just about lexico-grammar but equally about phonology and pragmatics. Phonology was of course the first level of language that received thorough consideration in the study of ELF (Jenkins 2000, 2002).[5] This is not surprising, for several reasons. Phonology is a comparatively closed system with a finite number of phonemes, intonation contours, etc. in any phonological system, so the task of describing its workings in intercultural communication, though methodologically very challenging, is therefore relatively more feasible than handling 'the whole' of lexico-grammar or pragmatics. Importantly, pronunciation has also been found to play a particularly crucial role in ELF talk as it 'emerged as by far the greatest factor in unintelligibility' (Jenkins 2000: 19f.) while at the same time being 'the area of greatest prejudice and preconception, and the most resistant to change on all sides' (ibid.: 4, and hence Jenkins 2007). But it is of course recognized as inevitable that virtually all ELF users with a first language other than English will speak the language with some trace (more or less pronounced, so to speak) of their L1 accent. From an ELF perspective, this accent is perfectly acceptable (and even desirable as an expression of identity) as long as it does not cause serious intelligibility problems. One might therefore wonder why the same degree of leeway is not granted to speakers' 'lexico-grammatical accent' and 'pragmatic accent'. A longer discussion of this intriguing question would lead us too far afield at this point, but we might just note that for one thing, pronunciation has been shown to be more inextricably linked to deep-seated feelings of identity that are relatively inaccessible to deliberate intervention in terms of 'accent reduction',[6] and secondly, that the role of grammar, which is relatively more amenable to conscious control, is really not so much about intelligibility, but—just like accents—often a matter of marking social membership of particular NS communities. As Widdowson explains:

> ... it is precisely because grammar is so often redundant in communicative transactions that it takes on another significance, namely that of expressing social identity. The mastery of a particular grammatical system, especially perhaps those features which are redundant, marks you as a member of the community which has developed that system for its own special purposes beyond the transaction of ordinary mundane matters. Conversely, of course, those who are unable to master the subtleties of the system are excluded from membership of the community. They do not belong. In short, grammar is a kind of shibboleth.
> (Widdowson 2003: 39)

We will come back to redundancy and consider how it is exploited by ELF users in section 6.4 below.

6.2 Communicative interaction and the idiom principle

Variation in language comes about as the natural consequence of communicative adaptation. This does not, of course, just come about proactively under its own steam, so to speak. The potential for variation is inherent in the virtual language and, as we have seen, can be exploited reactively to make appropriate reference ideationally as and when the occasion arises. I turn now to what Halliday refers to as the interpersonal function and consider how communication is enacted among ELF users.

I want to suggest that there are two main social forces which are activated in the communicative process, and which can be thought of as counter-currents pulling in different directions which the parties involved need to reconcile. In what follows I shall characterize these social forces, which Widdowson (1983, 1990: 109f.) terms the *cooperative* and the *territorial imperative*, and indicate how they operate in the use of English as a lingua franca as opposed to English as a native language and give rise to different formal realizations.

On the one hand, language use is influenced by the cooperative impera-tive: we need to continually modify and fine-tune our language in order to communicate with other people. On the other hand, we adjust our language in compliance with the territorial imperative to secure and protect our own space and sustain and reinforce our separate social identity, either as an indi-vidual or as a group. There is, of course, room for manoeuvre between these two options, but in principle one imperative urges us to lower our defences and reduce our differences in the interests of wider communication with other people while the other urges us to close ranks and enhance our differences vis à vis others to keep them out. Widdowson (1983) states that it is crucial for social life that interlocutors should get the balance right between these two forces. He relates the cooperative imperative to speakers' procedures for making their communicative intention accessible, and the territorial imperative to procedures for making what is said acceptable to others in the same 'territory'. Both are important for keeping interlocutors on board and engaged:

human communication involves the reconciliation of two opposing forces. One is a function of the territorial imperative, as powerful in humans as in other species of animal, which disposes the individual to maintain his own schematic life space against the threat of invading influence. The other is a function of the cooperative imperative which disposes the individual to assume a social role, for his own good, and to accept a modification to his world in return for social benefits. Survival depends on getting right the balance between these two forces. ...

Communication depends on interlocutors being receptive, and this means that both propositional information and illocutionary intent has to be expressed in such a way that it is both accessible and acceptable. In other words, procedures have to service both the cooperative and the territorial imperatives.
(Widdowson 1983: 47–8)

In reference to the issues discussed in the last chapter concerning conformity and creativity, the cooperative imperative would seem to relate to the former rather than to the latter. To co-operate with somebody involves some degree of conformity to the regulative conventions of usage assumed to be shared by both parties, which creativity will of its nature tend to disrupt. The idiomatic patterns that corpus analysis reveals can therefore be seen as the formal lin-guistic reflex of this conformity function. John Sinclair has proposed that such patterned usage is indicative of a general principle of language perform-ance, which he refers to as the 'principle of idiom':

The principle of idiom is that a language user has available to him or her a large number of semi-preconstructed phrases that constitute single choices, even though

they might appear to be analysable into segments. To some extent, this may reflect the recurrence of similar situations in human affairs; it may illustrate a natural tendency to economy of effort; or it may be motivated in part by the exigencies of real-time conversation.
(Sinclair 1991: 110)

So one motivation for the idiom principle, one can propose, is that it makes for effective communication—you cooperate with your interlocutors by using conventionally preconstructed phrases you are both familiar with, and you do not have to construct meanings by what Sinclair calls the 'open-choice principle'. If all parties in communication have access to these patterns as part of their competence in the language, then this clearly makes both production and processing of text easier for them—a matter of assembling pre-fabricated formulae rather than making sense of each linguistic component bit by bit. One linguistic item primes expectation for the occurrence of others, with different degrees of predictability. Thus, for many ENL speakers *unforeseen* anticipates *circumstances, foregone* anticipates *conclusion,* and so on. In some cases indeed, particularly where these formulaic patterns take the form of proverbial sayings, it is not even necessary to produce the whole phrase. The first person needs only to cue the second person into it, and just the beginning will suffice to do that. *When in Rome...* the former might say, leaving the (implicit) completion... *do as the Romans do* to the latter.[7]

So the idiom principle would seem to relate to the least effort principle in that it reduces the language user's on-line processing load and so facilitates communication. In other words, the idiom principle can be said to be motivated by the cooperative imperative in that it facilitates, in Widdowson's terms, accessibility.

But if this is so, then although the principle can be adduced from its established realizations, it does not stop working but continues to operate in the ongoing use of language to yield new realizations. The *idiomatizing function* as a communicative process is exemplified by the forms of particular idiomatic wordings, but it cannot, of course, be equated with them. The idiomatic patterning that typifies current usage is simply a snapshot, the static representation of a continuing process. Thus what we find described in grammars, dictionaries, and textbooks is just such a snapshot, based on large-scale corpus analysis of current ENL usage and revealing patterns of idiomatic wording attested as having been produced in ENL communities. But a corpus compiled in, say, 2005 is likely to reveal some patterns that are different from those gleaned from a corpus built in the 1990s. And since English is now being used on such a massive scale outside ENL communities, investigating ELF interactions affords us unprecedented opportunities of observing the *processes* of idiomatizing, of the idiom principle in action as it were, rather than only its conventionalized *products* as particular idiomatic wordings.

The idiom principle can be seen as a means whereby users of a language accommodate to each other by conforming to shared conventions of established phraseology. But what about the use of English as a lingua franca, where knowledge of such shared conventions cannot of course be taken for granted since the situations and purposes in and for which ELF speakers typically use the language vary greatly from ENL ones (as discussed at length in the preceding chapters)? There is no reason why ELF users should be familiar with these recurrent idiomatic features of ENL usage. But if the idiom principle is a natural feature facilitating language use, it cannot be in abeyance. It must be expressed in other ways. It cannot be restricted to the manifestation of previously established patterns of usage, the 'semi-preconstructed phrases' that Sinclair refers to. It must also involve the dynamic on-line application of the principle, and we would expect this to result in changes in wording, and the use of local idiomatic coinages devised to meet an immediate communicative need. And this is indeed what we do find in the use of English as a lingua franca, as the examples discussed in 6.3 and 6.4 below will show.

What then of the territorial imperative? Although the idiom principle would seem to be motivated by the cooperative imperative, the particular idiomatic wordings that the principle gives rise to in the usage of particular languages can take on a territorial function as well when they become established as a conventional resource for communication, as 'pre-constructions', within a particular community of first language users.

These patterns of usage are internalized by native speakers of a language by the natural process of acquisition and become habitual as the customary idiom of their community. They thus function as territorial markers of social identity and group membership, and many are so deeply embedded in intuitive behaviour that only with the arrival of the computer have they become observable by analysis and a matter of declarative knowledge. Procedural knowledge of them is a part of communicative competence as described by Hymes—a knowledge of the degree to which an expression is actually performed by a community of first language users (Hymes 1972: 281).

As with other aspects of sociocultural behaviour, these idiomatic patterns represent accepted norms which community members recognize as customary and usual. This is not to say that they always adhere to them. These norms are not binding. Like the maxims of the Gricean cooperative principle, they are default expectations, and of course people often intentionally depart from them to create effects or implicatures of one kind or another, for instance in literary or playful uses of language. But the point is that these departures can only be recognized if the norms are familiar. Obviously you can only tell what is unusual if you know what is usual. If you do not know the norms that are prevalent in a particular community of users, and your non-conformity is unintentional, this is likely to mark you as a non-member, an outsider. But what if we are dealing not with a clearly established community of users who know these presupposed norms, but with users of the language many of whom do not? What about contexts of use not in these primary social communities, but in the secondary and often global communities defined by common interests, professional aims, etc. as discussed in Chapter 4, in which the tables are turned, where the ELF users are in the majority and it is the native speakers that might well be perceived as the linguistic outsiders?

6.3 ELF and idiomatic usage

The prevailing assumption about second-language/non-L1 users of a language, whether this is English or any other, is that the closer they get to native speaker idiomatic behaviour the better. It needs to be borne in mind, however, that the more distinctively native-like the idiom they strive for, the greater the risk if they fail to 'get it right' in native-speaker contexts. The very attempt to replicate native speaker idiomatic usage could be taken as an attempted territorial encroachment, an outsider's invalid claim to community membership.

Moreover, in situations where EFL/ESL learners (as opposed to ELF users) aspire to native-speaker norms, it is not only a matter of producing the accepted wording of the idiom. It is also a matter of knowing the contexts in which it is appropriate to use such forms. Some kinds of recurrent patterning are of very general occurrence in native-speaker usage, but others are quite restrictive in range. Since the idiom principle is pragmatically motivated, its formal realizations in a particular language are naturally acquired by native speakers in association with the contexts in which it is appropriate to use them. The linguistic forms of idiomatic usage are acquired along with the contextual conditions of their use as part of the process of acculturation into a community. This process is not confined to first language acquirers, of course. Other people can acquire idiomatic competence of this kind by long exposure or experience within a particular community. And if it is their aim to be adopted, or at least accepted, as members, then it would make sense for them to acquire this competence in order to meet the conditions of membership.

But the crucial point to emphasize here is that not everybody learns a language with this aim in mind. Certainly not English, 'the most pluricentric and international of all languages', as Clyne (2006: 99) puts it. As has already been stressed in this book, the millions of people around the world who have learnt this language to varying degrees for the most part use it as a lingua franca, as a means of international communication, but not primarily to identify with, or accommodate to, the sociocultural values of its native speakers—or as a means of communicating primarily with them. On the contrary, since 'producing a speech act in someone else's cultural terms may go against the grain of a speaker' (Clyne 2006: 100), there are many users of English as a lingua franca who would want to challenge these ENL sociocultural values rather than subscribe to them. 'I don't think I should learn all this' was how a respondent in Adolphs' (2005) study of attitudes towards local varieties of ENL put it.[8] Many ELF speakers would certainly not want to have to recognize the territorial rights of ENL speakers as a condition of their learning and using English for international communication. And yet the insistence that the only authentic English is that which bears the particular idiomatic stamp of native speakers in Britain or the United States, etc. is still widespread in the ELT industry and in many people's minds, too.

Apart from the fact that this insistence is unwarranted when it comes to learning English for international purposes, it also makes the process of learning itself much more difficult. As I have already pointed out, the particular linguistic realizations of the idiom principle in English, or any other language, are acquired as pragmatic functions through an extended experience of language in use. With idioms, it is this pragmatic functioning that is crucial, and it will take precedence over semantic meaning: the segments in an idiomatic phrase will lose their independent semantic value. Indeed there are innumerable idiomatic expressions where the meaning of the separate segments is entirely irrelevant and not even thought about by native speakers. So, for example, their repertoire of idiomatic preconstructions may include the expressions *hoist with your own petard* or *getting short shrift*, which they will use without having the least idea what a *petard* is, or what *shrift* means. Native speaker 'insiders' are not inhibited by such ignorance. Experience has shown them that the phrase works pragmatically very well and that is all that matters: they don't need to worry about the semantics. But non-native 'outsiders' have not had the same experience. When confronted with such expressions they might 'let them pass' (Firth 1996) and trust that the context will come to their aid, but there will also be times when there will be a need to focus more closely on the message form and when the semantics of the segments is all they have to go on: *She made it in the nick of time*—in the what? *You are cutting it fine*—Cutting? And cutting what? *He came a cropper*— Came *a*? What kind of grammar is that? And what is a cropper? (for further discussion see Seidlhofer and Widdowson 2007).

What we need to remember, however, is that in ELF talk we are not on ENL territory, and so the territorial function of ENL idioms has to be understood as in abeyance. This switch in perspective is (yet another) conceptual challenge that ELF poses, in particular to language teaching professionals who tend to judge ELF interaction by EFL (English as a foreign language) habits and standards, leading them to the view—contrary to the one I am arguing for here—that 'as far as idiomaticity is concerned, L1-users are 'playing at home', with rules they can bend according to need. L2-users are 'playing away', and if they break the rules, they are penalized.' (Prodromou 2007: 24). As I will try to show, this view is only tenable if we adhere to a limited, static view of *idioms* as prefabricated forms of the code rather than understanding *idiomatizing* as a process that speakers will draw on dynamically and flexibly in any natural language use. Prodromou says that the 'successful users of English' he observed 'as far as idiomaticity is concerned [...] keep away from minefields' (ibid.). Pitzl, taking a different line on idiomaticity, comments as follows:

Staying out of harm's way by keeping away from the minefield of idiomaticity is a suggestion which is quite openly territorial. And indeed if we remember that a central function of idioms in ENL is to serve as territorial markers of group membership, then the tendency to adopt this territorial approach is quite understandable. Nevertheless,

when dealing with ELF, we need to be willing to shift our perspective and to adopt a new approach. The territorial imperative does not apply to ELF speakers in the same way as it applies to the members of any L1 speech community. We are therefore facing the challenge of having to leave behind the traditional territorial notion of why speakers use idioms and take into account the possibility that ELF speakers may use idioms for various other communicative purposes.
(Pitzl 2009: 312)

So in ELF interactions, conformity to particular idiomatic ENL manifestations is not only a needless requirement, but—especially in the case of the kind of semantically non-transparent phrases mentioned above—it may actually work against the cooperative function of the idiom principle itself. As we have already noted, this principle operates dynamically in the on-line pragmatic process of making meaning. It must, therefore, allow for non-conformity with any existing idiomatic expressions where this is necessary or appropriate, that is to say where shared knowledge of the exact wording cannot be taken for granted.

6.4 Unilateral idiomaticity

The point is that these manifestations of idiomaticity, these particular idiomatic ENL expressions, are effective as cooperative and territorial devices within certain native-speaking communities of users because they have common knowledge of their wording and the conditions of their use. But since no such common knowledge can be assumed in the case of countless ELF users of English, the idiom principle can only realize its cooperative (and possibly also a different territorial) function here if the users are able to develop their own idiomatic realizations as appropriate to the particular interactions they are engaged in. And they will be able to do this to the extent that they have the semantic resource available to them in the virtual language for them to use to such pragmatic effect, for it is this resource which enables them to assemble on-line idiomatic expressions by exploiting the open-choice principle.

In contrast, simply replicating the idiomatic behaviour of particular English-speaking communities cannot serve the cooperative function of the idiom principle in language use outside these communities. On the contrary, it sometimes happens that speakers in ELF interactions indulge in native-speaker idiomaticity, thus un-cooperatively and inappropriately positioning themselves in ENL rather than ELF 'territory'. This can result in what I have termed *unilateral idiomaticity* (Seidlhofer 2002), by which I mean the use by one speaker of marked idiomatic expressions attested in ENL that may well be unknown and unintelligible to the other participants in ELF interactions, especially those mentioned earlier in this section, such as *cutting it fine*, but also semantically non-transparent phrasal verbs, etc. These expressions frequently take the form of just the kind of fixed ENL expressions which corpora such as CANCODE are so good at revealing as being part and parcel of everyday native-speaker spoken English (cf. for example, Carter and McCarthy 1997)—the 'real' English that all users of the language are encouraged to emulate.

I use the adjective *unilateral* here to denote '[p]erformed or undertaken by or on the part of one side; made, enjoyed, shared in, felt, etc. by only one person or party' and '[d]ealing or concerned with, relating to, only one side of a subject; one-sided', for which the dictionary also gives a quotation that is very apt for our concerns here: 'This is a unilateral view of the social contract, and omits the element of reciprocity' (OED Online, s.v. *unilateral*). The term *unilateral idiomaticity* is thus intended to convey a sense of lack of concern for one's interlocutor, a neglect of the need for accommodation, for sensitively gauging the other person's likely familiarity with expressions of a particular kind—in short precisely the kind of awareness and skill that accomplished ELF speakers are so good at employing. Indulging in unilateral idiomaticity is thus a (usually unintentionally) unfriendly act, in the sense that it is unfriendly to impose your habits on somebody else, especially when you are not linguistically 'at home'. Here are a couple of examples from my field notes:

Some years ago, I was involved in the following ELF dinner conversation at a restaurant in southern Crete. On my left sat my English (native-speaker) friend Peter; on my right, three Norwegian acquaintances. Yannis, the (Cretan) restaurant owner's son, whom we know quite well, appears with several glasses of the local spirit called *raki*, usually complimentary at the end of a meal. He serves it in small glasses to the Norwegians with the words 'this is from the house' (maybe trying to use a phrase that Peter has taught him, but not quite 'getting it right'). The Norwegian woman on my right, Leila, says 'ja ja', nodding to Yannis. Her response sounds like an acknowledgement that she has received some information, maybe something like 'this is the house raki, we make it', but not like thanking. Peter and I notice this simultaneously, and Peter explains to Leila: 'Yannis meant that this is ON the house'. But from Leila's nonplussed facial expression it is clear that she is not familiar with this phrase. So I rephrase, saying 'Yannis meant that it is a PRESENT from them', upon which Leila immediately says 'Ahh!!' and, realizing that she should have thanked Yannis, looks round to see whether he is still within earshot.

Relaxed dinner conversations are occasions where such ripples in the talk can easily be smoothed out. There are other situations, however, when speakers feel (or actually are) more 'on record' and therefore more under pressure, such as when they are being broadcast live on an international radio programme. I have several examples of such interactions in my field notes, including the following. A British BBC journalist is interviewing a Chinese lawyer about human rights issues:

JOURNALIST: ... but that makes it a criminal offence, in my book!
LAWYER: eh sorry?
JOURNALIST: well don't you think this is criminally wrong?
LAWYER: eh you mean if it was (secret)—yes
(Author's data)[9]

The British journalist here uses the rather non-transparent idiomatic expression *in my book* to give his opinion, and it is clear that for his interlocutor this causes difficulties that are very unlikely to have arisen had he said *I think* or *in my opinion/judgement*. It is problems like the one illustrated here that prompted people I knew at the BBC to ask me whether on the basis of my ELF research I would be able to guide them in giving advice to British correspondents on how to engage with their countless non-native English speaker interlocutors, i.e. how their journalists would need to modify their speech so as to become more intelligible internationally, especially in live interviews. In the light of my observations of frequent communication difficulties on the BBC World Service this would have been a useful and promising project to embark on, but unfortunately the division that made the enquiry was radically restructured soon after and the idea was abandoned.

Recent research into the use of English among speakers from different linguacultural backgrounds provides further examples of unilateral idiomaticity. The following extract from an interaction between M, an American ENL speaker, S, a German, and H, a Chinese speaker, reported and discussed in Roberts (2005) illustrates this very clearly:

M: Let's say we need decorations and we need it cleaned up. What's your bottom line?
S: What's my what?
M: What is the bottom line. What, what's the-⎤
H: bottom line, yes   ⎦
M: least you can do it for? The least it can be done for?
S: The lowest, uh-⎤
M: Yeah   ⎦
S: price? Four thousand.
M: Four thousand.
ALL: @@@
(Roberts 2005: 151)

Roberts discusses this interaction in detail and remarks (about an episode that closely follows the one quoted above) that a speaker may on such occasions be 'assuming a superior posture and using vagueness and colloquial language to belittle their interlocutor's position' (Roberts 2005: 152). We cannot know, of course, whether M employs the idiomatic phrase *your bottom line* deliberately to put S down, and does paraphrase it when prompted by S's question. My own reading of the extract is that the phrase simply 'pops out'. I do agree however that the idiomatic expression employed in this case seems uncooperative: the use of this non-transparent phrase in an interaction with two non-native English speakers appears inappropriate and inconsiderate in this specific situation, and is in fact unsuccessful in that it requires repair by rephrasing. It is thus a clear example of conformity to a native-speaker norm of usage being communicatively dysfunctional in an ELF interaction.

Of course, unilateral idiomaticity may not always have a dysfunctional effect. As I observed earlier, interactants may be able, with the help of context, to 'let it pass' and infer enough meaning for the general communicative purpose of the interaction. All linguistic interaction, after all, is a pragmatic process of negotiating meaning whereby misunderstandings are resolved on-line. But the point is that the unilateral use of idiomatic expressions, often motivated by the desire to replicate ENL behaviour as closely as possible, can needlessly interfere with this process and make the interaction more effortful, especially in situations where many speakers are using an additionally acquired language that is the only common denominator, but often the L1 of just one participant, or of none. Where the idiomaticity is reciprocal, it can obviously enhance communicative effectiveness, but where it is unilateral, it will tend to work against it. So attempts to conform to native speaker norms may be communicatively counterproductive. To go back briefly to the Cretan restaurant, Yannis' expression *This is from the house* may (as I suggested parenthetically) have been intended as a ENL idiom—his version of *This is on the house*, with the preposition changed to make it more transparent to himself or to the others. We cannot be sure, of course, but if so, it was this aiming for an ENL idiom that brought about the misunderstanding, which would have been avoided if he had used an expression like *This is a present from the house* in the first place.

So although, as in the examples of unilateral idiomaticity quoted so far the 'culprits' are mostly ENL speakers, this is not necessarily the case. This again is evidenced in the following exchange between Natalie (N), whose first language is French, and Chie (Ch) an L1 speaker of Japanese:

CH: yeah (.) hmm (,) erm: what's- are you doing hmm in your free time?
N: ah my free time? well er i like spending my free time erm (..) first of all **chilling out**
CH: **what sorry?**
N: **chilling out** (.) @@ er i like doing nothing and er only putting
CH: ah
N: my feet up and relaxing (,) and reading as well
CH: yeah
(Dewey 2007b: 239)

Natalie, 'who had lived in London for about 6 months at the time of the recording, uses a phrasal verb common among young speakers of British and American English, *chill out*, meaning "relax"' (ibid.). What is particularly interesting about this example is that Dewey happened to capture two conversations in which Natalie uses the same phrasal verb: he quotes another extract of a conversation, recorded less than a month before the one above, in which Natalie causes the same (temporary) non-understanding when talking to a Korean interlocutor. Nevertheless, she continues to use it, presumably because she finds the expression 'cool' and is thus pleased to have it in her repertoire. In terms of ENL idiomaticity Natalie's expression is of course entirely appropriate. From the point of view of the communicative requirements of the ELF situation she is in, however, she inappropriately positions herself in ENL 'territory' despite the fact that she is not talking to an ENL speaker.[10]

6.5 ELF and the idiomatizing process

Sinclair defines the idiom principle by referring to the 'large number of semi-preconstructed phrases' that are available to 'a language user'. But which language user? As the above examples demonstrate, availability may well be limited for users of ELF. They may have some of the most commonly occurring fixed phrases available to them (*of course, on time, by the way*) but often not those which native speakers have intuitive access to due to extensive experience of the language, and some of which can really only be pinned down by corpus analysis. This being so, ELF users will tend to construct what they have to say more analytically, in a bottom-up fashion, drawing on what is semantically encoded in the grammar and lexis of the language—in other words, by recourse to Sinclair's 'open-choice' principle. Sinclair implies that this is essentially a principle of linguistic analysis that does not apply to what language users actually do. One can accept that this does not apply to native speakers. But it would seem to apply to other users. One needs to recognize that the mode of communication among ELF users may be quite radically different from that which characterizes the linguistic behaviour of ENL speakers, and that, given the number of ELF speakers and their spread across the whole globe, this mode of communication deserves serious scholarly attention.[11]

A study that investigates the frequency of pre-constructed phrases, or formulaic expressions in ELF talk is Kecskes (2007), and his findings bear out the observations made above. Kecskes points out that it is problematic to give figures for frequencies because the notion of just what constitutes a formulaic sequence or linguistic routine varies greatly. Schmitt and Carter 2004, for instance, provide an overview of characteristics of formulaic sequences, and they also quote figures in support of the observation that such patterns are ubiquitous in (native) language use, the highest of which, given by Erman and Warren 2000, is 58.6 per cent of the spoken English discourse analysed by them, and only slightly lower for written texts. In comparison to such figures, the portion of formulaic expressions Kecskes found in his ELF data, 7.6 per cent, is indeed low. Kecskes' database is small and thus does not allow much in the way of generalizations, but on the other hand the very limitation in size enabled him to carry out a triangulation procedure: a week after the interactions had been recorded, the thirteen participants listened to their conversations and verbalized their thought processes. The resulting think-aloud protocols showed that the interactants:

try to come as close to the compositional meaning as possible because they think that if there is no figurative/or metaphorical meaning involved their interlocutors will process the English words and expressions the way they meant them. Since lingua franca speakers come from different sociocultural backgrounds and represent different cultures the mutual knowledge they may share is the knowledge of the linguistic code. Consequently, semantic analyzability plays a decisive role in ELF speech production.[12]

(Kecskes 2007: 10)

So ELF users will tend to rely rather on the open-choice principle, and it is not surprising that this often results in creative expressions which do not conform to what native speakers would recognize as the established idiomatic wording. But this adherence to the open-choice principle by no means precludes ELF users from exploiting the idiom principle in their own terms. ELF users, while often not producing the familiar ENL idiomatic phrases, clearly do engage in the dynamic process of idiomatizing, but as they are operating in ELF rather than in ENL 'territory', they also coin their own idiomatic phrases, or use conventional phrases in their own way. Thus Mauranen (2005, 2009, forthcoming) analyses chunking in academic ELF and discusses the way ELF speakers make creative use of chunks for fulfilling various functions in discourse. The point is, then, that while the *products* of the workings of the idiom principle may at times look different in ELF talk, the *process* of idiomatizing is taking place as a process inherent in any natural language use.

This process is illustrated very clearly in the following interaction captured in VOICE, where a 'non-ENL' wording gets taken up and is creatively developed and appropriated. It shows how a non-conventional use of adjective–noun collocations works to this effect. The speech event is a working group discussion among 12 representatives from several European universities on the topic of joint degree programmes in Europe, and how academics in various disciplines might collaborate across national borders. The participants have met before but are not very well acquainted:[13]

S1 [L1=swe-SE]:	you you're talking about (.) er: er (.) i saw (.) er two factors the **enDANgered (.) factor** (.) so to say. you have low numbers and you have to have a (.) hh to have critical masses.
[...]	
S11 [L1=dan-DK]:	right. i don't <un> xxx </un> i just wanna say that (.) a:nd that small <6> or </6> (.)
S1:	<6>mhm </6>
S11:	and or er **endangered** (.) **endangered er programs** (.) could actually benefit tremendously by pooling resources.
[...]	
S1:	mhm <5> mhm </5>
S10 [L1=fre-FR]:	<5>so:</5> if there is no (.) confidence between er people from er both <6> inst</6>itution <7> it will </7> be very difficult f- (.)
S1:	<6>mhm </6>
S1:	<7>mhm </7>
S10:	to raise (.) er: a project and program from the very beginning. (.) <1> er:</1> just choosing the field <2> because </2> it's **endangered** o:r er: very er or could be very attractive for students. if you haven't er: (.)
[...]	
S9 [L1=scr-HR]:	the most natural way to cooperate i think (.) is (.) at the (.) doctoral level plus research. (1) in these (fields). (1) and to combine both somehow. and my second comment

regarding the the **endangered fields** is these is not o- these are not only the fields in which you we have a small number of students. (.) i would just like to mention that in in MY case of [place3] **endangered study** is a study of journalism for instance. because (.) we have a lot of ini- initiatives which are of a very low level in the region. (1) to establish the programs which are (.) usually very (.) er (1) just at a low ver- low level of quality.

[...]

S10: [...] i agree with this er this ideas that er [org1] could stimulate (.) a new (.) curricula in (.) mul- -tidisciplinary fields for example (.) and we didn't (2) talk very much (.) about er a topic (.) er: (3) we talk er yesterday. er: (.) the: case of er ended- **endangered fields**. er: fields where (.) er in university we have no more strategy (.) for development.

[...]

S1: are you talking about the the small areas <5> and the **endangered areas?**</5>

S10: <5>small areas (.) which which are not </5> in generally in (.) development strategy in any institution. (.) except closing

SX: mhm (3)

S1: mhm. (3)

[...]

S9: so in practice we will need a list of the **endangered disciplines** <4> at at </4> all uni<5>versities </5>

S4 [L1=por-PT, ger-AT]: <4> @@ </4>

[...]

S4: <6>industry mathematics (.) yes of course </6>

S9: hh the group theory should be (.) disappeared or not hh <7> this is </7> now the the en- **the LIST of endangered activities** which were (.)

S4: <7>yah </7>

S9: in the history or in the recent history very good (.) and are now **endangered.** (.)

S3: [L1=ger-AT]: mhm (.)

S9: er <soft><un> xx </un></soft>

S1: mhm

S9: mathematics (.) will prevail (.) it's for <1> sure but </1>

S1: <1>mhm </1> mhm

S9: what and er which kind which part of mathematics (.) are **in danger** and which parts are

S1: mhm <2> mhm mhm </2>

S9: <2>e:r in </2> good condition (2)

S1: yeah sh- e: r er w:e had other (.) opinions huh? [...]

(VOICE 2009: POwgd14)

In the course of this discussion, which lasted nearly three hours, the collocational range of *endangered* (the 'endangered factor' introduced by S1, still with the rider *so to say*) is collaboratively broadened to include the nouns *activities, areas, disciplines, field(s), program,* and *study,* and an in-group consensus is well and truly established. The process that unfolds here before our eyes is one of speakers collaborating, even colluding in the creation of their own collocational rules. The languaging 'game' is introduced by a slightly humorous use by the Swedish speaker, the chair, and then taken up and elaborated by the Swedish, Danish, French, and Croatian participants. We could say that we see both the cooperative and the territorial imperative at work here: the collocation is accepted and used by several speakers, and it also serves to create a sense of in-group belonging.

What I found fascinating when investigating this use of *endangered* in VOICE was that in a speech event recorded on the same day, but with a different group of speakers, the interlocutors also play with collocations with this premodifier:

S3 [L1=fre-CH]:   we don't have to think ONLY to european master multilingual problems <8> and </8> things like that but we also have to (.)
S1 [L1=nor-NO]:   <8>mhm </8>
S3:   think about (.) **ENdangered** (.) <9> e:r </9> (.)
S1:   <9>mhm </9>
S3:   **<1>fiel- </1>**
S2 [L1slo-SK]   **<1>spe</1>cies**
S3:   <2>**species** </2><3><@>**yes** </@> @ </3> (.)
S1:   <2>yeah </2>
S1:   <3>yes mhm </3>
S3:   **erm and also: sciences.** then it's quite wide i'm i'm not sure that we can today say oh let's: have (.) GREEK <4> or </4> let's <5> have </5> e:r (.)

(VOICE 2009: POwgd325)

We note at the beginning of this extract that the ELF interactants display some familiarity with what is idiomatically 'normal' in ENL: S3's first mention of *endangered fiel[ds]* (where the hesitation *e:r* between the two words might indicate that she is looking for an appropriate noun) prompts S2 to supply *species* (overlapping with S3's *fiel-)*, whereupon S3 acknowledges S2's *species* by echoing it and following this up by a laughingly spoken *yes* and more laughter. All this overlaps with S1's backchannels *yeah, yes mhm.* But after having indicated recognition of the collocation *endangered species* offered by S2, S3 brings the focus back to what she wanted to introduce originally, by saying *erm and also: sciences,* by which she seems to mean 'and also endangered sciences'.

We can thus see how the ELF speakers here exploit and at times expand the potential for modification to construct shared new adjective–noun collocations. Observe too, the territorial imperative at work here, the emerging comity: the interlocutors here 'collude' in their collocational extension of the attributive use of *endangered* to *field* [of study]. Their mention of *species,* accompanied by laughter, would seem to indicate that they are fully aware that this noun is by far the most frequent collocate of *endangered.*[14] The process unfolding here reminds us of what in sociocultural theory and second language acquisition research is referred to as *languaging*: 'the use of speaking and writing to mediate cognitively complex activities' through which our thinking is made 'available as a source of further reflection' (Swain and Deters 2007: 821f.). (See also the discussion of languaging in 5.2 above.) What we see in this example is the process of idiomatizing at work. These ELF users take up the expression *endangered* and idiomatically 'customize' it, so to speak, on-line by using it as a recurrent referential token. This serves a cooperative function in that it facilitates communication, but at the same time a territorial function in that it establishes their insider status in the particular discourse space they have co-constructed.

Idiomatization works in this example by the speakers going beyond the 'normal' ENL collocational range of the word *endangered* and so creating their own idiomatic wording. However, ELF users also exploit the creative possibilities of conventional idiomatic wordings in the reverse process of *de-idiomatization*. This happens when neutralized elements in idiomatic expressions are re-activated.

Pitzl (2009) demonstrates this with particular clarity. Using data from VOICE, her study shows that '[w]hile idioms may be formally varied in ways possibly considered unacceptable by native speakers, such formal variation of idioms does not inhibit their functionality in ELF' (2009: 316). One example of this functionality is lending emphasis to what is said, as in the following extract from a professional meeting. The participants are discussing a draft document, which S1, whose L1 is Danish, says they do not need to adapt *head and tails*:

234 S1:   but (1) as (.) i've already said to some of you when (.) i suddenly (1) decided
           to gi- give it a look over i (1) i was struck by the extent to which this: (1) in
           MY opinion at least meets a lot of (.) OUR needs in terms of (undeveloped)
           specification I mean we do NOT need to aDApt this: sort of (1) **head and
           tails** but i think there's there's a lot of good thinking in the way in which it
           is set up (.) there's a (1) and thank god (1) the mutual recognition project
           already at that time was (1) forward enough to recognize the value of (.)
           <1> integrating </1> the: THEN [org2] criteria =
235 SX-2: <1><soft> mhm </soft></1>
236 SX-2: = <soft> hm </soft>
(Pitzl 2009: 310/VOICE 2009: POmtg539)

Pitzl comments that the intended meaning, something like 'as a whole' or 'entirely' is easy to understand in this particular context, and that:

[t]he function the metaphor fulfills in the context of this ELF working group meeting is to give emphasis to S1's statement. So even though, at first glance, the expression resembles existing ENL idioms, it is actually not an ENL idiom 'gone wrong' but a newly created metaphor using terms of embodiment (*head* and *tails*).
(ibid.: 311)

'Metaphor' is the operative word here, as Pitzl shows: that it is through the process of what she calls re-metaphorization that dead, or rather, sleeping metaphors in the shape of conventional and fixed ENL idioms 'come alive' again in ELF talk, exhibit formal variation, and fulfil a wide range of communicative functions serving rapport and tact, humour, emphasis, and clarity and expression of cultural identity (see Pitzl 2009 and 2011 for more examples and discussion).

The phenomena of idiomatizing and metaphorizing are probably the most powerful illustration of a point that ELF researchers have been trying to make clear over recent years, but that seems quite hard to accept, particularly for English language professionals. It is that investigating how ELF works is not primarily about which *forms* it takes (although access to these is of course needed as the 'raw material' of empirical research) but about the *functions* it fulfils and the more general processes of language dynamics and communication that the forms we observe alert us to.

We see, then, that idiomatizing and metaphorizing are natural processes and can be said to realize the two basic functions of language that Halliday has identified: idiomatizing is second person/listener oriented in that it relates to the interpersonal function and so facilitates the management of the interaction by building up, and building on, familiarity. Metaphorizing, in contrast, goes against the familiar/expected: it relates more to the ideational function in that it represents how the first person/the speaker 'understands the environment' (see quotation from Halliday 1994 in 6.1 above) and gives it expression. This is how language normally functions, but in ELF this happens by not necessarily conforming to ENL norms: what we can observe is creative languaging on the basis of the virtual language (see Chapter 5), not just a replication of ENL forms.

6.6 The exploitation of redundancy

As we have seen, ELF users find ways of meeting their functional requirements by exploiting the resource of the virtual language, and this involves breaking free from the constraints of established norms, both those that define the standard code of English, and those of the attested usage of its native speakers. In the case of attested usage, I have argued that conformity to the patterns of conventional idiomatic wording is likely to inhibit rather than facilitate ELF communication, which is, on the contrary, more dependent on the open-choice principle. This principle, as Sinclair defines it, applies to the selection of items at the level of syntax, the constituents of sentences, the filling in of structural slots with lexical fillers. But the open-choice principle operates at other levels as well. Thus, to refer to the earlier discussion in Chapter 5, there are rules for word formation in the virtual language which allow for the possibility of combining free with bound morphemes and this possibility is realized in conventional combinations like *unhappy* or *weariness*, but can also be realized by way of the open-choice principle in unconventional combinations like *unformal* or *bigness* and *healthness* (as attested in VOICE). The same principle applies to inflectional as well as derivational morphology, and is indeed applied in the Ban Ki-moon example we considered earlier, where the plural morpheme is combined with a noun with which it would not conventionally be combined to produce *evidences*, rather than, say, *findings*. In these cases, and in innumerable others of like kind that are attested in ELF, users of the language are applying the open-choice principle beyond its conventional restrictions as a general regulative strategy.

This creative exploitation of the meaning potential of the virtual language is one strategy that regulates ELF usage. Another would on the face of it seem to work in the opposite way, to be reductive rather than productive. Here the user does not make elaborative use of a linguistic feature, but chooses to disregard it. Consider again plural marking. There are occasions when, as in the Ban Ki-moon example, the plural morpheme is attached to a noun which would not conventionally be considered eligible for pluralization. There are also occasions, however, when plural marking is not undertaken where it would be conventionally required, as in the StE plural form of demonstrative *this*, i.e. *these*:

S3 [L1=pol]   ... it will happen only if on the left-hand side you can adapt **this new washing habits** which are...
(VOICE 2009: PBmtg269)

S5 [L1=ukr]:   hh then goes political dimension and enlargement hh then environment and then er **all this humanitarian issues**
(VOICE 2009: EDwgd5)

S5 [L1=fin-FI]:   yes and it's linked with diversity that you got **all this ideas** er from different
(VOICE 2009: EDwsd15)

In the above examples from VOICE Online 1.0, the plural nouns are not preceded, as would be conventional, by the plural demonstrative *these* but by *this*.[15] The plural of the premodifier is, of course, redundant in the sense that the plural morpheme attached to the noun suffices to indicate plural number, and in two cases this is also done by *all*. Even more redundant would the use of *these* be in the following instances, where plural is already doubly marked by numerals (*four, three*) and the plural form of the premodified nouns:

S3 [L1=ukr]:   yeah (.) er:m (.) we have like er **this four presenters** (.) hh we have [S2] e:r we have [S8] erm: we have erm: you hh and we have e:r e:r <2> sorry </2><3> yeah er er </3> [S5] [S5]
(VOICE 2009: EDcon521)

S2 [L1=ger-AT]:   ...i feel very s- very familar to this region and erm it was more easier for me to identify with him not this exactly place where you see **this three trees** but erm the dis- the the the countryside
(VOICE 2009: EDsed364)

Another case of redundancy exploitation is that of the present tense morpheme, the third person singular *–s*, which is quite frequently not made use of in ELF speech. Breiteneder (2005, 2009a and b; see also 5.2 above) presents studies of this feature in ELF talk that again make plain that this is not to be dismissed as a haphazard 'error' but as the use of a reductive strategy that follows what might be called the principle of appropriate communicative economy. This principle also of course operates in native-speaker usage, in newspaper headlines, for example, where articles are frequently absent, and in colloquial speech where pronouns are dropped ('See you tomorrow', 'Sleep well last night?'), as well as in various ENL dialects. When native speakers make such reductions they are accepted as appropriate— legitimate examples of the principle of communicative economy in action. This principle, like the idiom principle discussed earlier, operates in ELF as it does in ENL, or any natural language, but is formally realized in different ways (see also Ranta 2009).[16]

The examples we have been looking at so far are of redundancy reduction. But redundancy is a feature of any natural language, and although as we have seen, ELF usage reduces redundancy in some aspects of the language, it increases it in others. Again, the communicative function remains but is realized formally in different ways. A case in point is adding emphasis with a preposition, as in *We reject against this idea* or *At the end of the show, he returns back to the stage*.[17] And again, the deviation from current ENL usage is usually perceived as an error. For instance, *return back* is listed on the website 'Common Errors in English Usage', where it says: 'A redundancy. Use just 'return,' unless you mean to say instead 'turn back.''[18]

An instance of additive redundancy which is widely attested in ELF usage is the occurrence of the expression 'discuss about'. According to the *Cambridge Grammar of English*, which carries on its cover a 'Real English Guarantee' and proclaims to be based on an international corpus, '*About is not used with the verb discuss*' (Carter and McCarthy 2006: 23). And yet on the actual evidence of the international ELF corpus VOICE, it is in fact used, and used by speakers from a wide variety of L1 backgrounds. Here are some examples:

S5 [L1=slv]:   actually there were some topics er we **discussed about** who will e:rm (1) come (.) up with a press conference who is going to (1) to be the (.) <pvc> hostman {host} </pvc> of the press conference so there were some topics...
(VOICE 2009: PBmtg269)

S4 [L1=dut-NL]:   yeah. we <5> can **discuss about** this </5>
(VOICE 2009: PBmtg414)

S10 [L1= fre-FR]:   they found a format (.) in when er: (1) for this system er: (1) and chemist **discuss about** another type (.) of project <un> xxx </un> of format.
(VOICE 2009: POwgd14)

S2 [L1=gre-CY]:   <3>it IS im</3>portant because yes (.) it gives you an idea whether the university (.) e:r will be ready or will be: (.) in our case (.) i mean the departments w- wouldn't even DISCUSS it. (.) wouldn't even **discuss about** joint degrees if they don't know ANYthing about the funding.

(VOICE 2009: POwgd317)

S1 [L1=tur-TR]:   so it is usually a prolonged <un> xx </un> seizure hypoxia and <un> xxx </un> (.) it can be infections which is very important because we have now (.) a:n distinguished neuroscientist we will **discuss about** this issue (.) it can be again trauma AND there are some patients which we cannot find any er significant risk factor.

(VOICE 2009: PRpan585)

In these examples, the use of the preposition *about* with the verb *discuss* can be seen as functionally effective in that it serves several purposes to do with accessibility, such as lending more weight to the verb, gaining processing time, or highlighting the object, i.e. what it is that is discussed.[19] It illustrates the process of regularization which, as was pointed out earlier, is also a feature of ELF usage. In the VOICE corpus there are many instances of the noun, *discussion*, followed by *about*, too, and conducting a search and seeing all of these listed together with occurrences of *discuss + about* makes one realize how irregular StE is in requiring a direct object with this verb, especially since semantically similar verbs such as *talk*, *speak*, *chat*, and *argue* are followed by *about*, which connects the verb with its complement. Extending the use of the preposition to the verb *discuss* is thus a process of regularization that seems to facilitate production as well as reception.[20] Dewey (2007b:144ff.) presents a perceptive analysis of prepositions in ELF, particularly *about*, in systemic–functional terms. He also quotes examples of *discuss + about* from the British National Corpus, noting that this construction may gradually be taking hold in ENL, too. Here we thus have a striking example of how far description and prescription can diverge, and how normative opinions tend to persist. So while there is clear evidence that *discuss + about* is being used, the *Oxford Advanced Learner's Dictionary* offers a 'Help' note under the entry *discuss*:

You cannot say 'discuss about something': I~~discussed about my problem with my parents.~~
(*Oxford Advanced Learner's Dictionary*: 8th edn. 2010)

However, the very reason why the OALD and the Cambridge Grammar quoted above make this statement in the first place is that *about* is indeed used with the verb *discuss,* and in the context of this book and as an ELF speaker, I feel the urge to say, in response to 'You cannot say...', 'Yes we *can*!'.

Another example of such regularization in ELF usage is the use of the preposition *to* with the verb *answer*. Here are two examples from VOICE:

S2 [L1=por-PT]:   ...i will also **answer to you.** i think (.) of COURSE there are some concerns <fast> in the public opinion about enlargement...

(VOICE 2009: POprc558)

S12 [L1=ger-AT]:   ...may i just <clears throat> (1) {parallel conversation starts} er erm er **answer to this** (.) {parallel conversation ends} e:r my my my my e:r feeling was that (.)...

(VOICE 2009: POwgd325)

Here, one can argue, the regularization by analogy is even more evident than in the case of *discuss about*. For the verb *answer* is not only semantically synonymous with the verb *reply*, with its obligatory preposition *to* in StE, but the noun *answer* (unlike the noun *discussion*) is morphologically identical with the verb. So *answer to*, as a form of words, is already sanctioned in standard usage and available for copying, so to speak, in a way that *discuss about* is not.

The preposition *to* used with the verb *ask* also seems to helpfully highlight the distinction between such phrases as *to ask a question* as opposed to *to ask a person (something)*, underlining the fact that in the latter case the speaker addresses a question or a request *to* somebody:

S1 [L1= ger-DE]:   i you can ask this or i can **ask to** [first name8] (.)

(VOICE 2009: PBmtg300)

S4 [L1=ita-IT]:   i think tha- i don- i don- really i don't know if it it will be possible to do so (.) but i think if er (.) the community **ask** (.) **to us** to push this kind (.) of er initiatives (.) i think that they have er also (.) to be able (.) no? to be FLEXIBLE (.) <6> in </6> regulation and rules.<7> the </7> rules and regulation of the master (.)

(VOICE 2009: POwgd325)

The general point to be made about all these examples we have considered is that instead of simply stigmatizing them as deviant forms, evidence of error, we need to consider what the functional motivation for ELF usages might be. As with idiomaticity, we need to distinguish the process in principle from its particular realizations, the regulative conventions of its actual wordings. As was pointed out earlier, though the idiomatic expressions that are attested in native-speaker usage are evidence of the idiom principle at work, these are by no means the only way in which the principle is acted upon. On the contrary, if the principle is to function effectively, it can only do so by the use of other forms, other wordings. The same point applies to redundancy. As with idiomaticity, redundancy as a general principle, serves a cooperative purpose in that it facilitates the processing of the message. But *realizations* of this principle as grammatical specifications, like the realizations of idiomaticity in idiomatic expressions, also serve a territorial function in that they represent the rules established as socially correct for a particular community and which define the conditions of membership. Such grammatical rules, then, like the patterns of idiomatic usage, also function as territorial markers of social identity and group membership, and if you want to be a member, you are required to conform. This, of course, is why ungrammaticality is so often seen as reprehensible: not because it affects communication, but because it offends social etiquette. With ELF users, however, there is no such social requirement to conform, and so there is no reason why they should not disregard those grammatical features if they are surplus to their communicative requirements. So they have to be cooperative by realizing the redundancy principle in other linguistic ways. And so they do.

6.7 Conclusion

The 'departures' from the norms of the standard code and native-speaker idiomatic usage that we have been considering in this chapter can then be seen as resulting from ELF users making effective strategic use of the language as a communicative resource. It has to be borne in mind that this formal unconventionality is defined only in reference to certain established actualized versions of the language, certain sets of conventions. These, the native-speaker versions of English, are, as we have noted, accorded a prestigious status, but it needs to be recognized that they are indeed only versions, historically shaped to suit the social and communicative requirements of certain communities and so necessarily of restricted relevance to other users of the language with very different needs and purposes. The formal features of ELF, like those of any natural language, are motivated by the functions they are required to serve and in this respect they are not abnormal at all but on the contrary conform to certain basic communicative principles which are incompatible with conformity to native-speaker norms (for further comments, see Seidlhofer 2009b).

What I have tried to show in this chapter is how ELF users draw on the possibilities inherent in the virtual language to produce linguistic forms in accordance with their functional needs. I have shown this to be an entirely natural process, which exemplifies how language evolves and, in Halliday's words (quoted at the head of this chapter), becomes what it is because of what it has to do. In this chapter, and throughout this book, the assumption has been that language development as exemplified by ELF is self-regulating and that the formal adaptations that are made can naturally enhance functional effectiveness.

But not everybody would share this assumption. There is also the view that language will not develop satisfactorily on its own accord, but needs to be adapted by deliberate design. It is of interest to see how far the principles of such design relate to the principles of natural development that are exemplified in ELF. This will be the theme of Chapter 7.

Notes

1 In the *British National Corpus*, as opposed to over 21,000 instances of the singular noun form *evidence*, there are only 31 instances of the plural form of the noun, *evidences* (and seven instances of the third person singular verb form *evidences*). When investigating the use of the pluralization of the noun *evidence*, I came

across this intriguing account by a US biochemist in a text entitled *29 + Evidences for Macroevolution,* subheading: 'Evidences'? on the website 'The TalkOrigins Archive':

"I've caught an enormous amount of flack for the title of this FAQ. Many a reader has reminded me that 'evidences' is only used in ecclesiastical contexts. True, the majority of references using the term 'evidences' are religious apologies, as evidenced by a simple Google search for 'evidences'. Others importune that 'evidences' is not even a valid English term, as 'evidence' is already a plural noun (formally known as a *mass noun* or a *non-count noun*). Originally, the title of this FAQ was diffidently christened 'Proofs of Macroevolution'—something used just to be a *tad* provocative, since science really cannot prove anything in the mathematical or logical sense of 'prove.' I was strongly urged to remove the overstated 'Proofs' (and I agreed it should be changed), so I decided to insert 'evidences' as an inside joke for all who realize how common that bit of language is in creation/evolution debates. Personally, I thought it was pretty funny. It also lends a nice eccentric air to the title, giving it some name recognition. Who would remember 'The Scientific Evidence for Common Descent' or some other insipid appellation? Recently, I've had some fun investigating the historical usage of the word 'evidences,' and I am surprised to report that it is not at all limited to Christian apologetics. It appears to be somewhat of an archaic usage, but was not and is not confined to theological discourse. In an effort to contribute even more verbiage to this logomachy, I have compiled a listing of authors, writers, politicians, documents, historians, scientists, etc. that have employed this particular etymon. My locution might be peculiar, but I have distinguished company." (http://www.talkorigins.org/faqs/comdesc/evidences.html)

2 Further non-conventional pluralizations attested in VOICE and produced by speakers from a wide variety of first-language backgrounds include *documentations, educations, fundings, recognitions, spendings*—and also related phenomena such as re-analysis in *criterias* and *medias*. Thanks go to Marie-Luise Pitzl for compiling a list of these.

3 For references to further studies, especially in the academic and business domains, see Chapter 8.

4 While compiling, testing, and using VOICE I have observed these tendencies in this larger corpus as well. A comprehensive investigation of article use would of course require part-of-speech tagging, which is, however, only now being prepared for VOICE at the time of writing.

5 Jenkins has repeatedly pointed out that her 'Lingua Franca Core' (LFC) may need to be modified in the light of more data, maybe from additional L1s, but to date no studies that investigated her findings from the perspective of such additional languages have falsified her results (cf. Deterding and Kirkpatrick 2006, Walker 2010). More such empirical work would certainly be very useful. Elements of Jenkins' (2000) LFC have recently also been subjected to empirical tests from a psycholinguistic perspective, and generally confirmed, by Osimk (2009a, b, 2010).

6 A loaded term, especially for ELF speech—see Jenkins (2000: 207f.) An alternative now getting more and more accepted is to think in terms of 'accent addition', i.e. adding to one's pronunciation repertoire in a way that is appropriate to one's needs and desires. But this is not to deny that there is still a lot of stigmatizing of accent and that 'accent reduction' is still big business, even in the UK.

7 This principle also operates in written language, of course. Aston (1995: 270) points out that 'proverbs and clichés are very rarely reproduced verbatim in a newspaper corpus, but the fact that they frequently form the basis of modified citations demonstrates that their prototypical forms are assumed to be available' and he illustrates this with the example *a bridge too far*, which newspapers tend to use 'either with a pun on the literal sense of *bridge*, or in allusive variants such as *a call/a fridge too far*' Aston (1995: 270). On idiom variation from a cognitive-linguistic perspective see Langlotz (2006).

8 See also the views expressed by Jenkins' numerous respondents in her 2007 book.

9 Author's field notes, BBC World Service, May 2001.

10 Marie-Luise Pitzl (personal communication) reminds me that several years on from when Dewey collected his data, the expression *chilling out*, or just *chilling*, is becoming very widespread among youngsters also in non-English speaking countries such as Austria. We thus have here another example of continuous language variation and spread, and a reminder that judgements about the appropriateness or otherwise of linguistic choices will of course always be very context-dependent.

11 It has indeed been the principal purpose of the VOICE project to create a sizeable empirical basis in order to make such research possible.

12 It should be noted that all of Kecskes' respondents had been resident in the USA for at least six months, so it is likely that they had, in principle, access to everyday idiomatic expressions in the first place (that they then tended not to use in the ELF interactions recorded). The case may be different with ELF users operating mainly or entirely outside English-speaking environments.

13 The extracts cited here come from different stages in this long discussion. The dots in square brackets occupying a line of their own indicate where stretches of talk are left out. The entire transcript and the text header with ample contextual information as well as the recording of the whole speech event can be found on the *VOICE Online* website: http://voice.univie.ac.at/index.xql

14 In the British National Corpus, for example, 253 of the 538 occurrences of *endangered* are directly followed by *species*, and the overwhelming majority of all attributive occurrences modify nouns denoting animals or other natural phenomena.

15 Here we are, of course, confronted with an intrinsic difficulty of transcription: transcribers can only note down as precisely as possible what they hear, not what the speaker intended to say – which *may* on occasion actually have been 'these', pronounced with a relatively short i-sound. There is no knowing what the interlocutor(s) actually heard, but at any rate we do not see any indications of intelligibility problems arising in these interactions due to all this variation.

16 For a detailed consideration of how 'third person zero' in ELF talk has been discussed in descriptive research, see Seidlhofer 2009b.

17 Author's field notes, BBC World Service, September 2008.

18 http://www.wsu.edu/~brians/errors/returnback.html (accessed 17 Sept 2010).

19 Similarly, the fact that the progressive aspect seems 'attractive' to ELF users would also partly seem due to reasons such as the presence of a form of *be* plus an *–ing* ending both signal that a verb is being used (which may be particularly useful in the case of the many monosyllabic verbs in English), helping both the listener in processing and the speaker in production by giving them more time. Similar obser-

vations have been made, on the basis of many analysed examples from ELFA and VOICE respectively, by Ranta (2006) and Dorn (2010).

20 The point about analogies with similar verbs, and of prepositions being used differently from StE in general (*discuss about, emphasize on, stress on*), has of course been made in the discussion of Outer Circle/'New Englishes' (see Platt, Weber, and Ho 1984: 85, and Schneider 2007).

7

Designing English as an international language

One of the unanticipated achievements of the twenty-first century was the rapid diffusion of Basic English as the lingua franca of the world and the even more rapid modification, expansion and spread of English in its wake. ...

No deliberate attempt was made to establish it as the world language. It had many natural advantages over its chief competitors, Spanish, French, Russian, German and Italian. It was simpler, subtler, more flexible and already more widely spoken, but it was certainly the use of Basic English which gave it its final victory over these rivals.

H. G. WELLS: *The Shape of Things to Come*

7.1 Linguistic description and prescription

In previous chapters, I have been drawing on the data of actually occurring usage, mainly in the VOICE corpus, to provide empirical evidence of how ELF functions as a naturally occurring phenomenon, one that exemplifies the dynamic processes of variation and adaptability that constitute the vitality of any living language—processes which are activated and regulated by the communicative needs of a globalized world. These chapters, then, have been concerned with giving an empirical description of how linguistic forms are actually used in ELF interactions. They are emphatically not intended to prescribe what forms of English people *should* use to ensure effective communication. It is important to emphasize this because the *descriptive* work on ELF that I have been discussing in this book has sometimes been confused with the *prescriptive* proposals that have been made for the specification of a simplified version of English.[1]

As we have seen in Chapter 2, not everybody is content just to allow natural linguistic processes to take their course, and some people feel obliged to intervene and arrest or direct their development in one way or another. There may, of course, be good reasons for intervention: natural processes can often be improved on, after all, whether they have to do with language or anything else. So far we have been concerned with a description of how English is actually used. In this chapter we consider prescriptions that have been put forward concerning how English *should* be used—the various proposals that have been made for intervening in linguistic affairs, for managing or planning the language with the aim of making it more effective.

This issue of prescription is of particular current relevance for an understanding of ELF. In previous chapters, I have tried to show how linguistic features of ELF are functionally motivated in subtle and complex ways. But superficially they can be misunderstood as a set of reduced forms that can be prescribed for use in rudimentary communication. And just such a prescription is in fact currently being marketed vigorously under the trade mark of 'Globish'. This term is also used, misleadingly, as synonymous with 'globalized English' (see McCrum 2010 passim) suggesting that Globish is a description of actual usage, so we need to be clear that it is nothing of the kind. It is in fact an example of linguistic engineering or language planning, the most recent of several other attempts that have been made in the past to devise a simpler and more elementary version of English.[2]

7.2 Language planning and linguistic intervention

The general field of language planning, as described for example in Kaplan and Baldauf (1997), covers a range of different kinds of intervention, all of which relate to the issues concerning ELF that have been discussed in the previous chapters of this book. The area that is usually called status planning, for example, involves the assigning of different languages or language varieties to certain domains of use so that they effectively complement each other. This question of status relates to the discussion of standard language ideologies in Chapter 3, but in particular it bears directly on the point made in Chapter 4 about the co-existence of English with other languages in a composite repertoire of linguistic resources. This co-existence is possible, and feasible, I argued, if the English is dissociated from its status as the language of its native speakers and reconceived as a lingua franca. My argument throughout this book is essentially that an understanding of ELF depends on the recognition not only of its independent status as a legitimate use of language in its own right, but also of its inter-dependent status as a complementary component in a plurilingual repertoire. Only when its status in this first sense is recognized can there be any realistic possibility of planning its status in the second.

A second kind of intervention via language planning is what is known, rather misleadingly perhaps, as corpus planning.[3] Whereas status planning deals with languages as they exist in their current form, corpus planning has to do with making changes in the formal properties of the languages themselves, often involving lexical and/or grammatical elaboration to make them measure up to a changed status (see Ferguson 2006: Chapter 2). In the case of ELF, it is the change of status, its role as an international means of communication, that brings about the linguistic changes. But these are not, of course, planned. As we have seen, they occur naturally as a contingent consequence of communicative adaptation. Furthermore, although there is some elaboration such as increasing explicitness, as we saw in the strategies of regularization and redundancy exploitation illustrated in the last two chapters, the tendency is to reduce the formal complexity of the language rather than to increase it. So, as with any other naturally occurring language, the forms of ELF derive, in Halliday's phrase, from the functions they have evolved to serve. But what if functions are identified that seem to be ill served by the existing 'evolved' state of the language? This is where it could be argued that there is a case for corpus planning, for proposing 'improvements' of one kind or another to make the language better suited to the demands made upon it.

This kind of corpus planning, based on the belief that intervention is necessary to improve on naturally occurring language and make it more effective, has a very long history, and it is worth considering how the different proposals that have been made relate to the issues I am concerned with in this book, how far they correspond with the natural adaptations that occur in the unplanned emergence of ELF. This is of particular relevance because whether linguistic modification is planned and deliberately imposed, or naturally occurs as an adaptive process, it has a direct bearing on a third aspect of language planning, referred to as 'acquisition planning' (see Ferguson ibid.: Chapter 2). This is concerned with the language that is to be prescribed for learning and teaching, with the planning and design, in other words, of the language subject. I shall be dealing with this kind of educational and pedagogic planning in the following chapter, and particularly as it relates to ELF, and so this present chapter will lead logically on to the next.

Corpus planning proposals to reform English to make it more functionally effective go back a long way. We find one, for example put forward by Sir Thomas Sprat, author of *The History of the Royal Society of London*, printed in 1667. The Royal Society was established in the mid-17th century for the purpose of the 'Improving of Natural Knowledge'. Such improvement, in Sprat's view, called for a corresponding improvement in language usage. This, according to Sprat, was at the time severely hampered by eloquence, which he refers to as 'the luxury and redundance of Speech, . . . this vicious abundance of phrase, this trick of metaphors, this volubility of tongue, that makes so great a noise in the world.'

Members of the Royal Society, he tells us, have taken corrective action against this mischief:

They have therefore been most rigorous in putting into execution, the only remedy that can be found for extravagance: and that has been, a constant resolution, to reject all the amplifications, digressions, and swellings of style: to return back[4] to the primitive purity, and shortness, when men delivered so many things, almost in an equal number of words. They have exacted from all their members, a close, naked, natural way of speaking, positive expressions; clear senses; a native easiness: bringing all things as near the mathematical plainness as they can.

This belief in the need for intervention to protect the language from unseemly abuse carries over from Sprat's century to the next. It is expressed stridently in Jonathan Swift's pamphlet entitled *A proposal for correcting, improving and ascertaining the English tongue,* written in 1712. Swift, like Sprat, deplores verbal extravagance, the 'succession of affected phrases and new conceited words' that have corrupted the language. It was for this reason that he proposed the setting up of a Society whose members would be empowered to exercise such beneficial control:

Besides the Grammar-part, wherein we are allowed to be very defective, they will observe many gross Improprieties, which however authorized by Practice, and grown familiar, ought to be discarded. They will find many Words that deserve to be utterly thrown out of our Language; many more to be corrected, and perhaps not a few, long since antiquated, which ought to be restored, on Account of their Energy and Sound. (Swift 1712)

This so-called 'complaint tradition' continues into the 20th century. We find it, for example, in George Orwell (1961). His essay, *Politics and the English Language,* begins: 'Most people who bother with the matter at all would admit that the English language is in a bad way' and goes on to stress the need to 'fight against bad English', by which he means something very similar to what Sprat stigmatizes as 'extravagance' and 'swellings of style'. Orwell, too, is affronted by the same kind of verbal abuse: empty phrases put in to 'pad each sentence with extra syllables', 'pretentious diction', 'inflated style', 'sheer cloudy vagueness', all of which, he says, amounts to a 'debasement of the language'. Like his 17th and 18th century precursors, Orwell makes an impassioned plea for plain language and again, like them, he does not advocate this on practical grounds alone. In his view, it is not just that plain language leads to a clearer and more direct conveyance of meaning, but it is also morally superior in that it lends itself more to expressing 'the truth'. Elaborate verbiage not only results in 'an increase in slovenliness and vagueness', he says, but also in 'swindles and perversions'.

All of these indignant complaints about the abuse of English (at times, we might note, expressed in the kind of language that is being complained about) call to mind the objections of Derwent May quoted in Chapter 2, to the 'new barbarisms' and 'corrupt English' of non-native users of English. The difference is that in the complaints we have been citing here, it is the native speakers of the language who are the perpetrators. And there is another difference we need to note, and a significant one that sets Sprat apart from complainers like Swift and Orwell. It is that the reform he is arguing for is meant to modify the language to make it better suited to a particular domain of use—the domain of scientific enquiry of the Royal Society. The 'improving' of the language is seen as a necessary requirement for the 'Improving of Natural Knowledge'.

In this respect, Sprat's proposals resemble more recent corpus planning prescriptions that have been proposed to regulate how the language is used in specific domains. These are not motivated by a general belief that 'the English language is in a bad way' but by the observation that in certain domains and for certain purposes, effective communication depends on language restriction, a reduction indeed to what Sprat calls 'plainness' and a rejection of 'amplifications, digressions and swellings of style'. These domains are typically those which involve the transactional exchange of information, where the ideational function takes precedence over the interpersonal (see Chapter 6). A typical example would be Seaspeak, the English prescribed for international maritime use, or the language of air traffic control. These specify a restricted set of expressions for the carrying out of operational procedures, versions of existing usage adapted to be as concise and as precise as possible to make them functionally appropriate for their purpose (see Strevens and Johnson 1983; Weeks, Glover, Johnson, and Strevens 1988; Wyss-Bühlmann 2005; Intemann 2005). Clearly, with such a purpose the possibility of any unpredictable variation and creativity is reduced to the absolute minimum. The dynamics of normal language use is arrested in favour of fixed formulaic routines, a kind of enforced idiom. We find the same kind of prescribed and pre-scripted language in the formulaic routines of certain service encounters, such as call centre transactions (see Cameron 2000; Baker, Emmison, and Firth 2005; Forey and Lockwood 2007; Bolton 2010).

The use of English as an international means of communication, however, is not confined to certain domains or certain purposes but ranges over all of them. The question then arises as to how far corpus planning can be applied to make the language as a whole better suited to this wide-ranging international role.

7.3 The prescription of an international language

The strategy of ELF users, as was illustrated in the last two chapters, is to exploit the resources inherent in the virtual language by focusing on features of maximal functional value and discarding those that are surplus to their communicative requirement. I have argued that in so doing, they can be seen as focusing on what is essential in the language to make it more efficient for their purposes, as well as projecting their non-ENL identities. But for many people, the variation that results gives rise to the worry that once the control of native-speaker norms is relaxed, the language will disintegrate and become unintelligible. Here, then, a case could be made for corpus planning, for prescribing adaptations to stabilize and regulate the language to suit its status as an international means of communication.

The rapid and all pervasive spread of English over recent years has, as we saw in earlier chapters, provoked a good deal of negative reaction, with expressions of foreboding about the decline of the language or about its dominance. But it has also encouraged popular pronouncements on how to improve the language and the devising of recipes for its effective use in communication. The most recent, and most vigorously promoted of these is Globish, which I mentioned earlier in the chapter. This consists of a list of 1,500 English words which its inventor, J. P. Nerrière, on the basis of impressionistic observation, has identified as the most commonly occurring in rudimentary transactions among non-native users of the language. These users, he has noted, claim ownership of the language for their own purposes and get by very effectively without conforming to native speaker norms. In other words, he recognizes the phenomenon of ELF. But then, rather than seek to understand or describe its variable complexities he reduces it to a recipe (see http://www.globish.com/?page=about_globish).[5] The most recent publication (Nerrière and Hon 2009), now translated into several languages, bears the title 'Globish The World Over' but we need to note that Globish is not the actual globalized use of English as a lingua franca the world over (as seems to be assumed in McCrum 2010 cited earlier) but a prescribed reduced version of the language that it is recommended *should* be used the world over. In the words of its inventor 'It is designed for trivial efficiency, always, everywhere, with everyone' (http://www.globish.com/?page=about_globish).

According to the website, in the section titled 'Talk the talk', the Globish recipe consists of the following instructions:

Use only words in the Globish glossary
Keep sentences short
Repeat yourself
Avoid metaphors and colourful expressions
Avoid negative questions
Avoid all humour
Avoid acronyms
Use gestures and visual aids

Clearly, this set of instructions for using the language is very different from how people do actually use it. The Globish glossary, for instance, proscribes the use of many words that have international currency, such as *piano*, *telephone*, and *university*. More importantly, no allowance is made here for the creative exploitation of linguistic resources, the negotiation of meaning and interpersonal relationships that, as we saw in Chapters 5 and 6, figure so prominently in ELF interactions. Nerrière argues against the validity and viability of ENL norms in international communication, as I have done in previous chapters of this book, but then replaces them with another set of norms that users are required to conform to. Globish is, like Seaspeak referred to earlier, essentially a restricted language. Seaspeak, however, was designed to meet specific purposes, for use in relatively well-defined and predicable situations, so there is a correspondence between linguistic and contextual restrictions. Globish, on the other hand, as its name indicates, is prescribed for universal use in all domains and all kinds of unpredictable contexts, 'always, everywhere, with everyone'. The question obviously arises as to where this prescription comes from, on what principles these restrictions are specified, or what empirical evidence supports the claim that they are universally effective for communication. With Seaspeak, the conceptual and empirical considerations that influenced its design are made explicit (in, for example, Strevens and Johnson 1983; Weeks, Glover, Johnson, and Strevens 1988). With Globish (in Nerrière and Hon 2009, for example; see also Grzega 2006), they are not.

This is a crucial difference. As I said at the beginning of this chapter, there may be good reasons for intervention, for regulating natural processes, linguistic or otherwise. But then we need to be clear about the principles that inform the intervention. If a corpus is to be planned, we need to know just what the plan is. There have been other proposals for regulating English and designing it to make it more effective as a means of international communication—proposals that are based on an explicit rationale and that deserve to be taken seriously. I will now consider two such corpus planning proposals. They bear directly on the concerns of this book because they both claim to provide a principled basis for acquisition planning, for the prescription of what English is to be taught as the language subject for international communication. Since I make the claim that descriptions of ELF also have implications for the design of the English language as a subject, it is of interest to see how the features of these proposals compare with the features of ELF that we have identified. This will prepare the ground for the consideration of the relevance of understanding ELF for language teaching and learning which we will take up in the next chapter.

7.4 Nuclear English

One such proposal comes from Quirk in a paper entitled 'International communication and the concept of Nuclear English'. What lends particular interest to this proposal is not only that, as I noted in Chapter 3, Quirk is an acknowledged authority on 'the English language', but also that his paper, originally published in Smith (1981) and then again in Brumfit (1982), appears in Bolton and Kachru (2006) in a section entitled 'Paradigms of Description'. This includes the celebrated paper by Kachru himself (Kachru 1985) in which he first proposed the Three Circles model frequently referred to earlier in this book. The clear implication is that both papers, and the paradigms they represent, are relevant to current discussion about the internationalization of English.

The denomination 'Nuclear English' might raise exaggerated expectations as it seems to suggest an entirely new model for English. However, what Quirk's proposal really amounts to is an airing of ideas about the ways in which native English might be modified to make it easier to learn as a foreign language and easier to use as an international language. So Quirk does not propose a completely reformed system; rather, he offers some examples of preferred forms, all of them already available in the existing standard language, especially in the area of grammar. Thus, he proposes that where meanings can be expressed in different structural ways, the simpler or more explicit alternative might be prescribed. For example, non-restrictive relative clauses might be replaced with adverbial clauses, as in:

I expressed my sympathy to the captain, who had been reprimanded. =>
I expressed my sympathy to the captain because he had been reprimanded.

Similarly, ditransitive constructions might be replaced with the correspond-ing prepositional alternative:

We offered the girl a drink. =>
We offered a drink to the girl.
(Quirk 1982: 20, 22)

In reference to the general functions of language discussed in the previous chapter, these proposals would relate to the ideational function in that they would facilitate the expression of propositional meaning. Other proposals relate to the interpersonal function and thus are concerned with modality. As Quirk points out, problems arise with modal verbs since the same forms encode distinct meanings. Thus the expression *He may come* may signal epistemic meaning ('It is possible that he will come') or deontic meaning ('It is permitted for him to come'). After reviewing two other possible ways in which such ambiguity might be resolved, he proposes the following as being a preferred alternative:

We would retain the full range of modalities but restrict their expression to carefully prescribed and maximally explicit paraphrases, banning the use of the normal modal verbs altogether...In requiring paraphrase, we would be insisting on a speaker's clarifying his own intention in advance, while yet expressing himself without departure from fully acceptable forms of ordinary English.
(Quirk 1982: 25f.)

Such a proposal, furthermore, would have an additional advantage:

Indeed, paraphrases of the kind 'It is possible that this is not true', 'It is not possible that this is true' present the means not only of separating modality from proposition but of stipulating such features as the scope of negation, frequently obscured in ordinary language.
(ibid.: 26)

Quirk's Nuclear English, then, would be a sub-set of 'fully acceptable forms of ordinary English' selected for their clarity and explicitness and in general for their greater communicative efficiency. But acceptability here has to do with conformity to the encoded standard language and not to the conventions of usage. By 'ordinary language' Quirk does not mean the 'real' or 'authen-tic' English of attested occurrence. On the contrary, as he makes quite clear, his Nuclear English would be quite inauthentic in respect to the 'ordinary' language of actual native-speaker performance. As he puts it earlier in his paper:

In none of these instances, it will be noticed, does the 'solution' lie in going beyond the rules of ordinary acceptable English. But equally noteworthy: nor has the proposed solution any bearing at all upon frequency of occurrence in ordinary English. If anything (as we shall see below with modal auxiliaries), the most frequent items are

those that are most likely to be excluded from Nuclear English since they are the most polysemous.
(ibid.: 21)

So Nuclear English is entirely ordinary in its conformity to the rules of the standard code, but entirely extraordinary in its contravention of the conventions of usage. Quirk wrote his paper, of course, before corpus linguistics came on the scene to provide a detailed account of such conventions, but their irrelevance in principle to his scheme remains the same. Nuclear English, far from reflecting idiomatic native-speaker usage, is designed to constrain its occurrence. As Quirk puts it:

It will be seen that Nuclear English is conceived as having great power but also as exercising drastic constraints. Not only is the language to be learned by the non-native carefully and explicitly restricted; so equally must the language of the native speaker be constrained to a precisely corresponding extent when he is using Nuclear English as an international medium.
(ibid.: 26)

Quirk's recognition that the effectiveness of English as a means of international communication depends on non-conformity rather than conformity to native-speaker norms of usage is, of course, in accord with the arguments for ELF that I have put forward in this book. But for him, there must still be conformity to the code of Standard English. What he is arguing for is restrictions on its use, but there is no questioning of the status of the standard itself as the only legitimate basis for international communication. This, of course, is entirely consistent with his position on language variation discussed in Chapter 3. Quirk rejects actual usage as a relevant factor in the design of an international language and instead constructs one directly out of selected features of the code itself. The basic assumption here is that the only usage that is to be considered is that of native speakers, and what he leaves completely out of account is the usage of non-native users of English. Thus, the actually occurring English as an international language as empirically attested is not seen as having any bearing on the planned development of English as an international language.

Nuclear English is an interesting speculative construct and as such can be seen as a kind of hypothesis that can be subjected to empirical validation. How far, we might ask, do the features of this imposed restricted usage correspond to those that characterize the naturally occurring unrestricted usage as exemplified in ELF? Do ELF speakers engage in paraphrase to get round the problems of modality? Do they prefer adverbial phrases to non-restrictive relative constructions? In general, do their strategies in any way reflect the structural simplifications that Quirk proposes? In many cases, it seems unlikely. To take one particular example, in considering the basic design principles of Nuclear English, Quirk comments that:

It might, for example, be decided that the English tag question (so often in the English of Wales and Southeast Asia replaced by the invariant *isn't it*) was disproportionately burdensome, with its requirement of reversed polarity, supply of tensed operator and congruent subject:

I'm late, *aren't I? am I not?*
She used to work here, *didn't she?*
They oughtn't to go there, *ought they?*
For all the italicized pieces, whose function as a response promotor is arguably worth retaining, we could achieve the same objective with *isn't that right?* or *is that right?*, in full English a perfectly acceptable expression though of course a minority one (except as shortened to "right" in AmE).
(ibid.: 20)

The formal complexity of tag questions is, as Quirk implies, disproportion-ate to their relatively simple communicative function, so it is no surprise to find that actual users of English in Wales and Southeast Asia have come up with the alternative *isn't it/is it?* One might add that this invariant tag is also a feature of many other varieties of English (cf. Kortmann, Schneider *et al.* 2004; Vol. 2), and that since Quirk's paper was written, it has been more gen-erally adopted and indeed further simplified in much British English spoken usage as the invariant *innit?*, mainly by young speakers. Tag simplification along the same lines has also been widely observed (though not systematically analysed to date) in the usage of ELF speakers, in part, of course, explained by the fact that an invariant tag is often a feature of their own language. But the way actual users of English have solved the complex tag problem[6] does not qualify for inclusion in Nuclear English because it involves 'going beyond the rules of ordinary acceptable English'. The only acceptable solution is a form of words 'in full English': *is(n't) that so?*, even though it is only used by a minority (but a minority, of course, of native speakers). So the English supposedly designed for international use rejects the forms that are interna-tionally used in favour of forms that are not.

As Quirk admits, expecting users of English (both native and non-native speakers) to conform to the 'drastic constraints' imposed by Nuclear English is, in his own words 'a tall order'. But he believes that drastic measures of this kind are called for 'if we take seriously the issue of international needs' (ibid.: 26). Just what these needs are is left undefined but it is assumed that they can only be met by keeping within certain rules of the standard lan-guage and steering clear of others. Nuclear English must be 'firmly within the grammar of ordinary English' (ibid.: 21) and this is taken to be axiomatic. Any form not sanctioned by this grammar is unacceptable, and since accept-ability is defined by conformity to native-speaker norms, it is hard to see how Nuclear English can, as claimed, be as 'culture-free as calculus' (ibid.: 19).[7] Quirk does not countenance the possibility of forms which are not already available in the grammar of (his) ENL. No allowance, therefore, is made for non-conformity, for the possibility of alternative realizations of the virtual language. This is hardly surprising, of course, since without reference to any data of actual communication, it is difficult to know what form such realiza-tions might take.

And Quirk makes no reference whatever to such data—and of course, such data was hardly available in 1982. He frequently stresses the importance of communicative needs in principle, but feels no obligation to consider how people actually cope with such needs in practice. His proposals are entirely speculative and hypothetical and based on native-speaker introspection—but introspection, of course, informed by particularly expert acquaintance with the English language. This is why it will be of some interest to see how his prescription of an international version of English corresponds with the description of international English as it actually occurs and is being described in current empirical ELF research.

7.5 Basic English

Quirk refers to the drastic constraints that Nuclear English would impose on its users. Even more drastic are the constraints imposed by another proposal for designing an international English—perhaps the best known proposal of all: Basic English. Its originator, the Cambridge philosopher and logician C. K. Ogden, was, like Quirk, motivated by an awareness of the need for an effective means for international understanding, which was felt particularly acutely after the First World War.

Basic English (Basic for short) bears a superficial resemblance to Globish and was similarly motivated by a zeal to regulate the language to make it a more effective means of global communication. But Ogden had much more than 'trivial efficiency' in mind: in his words, Basic was intended to be 'an International Auxiliary Language, i.e. a second language (in science, commerce and travel) for all who do not already speak English' (Ogden 1938: 9).

As with Globish, Basic consists of a number of words but whereas the 1500 of Globish seem simply to be an impressionistic selection of those that seem most frequently used, the 850 of Basic are abstract units of meaning identified and categorized on conceptual grounds. 600 of these are nouns denoting 'things', 400 of which are 'general' and 200 'pictured', the latter being susceptible to specific visual representation (for example, *apple, dog*), the former not (*fruit, animal*). 150 words are adjectives denoting 'qualities', 100 of which are again said to be 'general' (*male, fat*) and 50 'opposites' (*female, thin*). The remaining 100 words are so-called 'operations' and these are a miscellany of various kinds of 'function' words—adverbs, conjunctions, prepositions for the most part. It is these words, together with a brief list of rules, that constitute the necessary generative dynamism: they provide the means for combining the elements in the other lists into lexical compounds and grammatical structures.[8]

These 850 words, we are told, have been 'scientifically selected' and Ogden refers to a decade of research that went into their compilation. This was research in semantics that he engaged in with I. A. Richards, one result of which was the celebrated publication *The Meaning of Meaning* (Ogden and Richards 1923). As Richards puts it, '[t]here is a lot of theory behind Basic and Basic could no more do what it does than an aeroplane could fly the Pacific without the theoretical engineering behind its design' (Richards 1940: 19). Probably the best synoptic presentation of this thinking is to be found in Catford's 'The Background and Origins of Basic English', published as late as 1950, and, interestingly, in the journal *English Language Teaching*—that is to say, it must have seemed worthwhile and realistic then to expect 'ordinary' practising teachers to benefit from this quite demanding article. In it, Catford explains how Ogden drew on Jeremy Bentham's distinctions between 'real' entities and 'fictitious' entities, whereby 'every fictitious entity bears some relation to some real entity, and cannot otherwise be understood than in so far as that relation is perceived' (Ogden 1932: 12, quoted in Catford 1950: 37). Catford's example for illustrating this distinction is 'the belief... that in talking of such things as *freedom* and *redness* we are referring to independent entities not in space or time, instead of simply *free actions* and *red things*' (1950: 36). Bentham's distinction was crucial for Ogden's (and subsequently Ogden and Richard's 1923) work on definition, on getting at the 'central, pivotal or key meaning' of each word (Richards 1943: 22).

It would seem to have been Bentham's thinking, then, that informed the 'theoretical engineering' that resulted in Basic. As Ogden himself explains:

How is Basic able to get so far with only 850 words? The reason may be given in simplest language.

The greater part of the words used in science and for everyday talk are what may be called *shorthand* for other words. That is to say they are taking the place of other words which are clearly, in some sense, nearer the facts.

The greater part of the things we generally seem to be talking about are what may be named *fictions*: and for these again there are other words in common use which get nearer to fact...

The most important group of 'shorthand' words in European languages is made up of what are named 'verbs'—words like 'accelerate' and 'ascertain'; 'liberty' and 'blindness' are examples of fictions; 'credulous' and 'courteous' say something about our feelings in addition to their straightforward sense.

(Ogden 1930: 100–102)

It was the power of definition which made it possible to say essentially everything with a very limited vocabulary. Richards relates this discovery thus:

In our joint work we came to the theory and practice of definition. In comparing definitions—definitions of everything, from a sense quality to a force and from a rabbit to a concept—we were struck by the fact that whatever you are defining, certain words keep coming back into your definitions. Define them, and with them you could define anything. That suggests that there might be some limited set of words in terms of which the meanings of all other words might be stated. If so, then a very limited language—limited in its vocabulary but comprehensive in its scope—would be possible.

(ibid.: 23)

This then, in a nutshell, is the principal idea behind Basic. The word lists in essence constitute a defining vocabulary. If a lexical item can be decomposed into semantic features which are themselves lexicalized as an English word, then there is no place for it in Basic. Thus, to take Ogden's own examples, the words *puppy* and *bitch* can be dispensed with since they can be replaced by the expressions *young dog* and *female dog*. Similarly, *ascend* and *descend* can be replaced by *go up* and *go down* respectively—expressions which furthermore, as Ogden would say, are more 'straightforward' and 'nearer the fact'. With primacy given to this defining capability, it follows that where there are synonyms, it is the word that combines more readily with others that will be selected for inclusion. Basic, then, is a language stripped down to its conceptual essentials:

It is an English in which 850 words *do all the work* of 20,000, and has been formed by taking out everything which is not necessary to the sense. *Disembark*, for example, is broken up into *get off a ship*. *I am able* takes the place of *I can*; *shape* is covered by the more general word *form*; and *difficult* by the use of *hard*.

By putting together the names of simple operations—such as *get, give, come, go, put, take*—with the words for directions like *in, over, through*, and the rest, two or three thousand complex ideas, like *insert* which becomes *put in*, are made part of the learner's store.
(Ogden 1938: 92)

What we see here is the same procedure that Quirk uses to simplify modality: the replacement of existing expressions with 'carefully prescribed and maximally explicit paraphrases', but with Ogden the procedure is applied as a general principle to all aspects of the language.

Radical though Ogden's proposals are, however, they are, like those of Quirk, also essentially conservative in that they do not involve 'going beyond the rules of ordinary acceptable English.' The 850 words of the defining metalanguage are all drawn from actual lexical encodings and the manner in which they are combined is entirely in conformity with the code rules of Standard English. These rules in effect set constraints on the generative power of the Basic system. Consider, for example, the case of the operator *un-*. This according to Ogden can be applied to 50 words that appear in the list of Qualities 'to form negatives'. But as Ogden notes:

A certain number of these formations, e.g., *unregular, unprobable*, are departures from Standard English. All, however, can readily be avoided by the use of *not*, and the beginner who desires not to disturb the susceptibilities of the purist during the next few years can thus always attain his desire...
(ibid.: 52)

The Basic system allows for the possibility of using the *un-* operator indiscriminately for all the adjectives on the list, but it seems that avoidance is desirable where this results in a non-Standard formation, and in this case another negative operator, *not*, can be used instead to produce *not regular* rather than *unregular*, *not frequent* rather than *unfrequent*, *not normal* rather than *unnormal*, and so on. The difficulty with this suggestion is that it presupposes that Basic learners/users will know in advance which formations to avoid so as 'not to disturb the susceptibilities of the purist', but such knowledge of course depends on a familiarity with the Standard language, which they do not have. So even if they wished to defer to native-speaker norms so as not to disturb purist susceptibilities, they have no way of knowing what they are. So how are they to decide whether to use *un-* or *not-* (or *non-* if it comes to that) as the negative operator in particular cases? And why should these cases be confined to 50 adjectives and not to all 150 listed under Qualities? If we can have *unhealthy* and *unfit*, why not *unstrong, unfat, unviolent, unsharp, ungood*, and so on? If there is to be a negating operator in the system, why should there be any constraints on its use, and why should there be two of them doing the same work? Such constraints and such duplication would seem to indicate that, for all the claims that Basic was designed as an independent conceptual construct, it actually defers to the norms of StE.

So innovative though it is in many ways, Basic is also informed by conservative assumptions that constrain the application of its underlying principles. And though Ogden's proposals for simplification seem much bolder than those of Quirk, they are actually more conservative in that they not only defer to the code rules of the standard language, but also in some respects would seem to be influenced by conventions of usage as well. Whereas Quirk makes a point of ruling out the frequency of actual occurrence as a relevant consideration in the design of Nuclear English, Ogden insists that his Basic is 'sufficient for ordinary communication in *idiomatic* English' (Ogden 1938: 10, emphasis added). It is this, perhaps, that explains a rather striking inconsistency in the application of his central defining principle.

I refer to the 50 adjectives listed as Opposites alongside the 100 adjectives that are designated General under the heading of Qualities. Among words in the General list, we find *clean, happy, true,* and *wise,* and among those designated as Opposites, *dirty, sad, false,* and *foolish.* But since words in the latter group are negative versions of those of the former, further verbal economies could easily be made by means of the negative operator *un-* to make *unclean, unhappy, untrue,* and *unwise,* especially since all of these are established lexical items in the standard language anyway. One can only suppose that the opposites are included because they are more frequent or normal in usage than their negated counterparts. So having specified the operator *un-* as a coding device of Basic, Ogden then fails to apply it to reduce what he refers to as 'the wastage of words'. There are, we are told, no less than 50 adjectives 'which may form negatives, coinciding in many cases with the Opposites, by adding the prefix *un-*' (Ogden 1938: 52). But if these negative formations coincide with Opposites, they are redundant to a system that seeks maximal verbal economy and so could have been dispensed with.

Again, it seems that the design of Basic is influenced by considerations of what would be acceptable in reference to native-speaker norms—and not only those that concern the (constitutive) rules of the standard code, but also those that concern (regulative) conventions of usage (see Chapter 5). In the last analysis, it is the authority of ENL that is deferred to. But if Basic is to be, as Ogden intends it to be, 'a universal auxiliary language', an international lingua franca, then such deference to the code rules and usage conventions of a national language is not only unnecessary but is contrary to its purpose. But Ogden, like Quirk, can apparently only conceive of an international language as a reformed version of a national language, and this is actually made quite explicit in the very name Basic English. For this is not only used as a descriptive label (it is basic, necessary, essential English) but as an acronym that stands for British American Scientific International Commercial. So Basic is represented as an international English that still remains the national property of the British and the Americans. As such it obviously lends support to the view that any use of English is effectively hegemonic and necessarily furthers the interests of its native speakers.

I have suggested that Ogden's application of his own principles is inconsistent, modified by considerations of acceptability. But what would be the result if such principles were consistently and rigorously applied without such considerations? Ogden says that Basic English 'has been formed by taking out everything which is not necessary to the sense' (ibid.: 92), eliminating words 'unnecessarily coloured by some form of *feeling*' (ibid.: 101). This calls to mind another project that seeks to reduce 'the wastage of words' along similar lines: the well known fictional one that Orwell presents us with in his novel *1984*. Here too the aim is to devise a new form of English, Newspeak, designed to be a more efficient instrument of thought. And interestingly enough, one of the ways of doing this is by applying Ogden's defining principle and making use of the negative operator *un-*, but carrying the procedure through to its logical conclusion. This is how Symes, one of the researchers on the Newspeak project, enthusiastically puts it:

We're destroying words—scores of them, hundreds of them, every day. We're cutting the language down to the bone.
    It's a beautiful thing, the destruction of words. Of course the great wastage is in the verbs and adjectives, but there are hundreds of nouns that can be got rid of as well. It isn't only the synonyms; there are also the antonyms. After all, what justification is there for a word which is simply the opposite of some other word? A word contains its opposite in itself. Take 'good', for instance. If you have a word like 'good', what need is there for a word like 'bad'? 'Ungood' will do just as well—better, because it's an exact opposite, which the other is not. Or again, if you want a stronger version of 'good', what sense is there in having a whole string of vague useless words like 'excellent' and 'splendid' and all the rest of them? 'Plusgood' covers the meaning, or 'doubleplusgood' if you want something stronger still. Of course we use those forms already, but in the final version of Newspeak there'll be nothing else. In the end the whole notion of goodness and badness will be covered by only six words—in reality, only one word.

There are no opposites of the Basic kind in Newspeak: they are eliminated by systematic use of the *un-* operator. And 'vague useless words' like *excellent* and *splendid*—words that, as Ogden puts it, 'are unnecessarily coloured by some form of feeling'—are similarly dispensed with by means of the operators *plus* and *doubleplus*. Such clearing away 'the wastage of words' would drastically reduce the 850 words of Basic. Basic can be presented on a sheet of note paper. The final version of Newspeak could probably have been written on a postcard.

Of course, Newspeak is a fictional *reductio ad absurdum*, and nobody in fact, one might object, would seriously take the defining principle to such ridiculous extremes. But then how far *can* or *should* the principle be taken, and what other factors need to be considered in applying it? Ogden provides no clear answer to these questions. As we have seen, there is some ambivalence in his proposals. Since Basic is a reduction of English to its conceptual elements, these can only be compounded into new words or phrases or paraphrases by the open-choice principle (see Chapter 6) and yet Ogden wants Basic usage to be 'normal' and 'idiomatic' as well. These demands are naturally in conflict and, as we have seen, difficult to reconcile. The inclusion of the Opposites would seem to be motivated by the normality criterion, and is inconsistent with the defining principle. In other cases, the principle is given priority over normality. The words *ask* and *eat,* for example, are excluded from Basic and their sense has to be rendered by the paraphrases *make a request/put a question* and *take food*.[9] As Quirk observes in reference to his discussion of modality, paraphrase by its very explicitness quite naturally departs from normal idiomatic convention—the explicitness, we might add, necessarily bringing the open-choice principle into play (see Chapter 6). Not surprisingly, therefore, the required use of paraphrase in Basic results in English which is distinctly abnormal and unidiomatic, as several critics have pointed out.

For instance, Bongers (1947) juxtaposes several original texts with their Basic versions to illustrate this shortcoming, among them this extract from E. A. Poe's *The Gold Bug* and the Basic Version, *The Gold Insect,* devised by A. P. Rossiter (1932):

Basic	Original
As I was taking it, the deep-throated voice of a dog came to our ears, and then the sound of nails on the door. Jupiter went to it, and a great Newfoundland dog of Legrand's came loudly in, got its feet up on my arms, and kept putting its nose against me in a loving way: for I had given it much attention at other times.	As I received it a loud growl was heard, succeeded by scratching at the door. Jupiter opened it, and a large Newfoundland, belonging to Legrand, rushed in, leaped upon my shoulders, and loaded me with caresses; for I had shown him much attention during previous visits. Bongers (1947: 123)

Table 7.1 A text in Basic and the original version

It can be reasonably objected, however, that this is not a fair comparison since Basic was not designed to capture the nuances of literary style. Its function is limited to the explicit signalling of conceptual meaning, and this is readily recognized by its advocates:

Impromptu eloquence and after-dinner wit in Basic are tougher assignments. Its thrifty vocabulary is at its best in everyday dealings and explanations, and it is not naturally a spellbinder's medium.
(Richards 1943: 114)

[T]he language, while in universal use, cannot retain the charm and completeness of a native language. It is an expedient, a make-shift. It lacks the satisfying quality of an intimate and exclusive possession. ... Despite its awkwardness, its stop-gap phrases, its colourless vocabulary, it can yet convey many meanings. It cannot give flood to the human soul, but it can provide a bridge to human thought.
(Routh 1944: 6)

So one cannot reasonably expect that Basic can be used as a medium for eloquence or wit or the expression of intimate experience. After all, Ogden's aim is quite explicitly to get rid of the influence of feelings and to free the language from the distractions of any affective associations that might interfere with the clear conveyance of thought. The difficulty is, of course, that 'normal' language as it naturally occurs does not focus so exclusively on the conceptual meanings that Basic is designed to encode. Communication is a complex pragmatic process that necessarily involves affective factors and it cannot be reduced to the transmission of thought, the encoding, conveyance, and decoding of semantic concepts. So the use of Basic will always tend away from normal idiomatic English. Of course it will approximate to normality in different degrees depending on the domains in which it is used. For domains and purposes where the transmission of objective information is at a premium, the approximation could well be close. One might argue, therefore, that Basic would be well suited to the kind of restricted transactional routines that I referred to earlier in this chapter—maritime manoeuvres, air traffic control, call centre routines, and so on; or to other domains where the expression of conceptual meaning is prioritized and there is natural synergy between form and function. An interesting example of this is McGrath's book on architecture, *Twentieth Century Houses*, published in 1934 by Faber and Faber.

   This book is frequently referred to as a particularly successful, elegant work written entirely in Basic—in order to make it more accessible to an international readership. Ogden wrote an epilogue to it, and he points out (naturally in Basic) the close parallels between the austere functionalism and clear lines of the architecture of the day and the design of Basic:

In building with words there is the same pull between the science of structure and the art of ornament as there is in building with steel and stone and wood...
   Mr McGrath is an architect with a language-sense. In using Basic for his book, he has had in mind something more than the fact, important enough in itself, that this step would give him an international public. He saw in Basic a language which had the

same qualities as the buildings he was writing about, and which had, for this reason, a special value for his purpose.

Much has been said in this book about international forms in building, about the straightforward use of materials, clear statement, and reasoned design. All these qualities might equally well have been named in connection with Basic English. In fact, it is possible to give a clear account of Basic under these very heads. (McGrath 1934: 221f.)

There is no noticeable abnormality here. We should note, however, that Ogden had developed an expert skill in writing in Basic, and he would naturally have taken particular care in texts whose primary purpose was to extol the virtues of his scheme. The question is how far other users would be able to approximate to 'normal' English in the same way. To start with, the ability depends, as was previously noted, on a familiarity with normality which novice users would not have. One might take the example in the text cited above of the word *straightforward*. This is the result of the judicious selection of the operator *forward* to combine with the quality *straight* to make the compound form *straightforward*. Ogden, of course, knows that this result is an idiomatic expression, whose figurative sense is not actually directly derivable from the separate semantic meanings of its constituents. But how are other users to know this? Basic, as a code, permits all kinds of different combinations, none of them necessarily in conformity with what is 'normal'.

Users of Basic familiar with normal English usage can, of course, make it conform to the norm. Similarly they can exploit the multiple senses of its 850 word forms because they know in advance the different grammatical and lexical functions they can fulfil. They know, for example, which of the nouns in the Things list can be normally used and conjugated as verbs and which cannot, and how the change of word class results in a change of meaning. As West and Swenson (1934) point out in their critical examination of Basic English, Ogden's 850 words is 'a considerable understatement' (p. 10), and that he is practising a kind of conjuring trick (my term, not theirs) by, for instance, 'using a word in more than one part of speech, e.g. *back* (preposition), *back* (noun), *back-ing a car*' (p. 7), 'by compounding words, for example, verb + preposition, *come round, come about* (=happen)' (p. 8) and 'by extension in the use of a word, e.g. ...*flat* to *a flat* (=an apartment)' (ibid.). All of these examples (and one could give many more) constitute results of Ogden's 'simple rules [which] are given for making other words with the help of those in the list; such as *designer, designing* and *designed*, from *design*, or *air-plane* from *air* and *plane*'. But one needs to know what constraints there are, if any, on the application of these simple rules, and this is far from simple.

To refer to the distinction discussed in Chapter 5, what Ogden does in Basic is to devise a simplified set of constitutive rules for English, an alternative virtual language, but then seems to require that these rules should be actualized in accordance with established regulative conventions to produce normal idiomatic English. There are numerous alternative ways of playing the Basic game according to the rules, but apparently only those that conform to these conventions of normality are acceptable.

7.6 Basic English and ELF

Ogden then, having devised his alternative virtual language, proceeds to set constraints on the exploitation of its potential, thereby rather defeating the object of the exercise. With ELF, on the other hand, the only constraints on exploitation are those which are inherent in the virtual language itself. Thus, as we saw in Chapter 5, ELF users create new words by making use of morphological rules without regard to the norms of regulative convention. There is no reason, in principle, why users should not use Basic rules creatively in the same way. As an artificial construct, Ogden's reconstituted code, unlike a naturally occurring language, has no dynamism or vitality of its own, but this is not to say that it could not develop a dynamism in use. In effect, what Ogden does is to increase the artificiality of Basic by setting limits on its vitality.

Vitality is one of the four attributes of language that Stewart, in an influential paper, identifies as relevant to the definition of general language types (Stewart 1968). The other attributes are *standardization*, *autonomy*, and *historicity*. Thus in Stewart's typology, an artificial language like Basic has the attributes of autonomy and standardization, but lacks historicity and vitality, as compared, for example, with a classical language, like Latin, which has all three attributes except vitality. Stewart's typological scheme is a very general one, and it has been criticized for being over-simple (see for example Haugen 1972/2001), but the four attributes he identifies are helpful in understanding the nature of ELF, and in clarifying how it differs from Basic. The specification of the features of Basic as a new coding system constitutes standardization at the same time: its standards are its design features. It can also claim autonomy in that though rationally derived from an existing language, it is independent of it, except that this autonomy, as I have suggested, is somewhat compromised by the requirement that its use should conform to normal English usage. As originally proposed, it obviously lacked historicity and vitality since Ogden brought it ready-made into existence. But both of these features can be acquired once this new coding system is put into operation and naturalized by use. It is entirely possible for an artificial language to be vitalized as it is for a classical language to be re-vitalized, as in the case, for example, of modern Hebrew. As I have noted, Ogden and others did indeed seek to give Basic vitality by putting it to communicative use, and to the extent that it was so used it did acquire the feature of historicity. But the point is that Basic as an artificial construct is not in itself vital but has to be *made* vital. Vitality is a function of use and the question arises as to how far the natural conditions and requirements of use can be met by the Basic specifications, and how far they are actually constrained by them.

It is in this matter of vitality, I would argue, that ELF differs so crucially from Basic (and from artificial auxiliary languages such as Esperanto—and indeed Globish). For it is the *actual* vitality of ELF, as evidenced from its widespread and continuing use, that makes it autonomous, separate from native-speaker English and, as I have argued throughout this book, a phenomenon in its own right, with its own status as an international means of communication. And the vitality of ELF, as with any other natural language, has to do with the way formal linguistic properties are made to function, and are exploited and adapted to serve communicative purposes. Hence the emphasis in describing ELF not on linguistic forms as such but on their functional significance, on what they indicate about strategies of use. With ELF its formal properties are a reflex of communicative functions, but with Basic the formal properties are defined in advance and how they might actually function in use, how they might get vitalized, is a matter of speculation.

One speculation is provided by the quotation at the head of this chapter. This comes from a novel by H. G. Wells, *The Shape of Things to Come*, which is a projection of future world history, supposedly written by a Dr Philip Raven, from 1929 to 2106. What is of interest for the present discussion is that Basic English is represented as having achieved vitality, having become the international lingua franca by the 21st century. However, this is seen as a catalyst for the subsequent 'modification, expansion and spread of English *in its wake*' (my emphasis). It is this English that then takes over and prevails, modified in ways beyond the prescriptions of Basic. The two parts of the quotation at the head of this chapter are connected by a passage that reads as follows:

The English most of us speak and write today [i.e. in 2106] is a very different tongue from the English of Shakespeare, Addison, Bunyan or Shaw; it has shed the last traces of such archaic elaborations as a subjunctive mood; it has simplified its spelling, standardized its pronunciation, adopted many foreign locutions, and naturalized and assimilated thousands of foreign words.
(Wells: *The Shape of Things to Come*: Book 5: 7)

Away from fantasy and back to the present, we know that Basic did not in fact get adopted as Wells imagined it might, and that the rapid spread of English as a lingua franca has happened without its assistance. But its modifications, among them those that Wells mentions here (the shedding of archaic elaborations, for example, the adoption of foreign locutions, the assimilation of foreign words) are occurring in the natural adaptive processes of continuing vitalization that characterize ELF.

Nuclear English and Basic English are corpus planning proposals of considerable interest in themselves, but their relevance to the concerns of this book is that they bring into sharp relief the essential difference between the prescription of what should be and the description of what actually is. The difference is crucial, but not always recognized. In a recent book, for example, Ferguson, referring to Jenkins' empirically based proposals for a phonological Lingua Franca Core, makes the following comment:

These proposals bring to mind previous efforts to define a core English: Ogden's (1930) *Basic English* and Quirk's (1981) *Nuclear English*, for example. (Ferguson 2006: 166)

The implication of what Ferguson says here is clear: Jenkins' proposals are like previous efforts—why else would they call Basic and Nuclear English to mind—and descriptions of ELF and the prescriptions of Basic and Nuclear English are all essentially the same sort of thing. What I have attempted to do in this chapter is to counter such a misconception by showing that they are very different things indeed.[10]

7.7 Conclusion

In previous chapters of this book I have argued that in the present globalized world, it is inappropriate to insist that standard ENL should enjoy privileged status as an international means of communication. I have instead given reasons for recognizing that ELF assumes that status quite naturally as a function of its unplanned development. In this chapter, I have considered another aspect of language planning: so-called corpus planning, which can be seen as an alternative both to the maintenance of the status of the standard ENL and to the acceptance of naturally occurring ELF.

Because such corpus planning interventions, from Basic to Globish, prescribe alternative versions of the language that claim to be better suited to international use, it is obviously of interest to see how these prescriptions relate to the way English is actually used. Hence their relevance to an understanding of ELF. In this chapter I have paid particular attention to Basic English, since this is the most comprehensive and detailed prescription and brings out particularly clearly the issues involved.

The difficulties that arise when examining such corpus planning schemes suggest that rather than modify a code, or reconstruct one, and then seek to give it vitality by persuading people to use it, it would seem preferable to first find out and describe how people actually exploit the potential of an existing language (as illustrated in Chapters 5 and 6).

The question then arises, however, as to what relevance this description has for the third kind of language planning that was referred to in the first section of this chapter—the planning that involves decisions about what kind of English is appropriate for learning and teaching the language as a subject. This too is a kind of prescription, so how far can it be based on a corpus planning prescription like Basic? How far can it be derived in some way from the description of ELF? These are matters that I take up in the next chapter.

Notes

1 Examples include contributions to Rubdy and Saraceni 2006, notably Prodromou's, as well as the editors' own introduction; also several contributions to Dziubalska-Kolaczyk and Przedlacka (2008). The latter focus on pronunciation

models and are discussed in Jenkins 2007: 22ff. The question of description versus prescription will be dealt with in greater detail in Chapter 8.

2 As Deborah Cameron (2010) makes clear in her review of Robert McCrum (2010) *How the English Language Became the World's Language*, the author is 'conflating different kinds of global English. In interviews and comments McCrum has insisted that what he means by 'globish' is a reduced auxiliary language with no native speakers, like the version promoted by Nerrière; but many of the examples he uses in the book concern the varieties spoken in post-colonial societies such as India and Nigeria, which do have some native speakers, which serve a full range of communicative functions, and which are not globally intelligible or culturally neutral. At times he even uses 'globish' to refer to the language in which G8 leaders give international press conferences—though in fact this is simply English, used by non-native elites in a way that diverges minimally from native norms' (Deborah Cameron 2010).

3 I say 'misleadingly' because the term 'corpus planning' precedes and is independent of later work in corpus linguistics, which is the association most likely to be triggered in most of today's linguists by the use of the word 'corpus'.

4 Note the combination of *return* with *back*, which is used in 1667 by a writer railing against 'redundance of Speech' and 'vicious abundance of phrase'—while we saw in Chapter 6 that it is precisely such verb + preposition combinations that are called redundant and regarded as errors that learners of English should guard against.

5 To be found in an 'Extract from the TIMESONLINE, Dec. 2006 'Globish, the dialect of the 3rd Millennium' on the Globish Website (http://www.globish.com/).

6 As indicated, substantial empirical work on the use of what Quirk calls 'response promotor' is still outstanding, but the items *no?*, *yes?* and (less so) *or?* have often been mentioned as candidates for fulfilling this function. A brief check of VOICE 1.0 Online yielded a quite widespread use of *no?* as response promoter across speakers from a variety of L1's, as in:

S1 [L1= ita-IT]:   okay good. (2) copy it on the: er word file. (13) <smacks lips> hh o<yawning>kay (.) well i think we can go </yawning> (1) **no?** (5) hh i think i need a coffee as well (.)
(VOICE 2009: EDsed363)

S1 [L1=ger-AT]:   <10>brings you out of your </10> usual er perceptual habits **no?** (1) erm (.)
(VOICE 2009: EDsed363)

S2 [L1=dut-NL]:   you want to: have a contract together with with us and we make a (.) a HANDLING contract whatever it's it's so quite easy. **no?** THEY say (.)
(VOICE 2009: PBmtg300)

S1 [L1: swe-SE]:   er we we refrain then from (.) pointing out er besides what could be (.) of relevance for capital universities (.) as we have said **no?**<clears throat> and we.[...]
(VOICE 2009: POwgd14)

S1 [L1=rum-RO]   ...so of course the paper is a is a result of the negotiation **no?** between the different organizations [...]
(VOICE 2009: POwsd266)

7 The role of culture often figures in debates about ELF, too. What seems most important with regard to ELF is of course that no language use can ever be 'culture-free'; the point is that ELF can be imbued with speaker's own cultures and identities, not Anglo-American.

8 A more detailed presentation of the Basic construct would go beyond the scope of this chapter. For readers who want to find out more about BASIC, there are online resources made available by the Basic English Institute, in particular the section 'Ogden's Basic English' (available on http://ogden.basic-english.org/basiceng.html). Templer (2005), also available online, argues for the great potential of Basic for teaching English as an international language, especially to socially disadvantaged learners and in socioeconomically deprived areas. His article, as well as Seidlhofer (2002) give a concise outline of the main ideas behind BASIC, as well as many references to original publications by Ogden and Richards. Catford (1950) offers a more detailed discussion.

9 Ogden does, however, have a supplement of 'International words', and these, interestingly enough, include lexical items such as *piano*, *telephone*, and *university*, which Globish excludes (see <http://ogden.basic-english.org/wordalpi.html>, and section 7.3. above).

10 And this is (implicitly at least) acknowledged in Ferguson (2009), which engages closely with conceptual questions of ELF.

8

ELF and English Language Teaching

I have argued that setting objectives for learners to achieve must
take account of the way the language has been appropriated
internationally as a means of communication, and that this should
lead us to think again about defining such objectives in reference to
native-speaker norms. I have suggested that rather than seeking
to specify goals in terms of projected needs, which for most
part are highly unpredictable, it would be preferable, and more
practicable, to focus on the development of a more general
capability which would serve as an investment for
subsequent learning.

H. G. WIDDOWSON: *Defining Issues in English Language Teaching*

8.1 Prescriptions for use and learning

The prescriptions discussed in the last chapter were prescriptions for
use, exercises in corpus planning, concerned with making English more
effective as a means of international communication. We turn now to
prescriptions of a different kind, prescriptions for learning—the so-called
acquisition planning mentioned at the beginning of Chapter 7. In designing English as a subject, prescriptive decisions have to be made about
which features of the language are to be selected and how they are to be
presented. The question of particular relevance in this book, of course, is
what bearing ELF has on the making of these pedagogic decisions. This
chapter, then, is concerned with questions of pedagogic *principle* which I
take to be the basis which any particular classroom practice has to start
from. What decisions teachers will make for particular learners with their
particular needs will always be a local matter that a general book about
ELF cannot (or rather, should not) address.

   Acquisition planning for English, carried out under the more familiar
terms of syllabus design and teaching methodology, has, of course, a long
history (see Howatt 2004). Ideas about what is the best plan for acquisition, and what counts as acquisition of a language anyway, have varied very

considerably over the years. At one time primacy is given to linguistic forms and at another to communicative functions. Approaches and methods come and go, each with its own claims to validity based on different paradigms or fashions of linguistic description and psycholinguistic research (see Richards and Rodgers 2001; Rodgers 2009; Dörnyei 2009). So-called Structural Language Teaching (SLT) is superseded by Communicative Language Teaching (CLT), itself then mutating in recent years into Task Based Language Teaching (TBLT; see Ellis 2003) and Language and Content Integrated Learning (CLIL; see Wolff 2009).

Different though these approaches are in many respects, they are all, in one way or another, concerned with the same central pedagogic problem, still as relevant and as unresolved now as ever, of deciding what formal or functional features of the language as a whole are to be focused on as appropriate for learning. Attempts to resolve it go back a long way and have been extensively described elsewhere and it is not my purpose to review them here. What I want to do in this chapter is to focus attention on the essential nature of the problem and explore how an understanding of ELF might lead us to see it in a new light.

I take Ogden's Basic English as a starting point since it provides a link with what was discussed in the last chapter by raising the question of the relationship between corpus and acquisition planning and brings out the main issues of this basic pedagogic problem with particular clarity. As I hope to show, though the work of Ogden and his contemporaries belongs in a sense in the past, what they have to say still has direct relevance to our current concerns in English teaching pedagogy. And I believe that the fact that they are at one remove from us actually makes it easier to step back and look at the issues dispassionately. I therefore hope that readers will appreciate the advantages of first approaching these issues of principle with reference to the Basic English debate discussed in Chapter 7. The main focus of the present chapter will then be on the contribution that ELF research might make to current pedagogical thinking.

In the discussion of Basic English in the last chapter the focus of attention was on its claimed effectiveness as an international means of communication, comparable in function to Esperanto or Volapük, or, more recently, Globish. But it is important to note that Basic was conceived of not only as a basis for communication and as such an end in itself, but also as a basis for further learning, for the subsequent acquisition of what Richards refers to as an 'ampler' English:

It [Basic] is no rival to or substitute for an ampler English, where the use of that is feasible. It is an introduction and an exploratory instrument.
(Richards 1943: vi)

Ogden's idea was to extract the conceptual essentials of the language, to reveal what was most elemental about it as a communicative resource. The constraints of Basic, therefore, were designed to serve a crucial enabling function, to provide a basis for subsequent learning. So Basic was thought of not only as an exercise in corpus planning but in acquisition planning as well. The idea was that once you had acquired Basic, and therefore been made aware of its potential for getting your meaning across, you could then use it as 'an exploratory instrument' for extending your communicative range. In this respect, Basic was seen as a kind of investment which would ultimately yield returns in the form of an 'ampler' English, one which would presumably take on the full functional range of the language as it naturally and normally occurs.

As we have seen, however, for all Ogden's claims to the contrary, getting meaning across in Basic often resulted in an abnormal kind of English. Like Quirk's Nuclear English, Ogden's Basic was a conceptual contrivance that paid no heed to the criterion of naturalness as indicated by relative frequency in usage. In this respect Ogden's approach to the prescription of English for learning sets him apart from, and indeed in opposition to, his (probably more influential) contemporaries Harold Palmer (Palmer and Hornby 1937) and Michael West (1934, 1953), who were committed to pedagogic prescriptions which were essentially based on frequent words in 'natural' English (cf. Bongers 1947: 119 ff.).

In their criticism of Basic already referred to in the previous chapter, West and Swenson argue that instead of adhering to the defining principle that results in odd periphrastic combinations that might be confusing, it would have been preferable to include many frequently used, simple words, thus allowing 'ask' where Basic has 'make a request, put a question', 'eat' for Basic 'take food' and 'wife/husband' for Basic 'married woman/man' (op. cit.: 32f.). They also give examples of sentences written in West's own 1000-word vocabulary, selected with reference to frequency of occurrence, and compare these favourably with a 'translation' into Basic, such as:

West	Ogden
The priest thanked the ladies for their help in making the party so successful. (West and Swenson 1934: 34)	The servant of the church said it was very kind of the women of good birth to help him in making the meeting of friends come off so well.

Table 8.1 West and Swenson's text compared with a translation in Basic

Given this (no doubt carefully chosen) example one can see that West and Swenson have a point. As was conceded in the previous chapter, it may be possible to produce Basic that sounds 'natural' in that it respects frequency conventions, so long as one knows what these conventions are. Learners, however, usually do not know what these conventions are and so in using Basic will be likely to produce language which is unnatural as measured against the frequency norm. But does this matter? The question arises as to whether the language for learning should be 'natural' as measured against this frequency norm anyway.

8.2 Natural use and usefulness for learning

On the face of it, a pedagogic prescription based on 'natural' English has a more immediate and intuitive appeal than an 'unnatural' system which has been artificially constructed. There is, however, no necessary relationship between naturalness in respect to native-speaker usage and effectiveness for learning. The crucial question here is not whether the Basic prescription results in natural native-speaker-like performance, but whether it impedes the natural learning process rather than (as its proponents claim) facilitates it. What we need to ask is: how far does Basic indeed provide the basis for an 'ampler' language, whether this resembles the conventions of native-speaker usage or not?

What Ogden believed was that the effective use and learning of a foreign language were not a matter of replicating patterns that have been actualized as natural native-speaker behaviour, but on the contrary of getting through to the underlying conceptual essentials that these patterns tended to conceal or distort. In this view, what counts is not how much of the language is learnt, but how it is conceived. As Richards puts it:

> The language remains a mere means of repeating the same things in another code. And it is too often assumed that only an advanced knowledge of a language can be a liberating knowledge. That is a mistake; the liberation and enlargement of thought depend rather upon the *how*—with what understanding—the language is learned than upon *how much* of it is picked up. A small segment of a language, well learned with its meanings well explored, is more valuable—from this point of view, as allowing one to see how its thought patterns compare with those of one's vernacular—than a larger vocabulary learned as a code.
> (Richards 1943: 117)

The point that Richards makes here is that learning develops more from a qualitative rather than a quantitative prescription and that the primary consideration is to identify language which is likely to activate the learning process. A similar point is made by Widdowson some fifty years later:

> We need to recognize, it seems to me, that some things can be taught, and some things must be left to be learnt. What this means is that decisions always have to be taken as to what is the best *investment*, what it is that provides learners with an *effective basis for further learning*. Learners cannot be rehearsed in patterns of appropriate cultural behaviour, and of course they will not be prepared in every particular to cope with all the niceties of communication, but the crucial requirement is that they should have a basic *capacity which enables them to learn how to cope when occasion arises*. ... Such a context is bound to set limits on what language learners are explicitly taught, and these cannot of their nature contain 'real world communication'. But the crucial point is that this is not language to be learnt as such, but *language to be learnt from*.
> (Widdowson 1998: 331, emphases added)

The central question, of course, is what kind of language constitutes the best learning investment. Ogden and Richards claim it is Basic, since this represents the encoding of what is quintessentially conceptual in the language, that once acquired can be variously realized in actual use in all kinds of ways depending on emergent communicative requirement. West, on the other hand, believed that the best investment could not be inferred by such speculation, but had to be empirically substantiated, derived from the data of actually occurring usage. The extensive work that he and his colleagues undertook in vocabulary research (fully documented in Bongers 1947, and discussed in Howatt 2004) aimed at providing just such a substantiation by identifying the most essential words of the language in terms of their relative frequency.

Later, however, in what must be the most detailed and comprehensive analysis of language pedagogy ever written, Mackey points out that frequency of use is not a reliable indicator of usefulness and so not necessarily a good investment criterion. As he puts it:

Frequency does not reveal the relative importance of concepts. It is not concerned with the code of the language (langue), but rather with its manifestation, its use (parole). (Mackey 1965: 181)

Mackey goes on to propose that this conceptual importance can be accounted for by recognizing the coverage value of language items. This he defines as follows:

The coverage or covering capacity of an item is the number of things one can say with it. It can be measured by the number of other items which it can displace. (Mackey 1965: 184)

The most obvious way for a word to displace others is by definition, and this, of course, is the central guiding principle of Basic. So what Mackey is in effect proposing is that Ogden's conceptual analysis is needed to counter or complement the limitations of West's empirical approach based on frequency.

The two approaches, however, seem to be informed by incompatible principles, as Mackey himself recognizes:

Basic English, which was founded essentially on the principle of coverage, was a conscious reaction against the over-application of the principle of frequency in selection; it was not devised in ignorance of the principle. For at the time, Ogden had at hand the works of Horn, Thorndike and Dewey [i.e. on word counts and vocabulary selection]; but he believed that what a word will do for us is not the same as the number of times it is used. For him, it was not the frequency of a word which makes it useful; it was its usefulness which makes it frequent. (Mackey 1965: 187)

It has to be said, however, that West himself acknowledged that the prescription of language for learning needs to take other factors apart from frequency into account. In *A General Service List of English Words*, the final revised report of the findings of the Carnegie Committee's extensive research on word frequency, West makes mention of other considerations. Among these are *ease or difficulty of learning* (or *Cost*) and what he calls *Cover*:

An item may be frequent but unnecessary. Thus 'for the time being' is not uncommon, but it is adequately covered by 'for the present.'

In other words, the two expressions may be comparable in both frequency and cover value. But there is another factor involved in preferring the less frequent expression, and this is *Cost*. West continues:

'For the time being' is costly, since the word 'being' here is remote in meaning from To be, whereas 'present' is used in its normal, root sense. It is *a useful general rule* to prefer the item nearest to the root sense.
(West 1936: ix, emphasis added)

The question arises as to how far one should allow these other considerations to override frequency, and if one allows the inclusion of infrequent items on the grounds that they have more learning value, then what is to prevent one preferring items of low cost and high coverage that (like some of the oddities of Basic mentioned above) do not occur in the data at all, that have a frequency of zero? Since there is no indication as how these expedient and secondary pedagogic considerations are to be applied, there seems no way of preventing them from becoming primary considerations, comparable to Ogden's 'principle of coverage'. So although West is at pains to foreground criteria that are quite different from Ogden's, he ends up making similar recommendations.

Much the same point applies to another consideration that West mentions as overriding the frequency factor. This goes under the heading of *Intensive and emotional words*. These are described in a way which is entirely consistent with Ogden's rationale for Basic:

The foreigner is learning English to express ideas rather than emotion; for his emotional expression he has the mother-tongue. English is a rather unemotional language but it has its intensive words and items whose only function is to be the equivalent of underlining, or an exclamation mark, e.g., 'simply useless' = quite useless plus annoyance. It is *a useful general rule* that intensive words and items are of secondary importance to the foreign learner, however common they may be.
(West 1936: x, emphasis added)

A systematic application of these two 'useful general rules' would result in a language stripped down to its conceptual essentials and devoid of its normal idiomatic and affective features, an instrument for expressing ideas as simply and directly as possible.

So although West's starting point for pedagogic prescription is English that is actually attested in use, his subsequent doctoring effectively results in the same kind of reduced conceptual core artificially constructed by Ogden. It is interesting to note that West's justification for such reduction is that learners will only need English for the expression of ideas, that is to say, he assumes that any subsequent use of the learnt language will be exclusively for an ideational purpose with the expression of emotion confined to the mother tongue. This assumption of course runs counter to the evidence of ELF usage considered in Chapter 6, which makes it clear that the learnt language is naturally used across the whole functional range, including the expression of identity and affective meaning, and there is no intrinsic unemotional property in English that prevents this. So it is clear that the 'foreigner' will inevitably use English, like any other natural language, to express emotion as well as ideas—indeed the two are so closely integrated that it is not easy to see how they can be distinguished. West's restriction of prescribed language to what is essentially conceptual or ideational is based on the mistaken assumption that this is the only kind of language that learners will ever need to use.

West is thinking of what learners will need as *users* of the language. But what of their needs as *learners*? One can accept that the kind of restriction West and Ogden propose reduces the naturalness of use, but it does not follow that it is not effective as an investment for learning. One can argue that once this kind of conceptual knowledge is in place, it serves as a basis for the subsequent learning through use of how the language can be extended and adapted for the expression of emotion and other personal and interpersonal subtleties. The idea here, and it is of course a traditional one, is that the main consideration in deciding on what language to teach is not the extent to which it resembles actual usage but the extent to which it provides enabling conditions for further learning.

What Ogden, Richards, Mackey, and West had to say about English and English teaching is past history. What makes them relevant to the present, and to the present discussion, is that it brings out with particular clarity the central issue I referred to at the beginning of this chapter: how do we decide on what language should be prescribed as appropriate to the subject, how far and in what respects should it, or can it, approximate to the norms of native-speaker use?

8.3 English prescribed: objectives and processes

In designing the language subject, there are two considerations that have to be borne in mind. On the one hand, there is the need to take note of the eventual *objective*, and this would favour a focus on how the language is normally and naturally used. On the other hand there is the need to activate the learning *process*, to prescribe what Widdowson refers to as 'language to learn from', and this may well be very different from naturally occurring language. It is apparent that in the prescriptive proposals of both Ogden and West these two considerations are in opposition and difficult to reconcile. These proposals date back to the first half of the 20th century, of course, and it might be supposed that this problem of opposing considerations is equally dated, and has long since been resolved. However, the contrary is the case: developments in the study of language and language learning over recent years have tended to polarize these two aspects of pedagogic prescription and so to exacerbate the problem.

One of these developments has already been discussed earlier in this book (in Chapter 3). This is the vastly increased scope for linguistic description afforded by advances in computer technology. Whereas for West and his colleagues the collection and counting of words were slow, laborious, and limited, current corpus linguistics can assemble and analyse vast quantities of actually occurring language data, and reveal far more than the elementary facts of word frequencies. As was pointed out in Chapter 3, corpus analysis can now provide detailed profiles of actual language performance that reveal norms of usage that language users and analysts alike were hitherto unaware of. If it is assumed that the objective for learning English should be to match up with these norms as closely as possible, then it follows that it is their description that should determine what is prescribed for the subject.

And that, as we have already noted in Chapter 5, is essentially the position that is taken by the 'real English' advocates. As with West, the focus of attention here is on the pedagogic objective—on what learners of the language will need to use the learnt language for. But this objective was defined in very different ways. West, as we have seen, thought of the range of use as limited with no need for foreign users to aspire to be like native speakers. For the advocates of 'real English', on the other hand, there is no such limitation: the objective is defined on the assumption that learners should aspire to be as like native speakers as possible. It is the unquestioned universal validity of this assumption, of course, that I have been arguing against throughout this book. But apart from the question of how *valid* it is to specify the objective of learning in this way, there is the question of how *viable* it is in relation to the other crucial consideration that has to be taken into account in defining the subject: the *process* of learning.

Alongside the developments in the description of language based on corpus analysis have been developments in the study of language learning, most prominently in the research on second language acquisition (SLA), and this we would obviously expect to have some bearing on the process side of the subject. How far then are the findings of SLA consistent with the 'real language' objective?

What, in broad terms, SLA research has revealed is that the acquisition of the grammatical features of a second language follows a certain order, to some extent predetermined, and moves from one interlanguage stage to another. This 'natural order' necessarily controls the learnability of these features and therefore, the reasoning goes, provides guidance for how these features should be arranged in a teaching syllabus. This would prevent teachers wasting their (and their learners') time trying to teach something that learners are not ready to learn.

The advocacy of the authentic, however, tells teachers that they must present real language, get learners not just to use language communicatively but to replicate the communicative behaviour of native speakers. So we can see that what emerges from the study of the learning process is in direct contradiction to the real language precept. The problem is that even if one were to accept that the objective of learning is to replicate native-speaker behaviour, it makes no pedagogic sense to focus on this objective in complete disregard of how it might be achieved. The key issue here, as Widdowson has pointed out (Widdowson 2003, 2009), is the confusion between *samples* and *examples* of language. What can be taken from a corpus are samples of actually occurring language, but if these are to be learnt *from* they have to be understood as typical in one way or another, in other words they have to be understood as examples *of* something, tokens of types of lexical item, grammatical structure, idiomatic utterance, or whatever. If the samples cannot be processed by the learner in this way, although they may be real as samples of usage, they cannot be made real as examples for learning. The essential problem is that the objective-oriented presentation of 'real English' is incompatible with the learning process. One can, of course, get round this problem by redefining the learning process so that it is compatible. For example:

…it should not ever be necessary for students to 'unlearn' anything they have been taught. They cannot be taught everything at once, and because our knowledge of the textual detail of language has been so vague, they have been taught half-truths, generalities which apply only in some circumstances.
(Sinclair 1991: 499–500)

But on the evidence of second language acquisition research (see Dörnyei 2009), it is precisely by unlearning that students learn, moving from one 'half truth' to another, re-conceptualizing partial generalities as they go along. As Widdowson puts it:

Both psycholinguistic research and pedagogic experience make it obvious that the acquisition of competence is not cumulative but adaptive: learners proceed not by adding items of linguistic knowledge, but by a process of continual revision and reconstruction. In other words, learning is necessarily a process of recurrent unlearning and relearning, whereby encoding rules are modified, extended, re-aligned or abandoned altogether to accommodate new language data. The whole learning process is a matter of continual cognitive adaptation as the learner passes through different transitional stages, each of which is an adapted version of the one preceding. Learning can only progress by unlearning. So even if you presented real language only, as input, its reality would not survive, for it would be converted into processible data for learning, and the more real or authentic the input, the more difficult is the conversion likely to be.
(Widdowson 2009: 211)

From this perspective, then, teaching is mainly a matter of guiding this process of learning by unlearning, and the actual input presented by teachers is of secondary importance.

8.4 Objectives and processes reconsidered

At the heart of the problem of pedagogic prescription I have been discussing in this chapter is the entrenched assumption that the only English that is worth striving for in the language classroom is that which conforms to some native-speaker norms. This is taken to be self-evidently the proper objective for learning and overrides considerations about whether this is appropriate to the learning process. Proficiency is measured against this benchmark and it is taken for granted that the more closely learners approximate to these native-speaker norms, the more proficient they will become as users of the language—and conversely, of course, the less they conform, the less profi-cient they are bound to be. To refer back to the earlier discussion in Chapter 5 about regulative conventions, not only in this view is there only one real or proper way of playing this language game, but if you play it in any other way, this disqualifies you as an effective communicator.

Even when the focus of attention is on the process of learning it is this view of proficiency that prevails. Take the case of Task-based Language Teaching (TBLT). This is an approach to pedagogy that has been extensively promoted over recent years and it is endorsed by SLA researchers on the grounds that it can account for what they identify as three essential components of second lan-guage acquisition: complexity, accuracy, and fluency (CAF) (see Housen and Kuiken 2009), all three of which are defined in reference to native-speaker norms. According to Ellis, one of the most prominent advocates of TBLT (see Ellis 2003), for a classroom activity to qualify as a task it has to meet the criterion that '…Learners should largely have to rely on their own resources (linguistic and non-linguistic) in order to complete the activity' (Ellis 2009: 223).

However, we need to note that learners would not be able to call on *all* their linguistic resources. They would not, for example, be allowed to use the most reliable resource at their disposal, namely their own language. The only resource they have to rely on is what they are instructed to learn of the second language they are being taught. The imposition of this condition calls into question a second criterion of task design that Ellis specifies: 'There is a clearly defined outcome other than the use of language (i.e. the language serves as the means for achieving the outcome, not as an end in its own right)' (ibid.).

It is difficult to see how learners can take the outcome as anything else but the use of language if, in carrying out a task, the only language they can use is the one they are learning. They may go along with the pretence that this language is just the means for achieving an outcome, but they also know that achieving this outcome is not really an end in itself at all, but only a means to the real end, which is the learning of the language. In other words, they recognize full well that tasks are designed for language acquisition. As indicated earlier, this, according to TBLT, consists of the three components of CAF, each of which is defined exclusively in reference to native-speaker norms. Complexity is defined 'from the perspective of the L2 system or the L2 features', accuracy as 'the ability to produce error-free speech', and fluency as the ability to process the L2 with 'native-like rapidity' (Housen and Kuiken 2009: 461, 463). In short, tasks are designed not to develop communicative proficiency as such but proficiency in conforming to native-speaker norms.

It is this view of proficiency that determines the 'standards' of achievement in language education more generally and is particularly evident in measures of assessment. Even the *Common European Framework of Reference for*

Languages (Council of Europe 2001), despite its overall objective of further-ing a composite plurilingualism in which individuals' partial competences in various domains should be a desirable learning goal, persists in its orien-tation towards native-speaker norms. By and large, 'intelligibility' is taken to mean being intelligible to native speakers, and being able to understand native speakers. This orientation is also discernible in some descriptors of lan-guage proficiency developed for the Council of Europe's *European Language Portfolio*, for instance:

I can interact with a degree of fluency and spontaneity that makes regular interaction *with native speakers* quite possible. I can take an active part in discussion in familiar contexts, accounting for and sustaining my views.
(Spoken Interaction/B2)

I have no difficulty in understanding any kind of spoken language, whether live or broadcast, even when delivered *at fast native speed*, provided I have some time to get familiar with the accent.
(Listening/C2) (www.coe.int/portfolio, emphases added)

The European Language Portfolio is meant to apply to all languages and so of course fails to acknowledge the unique role of ELF in that English cannot be a 'foreign language' like any other.[1] The CEF's lack of differentiation between 'modern foreign languages' on the one hand and 'English' on the other is puzzling, as the socio-economic roles of these two categories of languages are so obviously different that the objectives for learning cannot be the same (see Seidlhofer 2003a). Of course 'English' *can* be studied like other foreign languages such as Italian or Japanese, but for most current learners and users of the language, the role of the language as a medium of intercultural commu-nication, its function as a (global) lingua franca, will be the more relevant one. So far, however, the call for a more differentiated categorization has hardly been taken up, and even publications that are quite critical of the CEF do not address this particular weakness (see Bausch *et al.* 2003).

The same is true of tests that take a narrow ENL view of proficiency even if they are called 'international' (see McNamara, 2011; Jenkins and Leung, forthcoming; Leung and Lewkowiz 2006, 2008, for similar criticism)[2]. To mention but one example, the following description of Pearson's Test of English (PTA) in a teachers' magazine indicates a complete lack of awareness of the role of ELF in the world:

To create an *international* exam we started by hiring item writers from *the UK, the US and Australia*...Because we are not using a single standard model of English we can grade all non-native students on a single scale. The first thing we look for is comprehensibility—are they understandable *to the native speaker*?
(*EL Gazette*, Sept 2008, emphases added)

However, as has been emphasized throughout this book, a failure to measure up to approved NS norms does not seem to prevent effective communica-tion in non-conformist ELF taking place on a global scale. This makes it abundantly clear that although the objective that is set is ENL, the objective that learners actually achieve is decidedly not. What is achieved, and put to use in ELF, is clearly not the English that has been *taught*, but the English that has been *learnt*. In other words, where there is a conflict between objective and process it is the process that prevails. In current pedagogical thinking, there are two possible reactions to this state of affairs.

One is to see this non-conformist English as an interim and incomplete kind of (inter)language that EFL learners produce in the process of moving towards proper competence, and which gets carried over in fossilized form into ELF use. On this account, ELF is simply the manifestation of arrested learning. But then the question naturally arises as to why the learning gets arrested, and why there is so much arrested language about—tens, even hundreds of millions of people use it, far more than use English of a supposedly complete and non-arrested kind. Furthermore all the evidence indicates that they use it to good effect to achieve their communicative purposes, so how can defective language be so effective?

The non-conformities of EFL learner language are stubbornly resistant to correction, as every teacher knows. One reason for this, it has been proposed (and widely accepted) on the basis of SLA research, is that what learners learn from the language they are presented with depends on a mental state of readiness to learn, and that this is largely determined by underlying acquisition processes beyond teacher control. Learners, in other words, have their own agenda and it is this they are conforming to rather than to that of the teacher.

From this second perspective, learners' non-conformities are to be categorized not as errors but as evidence of successful learning. This more positive view of learner efforts is, of course, to be welcomed, but the assumption generally remains that it is still only a means to an end, an interim interlanguage, a temporary and transitional kind of language that learners will subsequently improve upon as they approach the end point of approved native-speaker competence. In this view, what is needed is improved ways of teaching which will induce learners to move along the interlanguage scale to this desired end point. The idea is that these ways of teaching would then replace the failed attempts of the past and effectively eliminate the inadequacies of EFL learning. The practical feasibility of this idea is open to doubt, but leaving that aside, it is based on the assumption that acquisition can only be measured against the linguistic competence of the native speaker, and this, as I have already discussed in Chapter 4, is left undefined, so there is actually no clear end point to reach, and therefore no way of knowing where exactly learners are on the interlanguage scale.

Given these (not inconsiderable) difficulties, it seems reasonable to look for alternative ways of thinking that go beyond the two perspectives outlined above. One such alternative would be the proposition that I have been putting forward in this book: that we should recognize that native-speaker competence cannot be set up as a generally valid or viable objective, that ELF is not failed ENL, an arrested stage of interlanguage, but the result of learners putting their learnt language to use as an end in itself—as an end, one might say, in *itsELF*. Rather than persisting in setting ENL as the objective and measuring proficiency only in terms of degrees of conformity to NS norms, as has been the generally accepted practice in the past, it would seem reasonable to suggest that we should make reference to what people actually *do* with the language they have learnt, how they actually communicate in English as an additional language. As I have argued in previous chapters, ELF is no less real than that which has been performed in accordance with the set of regulative rules that has been sanctioned as the ENL standard.

There would seem to be a prima facie case then for considering the description of ELF as relevant to the prescription of learning *objectives* (on which more below). But as I have already argued, the objective is only one part of the language subject. How do these ideas about the potential relevance of ELF square with the crucial learning *process* side of things?

Although learners' intake does not correspond with teacher input, they do take in a good deal, picking up some bits of language, discarding others. The interesting question arises as to what motivates their selective learning. Why are some things learnt more readily than others? As I have noted, the explanation from an SLA point of view is that learning is a kind of self-generated mental process whereby the formal linguistic properties of the language are internalized in accordance with underlying acquisition rules. But one might also suggest that acquisition is regulated by functional factors, and speculate that what is most readily learnt is what learners intuitively recognize as having the greatest inherent valency, the most potential for exploitation, and so pick up aspects of the virtual language and actualize them in their own way.

What I am suggesting, then, is that learners have a tendency to home in on what is most conceptually salient or communicatively usable. They thereby do instinctively the kind of thing that Ogden does by rational analysis in his devising of Basic. But the difference is, of course, that whereas with Basic the features are speculative abstractions and there is no evidence that they have any psychological reality, or are indeed communicatively effective, the features that learners take in are naturally acquired and acted upon in ELF usage.

The key point here is that the language naturally acquired in the process of learning is the very language that is subsequently put to use. What is learnt is clearly useable as a resource for communication, as is attested by the findings of ELF research discussed in earlier chapters. Learners of English as a foreign language assume the role of users of English as a lingua franca. As they move into contexts of use outside the classroom, EFL learners become ELF users. If this is so, then the very *process* of acquiring this resource is itself a valid and viable *objective*. The problem of the disparity between the objective and the process of learning effectively disappears: both involve the development in learners of what Widdowson, in the quotation heading this chapter, refers to as a *capability* for realizing the potential for making meaning that is virtually inherent in the language. The focus now is, in the words of Richards quoted earlier, on 'the *how*—with what understanding—the language is learnt' rather than on '*how much* of it is picked up'. This, as he suggests, can have a liberating effect on learners: they are released from the strict confinement to conformity and enabled, empowered indeed, to appropriate the language for themselves. If, as is so often declared, teaching should, as a matter of principle, be learner-centred so as to encourage learner initiative and auton-omy, this is one obvious way of putting the principle into practice. But if this principle of learner-centredness is to be taken seriously, then there are other considerations that need to be taken into account, too.

To begin with, we need to follow through the implications of the obvious fact that learners of an additional language have previous experience of at least one other language, which they will quite naturally and inevitably draw upon. One can safely assume that this experience will have made them aware that not all features of what is linguistically encoded are of equal valency, that some are of greater functional value for them than others. It should therefore come as no surprise if this awareness is brought to the learning of another language and will prime learners to home in on aspects of the language that have a relatively high meaning potential while disregarding those that do not because they are surplus to communicative requirement. Generally speaking, in foreign language pedagogy, linguistic features tend to be assigned equal value in the teaching input whatever their degree of functional saliency.[3] But learners, on the basis of their previous experience of how language actually functions in use, will for their part naturally seek to restore the value differen-tial and are, of course, generally penalized for this.

This part of the learners' previous experience has to do with their sense of how language in general works. But they also bring with them the experience of their own language in particular. In a foreign language classroom there are always at least two languages present and there will always be the natural ten-dency to make the foreign language less foreign by relating it to the language that is familiar, in other words by translating. Again, the typical pedagogic response is to discourage the tendency, to deny that translation has any place in language pedagogy (for arguments against this position, see Cook 2010) and to maintain the pretence that the English of the classroom is a monolin-gual subject. But it cannot be monolingual for the learners (see Widdowson 2003: Chapter 11). The English they produce, I would argue, results from an entirely natural exploitation of their previous linguistic experience. This English is usually, of course, taken as erroneous, and it can be considered as such, *if* we assume that the only possible objective for learning is the acqui-sition of ENL norms. But if we consider the alternative I have suggested, and think of the objective in quite different terms—as the development of a capability for exploiting linguistic resources, then these so-called 'errors' can be seen as positive signs of effective learning. And this learning is not just that which is directed at ENL as the only legitimate ultimate goal, but learn-ing with a view to functioning in whatever English works for the purpose it is used for. From this perspective, what learners are doing, and should be encouraged to do, is engaging in the same strategic process of appropriation and adaptation that typifies the language of ELF users. To refer to what was said in Chapter 5, they are learning how to 'language', how to exploit the potential in the language for making meaning.

It is commonly assumed that language use and learning are two different processes, and that the first is dependent on the second. You first learn a language and then use it, and if you do not learn it properly, you cannot use it effectively. I would argue, on the contrary, that learning and using are *not consecutive but simultaneous* processes. For me the essential point is that language learners are already language users and will quite naturally be inclined to exploit the foreign language as they exploit the one they are familiar with. Such exploitation is generally regarded as interference and usually measures are taken in teaching to suppress it. Although lip service is paid to the idea that learners should be encouraged to put the language to communicative use, they are generally only allowed to do so on and in the teacher's terms and not their own, and as a means to an end, namely the eventual conformity with NS norms that counts as competence. The basic assumption is that you cannot be an effective user of the language until you have learnt it 'properly'. My assumption, in contrast, is that learners learn the language by making use of it on and in their own terms and that in using it they develop the capability for further learning.

The wide use of ELF brings home the simultaneity of learning and using in a particularly striking way. I would suggest that learning and using English are best thought of as aspects of the same process of exploiting the meaning-making potential virtually inherent in the language. It is not surprising to find, therefore, that ELF usage bears a resemblance to learner language. It would indeed be surprising if it did not. Users of ELF, having in Halliday's phrase, learnt 'how to mean' (Halliday 1975) make communicative use of the language they have learnt, and extend their learning quite naturally as they extend its use. But this does not mean that ELF usage is to be equated with learner language, as the latter is usually understood as representing some stage on the interlanguage continuum of development towards NS competence (see Granger 2008; Gilquin 2008).

What we see in ELF is people *languaging* (see Chapter 5), 'having a go, trying to make sense and getting somewhere against all the odds' (Phipps 2006: 1), and this makes evident that however 'defective' the English may be as a product measured against native-speaker competence on an interlanguage scale, they have managed to acquire a capability for putting the language they have learnt to effective communicative use (see also the personal accounts in Kramsch 2009, and Todeva and Cenoz 2009). Setting native-speaker competence as the only valid objective for English as a subject, I have argued, and insisting on learners conforming to it in the learning process can only inhibit the development of this capability. But on the evidence of ELF, it is this very capability that is learnt, and by being put to effective use it also provides for further learning. As Swain puts it (Swain 2006: 98): 'Languaging...refers to the process of making meaning and shaping knowledge and experience through language. It is part of what constitutes learning'. This further learning will then take individual routes determined by the language users' needs (academic or business, for example) but these are not predictable during schooling.

So it seems perverse to discourage the development of this capability through ELF use and to persist instead in attempting to get learners to reach some undefined level of competence that is, for the most part, both unnecessary and unattainable.

8.5 English as a subject and the relevance of ELF

The radically changed role of English in the world and the continuing spread of ELF as a global reality should at the very least prompt us to reconsider how realistic and relevant is the traditional way of thinking about the subject to be taught and learnt.

This is not, of course, a view that is generally shared. On the contrary, in the ELT establishment the conservative Anglo-Saxon attitudes I discussed in Chapter 2 still persist: that standard native-speaker English is the one and only English that counts. There is little indication here that the unprecedented global reality of ELF might prompt a reconsideration of traditional ways of thinking: it is generally just ignored as if it simply did not exist. This may not be surprising in the case of governments, ministries of education, and employers, as there is usually quite a long time lag before new insights have any impact on established procedures (such as curriculum design and job descriptions) in these quarters. But the same conservative attitude is also evident in the ELT profession itself, and here the degree of inertia is quite striking. In most cases, ignoring the pervasive reality of ELF seems to be not so much a deliberate act, but rather a general lack of awareness that traditional assumptions could, or should, be questioned. There appears to be very little desire in ELT to do so—the general tendency is to carry on with business as usual. This is perhaps most clearly shown by the reference books that are explicitly designed for learners of English. The *Oxford Advanced Learner's Dictionary* (8th edn. published in 2010) is a case in point. There seems to be some recognition that English exists outside the UK and the USA in that a list is given in the front matter of the book of 'Advisers on World English'. Presumably on their advice, some concession is made in the dictionary to Outer Circle varieties of English by the token inclusion of certain lexical items: *dwaal* (marked *SAfrE*) and *prepone* (*IndE*), for example. However, the dictionary does not only deal with words and meanings, but also with their grammatical features and conventions of usage. And here there is no such concession to 'World English' but on the contrary a rigid insistence on standard ENL norms. Thus, under the entry *discuss*, the learners for whom this dictionary is designed are told that they cannot say *discuss about something* (see Chapter 6). Similarly, they are advised that *enjoy* cannot be used intransitively or be followed by the infinitive, and this point is driven home graphically with strikethrough: '~~Thanks, I really enjoyed~~' (see OALD 8th edn. s.v. *enjoy*, Grammar Point). Learners are also told that *a lot of* or *lots of* 'are not used with measurements of time and distance': '~~I stayed in England a lot of weeks~~' (8th edn. s.v. *many*, Grammar Point) and so on, even though such forms are in fact attested in 'World English'.[4] It is clear from these examples that the focus of attention of OALD is firmly on ENL (to which, it must be said, it does provide excellent guidance), and this is further confirmed by the inclusion of maps and lists of town and cities of Australasia, the British Isles, and North America only and, in the Reference Section, of first names common in these regions.

The Longman Dictionary of English Language and Culture (3rd edn. 2005) is even more explicit, or blatant, in its exclusive promotion of ENL, as its very title indicates. The slogan on its cover reads: 'Gets to the heart of the language' and by 'the language' is meant the language as used to express the culture of its native-speaking communities, more specifically those of Britain and (North) America. A promotional statement reads as follows:

No matter how advanced your level of English, it's difficult to fully understand the language unless you understand the many cultural references that you see when reading books or newspapers. This dictionary gives you a deeper insight into the language by explaining cultural references, and helps you easily answer those difficult questions students might ask you about British and American culture.
(Pearson Longman Catalogue, see http://eltcatalogue.pearsoned-ema.com/Product.asp?CallingPage=CatalogueandISBN=9780582853126and SearchTerm =)

Here English is clearly taken to be the exclusive property of its native speakers and so inextricably bound up with their culture that understanding this culture is a necessary condition for 'fully' understanding 'the language' (see also Holliday 2009a on this topic).[5]

So one reaction to ELF is to be oblivious to it, or to pretend it does not exist, so the question of what thinking it might stimulate about its possible relevance for language pedagogy simply does not arise. Another reaction, found quite frequently in publications whose main readers are teaching professionals, is to acknowledge the existence of ELF but to see it not positively as a stimulus for reflection but on the contrary negatively as a threat to the established pedagogic order. In some cases, reactions to the suggestion that ELF might have pedagogic implications worth considering are surprisingly vehement, with quite strong emotional expressions being used. There is talk about 'bring[ing] the ideal down to the gutter, with no check-point on the way' (Sobkowiak 2005: 141), 'inventing a new variety' and 'installing a fledgling ugly duckling' (Maley 2009: 194, 196) and offering a 'broken weapon' for L2 users that 'risks bringing them stuttering onto the world stage of ELF' (Prodromou 2008: 250). These attitudes have been amply illustrated and discussed in

Jenkins 2007, so there is no need to go into detail about them here. Instead, a short quotation from a German university professor of English linguistics will suffice as a summary of the kind of perceptions, fears, and defiance that are frequently found:

> The demand for English will continue and possibly increase, which means that more and more people will acquire broken, deficient forms of English which are adequate to the extent that they permit the communicational functions they were learnt for. ... However, the incomplete acquisition reflected in such instances will never become the basis for a linguistic norm, which is, and has always been, based on the consent of the learned and guided by the accepted written norm, which has remained surprisingly homogeneous around the globe.... There is no danger of such deviant uses 'polluting' the standards of native speakers even if they become a minority in the global anglophone community. Int[ernational] E[nglish] will not be corrupted by such uses...
> (Görlach 2002: 12f.)

In the views expressed here, suggestions about the pedagogic relevance of ELF are denounced as potentially damaging. Most of, perhaps even all, such fairly extreme reactions, however, upon further scrutiny turn out to be objections not to proposals concerning ELF research that have actually been made, but to people's own interpretations and assumptions. These include the misapprehensions, repeated again and again, that ELF interactions are defined as excluding ENL speakers, that ELF is claimed to be 'a new variety' with features that are unique to it, and that recurrent patterns and features identified in empirical ELF research are proposed as a monolithic model that should replace any others for teaching and be offered for imitation in learners' actual production. I hope that this book so far has provided a sufficiently full picture of ELF to make clear that these assumptions are mistaken.

Another reaction to ELF is to see it as a threat to teachers' peace of mind against which they need to be protected. For instance, we sometimes encounter concerns expressed by practitioners (or more usually, teacher educators and authors speaking on teachers' behalf) to the effect that teachers' lives are difficult enough without the added complication of having to 'teach ELF', combined with the fear that once linguistic descriptions become available of how ELF interactions work this will be interpreted as binding prescription for teaching.[6]

If teacher education really does educate teachers linguistically and pedagogically rather than just train them, it is difficult to see how such ideas can even arise. Maley (2006), after a very brief (and inaccurate) summary of the goals of descriptive research into ELF comments:

> This project, while a perfectly legitimate, indeed valuable, piece of academic research does seem to raise a number of practical questions. As so often happens, the positive aspects of the research have been seized upon by enthusiasts and hastily assumed to offer seemingly simple solutions to a very complex problem area.
> (Maley 2006: 5)

We are not told who these hasty enthusiasts are, but presumably they are teaching professionals such as materials writers or teacher trainers, who should know better.

Despite all these difficulties, however, my overall impression is an optimistic one, namely that ELF research and the consideration of its potential implications for pedagogy is entering a phase of genuine engagement with and examination of the issues from which really productive discussions can unfold.[7] If the debate on ELF has the effect of making practitioners more reflective then this must be a good thing. Much recent writing about and against ELF is engaging with crucial questions; what is still happening, however, is that certain assumptions about ELF research are made, and repeated, that are simply unfounded, and these could easily be remedied by careful reading of publications on the subject.

The reactions mentioned above represent ELF as a threat to be resisted. A rather different reaction is simply to discount its pedagogic relevance altogether. This has been expressed with particular clarity by Michael Swan, and since he is an acknowledged authority in the field of English teaching, it is important to consider carefully what he has to say.[8]

In a recent book review, Swan states that ELF 'has not changed the pedagogic issues significantly from what they were 50 or 100 years ago' (2009: 80). I would agree that the pedagogic issues themselves have not changed and it was the purpose of the first part of this chapter to point this out—issues concerning the criteria for deciding on the language to be taught are indeed as current now as they were in the past. My claim is not that ELF changes the issues but that it changes the way we need to think about and act upon them. Swan does not see the need for any such change and this is where we differ.

All non-native speakers (NNSs) of English, he says, derive their language, directly or indirectly, from native-speaker (NS) models, and I would not want to disagree with that. But it raises the question of just how this language is derived, and if one allows the derivation to be indirect, what the nature of this indirect process might be. Swan indicates that one kind of derivation takes the form of deliberate pedagogic adjustment designed to demonstrate 'those aspects of the chosen variety that are likely to be most useful for successful NNS communication' (ibid.). How such usefulness is to be determined is, of course, the key question that I have been considering in this chapter, and Swan concedes that the study of successful NNS communication of ELF might provide an empirical basis for deciding what these aspects might be. So here empirical work on ELF *can* actually make a considerable difference. He also acknowledges the role of the learners themselves in the derivation process: 'NNS learners are selective in their turn, taking from these partial models the elements that they choose to, and are able to, assimilate.' (ibid.). Again, agreed—but of course this raises the very question that I considered earlier as to what motivates the choosing, and what constrains the assimilation.

At all events, however one defines these processes of teacher and learner activity, the result, according to Swan, is that 'NNSs thus necessarily end up

194 Understanding English as a Lingua Franca

with their own individual varieties of English' but these cannot be communicatively effective in their own right and in their own terms, for they 'need to conform to NS norms sufficiently to permit effective communication' (ibid.: 81). In other words, given that NNS English will be varied, its effectiveness as communication depends on a 'sufficient' degree of adherence to the rules of ENL. However, just what degree of sufficiency is enough to permit communication, or in what contexts and what purposes, is left unspecified. This omission, however, is crucial: it is precisely the contexts and purposes that determine what is 'sufficient' to ensure effective communication. But it is clear that the logical implication of what Swan says is that there is a direct correlation between conformity to NS norms and communicative success.

According to Swan, the varieties that NNS learners end up with are necessarily individual and 'may differ considerably from NS English and from each other (depending on learners' mother tongues and other factors) in ways that have already been extensively documented: learner English is not a new subject of study' (ibid.). Whatever is meant by 'individual varieties', it is clear that in this view, no matter how extensively and effectively they are put to communicative use, they remain only examples of learner English. The fact that the language has been appropriated worldwide as an international means of communication is in this view pedagogically irrelevant since the English taught must still conform to the ENL norm, even though the English that is actually learnt—and subsequently used—does not: proper English is proper English and that must be the English taught as a subject, and an error is an error no matter what other euphemistic term you use for it. It is this line of reasoning that leads to the conclusion that 'For teaching purposes, therefore, "ELF" is not in principle something different from "EFL"' (Swan 2009: 80–1).

Swan's position is probably widely shared, if not so explicitly and elegantly argued, and can be assumed to represent a sizeable section of orthodox opinion in the English teaching world, so it is of some interest and importance to see how it relates to the thinking I have pursued in this book. To begin with, it takes for granted that there is a norm of ENL, a well defined set of regulative rules that constitute proper English, and that ELF can only be accepted as an alternative mode of use in its own right if it can be shown that it constitutes a well defined variety, a different *kind* of English. Otherwise, all we have in ELF are different manifestations of unsuccessful efforts to learn EFL modelled on ENL. In this view, the E of ENL is the only admissible model for the E of (any kind of) ELT even though it may be rarely achieved as a target.

EFL is said to be 'the traditional label for English taught to and learnt by speakers of other languages for international communication' (ibid.). But although this may be the English that is taught, it is usually not the English that is learnt, and, as we have seen, it is the English that is learnt that is put to use in international communication. If English is really to be taught for international communication, then it would seem to make sense to find out how it is actually *used* for international communication, that is to say how it functions as a lingua franca.

As I have noted, Swan accepts that the English of NNS will vary from NS norms but he takes this variation to be the result of something like a one-way, pretty deterministic process. In this view, when EFL learners find themselves in an ELF user role, the 'individual varieties' they have been constrained to learn in the context of classrooms will be directly projected into contexts of use. And since, the argument goes, the English that is learnt will be affected by the learners' L1 (among other factors) these varieties are bound to differ not only from NS English but from each other as well. This being so, it is concluded, ELF uses, being a direct projection of EFL learning, will also necessarily differ from each other, and it would follow from this that we are likely to have as many different kinds of ELF as there are different mother tongues of learners, or even individual learners' idiolects.

On the face of it, this argument is persuasive, and calls for close consideration. It is an accepted fact that learner English bears marks of the influence of the first language. The previous linguistic experience of learners is necessarily involved in their learning of English as a foreign or other language and this, as I have argued earlier, helps them to 'naturalize' the new language, counter its foreignness and appropriate it as a communicative resource. But if this is the case, it is not the non-conformities of the linguistic forms themselves that should be focused on, whether they are taken as errors to be corrected or as interim elements of interlanguage. The focus should rather be on *how* they are used, how they function in the conceptualization and communication of meaning. In short, the focus should not be on the *forms* of learner language and how far they deviate from NS norms, but on how effectively they *function* in making meaning. But although an emphasis on the conceptual and communicative value or valency of linguistic forms would, I have argued, have the enabling effect of naturalizing the language along ELF lines, in certain respects classroom conditions set limits on how ELF-like learner language can be. This is because learner language produced in classrooms does not just naturally occur but always comes about through pedagogical contrivance of one kind or another. Even when there is a simulation of communicative interaction, if the learners have the same mother tongue, there has to be some degree of pretence, a willing (or unwilling) suspension of disbelief, and of course if their language varies because of L1 influence, the variation will be shared, and reinforced. More often than not, the L1 is a common factor in EFL settings, which makes it all the more natural for learners to have recourse to it in the activities they are required to perform. But it is, of course, precisely the absence of this common factor that motivates ELF use, and learners can be better prepared for this if the forms that are prioritized in their classes are those with particular functional value in that they have been found to be crucial to international intelligibility rather than those that conform to NS norms. Whereas learners in largely monolingual classrooms have their own language to revert and refer to as a back-up if and when necessary, ELF users typically do not. What they have in common as a resource is whatever English they have learnt, and they need to be resourceful in its use in order to cope

with the exigencies of actual communication and negotiate common understanding dynamically on-line (see Chapter 5). In this process, any features
of their learnt English that impede communication will quite naturally be
adjusted in the interests of accommodation, and these are likely, of course, to
include features which derive from L1 influence and which make one learner
'variety' different from another. The key point is that since the very *raison
d'être* of ELF is to mediate meanings to establish common understanding, this
will quite naturally regulate diversity in the interests of intelligibility.[9]

So the conditions of actual use will generally require continual adaptation and preclude the direct projection of learnt language. Therefore, with
reference to Swan's argument, it cannot be assumed as self-evident that the
variations in the learner language of EFL will carry over as variations in the
user language of ELF. The crucial point is that classrooms have to provide
opportunities for learners to develop a capability in English that will enable
them to make adaptive and actual use of the virtual language. They do not
just need to learn words but, to borrow the title of Austin 1962, 'how to do
things with words'. Or, in other words (this time those of Halliday quoted
above) they have to 'learn how to mean'.

As Swan says, 'English...is learnt and used by NNSs to cross language
barriers'. Agreed. But the essential question is: what is to be learnt *of* English
that enables NNSs (and NSs) to put it to effective use in crossing barriers that
impede communication? The traditional view is that what is to be learnt as a
necessary condition for any effective use is a number (of some undefined sufficiency) of standard items and rules of the language, and that the ability to
communicate in English is determined by an approximation to native-speaker
competence. But quite apart from the difficulty of defining such competence
(as discussed in Chapter 4), such a view runs directly counter to the evidence
of ELF use. What has been learnt and is successfully used by vast numbers of
NNSs to cross language barriers does not meet these conditions. ELF users
are capable of effective communication without being confined to such conformity. If the language really is to be taught as a means for crossing language
barriers, then it would surely make better sense to take into account how
this is actually done. So I would argue against Michael Swan that ELF, far
from being irrelevant, calls for a quite radical rethinking of taken-for-granted
assumptions about objectives and processes in English teaching.

8.6 Rethinking the subject

Throughout this chapter, I have argued that an understanding of the E of ELF
usage has implications for how the E in EFL or ESOL is to be defined. I want
now to bring these implications together and consider how the conceptualization of English as a subject they point to would differ from that which is
generally accepted at present.

The design of English as a subject to be taught—the definition of the E in
EFL or TESOL—involves decisions on two things: the *objective* that is to be

eventually attained and the *process* whereby it is to be reached, that is to say, the specification of ends and means. As I mentioned earlier, the eventual objective for some learners will indeed be to achieve NS norms but though this may be an ultimate aspiration, it does not mean it needs to be set as a teaching objective. It can only be achieved through a subsequent learning process if the socio-psychological conditions are favourable—conditions that it is actually impossible to replicate in classrooms. So the E in EFL/ESOL is the E that facilitates the learning process whether this subsequently leads to NS norms or not.

How then would the thinking about English as a subject be different if we assume an ELF perspective?

1 Most users of English in the world are non-native speakers who use the language effectively for their purposes. Vast numbers of them are communicatively capable but in reference to native-speaker norms, incompetent. Observations of ELF interactions show that conformity to these norms is not a necessary requirement for communication.

2 This NNSs' communicative capability has been achieved in spite of a failure of attainment as measured by conventional means. It turns out that language that from the conventional point of view has been only partially and imperfectly learnt can be put to communicative use. 'Failed' learners can be(come) effective users of English.

3 Given this state of affairs, two courses of action suggest themselves. Either one can persist in teaching a competence that learners rarely attain, and apparently do not need as subsequent users of the language. Or one can consider the possibility of setting objectives that are realistic in that they both reflect the learning process and are attainable, and correspond more closely to the requirements of the majority of actual users of the language.

4 The first option would be to continue with a pedagogy based on the ideal and ideological assumption that eventually all uses of English in the world should match up with native-speaker competence and that somehow an approach to teaching will eventually be discovered which enables learners to acquire it. The record shows that this is in effect a pedagogy predicated on failure, with vast numbers of people who put their learning to use in ELF stigmatized as incompetent and relegated to the limbo of interlanguage.

5 The second option would be to accept the reality that what is learnt of English does not, and cannot, correspond with the language that is currently taught and that the specification of NS competence as the primary objective has to be abandoned. Instead, the purpose of teaching becomes the development of a capability for effective use which involves the process of exploiting whatever linguistic resources are available, no matter how formally 'defective'.

6 The focus here is genuinely on communicative function and whatever forms are used are evaluated in terms of their functional effectiveness and not their degree of approximation to NS norms. Essentially, in this view, learners are not learning *a language* but learning *to language*.

7 Learning to language involves the use of strategies for making sense, negotiating meaning, co-constructing understanding, and so on, in short the strategic exploitation of the linguistic resources of the virtual language that characterizes the use of ELF, as illustrated in earlier chapters of this book.

8 The linguistic resources are virtual and their realization may not correspond to the regulative conventions of standard English, nor do they necessarily have an English source. The learners' own language(s) may also be exploited in the languaging process (as it often is in ELF). This is not seen as interfering with the process but as facilitating it.

9 A pedagogy that focuses on capability along these lines results in a partial acquisition of English. But unlike a pedagogy that focuses on NS competence this is not seen as a deficiency. It accepts that the notion of 'a language' and native-speaker competence in it are fictions, and that therefore all language acquisition is partial and can never be otherwise. Nobody can know a language, the whole language, and nothing but the language, whether this is thought to be one's own or somebody else's.

10 How much language learners acquire is ultimately irrelevant. What matters is the extent to which whatever parts they have learnt can serve to activate their capability for using, and therefore for further extending, their linguistic resource. This capability will then also serve them well subsequently, for instance when they do find they need (or wish) to conform to standard norms where such conformity is contextually appropriate.

These then, I would argue, are general principles of a pedagogy for teaching and learning English as a subject that can be proposed on the basis of an understanding of ELF—particularly, but perhaps not only, when learners already know that in their future lives, 'English' will largely mean ELF.

But let me make it quite clear that I am not advocating that descriptions of ELF should directly and uniquely determine what language is to be taught in the language classroom. As was discussed at length in Chapter 6, what is significant about ELF is not the non-conformist forms it takes but how the forms function, how they are put to strategic use in communication. So it would, in my view, be just as pedagogically pointless to prescribe a set of ELF forms as a set of ENL forms in dissociation from their function. What really matters is that the language should engage the learners' reality and activate the learning process. Any kind of language that is taught in order to achieve this effect is appropriate, and this will always be a matter of local decision. So what is crucial is not so much what language is presented as input but what learners make of it, and how they make use of it to develop the capability for languaging. The pedagogic significance of an ELF perspective is that it shifts the focus of attention to the learner and the learning process. It points to the need to reconsider how teaching might provide impetus and support for this process by attending to what learners do, not in terms of correctness and conformity to input, but as legitimate uptake in their learning and using. So an understanding of ELF leads not to the specification of ELF-like language content (although it might suggest some adaptation of priorities), but to the need for a change in teacher attitude. And this, in turn, would of course be likely to change the learners' own attitude, with a positive effect on their motivation.

So the criterion for selecting language to be taught is not whether it is proper English as measured against standard norms or the conventions of NS usage but whether it is appropriate English—locally appropriate to the purpose of developing a capability in the language. This capability will, of its nature, provide learners with the means of extending their knowledge of linguistic forms and their functional value in the process, and this will continue as they exploit their learning as ELF users—even approximating to ENL norms if this is appropriate to their purposes. There will be occasions when learners will want to eventually attain NS competence, whatever NSs they find they need or want to emulate. But this they can only do through the exercise of their capability. So for teaching, capability remains the primary concern.

The essential overall point is that the extension of formal knowledge is motivated by functional need. How people make the language work for themselves is primary, and the forms they produce are simply a consequence of this process. As was demonstrated in Chapter 6, users of ELF put the language they have learnt to communicative effect, and in exploiting the language in this way, they quite naturally explore its further possibilities. To return to the Halliday dictum referred to in Chapter 6, language takes the forms it does because of the functions it is required to serve. This applies as much to EFL learning and ELF usage as to the standard codes and regulative conventions of ENL. Through the experience of using what they have learnt of the language, ELF users inevitably learn more of it and acquire what Richards refers to as an 'ampler' language—ampler for any further communicative requirements they want to meet.

It might be (and indeed has been) argued that if learners do not have a norm to aspire to they will not even get that far, that it is necessary to set impossible goals because if you don't, people won't achieve anything. I am not aware of any empirical evidence in the motivation literature in support of this assumption, but the fact that learners generally fall short of the goal that has been set is not in itself sufficient argument for adhering to the goal. The alternative, setting achievable goals, would seem to be more consistent with a learner-centred pedagogy and, as I have argued, empirical work on ELF should prompt us to give it serious consideration.

Some of the requirements English users want to meet might, of course, contingently involve a closer approximation to ENL norms. But this approximation is indeed contingent. It will only happen as a consequence of, or corollary to the functions that English is required to serve. Users of the language will naturally be required to adjust and extend their language to make it appropriate to purpose; and where it is in their communicative interests to conform to ENL convention, they will, of course, seek to conform. Some learners of the language will want or need to conform to the approved NS conventions of the standard language, and for certain purposes adherence to canonical forms will be important. But this has to be established as and when locally appropriate rather than be assumed a priori to be generally and always valid. Given the role of English in the world, this should no longer be the default assumption. On the contrary we might start thinking of learning speaking and writing ENL as ESP—English for Specific Purposes, and where such purposes can be specified in advance, adherence to NS norms is obviously an entirely appropriate objective. But most learners have other and far less specific and predictable purposes, and it does not seem reasonable to impose such ESP objectives on them, especially since they are unlikely to attain them anyway. What they need is what is usually referred to as EGP—English for General Purposes—English that can be adapted to any purpose and made appropriate to any context. This is still generally assumed to be standard ENL, but as far as international uses of English are concerned, it is clearly not this English but ELF that serves these general purposes: it is ELF that is EGP. The pedagogic implication of this is that if the language subject is to prepare learners to use English for general purposes, it needs to develop not a *specific competence* but a *general capability* for use.

As I have indicated earlier in this chapter, what I am suggesting here, of course, goes against deep-seated belief and established custom, not to speak of vested interests, and has been, and will be, resisted and rejected on the grounds that it promotes a reduced, impoverished, pidgin-like kind of English and that it gives legitimacy to incompetence, or disadvantages learners. Much of this book is devoted to spelling out the reasons why such a view, which essentially re-affirms and perpetuates the privileged status of standard native-speaker English and denies the status of ELF as a legitimate use of language, is no longer tenable.

But of course, the assumption of the superior status of standard English is deeply ingrained, and taken as self-evident in linguistics and language pedagogy. This, as has been frequently asserted, is what learners and teachers of English alike want: the English as recorded in standard grammars and dictionaries, proper English, the real thing, and not some inferior ersatz version. This, of course, is not surprising since teachers and learners have been well schooled in the assumption that anything that does not conform to standard ENL is by definition defective, incorrect, undesirable. From this perspective, it is unsurprising that 'there is still some desire among students to conform to native-speaker norms, and this desire is not necessarily restricted to those students who use, or anticipate using English primarily with native speakers' (Timmis 2002: 248).

But there are quite different reasons brought forward for opposing the consideration of the possible pedagogic relevance of thinking along ELF lines. Thus Holliday (2009b: 22) observes that 'there are accusations that the English as a lingua franca movement is yet another device to maintain Centre dominance'.[10] He does not give references other than to Kuo (2006), but I might add, for example, that the 2005/2008 book edited by Dziubalska-Kołaczyk and Przedlacka contains a number of papers expressing this very sentiment. In this regard, Llurda (2009) offers an analysis into how non-native English speaking teachers 'have accepted formulations, proposals, and attitudes that relegate them to mere spectators and at times executioners of native speaker (NS) norms', and he very strikingly likens this phenomenon to the *Stockholm Syndrome*, which 'describe[s] a victim's psychological identification with their captor' (Llurda 2009: 119). Maley (2006), on the other hand, asserts that ELF researchers 'propose to emancipate the repressed learning masses from the stifling coils of "Standard English" '. He then goes on to observe that:

> the task of implementing teaching based on EIL would be enormous for it would require the re-tooling of teachers worldwide so that they became expert users of EIL, putting aside their years of effort invested in teaching a standard variety. It would involve turning around the oil tanker of vested interests in international examinations, in textbook publishing, in teacher training provision, in quality-control bodies and so on.
> (Maley 2006: 5)

True, the only English represented in textbooks, grammars, and dictionaries generally is ENL, and no real alternatives are on offer. And, of course, for teachers these books represent not only authority, but security. They give them clear guidelines about what to teach. And so, it can be argued, talk about capability and ELF as indicating an alternative is only likely to cause alarm and despondency, undermining teachers' belief and confidence in what they are doing without providing any feasible alternative. It is all very well to encourage teachers into a new way of thinking, but where are the textbooks that would enable them to put it into practice?

But this is not an argument against a change of thinking, or even against attempts at 'turning round the oil tankers of vested interests'. The case for an ELF-informed pedagogy in principle that I have been arguing for in this chapter is not invalidated by the current absence of teaching materials that would put it into practice. As I have already said, what matters is not the language content but how it is exploited for learning. What is crucial therefore is not *what* teaching materials are used but *how* they are used. If what we think about language teaching had to be determined by what textbooks are available there would be no possibility of adaptation to changing circumstances at all and pedagogy would simply petrify. Change always has to start somewhere. And the obvious place to start is in language teacher education.

8.7 ELF and teacher education

My purpose in this book is not to promote a whole new and superior pedagogic paradigm, but to suggest how an understanding of ELF could lead to a change in our thinking about English and the way it is generally taught, and to point out what implications ELF might have for how English as a subject might be defined. If teachers are to be 'reflective practitioners' as they are so frequently urged to be, then here, surely, is something they need to reflect about. So, it is not my intention to advocate abandoning traditional practices and ways of thinking out of hand, but rather to argue the need for a reconsideration of the *assumptions* on which they are based, for it is just as unreasonable to reject as it is to accept established ideas without critical appraisal. Any proposal for a change in practice has to be based on an under-standing of principle, and it is how the English subject is defined in principle that I am concerned with here.

Traditionally, English as a subject is designed from a teaching rather than a learning perspective on the unquestioned assumption that the purpose of pedagogy is to direct learners towards native-speaker competence. From this perspective learner achievement is measured only as degrees of success in approximating to this goal. The question is how far this remains a generally valid way of thinking. Is it not worth considering an alternative principle of approach which, as I have argued, can be drawn from an understanding of ELF? This would be to focus attention not on the language as product, on how much English learners manage to accumulate, but on the process of 'languaging', on how learners make use of what they know of the language. To do this would be to look at English as a subject from a learning rather than a teaching perspective, whereby credit is given for what the learner achieves by way of usable language for his/her purposes, whatever the degree of conformity to NS norms. Here it is not the level of competence that counts but the capability for using the language by exploiting its communicative potential. Instead of seeing the process of learning as subordinate to the objective of attaining the goal of native-speaker proficiency which can be subsequently put to use, *learning* and *using* are now seen as essentially aspects of the same process, upon which any particular objective that might be specified is necessarily dependent.

How this capability principle can be put into methodological practice to influence the content of courses and the design of classroom activities is an open question, and above all a *local* question, too. It is also an open question as to how such a principle can be made consistent with institutional requirements. Curricula have to be planned, instruction designed with objectives specified at different stages so as to produce measurable outcomes, and it is obviously convenient to take as benchmark the English that is most extensively described and documented, and sanctioned by authority, namely the standard language. But such institutional constraints should not prevent us from raising questions of pedagogic principle and thinking again about the validity or relevance of current conventional ways of thinking.

And this process of rethinking is well under way, even if it does not yet form part of the ELT 'mainstream'. After a period in which a general awareness had been gradually growing as to the need for a reorientation (see Burger 2000; Jenkins 2000; McKay 2002), recent years have seen a spate of very specific discussions and suggestions that build on insights arising from descriptive ELF research and reconnect these with local pedagogical concerns. As I see it, this constitutes a new and genuinely productive phase that has now gathered momentum. For example, in the 40th anniversary issue of *TESOL Quarterly* 2006 (40/1), issues arising out of the development of World Englishes and English as a Lingua Franca loom large. The editor of the journal, Suresh Canagarajah, in his introductory article 'TESOL at Forty: What Are the Issues?' emphasizes that:

geopolitical changes related to new forms of globalization have more recently reconfigured the relationship between English varieties and speech communities, sending us in search of new models. ... English's greatest use is as a contact language. Therefore, the outer and expanding circles are quite central to the currency of English today, recasting claims of ownership and reconfiguring relationships between varieties.
(Canagarajah 2006b: 23)

In the same year, David Graddol highlights ELF in the section on 'Learning English' in his *English Next*, observing that:

[t]eaching and learning English as a lingua franca (ELF) is probably the most radical and controversial approach to emerge in recent years. It squarely addresses some of the issues which global English raises.
(Graddol 2006: 87)

Also in 2006, Gibson Ferguson, in his book *Language Planning and Education* concludes two chapters dedicated to implications of the global spread of English thus:

The conclusion we are driven to, then, is not that the pursuit of an ELF model is valueless or pointless. Far from it, despite the methodological and conceptual difficulties involved. But rather that gaining acceptance is a formidable obstacle that can probably only be overcome by convincing teachers, students and the wider public not just that English is sociolinguistically in a different position from all other languages, which is obvious, but that this sociolinguistic uniqueness justifies the abandonment of a popular assumption that by and large holds sway for most languages; the assumption, namely, that native-speaker-like proficiency, and conformity to native speaker norms, is the truest measure of achievement in second language learning.
(Ferguson 2006: 177)

Subsequently, numerous other publications over recent years have provided testimony to the increasing critical awareness of the pedagogic implications of ELF. For instance, 2007 saw (in addition to Jenkins' *English as a Lingua Franca: Attitude and Identity*) the publication of three articles on questions of ELF and teacher education in one issue of the *International Journal of Applied Linguistics* (Dewey 2007a; Sifakis 2007; Kirkpatrick 2007a), as well as Kohn 2007, in a German-language volume. A special 2008 issue of the *Australian Review of Applied Linguistics* was dedicated to the theme 'English as an international language. Challenges and possibilities' (Clyne and Sharifian 2008). Phan Le Ha's (2008) *Teaching English as an Intercultural Language: Identity, Resistance and Negotiation*, as well as the second edition of Gnutzmann and Intemann's collection *The Globalisation of*

English and the English Language Classroom appeared in the same year. The following year, 2009, the first special issue of an international journal was published in which World Englishes 'met' ELF, the Symposium 'Englishes in world contexts' (*World Englishes* 28/2), as well as the collection *English as an International Language: Perspectives and Pedagogical Issues* (Sharifian 2009). Smit (2010) is the first substantial longitudinal study of ELF in higher education, and two further 2010 books, *The Routledge Handbook of World Englishes* (Kirkpatrick 2010b) and Saxena and Omoniyi (2010), though not primarily about ELT, both dedicate considerable space to issues of language education that arise when *Contending with Globalization in World Englishes* (the latter's title). Cogo and Dewey (2011), resulting from two early PhD theses on ELF, offers substantial descriptive findings but also important implications for pedagogy. And the journal *Language Teaching* commissioned a state-of-the-art review article on 'Research into English as a Lingua Franca' for publication in 2011 (Jenkins, Cogo, and Dewey 2011).

Looking at what might be most immediately relevant for practitioners, the concluding chapter of Kirkpatrick's book *World Englishes* entitled 'Implications for English language teaching' offers an even-handed consideration of the relative advantages and disadvantages of choosing an exonormative native-speaker model versus an endonormative nativized model. Kirkpatrick then briefly sketches the strengths of 'a *lingua franca approach* based on the goal of successful intercultural communication' (Kirkpatrick 2007b: 193), and he comments that if such an approach is adopted, '[n]either teachers nor students would be asked to aim for an unattainable or inappropriate model' (ibid.: 194). This, broadly speaking, is the perspective that I have developed in more detail in this chapter. In a particularly strong (short) section on '[R]equirements for ELT teachers and training courses' (ibid.: 195), Kirkpatrick outlines a teacher preparation course for a specialist Diploma in Teaching English to Speakers of Asian Languages, which he says could be adapted to other contexts. This course aims to produce teachers with (contrastive) linguistic understanding of English and their own language(s) as well as language variation, with an understanding of 'the role(s) of English(es) in their teaching community' that also 'informs their practice', and with sufficient knowledge and flexibility to enable them to 'evaluate teaching methods and materials and…adapt their teaching styles and methods to suit the needs of different contexts and cultures' (ibid.: 196).

This does indeed seem to be the way to go, and I agree with Kirkpatrick that the hope lies in teacher education.[11] While actual teacher education curricula would of course have to be tailored to local purposes, there are certain priorities that they should generally focus on in the education (not just training) of teachers so as provide the essential understanding of the nature of language and its use that underpins their pedagogic practices and that would enhance their status as well informed and self-reliant professionals.

Generally speaking, such a framework for teacher education would privilege process over form and awareness over certainty, and it would treat knowledge of language and knowledge about language as equally important. On the macro-level, there is an enormous body of work about the nature of language and communication that can be drawn on and combined into truly 'empowering' teacher education curricula. Together with work on language awareness (Hawkins 1984; Carter 1990; Brumfit 1992; van Lier 1995; Thornbury 1997; Widdowson 1997b; Andrews 2007; Cenoz and Hornberger 2008; Edmondson 2009), this would include research on communication strategies (Bialystok 1990; Kasper and Kellerman 1997; Cohen 1998; Oxford 2000), intercultural communication (Knapp 1987; Hofstede 1991; Kramsch 1993; Bremer *et al.* 1996; Byram 1997; Spencer-Oatey 2000; Corbett 2003, 2010; Scollon and Wong Scollon 2001; Holliday *et al.* 2004; Bührig and ten Thije 2006; Kotthoff and Spencer-Oatey 2009; Alptekin 2010); and other work on sociolinguistics (especially language variation) and social psychology (especially the study of accommodation).

I am not suggesting that prospective and in-service teachers should be fed an unrelieved diet of theory. Clearly there has to be a process of selection and adaptation to bring out the potential pedagogic relevance of these areas of enquiry. But there needs to be some awareness of this potential first before procedures for making it relevant can be designed. Building on insights in these and related areas and moving closer to the micro-level, a curriculum can be developed that fosters understanding in teachers of how the language they are studying and will be teaching figures in a more general framework of communication. The objective here would be to counteract the 'code-fixation' of much current language pedagogy that tends to be focused on developing proficiency in language forms rather than an awareness of the nature of language itself and its creative potential. And here recent research into ELF links up with the areas mentioned above in that it makes tangible that communication should never be expected to be 'complete' or 'perfect'.

The analyses of ELF interactions discussed in Chapters 5 and 6 indicate the high functional load that various strategies and processes have for achieving understanding. A particular focus in teacher education would therefore need to be put on appreciating these aspects and on encouraging teachers to actively teach them. Examples include close and active listening (cf. Lynch 2009), communicative awareness, such as gauging one's interlocutor's linguistic resources, 'letting it pass' (Firth 1996), various interaction strategies such as indicating understanding or non-understanding, regulating backchannel behaviour, asking for repetition, paraphrasing, avoiding 'unilateral idiomaticity', giving preference to 'transparent' expressions, being explicit, exploiting or adding redundancy, and attending to non-verbal communication. All of these could be demonstrated as fostering accommodation and building rapport amongst interlocutors (Aston 1988 calls it 'comity'). With these foci, there actually is substantial overlap with what some practitioners (Maley 2009; Saraceni 2009) say about teaching, in spite of their pronounced scepticism about ELF based on a fundamental misunderstanding of the concept. Thus Maley 2009 echoes the pedagogic implications of some ELF writers (for example, several contributions in Mauranen and Ranta 2009; Seidlhofer 2001, 2004) when he proposes that 'in terms of teaching, we need to move away from a product-based to a process-based approach.' He continues:

Rather than attempting to incorporate the Core features into our teaching, we should be inducting students into an awareness of diversity and of strategies for dealing with it (and this is something which could also profitably be extended to NSs!).
(Maley 2009: 197)

It would seem, however, that the 'either-or' position he sets up is not necessary, and that most learners would benefit from a focus on communication processes and strategies, combined with an initial focus on priorities derived from descriptive ELF research into the functional value of linguistic features on all levels of language.

This is in fact the direction in which the teaching of Business English, and in particular 'BELF' (Business ELF) seems to have been developing, at least as far as the innovators in the field are concerned. Thus Vicki Hollett, a recognized authority (as a teacher and coursebook author) in the areas of business, technical, and professional English, confirms that communication awareness, rapport building, and accommodation skills are among the most valuable aspects for her students. She agrees with what Mark Powell (2010) said in a plenary talk to teachers of Business English:

He argues strongly for paying attention to ELF innovations: 'We could do worse than listen to what they do and work with that instead of hammering them with what we've got in the course books.' . . . So I think one of the other helpful things about ELF research is that it will hopefully enable us as teachers to be more aware of language and strategies we unconsciously use—and hence help us to make better choices about what to teach.
(Vicki Hollett, personal communication)

On her blog she comments further on this talk:

Like 'English as a lingua franca' (ELF) researchers, Mark is urging us to set sensible priorities for what we teach and it makes a lot of sense. For the many English learners who won't be needing English to communicate with native speakers (NSs), why faff around with frilly stuff that will have little value when we can go 'lean'. . . . He describes a class with French and German speakers where his students were converging on forms that worked for all. Speech accommodation like this seems to be a key feature in ELF conversations.
(http://www.vickihollett.com/?p=3031, 19 December 2010) . . .

. . . one of the complaints that's often leveled against ELF researchers is that they are suggesting we teach an impoverished form of English, which your students cloudy faces indicate they are definitely don't want. But as I understand it, that's not what they are saying. They want to know more what's happening to the language as it changes so the choices we make about what we teach can be better informed.
(http://www.vickihollett.com/?p=3031, 2 January 2011)

A substantial body of ELF research in business contexts does indeed investigate 'what's happening to the language as it changes', how ELF professionals rise to the challenges of transcultural communication, and how teachers can best support them—generally by fostering intercultural communication skills rather than mastery of 'correct' ENL linguistic forms and 'anglo' cultural norms (see Ehrenreich 2010; Gramkow Anderson 1993; Kankaanranta and Planken 2010; Louhiala-Salminen, Charles, and Kankaanranta 2005; Charles and Marschan-Piekkari 2002; Pitzl 2010; Poncini 2004; Pullin 2010; Rogerson-Revell 2008, 2010; Thompson 2006; Wolfartsberger in press; and Koester 2010 for an overview).

A similar tendency towards focusing on awareness and communication strategies can also be observed in the other domain where descriptive ELF research dovetails with the reality 'on the ground', namely English for academic purposes (EAP). As higher education and research are becoming more and more globalized, the 'unmarked form' of EAP increasingly is ELFA, ELF in academic settings. As Mauranen, Pérez-Llantada, and Swales (2010: 640) point out, academia is an area 'where international communication characterizes the domain across the board'. Not surprisingly then, a substantial body of descriptive research on academic ELF has been undertaken that can offer guidance for important insights for teacher education. Many studies are based on the English as a Lingua Franca in Academic Settings (ELFA) corpus, for example, Mauranen 2006, 2009, forthcoming; Metsä-Ketelä 2006; Ranta 2009; and further references on the ELFA website.[12] Björkman (2008, 2009, 2010) investigates spoken ELF as used in engineering courses at a Swedish technical university, Schaller-Schwaner (2008) at different departments at a trilingual Swiss university, Smit (2010) at an international tourism course in Austria, and Watterson (2008) at a university in South Korea. All these studies point to the importance of strategic skills and the way academics and students use ELF and shape it to their specific requirements.

For these different settings, various cognitive-'linguisticky' activities in teacher education might be very useful and eye-opening: hands-on work could be done on transcripts of ELF interactions to develop an understanding of the functional value of 'non-native' features that are usually referred to as 'incorrect', 'unidiomatic', or 'overuse/underuse'. Having a close look (either with pre-selected extracts or by directly consulting a corpus) at how specific utterances function in an interaction would help teachers appreciate that these features are often there for good communicative reasons and thus demonstrate the fusion of using and learning that I elaborate on earlier in this chapter. Needless to say, a lot of exposure to the language used by successful ELF speakers would be essential, and as Kirkpatrick (above) emphasizes, local bilingual teachers would provide for just such exposure.

And of course, the identification of features of ELF usage can also make a valuable contribution to rethinking priorities for teaching. That is to say, if the absence or substitution of linguistic elements of ENL has been shown, by and large, not to cause communication problems in ELF interactions while other elements turn out to be crucial, this relative communicative value should be taken into account for pedagogic decisions as to what the limited teaching time should primarily be spent on. Communicatively salient features will then receive more attention in teaching for production than less salient ones. With regard to pronunciation, for example, Walker (2010), following the work of Jenkins (2000) points to ways in which such selective attention can be implemented in practical pedagogic terms. It is not surprising that guidance on pronunciation should come first since it deals with the relatively closed phonological system. But the same principle applies to other levels of language and use, and as the descriptive work on ELF proceeds, it is likely that other salient features can be identified as priorities (or otherwise) for teaching.

As earlier chapters of this book have made clear, the very concept of English has radically changed as it has been appropriated and adapted as an international language. It is this that justifies the equally international inclusion of English as a subject in virtually every school curriculum. The changed nature of English as a global means of communication surely calls for some reconsideration of how English as a subject has been conventionally conceived, and how such alternative conceptualizations also require new orientations in English language teaching and teacher education.

8.8 Conclusion

In designing English as a subject, prescriptive decisions have to be taken about what aspects of the language are best suited to the *objectives* and *processes* of learning. The debate about what factors need to be considered and how they can be reconciled has a long history. The main issue in contention, as illustrated by the disagreement between Ogden and West, has to do with how 'natural' or 'normal' the English prescribed for learning should be, and this issue continues to be contentious and remains unresolved. I have said that the traditional way of prescribing the English of the subject needs to be reconsidered because it is based on assumptions about the objectives and processes of learning that are outdated, and irrelevant, and unrealistic for most learners. The pedagogic relevance of ELF, I have argued, is that it suggests an alternative way of thinking.

Descriptions of ELF interactions reveal what its users can really do with the language they have learnt. Such descriptions represent what learners actually achieve as a communicative capability rather than what they are directed to achieve in the way of NS linguistic competence but very rarely do. Characteristics of ELF usage, therefore, give some indication of where priorities might lie in setting objectives—which communication processes and features might be focused on as having greater saliency or potential for use, which elements, in other words, are more likely to activate the languaging process and so represent the best pedagogic investment. *Understanding ELF* as a naturally occurring use of language provides a new perspective on how, in principle, English as a subject might be defined.

Notes

1 But see McNamara (2011).

2 Changes in testing are now at least being discussed. As Leung and Lewkowicz (2006: 229) observe: 'The next few years will very likely see a finer-grained discussion on greater recognition of use- and context-referenced language norms to accommodate both ELF and local varieties of English in some types of contextualized assessment of English'.

3 A case in point is the teaching of pronunciation, where the literature is full of the communicative importance of intonation, but intonation usually loses out to the more teachable sound segments in most courses (see Dalton and Seidlhofer 1994).

4 See, for instance, Platt, Weber, and Ho 1984: 117: 'In the New Englishes, there is a tendency, particularly in colloquial speech, to imply the subject or the object pronoun of a sentence rather than state it explicitly. The meaning is usually quite clear from the context'. The examples they give include the following, from Sri Lankan English: 'For example, back home the currency notes – if it is torn, people are reluctant to accept (it)', where 'it' is implied rather than explicitly stated (op. cit.: 118). Many more relevant examples can be found in Schneider 2007. Dewey (2007b) discusses transitivity in ELF, in particular the ellipsis of objects and complements of Standard English transitive verbs as indication of 'exploited redundancy' (p. 140), and he makes intriguing observations about emergent regularities in ELF usage in this respect.

5 It is, of course, a common assumption that language and culture are so bound up with each other that you cannot teach one without the other. This may apply to languages of relatively well defined communities, but obviously cannot apply to the global use of ELF which provides for the expression of different cultures and identities.

6 Some even claim that due to 'the nature of language to change (and thus render descriptions of it always out of date)' (Moore and Bounchan 2010: 115), there is no need for linguistic description at all, as if this changeability did not apply to all usage, including Standard Englishes. And a teacher educator and textbook writer on the online forum described in the next endnote writes: 'You ask why bother to teach them when they don't affect comprehsibility [sic]? I would suggest that again this kind of notion feeds in to what I termed an implicit "anti-teaching" mood among teachers. This is my gripe with the way in which Jennifer Jenkins' and Barbar [sic] Seidlhofer's research in this area can be interpreted as well.' So this contributor seems to think that descriptive research should be subject to censorship lest it might be misinterpreted as prescription by teachers. In my view, it would be up to teacher education to help teachers understand the difference between linguistic description and prescription for pedagogy.

7 An interesting example is provided by the way in which an online discussion about ELF and teaching evolved. Following the 42nd IATEFL Conference in Exeter in April 2008, an online forum was created (http://exeteronline.britishcouncil.org/mod/forum/discuss.php?d=392andmode=1, accessed 17/10/2010). Many of the early postings were opinions voiced in a very emotional and bellicose tone, but gradually real and probing questions of content were introduced by participants who had read up on the subject. The tone of the postings became much more tempered, and within a week a serious, rational engagement with genuine issues had developed and the participants confirmed that they had learnt a lot from each other.

8   I make special reference here to Michael Swan as a prominent exponent of this view, which would be supported by a sizeable number of ELT professionals, because his review appeared at a time when I was grappling with these issues and it thus helped me to clarify my own thinking.

9   This is not to deny that there will be occasions when diversity will not be regulated but will create conflict, as in the case of the asylum seekers and immigration officers discussed in Guido (2008) and referred to in Chapter 3.

10 It will probably be easy to see that as a non-native speaker of English myself, but also explicitly as a target of writings that criticize aspects of ELF work, I find myself confronted with rather perplexing accusations in this respect, as somebody who is accused of a 'dominance' that I never had in the first place.

11 The crucial role of teacher education has, of course, been emphasized in virtually all ELF publications that consider implications for pedagogy from the very beginnings (see Jenkins 1998, 2000: Chapter 8; Seidlhofer 1999, 2001, 2004).

12 ELFA website: <http://www.uta.fi/laitokset/kielet/engf/research/elfa/corpus.htm>, and see Chapter 1, endnote 19.

Bibliography

Abbott, G. and P. Wingard (eds.). 1981. *The Teaching of English as an International Language*. Glasgow and London: Collins.

Achebe, C. 1975. *Morning Yet in Creation Day*. New York: Doubleday.

Adolphs, S. 2005. ' "I don't think I should learn all this"—A longitudinal view of attitudes towards "native speaker" English' in C. Gnutzmann (ed.): *The Globalisation of English and the English Language Classroom*. Tübingen: Gunter Narr.

Akoha, J., Z. Ardo, J. Simpson, B. Seidlhofer, and H. G. Widdowson. 1991. 'Nationalism is an infantile disease. (Einstein) What about native-speakerism?' *BAAL Newsletter* 39: 21–26.

Alatis, J. (ed.). 1991. *Linguistics and Language Pedagogy: The State of the Art*. Georgetown: Georgetown University Press.

Allwright, D. and J. Hanks. 2008. *The Developing Language Learner: An Introduction to Exploratory Practice*. Basingstoke: Palgrave Macmillan.

Alo M. A. and R. Mesthrie. 2004. 'Nigerian English: morphology and syntax' in B. Kortmann, K. Burridge, R. Mesthrie, E. Schneider, and C. Upton (eds.): *A Handbook of Varieties of English*. Vol. II: *Morphology and Syntax*. Berlin, New York: Mouton de Gruyter.

Alptekin, C. 2010. 'Redefining multicompetence for bilingualism and ELF'. *International Journal of Applied Linguistics* 20/1: 95–110.

Ammon, U. 2000. 'Towards more fairness in international English: linguistic rights of non-native speakers?' in R. Phillipson (ed.): *Rights to Language: Equity, Power, and Education*. Mahwah, NJ: Lawrence Erlbaum Associates.

Ammon, U. (ed.). 2001. *The Dominance of English as a Language of Science: Effects on Other Languages and Language Communities*. Berlin: Mouton de Gruyter.

Ammon, U. 2006. 'Language conflicts in the European Union'. *International Journal of Applied Linguistics* 16/3: 319–38.

Ammon, U., K. Mattheier, and P. Nelde (eds.). 1994. *English only? in Europa/in Europe/en Europe. Sociolinguistica* 8. Tübingen: Niemeyer.

Ammon, U., N. Dittmar, K. Mattheier, and P. Trudgill (eds.). 2004. *Sociolinguistics. Soziolinguistik. An International Handbook of the Science of Language and Society. Ein internationals Handbuch zur Wissenschaft von Sprache und Gesellschaft* (2nd edn.). Berlin and New York: Walter de Gruyter.

Anderman, G. and M. Rogers (eds.). 2005. *In and Out of English: For Better, For Worse?* Clevedon: Multilingual Matters.

Anderson, J. 2009. 'Codifying Ghanaian English: problems and prospects' in E. Hoffmann and L. Siebers. (eds.): *World Englishes—Problems, Properties and Prospects*. Selected papers from the 13th IAWE conference. Amsterdam: John Benjamins.

Andrews, S. 2007. *Teacher Language Awareness*. Cambridge: Cambridge University Press.

Archibald, A., A. Cogo, and J. Jenkins. (eds.). 2011. *Latest Trends in ELF Research*. Newcastle upon Tyne: Cambridge Scholars Press.

Argaman, E. 2008. 'In the same boat? On metaphor variation as mediating the individual voice in organizational change'. *Applied Linguistics* 29/3: 483–502.

Aston, G. 1995. 'Corpora in language pedagogy: matching theory and practice' in G. Cook and B. Seidlhofer (eds.): *Principle and Practice in Applied Linguistics*. Oxford: Oxford University Press.

Aston, G. 1988. *Learning Comity. An Approach to the Description and Pedagogy of Interactional Speech*. Bologna: CLUEB.

Aston, G. 2008. 'It's only human...' in A. Martelli and V. Pulcini (eds.): *Investigating English with Corpora. Studies in Honour of Maria Teresa Prat*. Monza: Polimetrica International Scientific Publisher.

Aston, G. and L. Burnard. 1998. *The BNC Handbook: Exploring the British National Corpus with SARA*. Edinburgh: Edinburgh University Press.

Atkinson, T. and G. Claxton (eds.). 2000. *The Intuitive Practitioner*. Buckingham: Open University Press.

Auer, P. and L. Wei (eds.) 2009. *Handbook of Multilingualism and Multilingual Communication*. Berlin: Mouton de Gruyter.

Austin, J. L. 1962. *How to Do Things with Words*. Oxford: Oxford University Press.

Ayto, J. 1999. *Twentieth Century Words*. Oxford: Oxford University Press.

Baker, C. D., M. Emmison, and A. Firth. 2005. *Calling for Help: Language and Social Interaction in Telephone Helplines*. Amsterdam: John Benjamins.

Bamgbose, A. 1992. 'Standard Nigerian English: issues of identification' in B. B. Kachru (ed.): *The Other Tongue: English across Cultures* (2nd edn.). Chicago: University of Illinois Press.

Bamgbose, A. 1996. 'Post-Imperial English in Nigeria 1940–1990' in J. A. Fishman, A. W. Conrad, and A. Rubal-Lopez (eds.): *Post-Imperial English: Status Change in Former British and American Colonies, 1940–1990*. Berlin and New York: Mouton de Gruyter.

Bamgbose, A. 1998. 'Torn between the norms: innovations in world Englishes'. *World Englishes* 17/1: 1–14.

Bamgbose, A., A. Banjo, and A. Thomas (eds.). 1995. *New Englishes. A West African Perspective*. Ibadan: Mosuro and The British Council.

Banjo, A. 1997. 'Aspects of the syntax of Nigerian English' in E. W. Schneider (ed.): *Englishes around the World, Volume 2: Caribbean, Africa, Asia, Australasia*. 85–95.

Bauer, L. 1994. *Watching English Change: An Introduction to the Study of Linguistic Change in Standard Englishes in the Twentieth Century*. London: Longman.

Bauer, L. 2007. *The Linguistic Student's Handbook*. Edinburgh: Edinburgh University Press.

Bausch, K.-R., H. Christ, F. G. Königs, and H.-J. Krumm (eds.). 2003. *Der Gemeinsame europäische Referenzrahmen für Sprachen in der Diskussion*. Tübingen: Gunter Narr.

Becker, A. L. 2000. *Beyond Translation: Essays toward a Modern Philology*. Ann Arbor: University of Michigan Press.

Beneke, J. 1991. 'Englisch als *lingua franca* oder als Medium interkultureller Kommunikation' in R. Grebing (ed.): *Grenzenloses Sprachenlernen*. Berlin: Cornelsen.

Berns, M., K. de Bot, and U. Hasebrink (eds.). 2007. *In the Presence of English: the Media and European Youth*. New York: Springer.

Bex, T. and R. J. Watts (eds.). 1999. *Standard English: The Widening Debate*. London: Routledge.

Bhatia, T. K. and W. C. Ritchie. 2006. *The Handbook of Bilingualism*. Malden, MA: Blackwell.

Bialystok, E. 1990. *Communication Strategies: A Psychological Analysis of Second-language Use*. Oxford: Basil Blackwell.

Biber, D., S. Johansson, G. Leech, S. Conrad, and E. Finegan. 1999. *Longman Grammar of Spoken and Written English*. Harlow: Pearson.

Björkman, B. 2008. ' "So where we are?" Spoken lingua franca English at a technical university in Sweden'. *English Today*. 24/2: 35–41.

Björkman, B. 2009. 'From code to discourse in spoken ELF' in A. Mauranen and E. Ranta (eds.): *English as a Lingua Franca: Studies and Findings*. Newcastle upon Tyne: Cambridge Scholars Publishing.

Björkman, B. 2010. 'Spoken lingua franca English at a Swedish Technical University: an investigation of form and communicative effectiveness'. PhD dissertation, Stockholm University, Department of English.

Björkman, B. (ed.). 2011. 'The pragmatics of English as a lingua franca in the international university'. *Journal of Pragmatics* 43 (special issue).

Blackledge, A. 2005. *Discourse and Power in a Multilingual World*. Amsterdam: John Benjamins.

Blackledge, A. and A. Creese, with Tas Kin Barac, A. Bhatt, S. Hamid, L.Wei, V. Lytra, P. Martin, C.-J. Wu, and D. Yağcioğlu. 2008. 'Contesting "language" as "heritage": negotiation of identities in late modernity'. *Applied Linguistics* 29/4: 533–54.

Block, D. and D. Cameron (eds.). 2002. *Globalization and Language Teaching*. London: Routledge.

Böhringer, H., C. Hülmbauer, and E. Vetter (eds.). 2010. *Mehrsprachigkeit aus der Perspektive zweier EU-Projekte: DYLAN meets LINEE*. Frankfurt am Main: Peter Lang.

Bolton, K. 2006. 'World Englishes today' in B. B. Kachru, Y. Kachru, and C. Nelson (eds.): *The Handbook of World Englishes*. Oxford: Wiley-Blackwell.

Bolton, K. 2010. ' "Thank you for calling": Asian Englishes and "native-like" performance in Asian call centres' in A. Kirkpatrick (ed.): *The Routledge Handbook of World Englishes*. Abingdon: Routledge.

Bolton, K. and B. B. Kachru. (eds.) 2006. *World Englishes. Critical Concepts in Linguistics*. Volume III. Abingdon: Routledge.

Bongers, H. 1947. *The History and Principles of Vocabulary Control as it Affects the Teaching of Foreign Languages in General and of English in Particular*. Woerden (Holland): WOCOPI.

Borg, S. 2003. 'Teacher cognition in language teaching: a review of research on what language teachers think, know, believe and do'. *Language Teaching* 36/2: 81–109.

Bourdieu, P. and J.-C. Passeron. 1970. *Reproduction in Education, Culture and Society* (transl. R. Nice). London: Sage.

Braine, G. (ed.). 1999. *Non-native Educators in English Language Teaching*. Mahwah, NJ: Erlbaum.

Breen, M. 2007. 'Appropriating uncertainty: ELT professional development in the new century' in J. Cummins and C. Davison (eds.): *International Handbook of English Language Teaching*. Part II. New York: Springer, 1067–1084.

Breen, M., B. Hird, M. Milton, R. Oliver, and A. Thwaite. 2001. 'Making sense of language teaching: teachers' principles and classroom practices'. *Applied Linguistics* 22/4: 470–501.

Breiteneder, A. 2005. 'The naturalness of English as a European lingua franca: the case of the "third person –s" '. *Vienna English Working Papers*, 14/2: 3–26. (Available at http://anglistik.univie.ac.at/fileadmin/user_upload/dep_anglist/weitere_Uploads/Views/Views0502ALL.p

Breiteneder, A. 2009a. 'English as a lingua franca in Europe: An empirical perspective'. *World Englishes* 28/2: 256–69.

Breiteneder, A. 2009b. *English as a Lingua Franca in Europe. A Natural Development*. Saarbrücken: VDM-Verlag Müller.

Bremer, K., C. Roberts, M.-T. Vasseur, M. Simonot, and P. Broeder. 1996. *Achieving Understanding: Discourse in Intercultural Communication*. Harlow: Longman.

Britain, D. 2002. 'Space and spatial diffusion' in J. K. Chambers, P. Trudgill, and N. Schilling-Estes (eds.): *Handbook of Language Variation and Change*. Oxford: Blackwell.

British Council: *Annual Report 1987–8*. London: British Council.

British Council: *The British Council Conference prospectus*. ELT conference 1998.

British National Corpus, version 3 (BNC XML Edition). 2007. Distributed by Oxford University Computing Services on behalf of the BNC Consortium. http://www.natcorp.ox.ac.uk/

British National Corpus. BYU-BNC: The British National Corpus. http://corpus.byu.edu/bnc

Brumfit, C. J. (ed.). 1982. *English for International Communication*. Oxford: Pergamon.

Brumfit, C. J. 1992. 'Language awareness in teacher education' in C. James and P. Garrett (eds.): *Language Awareness in the Classroom*. London: Longman.

Brumfit, C. J. 2001. *Individual Freedom in Language Teaching: Helping Learners to Develop a Dialect of their Own*. Oxford: Oxford University Press.

Brumfit, C. J. 2002. *Global English and Language Teaching in the Twenty-first Century*. Centre for Language in Education. Occasional Papers No. 59. Southampton: University of Southampton.

Bruthiaux, P. 2003. 'Squaring the circles: issues in modeling English worldwide'. *International Journal of Applied Linguistics* 13/2: 159–78.

Brutt-Griffler, J. 1998. 'Conceptual questions in English as a world language'. *World Englishes* 17/3: 381–92.

Brutt-Griffler, J. 2002. *World English. A Study of its Development*. Clevedon: Multilingual Matters.

Brutt-Griffler, J. 2004. 'Comment'. *World Englishes* 23/2: 331–32.

Brutt-Griffler, J. 2009. 'The political perspective' in K. Knapp and B. Seidlhofer (eds.): *Handbook of Foreign Language Communication and Learning (Handbooks of Applied Linguistics, Volume 6)*. Berlin and New York: Mouton de Gruyter.

Brutt-Griffler, J. and K. Samimy. 1999. 'Revisiting the colonial in the postcolonial: critical praxis for nonnative-English-speaking teachers in a TESOL program'. *TESOL Quarterly* 33/3: 413–31.

Brutt-Griffler, J. and K. Samimy. 2001. 'Transcending the nativeness paradigm'. *World Englishes* 20: 99–106.

Burger, G. 2000. 'Englisch als globale lingua franca: Überlegungen zu einer notwendigen Neuorientierung des Englischunterrichts'. *Fremdsprachenunterricht* 53: 9–14.

Burns, A. 2007. 'Action research: contributions and future directions in ELT' in J. Cummins and C. Davison (eds.): *International Handbook of English Language Teaching*. Part II. New York: Springer. 987–1002.

Burridge, K. and B. Kortmann. 2008. *Varieties of English: the Pacific and Australasia*. Berlin: Mouton de Gruyter.

Bussmann, H. 1996. *Routledge Dictionary of Language and Linguistics*. G. Trauth and K. Kazzazi (transl. and eds.). London: Routledge.

Butler, J. 1997. *Excitable Speech: A Politics of the Performative*. London: Routledge.

Butler, S. 2009. *The Macquarie Dictionary* (5th edn.). Sydney: Macquarie Library.

Bührig, K. and J. D. ten Thije (eds.). 2006. *Beyond Misunderstanding. The Linguistic Analysis of Intercultural Communication*. Amsterdam: John Benjamins.

Byram, M. 1997. *Teaching and Assessing Intercultural Communicative Competence*. Clevedon: Multilingual Matters.

Byram, M. and M. Fleming (eds.). 1998. *Language Learning in Intercultural Perspective: Approaches through Drama and Ethnography*. Cambridge: Cambridge University Press.

Cambridge International Corpus Website. 2009. 'Corpus-based publications'. http://www.cup.cam.ac.uk/elt/corpus/corpus_based_books.htm, accessed Oct. 30, 2009.

Cameron, D. 1995. *Verbal Hygiene*. London: Routledge.

Cameron, D. 2000. *Good to talk? Living and Working in a Communication Culture*. London: Sage.

Cameron, D. 2010. 'Globish by Robert McCrum'. Review of McCrum 2010. *The Guardian*, 5 June 2010, Guardian Review section, p. 9. Also on: http://www.guardian.co.uk/books/2010/jun/05/globish-robert-mccrum-review, accessed 14 Sept 2010.

Cameron, L. and D. Larsen-Freeman. 2007. 'Complex systems and applied linguistics'. *International Journal of Applied Linguistics* 17: 226–40.

Canagarajah, S. 1999. *Resisting Linguistic Imperialism in Language Teaching*. Oxford: Oxford University Press.

Canagarajah, S. (ed.). 2005. *Reclaiming the Local in Language Policy and Practice*. Mahwah, NJ: Lawrence Erlbaum.

Canagarajah, S. 2006a. 'Negotiating the local in English as a lingua franca'. *Annual Review of Applied Linguistics* 26: 197–218.

Canagarajah, S. 2006b. 'TESOL at forty: What are the issues?' *TESOL Quarterly* 40/1: 9–34.

Canagarajah, S. 2006c. 'Constructing a diaspora identity in English: the case of Sri Lankan Tamils' in J. Brutt-Griffler and C. Evans Davies (eds.): *English and Ethnicity (Signs of Race)*. Basingstoke: Palgrave Macmillan.

Canagarajah, S. 2007a. 'The ecology of Global English'. *International Multilingual Research Journal* 1931–3160, Volume 1, Issue 2: 89–100.

Canagarajah, S. 2007b. 'Lingua franca English, multilingual communities, and language acquisition'. *Modern Language Journal* 91 (focus issue): 923–39.

Carter, R. (ed.) 1990. *Knowledge about Language and the Curriculum*. Sevenoaks: Hodder and Stoughton.

Carter, R. 1998. 'Orders of Reality: CANCODE, communication, and culture'. *ELT Journal* 52/1: 43–56.

Carter, R. 2004. *Language and Creativity. The Art of Common Talk*. Abingdon: Routledge.

Carter, R. and M. McCarthy. 1997. *Exploring Spoken English*. Cambridge: Cambridge University Press.

Carter, R. and M. McCarthy. 2006. *Cambridge Grammar of English: A Comprehensive Guide. Spoken and Written English Grammar and Usage*. Cambridge: Cambridge University Press.

Catford, J. C. 1950. 'The background and origins of Basic English'. *English Language Teaching* 5: 36–47.

Cenoz, J. and N. Hornberger. (eds.). 2008. *Encyclopedia of Language and Education* (2nd edn.). Volume 6: *Knowledge about Language*. New York: Springer Science.

Chambers, J. 2002. 'Patterns of variation including change' in J. Chambers, P. Trudgill, and N. Schilling-Estes (eds.): *The Handbook of Language Variation and Change*. Oxford: Blackwell.

Chambers, J. 2004. 'Dynamic typology and vernacular universals' in B. Kortmann (ed.): *Dialectology Meets Typology*. Berlin: Mouton de Gruyter.

Chambers, J. K. and P. Trudgill. 1998. *Dialectology* (2nd edn.). Cambridge: Cambridge University Press.

Chambers, J. K., P. Trudgill, and N. Schilling-Estes (eds.). 2002. *Handbook of Language Variation and Change*. Oxford: Blackwell.

Charles, M. and R. Marschan-Piekkari. 2002. 'Language training for enhanced horizontal communication: a challenge for MNCs'. *Business Communication Quarterly* 65/2: 9–29.

Chevillet, F. 1994. *Histoire de la langue anglaise*. Paris: Presses universitaires de France.

Chomsky, N. 1965. *Syntactic Structures*. London: Mouton.

Clyne, M. 2006. 'Some thoughts on pragmatics, sociolinguistic variation, and intercultural communication'. *Intercultural Pragmatics* 3: 95–105.

Clyne, M. and F. Sharifian. (eds.). 2008. 'English as an international language: challenges and possibilities'. Special forum issue, *Australian Review of Applied Linguistics* 31/3.

Cogo, A. 2007. 'Intercultural communication in English as a lingua franca: a case study'. PhD dissertation, King's College London.

Cogo, A. 2009. 'Accommodating difference in ELF conversations: a study of pragmatic strategies' in A. Mauranen and E. Ranta (eds.): *English as a Lingua Franca: Studies and Findings*. Newcastle upon Tyne: Cambridge Scholars Publishing.

Cogo A. 2010. 'Strategic use and perceptions of English as a lingua franca'. *Poznań Studies in Contemporary Linguistics*, 46/3: 295–312.

Cogo, A. and M. Dewey. 2006. 'Efficiency in ELF communication: from pragmatic motives to lexico-grammatical innovation'. *Nordic Journal of English Studies* 5/2: 59–93.

Cogo, A. and M. Dewey. 2011. *Analysing English as a Lingua Franca. A corpus-driven investigation*. London: Continuum.

Cohen, A. 1998. *Strategies in Learning and Using a Second Language*. London: Longman.

Cohen, A. and E. Macaro. 2007. *Language Learner Strategies: Thirty Years of Research and Practice*. Oxford: Oxford University Press.

Collins English Dictionary. 2010. (30th edn.). London: Harper Collins.

Collins Website. 2004. http://www.collins.co.uk/books.aspx?group=57, accessed Oct. 30, 2009.

Compact Oxford English Dictionary of Current English. 2008. Oxford: Oxford University Press.

Cook, G. 2010. *Translation in Language Teaching*. Oxford: Oxford University Press.

Cook, V. 1999. 'Going beyond the native speaker in language teaching'. *TESOL Quarterly* 33: 185–209.

Cook, V. (ed.). 2002. *Portraits of the L2 User*. Clevedon: Multilingual Matters.

Cook, V. (ed.). 2003. *Effects of the Second Language on the First*. Clevedon: Multilingual Matters.

Cook, V. 2007. 'The goals of ELT: Reproducing native-speakers or promoting multicompetence among second language users? in J. Cummins and C. Davison (eds.): *International Handbook of English Language Teaching*, Part 1, 237–248.

Coppieters, R. 1987. 'Competence differences between native and near-native speakers'. *Language* 63: 544–73.

Corbett, J. 2003. *An Intercultural Approach to English Language Teaching*. Clevedon: Multilingual Matters.

Corbett, J. 2010. *Intercultural Language Activities*. Cambridge: Cambridge University Press.

Coulmas, F. (ed.). 1981. *A Festschrift for Native Speaker*. Gravenhage: Mouton.

Council of Europe. 2001. *Common European Framework of Reference for Languages: Learning, teaching, assessment*. Cambridge: Cambridge University Press.

Coupland, N. 2000. 'Sociolinguistic prevarication about standard English'. *Journal of Sociolinguistics* 4/4: 622–34.

Coupland, N. (ed.) 2010. *The Handbook of Language and Globalization*. Malden, MA and Oxford: Wiley-Blackwell.

Crystal, D. 2003*a*. *The Cambridge Encyclopedia of the English Language* (2nd edn.). Cambridge: Cambridge University Press.

Crystal, D. 2003*b*. *English as a Global Language* (2nd edn.). Cambridge: Cambridge University Press.

Crystal, D. 2004. *The Language Revolution*. Cambridge: Polity Press.

Crystal, D. 2006*a*. 'English worldwide' in R. Hogg and D. Denison (eds.): *A History of the English Language*. Cambridge: Cambridge University Press.

Crystal, D. 2006*b*. *Language and the Internet* (2nd edn.). Cambridge: Cambridge University Press.

Cummins, J. and C. Davison (eds.). 2007. *International Handbook of English Language Teaching*. New York: Springer.

Dalton, C. and B. Seidlhofer. 1994. *Pronunciation (A Scheme for Teacher Education)*. Oxford: Oxford University Press.

Dam, L. (ed.). 2001. *Learner Autonomy: New Insights/Autonomie de l'apprenant: nouvelles pistes*. Special issue of AILA Review, 15. Amsterdam: Free University Press.

Daniels, H. 1995. 'Psycholinguistic, psycho-affective and procedural factors in the acquisition of authentic L2 pronunciation'. *Speak Out!* 15, 3–10. Reprinted in McLean, A. (ed.) (1997): *SIG Selections 1997*. IATEFL: Whitstable.

Davies, A. 2003. *The Native Speaker: Myth and Reality*. Clevedon: Multilingual Matters.

Davies, M. 2004. BYU-BNC: *The British National Corpus*. Available online at http://corpus.byu.edu/bnc.

Delbridge, A., J. Bernard, D. Blair, W. Ramson, and S. Butler (eds.). 1981. *The Macquarie Dictionary*. Sydney: Macquarie Library.

Deterding, D. and A. Kirkpatrick. 2006. 'Intelligibility and an emerging ASEAN English lingua franca'. *World Englishes* 25 (3/4): 391–410.

Dewey, M. 2007*a*. 'English as a lingua franca and globalization: an interconnected perspective'. *International Journal of Applied Linguistics* 17/3: 332–54.

Dewey, M. 2007*b*. 'English as a lingua franca: an empirical study of innovation in lexis and grammar'. PhD dissertation, King's College London.

Dewey, M. 2009. 'English as a lingua franca: heightened variability and theoretical implications' in A. Mauranen and E. Ranta (eds.): *English as a Lingua Franca: Studies and Findings*. Newcastle upon Tyne: Cambridge Scholars Publishing.

Dewey, M. and A. Cogo. 2007. 'Adopting an ELF perspective in ELT'. *IATEFL Voices*, Issue 1999.

Dorn, N. 2010. 'Exploring *–ing*: the progressive in English as a lingua franca'. MA dissertation, University of Vienna.

Dörnyei, Z. 2009. *The Psychology of Second Language Acquisition*. Oxford: Oxford University Press.

Dunbar, R. 1996. *Grooming, Gossip, and the Evolution of Language*. Cambridge, MA: Harvard University Press.

Dziubalska-Kołaczyk, K. and J. Przedlacka. (eds.). 2005/2008. *English Pronunciation Models: A Changing Scene* (2nd edn.). Frankfurt am Main: Peter Lang.

Eckert, P. and S. McConnell-Ginet. 1992. 'Think practically and look locally: language and gender as community-based practice'. *Annual Review of Anthropology* 21: 461–90.

Edmondson, W. 2009. 'Language awareness' in K. Knapp and B. Seidlhofer (eds.): *Handbook of Foreign Language Communication and Learning (Handbooks of Applied Linguistics, Volume 6)*. Berlin and New York: Mouton de Gruyter.

Ehlich, K. and H.-J. Meyer. 2011. Zur künftigen Rolle des Deutschen in der Wissenschaft und zu den Chancen wissenschaftlicher Mehrsprachigkeit. Mimeo. http://www.adsic.de/admin/upload/navigation/data/K.%20Ehlich%20-%20H.%20J.%20Meyer%20Thesen%20Tutzing%2010%2001%2011.pdf

Ehrenreich, S. 2009. 'English as a lingua franca in multinational corporations–exploring business communities of practice' in A. Mauranen and E. Ranta (eds.): *English as a Lingua Franca: Studies and Findings*. Newcastle upon Tyne: Cambridge Scholars Publishing.

Ehrenreich, S. 2010. 'LT English as a Business Lingua Franca in a German Multinational Corporation: Meeting the Challenge'. *Journal of Business Communication*, September 9, 2010 Vol. 4/4: 408–31; *EL Gazette*, September 2008.

Ellis, R. 2003. *Task-based Language Learning and Teaching*. Oxford: Oxford University Press.

Erman, B. and B. Warren. 2000. 'The idiom principle and the open choice principle'. *Text* 20/1: 29–62.

Facchinetti, R., D. Crystal, and B. Seidlhofer (eds.). 2010. *From International to Local English—and Back Again*. Frankfurt: Peter Lang.

Ferguson, G. 2006. *Language Planning and Education*. Edinburgh: Edinburgh University Press.

Ferguson, G. 2009. 'Issues in researching English as a lingua franca: a conceptual enquiry'. *International Journal of Applied Linguistics* 19/2: 117–217.

Filppula, M., J. Klemola, and H. Paulasto (eds.). 2009. *Vernacular Universals and Language Contacts: Evidence from Varieties of English and Beyond*. London: Routledge.

Firth, A. 1996. 'The discursive accomplishment of normality. On "lingua franca" English and conversation analysis'. *Journal of Pragmatics* 26: 237–59.

Firth, A. 2009. 'The lingua franca factor'. *Intercultural Pragmatics*. Band 6/2:147–70.

Firth, A. and J. Wagner. 1997. 'On discourse, communication, and (some) fundamental concepts in SLA research'. *The Modern Language Journal* 81/3: 285–300.

Firth, A. and J. Wagner. 2007. 'Second/foreign language learning as a social accomplishment: elaborations on a reconceptualized SLA'. *The Modern Language Journal* 91/1: 800–19.

Fishman, J. A. 1971. 'The sociology of language: an interdisciplinary social science approach to language in society' in J. A. Fishman (ed.): *Advances in the Sociology of Language*. The Hague: Mouton.

Fishman, J. A., A. W. Conrad, and A. Rubal-Lopez (eds.). 1996. *Post-Imperial English: Status Change in Former British and American Colonies, 1940–1990*. Berlin, New York: Mouton de Gruyter.

Forey, G. and J. Lockwood. 2007. ' "I'd love to put someone in jail for this": an initial investigation of English in the business processing outsourcing (BPO) industry'. *English for Specific Purposes* 26: 308–26.

Gal, S. 2010. *Linguistic Regimes and European Diversity*. Abstract for plenary talk at the New Challenges for Multilingualism in Europe Conference, Dubrovnik, 11–15 April 2010. (http://www.amiando.com/lineeconference.html?page=295530)

Gavioli, L. and G. Aston. 2001. 'Enriching reality: language corpora in language pedagogy'. *ELT Journal* 55/3: 238–46.

Giles, H. and N. Coupland. 1991. *Language: Contexts and Consequences.* Milton Keynes: Open University Press.

Giles, H., N. Coupland, and J. Coupland. (eds.). 1991. *Contexts of Accommodation: Developments in Applied Sociolinguistics.* Cambridge: Cambridge University Press.

Gilquin, G. 2008. 'Hesitation markers among EFL learners: Pragmatic deficiency or difference?' in J. Romero-Trillo (ed.): *Pragmatics and Corpus Linguistics: A Mutualistic Entente.* Berlin: Mouton de Gruyter.

Gilquin, G. and Å. Viberg. 2009. 'How to make do with one verb: a corpus-based contrastive study of DO and MAKE'. *Revue française de lingüistique appliquée*, 14/1: 67–82.

Gleick, J. 1987. *Chaos: Making a New Science.* New York: Penguin Books.

Gnutzmann, C. (ed.). 1999. *Teaching and Learning English as a Global Language. Native and Non-native Perspectives.* Tübingen: Stauffenburg.

Gnutzmann, C. and F. Intemann (eds.). 2008. *The Globalisation of English and the English Language Classroom* (2nd edn.). Tübingen: Gunter Narr.

Goebl, H., P. H. Nelde, Z. Starý, and W. Wölck (eds.). 1996. *Contact Linguistics/Lingüistique de Contact/Kontaktlinguistik. An International Handbook of Contemporary Research/ Manuel international des recherches contemporaines/Ein internationales Handbuch zeitgenössischer Forschung.* Vol.1 and 2. Berlin and New York: Walter de Gruyter.

Gordon, E. and T. Deverson. 1998. *New Zealand English and English in New Zealand.*

Görlach, M. 1991. *Englishes: Studies in Varieties of English, 1984–1988.* Amsterdam: John Benjamins.

Görlach, M. 1995. *More Englishes: New Studies in Varieties of English, 1988–1994.* Amsterdam: John Benjamins.

Görlach, M. 1998. *Even More Englishes: Studies, 1996–1997.* Amsterdam: John Benjamins.

Görlach, M. 1999. 'Varieties of English and language teaching' in C. Gnutzmann (ed.): *Teaching and Learning English as a Global Language. Native and Non-Native Perspectives.* Tübingen: Stauffenburg. 3–21.

Görlach, M. 2002. *Still More Englishes.* Amsterdam: John Benjamins.

Grace, G. 1981. 'Indirect inheritance and the aberrant Melanesian languages' in J. Hollyman and A. Pawley (eds.): *Studies in Pacific Languages and Cultures in Honour of Bruce Biggs.* Auckland: Linguistic Society of New Zealand.

Graddol, D. 1997. *The Future of English?* London: British Council.

Graddol, D. 2006. *English Next: Why Global English May Mean the End of 'English as a Foreign Language'.* London: British Council.

Gramkow Anderson, K. 1993. 'Lingua franca discourse: an investigation of the use of English in an international business context'. Unpublished MA dissertation, Alborg University.

Granger, S. 2003. 'The international corpus of learner English: a new resource for foreign language learning and teaching and second language acquisition research', *TESOL Quarterly*, 373 538–546.

Granger, S. 2008. 'Learner corpora' in A. Lüdeling and M. Kytö (eds.): *Corpus Linguistics. An International Handbook. Volume 1.* Berlin: Mouton de Gruyter.

Greenbaum, S. (ed.). 1996. *Comparing English Worldwide. The International Corpus of English.* Oxford: Clarendon.

Grzega, J. 2006. 'Globish and Basic Global English (BGE): two alternatives for a rapid acquisition of communicative competence in a globalized world'. *Journal for EuroLinguistiX* 3: 1–13.

Guido, M. G. 2008. *English as a Lingua Franca in Cross-cultural Immigration Domains.* Frankfurt am Main: Peter Lang.

Gut, U. 2004. 'Nigerian English—phonology' in B. Kortmann and E. Schneider (eds.): *A Handbook of Varieties of English.* Amsterdam: Mouton de Gruyter.

Hall, S. 1990. 'Cultural identity and diaspora' in J. Rutherford: *Identity. Community, Culture, Difference.* London: Lawrence and Wishart.

Halliday, M. A. K. 1975. *Learning How to Mean: Explorations in the Development of Language.* London: Edward Arnold.

Halliday, M. A. K. 1978. *Language as Social Semiotic*. London: Edward Arnold.

Halliday, M. A. K. 1994. *An Introduction to Functional Grammar* (2nd edn.). London: Arnold.

Halliday, M. A. K., A. McIntosh, and P. Strevens. 1964. *The Linguistic Sciences and Language Teaching*. London: Longman.

Halliday, M. A. K. and C. M. I. M. Matthiessen. 2004. *An Introduction to Functional Grammar* (3rd edn.). London: Arnold.

Haugen, E. 1972. *The Ecology of Language: Essays by Einar Haugen*. Selected and introduced by Anwar S. Dil. Stanford: Stanford University Press.

Haugen, E. 2001. 'The Ecology of Language' (reprint of Haugen 1972) in A. Fill and P. Mühlhäusler (eds.): *The Ecolinguistics Reader: Language, Ecology and Environment*. London and New York: Continuum.

Hawkins, E. 1984. *Awareness of Language: An Introduction*, Cambridge: Cambridge University Press.

Held, D. and A. McGrew. 2001. 'Globalization' in J. Krieger (ed.): *The Oxford Companion to Politics of the World* (2nd edn.). Oxford: Oxford University Press; also available online at: http://www.polity.co.uk/global/globalization-oxford.asp (29.10.09).

Heller, M. (ed.). 2007. *Bilingualism. Advances in Linguistics*. London, Basingstoke: Palgrave Macmillan.

Herdina, P. and U. Jessner. 2002. *A Dynamic Model of Multilingualism: Changing the Psycholinguistic Perspective*. Clevedon: Multilingual Matters.

Hickey, R. (ed.). 2010. *The Handbook of Language Contact*. Oxford: Wiley-Blackwell.

Hoffman, C. 2000. 'The Spread of English and the Growth of Multilingualism with English in Europe' in J. Cenoz and U. Jessner: *English in Europe: The Acquisition of a Third Language*. Clevedon: Multilingual Matters.

Hoffmann, T. and L. Siebers (eds.). 2009. *World Englishes—Problems, Properties and Prospects. Selected papers from the 13th IAWE conference*. javascript:zoom('Hardbound, e-Book,/178/veaw_g40.png')Amsterdam: John Benjamins.

Hofstede, G. 1991. *Cultures and Organizations*. London: McGraw Hill.

Holliday, A. 1994. *Appropriate Methodology and Social Context*. Cambridge: Cambridge University Press.

Holliday, A. 2005. *The Struggle to Teach English as an International Language*. Oxford: Oxford University Press.

Holliday, A. 2009a. 'The role of culture in English language education: key challenges'. *Language and Intercultural Communication* 9/3: 144–55.

Holliday, A. 2009b. 'English as a lingua franca, "non-native speakers" and cosmopolitan realities' in F. Sharifian (ed.): *English as an International Language. Perspectives and Pedagogical Issues*.

Holliday, A., M. Hyde, and J. Kullman. 2004. *Intercultural communication* London: Routledge.

Honna, N. 2008. *English as a Multicultural Language in Asian Contexts: Issues and Ideas*. Tokyo: Kurosio Publishers.

Hopper, P. 1998. 'Emergent grammar' in M. Tomasello (ed.): *The New Psychology of Language*. Mahwah, NJ: Lawrence Erlbaum.

House, J. 1999. 'Misunderstanding in intercultural communication: interactions in English as a *lingua franca* and the myth of mutual intelligibility' in C. Gnutzmann (ed.): *Teaching and Learning English as a Global Language*. Tübingen: Stauffenburg.

House, J. 2002. 'Developing pragmatic competence in English as a lingua franca' in K. Knapp and C. Meierkord (eds.): *Lingua Franca Communication*. Frankfurt: Peter Lang.

House, J. 2003. 'English as a lingua franca: a threat to multilingualism?' *Journal of Sociolinguistics* 7/4: 556–78.

Housen, A. and F. Kuiken. 2009. 'Complexity, accuracy, and fluency in second language acquisition'. *Applied Linguistics* 30/4: 461–73.

Howatt, A. P. R. with H. G. Widdowson. 2004. *A History of English Language Teaching* (2nd edn.). Oxford: Oxford University Press.

Huddleston, R. 2008. 'Review of Ronald Carter and Michael McCarthy *Cambridge Grammar of English: A comprehensive guide.* Cambridge: Cambridge University Press 2006'. *English Language and Linguistics* 12/1: 169–87.

Huddleston, R. and G. K. Pullum, in collaboration with L. Bauer (ed.). 2002. *The Cambridge Grammar of the English Language.* Cambridge: Cambridge University Press.

Hülmbauer, C. 2007. ' "You moved, aren't?"—The relationship between lexicogrammatical correctness and communicative effectiveness in English as a lingua franca'. *Vienna English Working Papers* 16/2: 3–35. Available at: http://anglistik.univie.ac.at/fileadmin/user_upload/dep_anglist/weitere_Uploads/Views/Views_0702.pdf).

Hülmbauer, C. 2009. ' "We don't take the right way. We just take the way that we think you will understand"—the shifting relationship between correctness and effectiveness in ELF' in A. Mauranen and E. Ranta (eds.): *English as a Lingua Franca: Studies and Findings.* Newcastle upon Tyne: Cambridge Scholars Publishing.

Hülmbauer, C. and B. Seidlhofer. 2011. 'Common sense and common practice: ELF research and conceptions of multilingualism'. Working Paper 5 of Research Team 4.2. Project DYLAN (Language Dynamics and Management of Diversity).

Hymes, D. 1962. 'The ethnography of speaking' in T. Gladwin and W. C. Sturtevant (eds.): *Anthropology and Human Behavior.* Washington, DC: Anthropological Society of Washington.

Hymes, D. 1972. 'On communicative competence' in J. B. Pride and J. Holmes. (eds.): *Sociolinguistics.* Harmondsworth: Penguin.

Hymes, D. 1989. 'Ways of Speaking' in R. Bauman and J. Sherzer (eds.): *Explorations in the Ethnography of Speaking* (2nd edn.). Cambridge: Cambridge University Press.

ICE (International Corpus of English) Website. 2009. http://ice-corpora.net/ice/index.htm Accessed Oct. 30, 2009.

ICE (International Corpus of English) Website. 2009. 'Joining the ICE Project.' http://ice-corpora.net/ice/joinice.htm. Accessed Oct. 30, 2009.

ICE Nigeria website. N.d. http://ice-corpora.net/ice/icenige.htm. Accessed Oct 30, 2009.

Igboanusi, H. 2002. *A Dictionary of Nigerian English Usage.* Ibadan: Enicrownfit.

Intemann, F. 2005. 'Taipei ground, confirm your last transmission was in English … ?' an analysis of aviation English as a world language, in C. Gnutzmann and F. Intemann: *The Globalisation of English and the English Language Classroom* (2nd edn.). 2008.

Jaquemet, M. 2005. 'Transidiomatic practices: language and power in the age of globalization'. *Language and Communication* 25/3: 257–77.

James, A. 2000. 'English as a European lingua franca. Current realities and existing dichotomies' in J. Cenoz and U. Jessner: *English in Europe. The Acquisition of a Third Language.* Clevedon: Multilingual Matters.

Jenkins, J. 1998. 'Rethinking phonology in teacher education'. *Vienna English Working Papers* 7/1: 40–6.

Jenkins, J. 2000. *The Phonology of English as an International Language. New Models, New Norms, New Goals.* Oxford: Oxford University Press.

Jenkins, J. 2002. 'A sociolinguistically based, empirically researched pronunciation syllabus for English as an International Language'. *Applied Linguistics* 23/1: 83–103.

Jenkins, J. 2006a. 'Points of view and blind spots: ELF and SLA'. *International Journal of Applied Linguistics* 16/2: 137–62.

Jenkins, J. 2006b. 'Current perspectives on teaching World Englishes and English as a Lingua Franca'. *TESOL Quarterly* 40/1: 157–81.

Jenkins, J. 2006c. 'The spread of EIL: A testing time for testers'. *ELT Journal* 60/1: 42–50.

Jenkins, J. 2006d. 'The times they are (very slowly) a-changin'. *ELT Journal* 60/1: 61–2.

Jenkins, J. 2007. *English as a Lingua Franca: Attitude and Identity.* Oxford: Oxford University Press.

Jenkins, J. 2009. *World Englishes: A Resource Book for Students* (2nd edn.). London: Routledge.

Jenkins, J., A. Cogo, and M. Dewey. 2011. 'Review of developments in research into English as a lingua franca'. *Language Teaching* 44/3: 281–315. Cambridge: Cambridge University Press.

Jenkins, J. and C. Leung. 2011. 'Testing English as a lingua franca' in A. J. Kunnan (ed.): *The Companion to Language Assessment*. Oxford: Blackwell.

Jessner, U. 2006. *Linguistic Awareness in Multilinguals: English as a Third Language*. Edinburgh: Edinburgh University Press.

Jones, S. and P. Bradwell. 2007. *As You Like It. Catching up in an Age of Global English*. London: Demos. Also available on: http://www.demos.co.uk/publications/asyoulikeitpamphlet, 22/10/2010)

Jørgensen, J. N. 2008. 'Polylingual languaging around and among children and adolescents'. *International Journal of Multilingualism* 5/3: 161–76.

Joseph, J. E. 2004. *Language and Identity: National, Ethnic, Religious*. Basingstoke: Palgrave Macmillan.

Jowitt, D. 1991. *Nigerian English Usage. An Introduction*. Ikeja: Longman Nigeria.

Kachru, B. B. 1985. 'Standards, codification and sociolinguistic realism: the English language in the outer circle' in R. Quirk and H. G. Widdowson (eds.): *English in the World: Teaching and Learning the Languages and Literatures*. Cambridge: Cambridge University Press. 11–30.

Kachru, B. B. (ed.). 1992. *The Other Tongue: English across Cultures* (2nd edn.). Chicago: University of Illinois Press.

Kachru, B. B. 1996a. 'English as lingua franca / Englisch als lingua franca / L'anglais comme «lingua franca»' in H. Goebl, P. H. Nelde, Z. Starý, and W. Wölck (eds.): *Contact Linguistics Linguistique de Contact/Kontaktlinguistik. An International Handbook of Contemporary Research/Manuel international des recherches contemporaines/Ein internationales Handbuch zeitgenössischer Forschung*. Volume 1. Berlin and New York: Walter de Gruyter.

Kachru, B. B. 1996b. 'The paradigms of marginality'. *World Englishes* 15: 241–55.

Kachru, B. B. 1997. 'World Englishes and English-using communities'. *Annual Review of Applied Linguistics* 17: 66–87. Cambridge and New York: Cambridge University Press.

Kachru, B. B. 2005. *Asian Englishes. Beyond the Canon*. Hong Kong: Hong Kong University Press.

Kachru, B. B. 2006. 'Standards, codification and sociolinguistic realism: the English language in the outer circle' (reprint of Kachru 1985) in K. Bolton and B. B. Kachru (eds.): *World Englishes. Critical Concepts in Linguistics*. Abingdon: Routledge.

Kachru, B. B., Y. Kachru, and C. Nelson (eds.). 2006. *The Handbook of World Englishes*. Malden, MA: Blackwell.

Kachru, Y. 2005. 'Teaching and learning of World Englishes' in E. Hinkel (ed.): *Handbook of Research in Second Language Learning and Teaching*. Mahwah, NJ: Lawrence Erlbaum.

Kamhi-Stein, L. D. (ed.). 2004. *Learning and Teaching from Experience: Perspectives on Nonnative English Speaking Professionals*. Ann Arbor, MI: University of Michigan Press.

Kankaanranta A. and B. Planken. 2010. 'BELF competence as business knowledge of internationally operating business professionals'. *Journal of Business Communication* 47/4: 380–407.

Kaplan, R. B. and R. B. Baldauf. 1997. *Language Planning from Practice to Theory*. Clevedon. Multilingual Matters.

Kasper, G. and E. Kellerman, E. (eds.) 1997. *Communication Strategies*. London: Longman.

Kaur J. 2009. 'Pre-empting problems of understanding in English as a lingua franca' in A. Mauranen and E. Ranta (eds.).

Kecskes, I. 2007. 'Formulaic language in English lingua franca' in I. Kecskes and L. Horn (eds.): *Explorations in Pragmatics: Linguistic, Cognitive and Intercultural Aspects*. Berlin and New York: Mouton de Gruyter.

Kecskes, I. and T. Papp. 2000. *Foreign Language and Mother Tongue*. Hillsdale, NJ: Lawrence Erlbaum.

Kerswill, P. 2002. 'Koineization and accommodation' in J. K. Chambers, P. Trudgill, and N. Schilling-Estes (eds.): *Handbook of Language Variation and Change*. Oxford: Blackwell.

Kirkpatrick, A. 2007a. 'Setting attainable and appropriate English language targets in multilingual settings: a case for Hong Kong'. *International Journal of Applied Linguistics* 17/3: 376–91.

Kirkpatrick, A. 2007*b*. *World Englishes: Implications for International Communication and English Language Teaching*. Cambridge: Cambridge University Press.

Kirkpatrick, A. 2010*a*. *English as a Lingua Franca in ASEAN: A Multilingual Model*. Hong Kong: Hong Kong University Press.

Kirkpatrick, A. 2010*b*. *The Routledge Handbook of World Englishes*. Abingdon: Routledge.

Klimpfinger, T. 2009. ' "She's mixing the two languages together"—forms and functions of code-switching in English as a lingua franca' in A. Mauranen, and E. Ranta (eds.): *English as a Lingua Franca: Studies and Findings*. Newcastle upon Tyne: Cambridge Scholars Publishing.

Knapp, K. 1987. 'English as an international *lingua franca* and the teaching of intercultural communication' in W. Lörscher and R. Schulze (eds.): *Perspectives on Language in Performance. Tübinger Beiträge zur Linguistik* 317/2. Tübingen: Narr.

Knapp, K. and C. Meierkord (eds.). 2002. *Lingua Franca Communication*. Frankfurt am Main: Peter Lang.

Koester A. 2010. *Workplace Discourse*. London: Continuum.

Kohn, K. 2007. 'Englisch als globale Lingua Franca. Eine Herausforderung für die Schule' in T. Anstatt (Hg.): *Mehrsprachigkeit bei Kindern und Erwachsenen*. Tübingen: Gunter Narr.

Kortmann, B. 2010. 'Variation across Englishes syntax' in A. Kirkpatrick (ed.): *The Routledge Handbook of World Englishes*. Abingdon: Routledge.

Kortmann, B. and E. W. Schneider, with K. Burridge, R. Mesthrie, and C. Upton (eds.): 2004. *A Handbook of Varieties of English*. Vol. 2: *Morphology and Syntax*. Berlin and New York: Mouton de Gruyter.

Kortmann, B. and E. W. Schneider. (eds.). 2008. *Varieties of English* (4 vols.). Berlin: Mouton de Gruyter.

Kotthoff, H. and H. Spencer-Oatey. (eds.). 2009. *Handbook of Intercultural Communication (Handbooks of Applied Linguistics, Volume 7)*. Berlin and New York: Mouton de Gruyter.

Kramsch, C. 1993. *Context and Culture in Language Teaching*. Oxford: Oxford University Press.

Kramsch, C. 1997. 'The privilege of the non-native speaker' in *Publications of the Modern Languages Association* 112/3: 359–69.

Kramsch, C. 1998. 'The privilege of the intercultural speaker' in M. Byram and M. Fleming (eds.): *Language Learning in Intercultural Perspective: Approaches through Drama and Ethnography*. Cambridge: Cambridge University Press.

Kramsch, C. 2009. *The Multilingual Subject*. Oxford: Oxford University Press.

Kramsch, C. and P. Sullivan. 1996. 'Appropriate pedagogy'. *ELT Journal* 50/3: 199–212.

Kuhn, T. S. 1962. *The Structure of Scientific Revolutions* (1st edn.). Chicago: University of Chicago Press.

Kujore, O. 1985. *English Usage: Some Notable Nigerian Variations*. Ibadan: Evans.

Kuo, I-C. 2006. 'Addressing the issue of teaching English as a lingua franca'. *ELT Journal* 60/3: 213–21.

Labov, W. 1972. *Sociolinguistic Patterns*. Philadelphia: University of Pennsylvania Press.

Labov, W. 1984. 'Field methods of the project on linguistic change and variation' in J. Baugh, and J. Scherzer (eds.): *Language in Use*. New York: Englewood Cliffs 28–53.

Lambert, W. E., R. C. Hodgson, R. C. Gardner, and S. Fillenbaum. 1960. 'Evaluational reactions to spoken language'. *Journal of Abnormal and Social Psychology* 60/1: 44–51.

Langlotz, A. 2006. *Idiomatic Creativity: A Cognitive-linguistic Model of Idiom-representation and Idiom-variation in English*. Amsterdam: John Benjamins.

Lantolf, J. P. and S. L. Thorne (eds.). 2006. *Sociocultural Theory and the Genesis of Second Language Development*. Oxford: Oxford University Press.

Larsen-Freeman, D. and L. Cameron. 2008. *Complex Systems and Applied Linguistics*. Oxford: Oxford University Press.

Le Page, R. B. and A. Tabouret-Keller. 1985. *Acts of Identity: Creole-based Approaches to Ethnicity and Language*. Cambridge: Cambridge University Press.

Leech, G. 2004. 'Review of D. Crystal. 2003. *English as a global language*' (2nd edn.). Cambridge: Cambridge University Press. *Journal of Pragmatics* 36/11: 2077–2080.

Leung, C. 2005. 'Convivial communication: recontextualizing communicative competence'. *International Journal of Applied Linguistics* 15/2: 119–44.

Leung, C. and J. Lewkowicz. 2006. 'Expanding horizons and unresolved conundrums: language testing and assessment'. *TESOL Quarterly* 40/1: 211–34.

Leung, C. and J. Lewkowicz. 2008. 'Assessing second/additional language of diverse populations' in E. Shohamy and N. Hornberger (eds.) (2nd edn.): *Encyclopedia of Language and Education, Volume 7: Language Testing and Assessment*, 301–17.

Lichtkoppler, J. 2007. ' "Male. Male."—"Male?"—"The sex is male." The role of repetition in English as a lingua franca conversations'. *Vienna English Working Papers* 16/1: 39–65. Available at: http://anglistik.univie.ac.at/fileadmin/user_upload/dep_anglist/weitere_Uploads/Views/views_0701.PDF).

Llurda, E. (ed.). 2005. *Non-native Language Teachers: Perceptions, Challenges and Contributions to the Profession*. New York, NY: Springer.

Llurda, E. 2009. 'Attitudes towards English as an international language: The pervasiveness of native models among L2 users and teachers' in F. Sharifian, 2009.

Longman Dictionary of English Language and Culture. 2005. (3rd. edn.). London: Longman Pearson.

Louhiala-Salminen, L., M. Charles, and A. Kankaanranta. 2005. 'English as a lingua franca in Nordic corporate mergers: two case companies'. *English for Specific Purposes* 24/4: 401–21.

Lowenberg, P. 2002. 'Assessing English proficiency in the expanding circle.' *World Englishes* 21/3: 431–35.

Lüdi, G. and B. Py. 2009. 'To be or not to be . . . a plurilingual speaker'. *International Journal of Multilingualism* 6/2: 154–167.

Lynch, T. 2009. *Teaching Second Language Listening*. Oxford: Oxford University Press.

Lyotard, J.-F. 1984. *The Postmodern Condition: A Report on Knowledge*. Manchester: Manchester University Press.

Mackey, W. F. 1965. *Language Teaching Analysis*. London: Longman.

Mair, C. 2003. 'Kreolismen und verbales Identitätsmanagement im geschriebenen jamaikanischen Englisch' in E. Vogel, A. Napp, and W. Lutterer (eds.): *Zwischen Ausgrenzung und Hybridisierung*. Würzburg: Ergon.

Mair, C. 2006. *Twentieth-century English: History, Variation, and Standardization*. Cambridge: Cambridge University Press.

Makoni, S. and A. Pennycook (eds.). 2007. *Disinventing and Reconstituting Languages*. Clevedon: Multilingual Matters.

Maley, A. 2006. 'Questions of English'. *English Teaching Professional* 46: 4–6.

Maley, A. 2009. 'ELF: a teacher's perspective'. *Language and Intercultural Communication* 9/3: 187–200.

Mauranen A. 2005. 'English as a lingua franca: an unknown language?' in G. Cortese and A. Duszak (eds.): *Identity, Community and Discourse: English in Intercultural Settings*. Frankfurt: Peter Lang.

Mauranen, A. 2006. 'A rich domain of ELF: the ELFA corpus of academic discourse'. *Nordic Journal of English Studies* 5/2: 145–59.

Mauranen A. 2009. 'Chunking in ELF: Expressions for managing interaction'. *Intercultural Pragmatics* 6/2: 217–33.

Mauranen A. Forthcoming. *Exploring ELF in Academia*. Cambridge: Cambridge University Press.

Mauranen, A. and E. Ranta. 2008. 'English as an academic lingua franca – The ELFA Project'. *Nordic Journal of English Studies* 7/3: 199–202.

Mauranen, A. and E. Ranta (eds.). 2009. *English as a Lingua Franca: Studies and Findings*. Newcastle upon Tyne: Cambridge Scholars Publishing.

Mauranen A., C. Pérez-Llantada, and J. M. Swales. 2010. 'Academic Englishes. A standardized knowledge?' in A. Kirkpatrick (ed.): *The Routledge Handbook of World Englishes*. Abingdon: Routledge.

May, D. 2000. 'It just isn't English'. *The Times*, 24 March 2000: 4.

McArthur, T. 1998. *The English Languages*. Cambridge: Cambridge University Press.

McArthur, T. 2001. 'World English and world Englishes: trends, tensions, varieties and standards'. *Language Teaching* 34/1: 1–20.

McArthur, T. 2002. *The Oxford Guide to World English*. Oxford: Oxford University Press.

McCrum, R. 2010. *Globish: How the English Language Became the World's Language*. London: Viking.

McGrath, R. 1934. *Twentieth Century Houses*. London: Faber and Faber.

McKay, S. 2002. *Teaching English as an International Language: Rethinking Goals and Approaches*. Oxford: Oxford University Press.

McKay, S. and W. Bokhorst-Heng. 2008. *Interactional English in its Sociolinguistic Contexts. Towards a Socially Sensitive EIL Pedagogy*. New York: Routledge.

McNamara, T. 2011. 'Managing learning: authority and language assessment'. *Language Teaching* 44/3.

McNamara, T. and C. Roever. 2006. *Language Testing: The Social Turn*. Oxford: Blackwell.

Medgyes, P. 1994/1999. *The Non-Native Teacher*. London: Macmillan. Revised edition 1998: Ismaning: Max Hueber Verlag.

Metsä-Ketelä M. 2006. 'Words are more or less superfluous'. *Nordic Journal of English Studies* 5/2: 117–43.

Meierkord, C. 2002 ' "Language stripped bare" or "linguistic masala"? Culture in lingua franca communication' in K. Knapp and C. Meierkord (eds.): *Lingua Franca Communication*. Frankfurt am Main: Peter Lang.

Melchers, G. and P. Shaw. 2003. *World Englishes*. London: Arnold.

Mesthrie, R. and R. M. Bhatt. 2008. *World Englishes. The Study of New Linguistic Varieties*. Cambridge: Cambridge University Press.

Milroy, J. 2001. 'Language ideologies and the consequences of standardization'. *Journal of Sociolinguistics* 5/4: 530–55.

Mollin. L. 2006. *Euro-English: Assessing Variety Status*. Tübingen: Gunter Narr.

Mondada, L. 2004. 'Ways of "doing being plurilingual" in international work meetings' in R.Gardner and J. Wagner (eds.): *Second Language Conversations*. London: Continuum.

Moore, S. and S. Bounchan. 2010. 'English in Cambodia: changes and challenges'. *World Englishes* 29/1: 114–26.

Mufwene, S. S. 2001. *The Ecology of Language Evolution*. Cambridge: Cambridge University Press.

Mufwene, S. S. 2004. 'Language birth and death'. *Annual Review of Anthropology* 33: 201–22.

Mühlhäusler, P. 1996. *Linguistic Ecology. Language Change and Linguistic Imperialism in the Pacific Region*. London: Routledge.

Mühlhäusler, P. 2000. 'Language planning and language ecology'. *Current Issues in Language Planning* 1/3: 306–67.

Myers-Scotton, C. 2002. *Contact Linguistics: Bilingual Encounters and Grammatical Outcomes*. Oxford: Oxford University Press.

Nelson, G. (ed.) 2004. *World Englishes*. Special Issue on ICE: Volume 23/2: 225–337.

Nerrière, J.-P. and D. Hon. 2009. *Globish The World Over*. E-book, available from http://www.globish.com/estore/catalog.php?item=44. Accessed 14 Sept 2010.

Ngugi wa Thiong'o. 1981a. *Education for a National Culture, 1981*. Harare: Zimbabwe Publishing House.

Ngugi wa Thiong'o. 1981b. *Detained: A Writer's Prison Diary, 1981*. Nairobi: Heinemann Educational Publishers.

Norton, B. 2000. *Identity and Language Learning: Gender, Ethnicity and Educational Change*. Harlow: Longman.

Ogden, C. K. 1930/1938. *Basic English. A General Introduction with Rules and Grammar*. London: Kegan Paul.

Ogden, C. K. (ed.). 1932. *Bentham's Theory of Fictions*. London: Kegan Paul.

Ogden, C. K. and I. A. Richards. 1923. *The Meaning of Meaning*. New York: Harcourt Brace and Co.

Ortega, L. 2010. *The Bilingual Turn in SLA*. Plenary delivered at the Annual Conference of the American Association for Applied Linguistics. Atlanta, GA, March 6–9.

Orwell, G. 1961. *Collected Essays*. London: Secker and Warburg.

Osimk, R. 2009a. 'Decoding sounds: an experimental approach to intelligibility in ELF'. *Vienna English Working Papers* 18/1: 64–89. (Available at http://anglistik.univie.ac.at/fileadmin/user_upload/dep_anglist/weitere_Uploads/Views/0901final.pdf)

Osimk, R. 2009b. Verständlichkeit in Englisch als Lingua Franca. Die Rolle von Aspiration, [θ]/[ð] und /r/. Saarbrücken: VDM-Verlag Müller.

Osimk, R. 2010. 'Testing the intelligibility of ELF sounds'. *Speak Out!* 42: 14–18.

Ostler, N. 2010. *The Last Lingua Franca. English Until the Return of Babel*. London: Allen Lane.

Oxford Advanced Learner's Dictionary (8th. edn.). 2010. Oxford: Oxford University Press.

Oxford Compact English Dictionary of Current English (3rd edn.). 2005. Oxford: Oxford University Press.

Oxford English Dictionary. 1989. (2nd edn.). Oxford: Oxford University Press.

Oxford, R. 2000. 'Communicative strategies' in M. Byram (ed.): *Routledge Encyclopedia of Language Teaching and Learning*. Abingdon: Routledge

Palmer, H. E. and A. S. Hornby. 1937. *Thousand-Word English. What it is and what can be done with it*. London: Harrap.

Park, J. and L. Wee, L. 2009. 'The three circles redux: a market-theoretic perspective on world Englishes'. *Applied Linguistics* 30/3: 389–406.

Pavlenko, A. and A. Blackledge (eds.). 2004. *Negotiation of Identities in Multilingual Contexts*. Clevedon: Multilingual Matters.

Pavlenko, A. and J. P. Lantolf. 2000. 'Second language learning as participation and the (re)construction of selves' in J. P. Lantolf (ed.). 2000: *Sociocultural Theory and Second Language Learning*. Oxford: Oxford University Press.

Pennycook, A. 1994. *The Cultural Politics of English as an International Language*. London: Longman.

Pennycook, A. 1999a. 'Introduction: critical approaches to TESOL'. *TESOL Quarterly* 33/3: 329–48.

Pennycook, A. 1999b. 'Pedagogical implications of different frameworks for understanding the global spread of English' in C. Gnutzmann (ed.): *Teaching and Learning English as a Global Language. Native and Non-native Perspectives*. Tübingen: Stauffenburg.

Pennycook, A. 2007. *Global Englishes and Transcultural Flows*. London: Routledge.

Pennycook, A. 2009. 'Plurilithic Englishes: towards a 3D model' in K. Murata and J. Jenkins (eds.): *Global Englishes in Asian Contexts. Current and Future Debates*. London: Continuum.

Peters, P., P. Collins, and A. Smith (eds.). 2009. *Comparative Studies in Australian and New Zealand English. Grammar and Beyond*. javascript:zoom('Hardbound,e-Book,/178/veaw_g39.png') Amsterdam: John Benjamins.

Phan Le Ha. 2008. *Teaching English as an Intercultural Language: Identity, Resistance and Negotiation*. Clevedon: Multilingual Matters.

Phillipson, R. 1992. *Linguistic Imperialism*. Oxford: Oxford University Press.

Phillipson, R. 2003a. *English-Only Europe?* London: Routledge.

Phillipson, R. 2003b. ' "World English" or "World Englishes"? On negating polyphony and multicanonicity of Englishes.' (Review of Brutt-Griffler: *World English: A study of its Development*)' Point-Counterpoint, Perspective 2. *World Englishes* 22/3: 324–26.

Phillipson, R. 2004. ' "Response" to a comment by Janina Brutt-Griffler'. *World Englishes* 23/2: 333–4.

Phillipson, R. 2009. *Linguistic Imperialism Continued*. New York and London: Routledge.

Phillipson, R. and T. Skutnabb-Kangas. 1999. 'Englishisation: one dimension of globalisation' in D. Graddol and U. H. Meinhof (eds.): *English in a Changing World. AILA Review* 13: 19–36.

Phipps, A. M. 2006. *Learning the Arts of Linguistic Survival: Languaging, Tourism, Life.* Clevedon: Multilingual Matters.

Pitzl, M.-L. 2009. ' "We should not wake up any dogs": idiom and metaphor in ELF' in A. Mauranen and E. Ranta (eds.): *English as a Lingua Franca: Studies and Findings.* Newcastle upon Tyne: Cambridge Scholars Publishing.

Pitzl, M.-L. 2010. *English as a Lingua Franca in International Business: Resolving Miscommunication and Reaching Shared Understanding.* Saarbrücken: VDM.

Pitzl, M.-L. 2011. 'Creativity in English as a lingua franca: idiom and metaphor'. Ph.D dissertation, University of Vienna.

Pitzl, M.-L., A. Breiteneder, and T. Klimpfinger. 2008. 'A world of words: processes of lexical innovation in VOICE'. *Vienna English Working Papers* 17/2: 21–46. (Available at http://anglistik.univie.ac.at/fileadmin/user_upload/dep_anglist/weitere_Uploads/Views/views_0802.pdf)

Platt, J., H. Weber, and M. L. Ho. 1984. *The New Englishes.* London: Routledge and Kegan Paul.

Pölzl, U. and B. Seidlhofer. 2006. 'In and on their own terms: the "habitat factor" in English as a lingua franca interactions'. *International Journal of the Sociology of Language* 177: 151–76.

Poncini, G. 2004. *Discursive Strategies in Multicultural Business Meetings.* Bern: Peter Lang.

Popper, K. 1959. *The Logic of Scientific Discovery* (transl. of *Logik der Forschung*). London: Hutchinson.

Powell, M. 2010. 'Lean language: streamlining business English'. Plenary talk at BESIG annual conference, Bielefeld. (Video viewable at: http://www.youtube.com/watch?v=oApWoAhSC8g)

Procter, P. (ed.) 1995. *Cambridge International Dictionary of English.* Cambridge: Cambridge University Press.

Prodromou, L. 2007. 'Bumping into creative idiomaticity'. *English Today* 23/1: 14–25.

Prodromou, L. 2008. *English as a Lingua Franca. A Corpus-based Analysis.* London: Continuum.

Pullin, P. 2010. 'Small talk, rapport and international communicative competence: Lessons to learn from BELF'. *Journal of Business Communication* 47/4: 455–76.

Quirk, R. 1962. *The Use of English* (With supplements by A. C. Gimson and J. Warburg). London: Longman.

Quirk, R. 1981. 'International communication and the concept of Nuclear English' in L. E. Smith (ed.): *English for Cross-Cultural Communication.* Basingstoke: Macmillan.

Quirk, R. 1982. 'International communication and the concept of Nuclear English' (reprint of Quirk 1981) in C. Brumfit (ed.): *English for International Communication.* Oxford: Pergamon.

Quirk, R. 1985. 'The English language in a global context' in R. Quirk and H. G. Widdowson (eds.): *English in the World: Teaching and Learning the Languages and Literatures.* Cambridge: Cambridge University Press.

Quirk, R. 1990. 'Language varieties and standard language'. *English Today* 21: 3–10.

Quirk, R. 1995. *Grammatical and Lexical Variance in English.* London: Longman.

Quirk, R. 2006. 'International communication and the concept of Nuclear English' (reprint of Quirk 1981) in K. Bolton and B. B. Kachru (eds.): *World Englishes. Critical Concepts in Linguistics.* Abingdon: Routledge.

Quirk, R., S. Greenbaum, G. Leech, and J. Svartvik. 1972. *A Grammar of Contemporary English.* London, New York: Longman.

Quirk, R. and H. G. Widdowson (eds.). 1985. *English in the World: Teaching and Learning the Languages and Literatures.* Cambridge: Cambridge University Press.

Rampton, B. 1990. 'Displacing the "native speaker": expertise, affiliation and inheritance'. *ELT Journal* 44/2: 97–101.

Rampton, B. 1997. 'Second language research in late modernity'. *The Modern Language Journal* 81: 329–33.

Ranta, E. 2006. 'The "attractive" progressive—Why use the *-ing* form in English as a lingua franca?' *Nordic Journal of English Studies* 5/2: 95–116. NJES Special Issue: *English as a Lingua Franca*: Anna Mauranen and Maria Metsä-Ketelä (eds.).

Ranta, E. 2009. 'Syntactic features in spoken ELF–learner language or spoken grammar?' in A. Mauranen and E. Ranta (eds.): *English as a Lingua Franca: Studies and Findings*. Newcastle upon Tyne: Cambridge Scholars Publishing.

Richards, I. A. 1940. 'Basic as the International Language'. *The Basic News* 9: 17–22.

Richards, I. A. 1943. *Basic English and Its Uses*. London: Kegan Paul, Trench, Trubner and Co.

Richards J. C. and T. S. Rodgers. 2001 (2nd edn.). *Approaches and Methods in Language Teaching*. Cambridge: Cambridge University Press.

Ridley, M. 1996. *The Origins of Virtue*. London: Penguin.

Riley, P. 2007. *Language, Culture and Identity: An Ethnolinguistic Perspective*. London: Continuum.

Roberts, P. 2005. 'Spoken English as a world language: international and intranational settings'. Unpublished PhD dissertation, University of Nottingham.

Rogerson-Revell P. 2008. 'Participation and performance in international business meetings'. *English for Specific Purposes* 27: 338–60.

Rogerson-Revell P. 2010. ' "Can you spell that for us nonnative speakers?" Accommodative strategies in international business meetings'. *Journal of Business Communication* 47/4: 432–54.

Rodgers, T. S. 2009. 'The methodology of foreign language teaching' in K. Knapp and B. Seidlhofer (eds.): *Handbook of Foreign Language Communication and Learning (Handbooks of Applied Linguistics, Volume 6)*. Berlin and New York: Mouton de Gruyter.

Rossiter, A. P. 1932. *Gold Insect: Being The Gold Bug Put into Basic English*. London: George Routledge and Sons.

Routh, H. V. 1944. *Basic English and the Problem of a World-Language*. London: The Royal Society of Literature.

Rubdy, R. 2009. 'Reclaiming the local in teaching EIL'. *Language and Intercultural Communication* 9/3: 156–74.

Rubdy, R. and M. Saraceni (eds.). 2006. *English in the World: Global Rules, Global Roles*. London: Continuum.

Rubin, D. 1992. 'Nonlanguage factors affecting undergraduates' judgments of nonnative English-speaking teaching assistants'. *Research in Higher Education* 33/4: 511–31.

Samarin. W. 1987. 'Lingua franca' in U. Ammon, N. Dittmar, and K. Mattheier (eds.): *Sociolinguistics: An International Handbook of the Science of Language and Society*. Berlin: Walter de Gruyter.

Sand, A. 2008. 'Angloversals? Concord and interrogatives in contact varieties of English' in T. Terttu Nevalainen, I. Taavitsainen, P. Päivi Pahta, and M. Korhonen, M. *The Dynamics of Linguistic Variation. Corpus Evidence on English Past and Present*. Amsterdam: John Benjamins.

Sankoff, G. 2002. 'Linguistic outcomes of language contact' in J. K. Chambers, P. Trudgill, and N. Schilling-Estes (eds.). 2002. *Handbook of Language Variation and Change*. Oxford: Blackwell.

Saraceni, M. 2009. 'Relocating English: towards a new paradigm for English in the world'. *Language and Intercultural Communication* 9/3: 175–86.

Saville-Troike, M. 2003. (3rd edn.). *The Ethnography of Communication: An Introduction*. Oxford: Blackwell.

Saxena, M. and T. Omoniyi (eds.). 2010. *Contending with Globalization in World Englishes*. Clevedon: Multilingual Matters.

Schaller-Schwaner, I. 2008. 'ELF in academic settings: working language and edulect, prestige and solidarity'. Paper presented at the ELF Forum: The First International Conference of English as a Lingua Franca, Helsinki University, March.

Schegloff, E. A. 1972. 'Notes on a conversational practice: formulating place' in D. Sudnow (ed.): *Studies in Social Interaction*. New York: Free Press.

Schmitt, N. and R. Carter. 2004. 'Formulaic sequences in action. An introduction' in N. Schmidt (ed.): *Formulaic Sequences*. Amsterdam: John Benjamins.

Schneider, E. W. (ed.). 1997. *Englishes around the World. Vol. I: General Studies, British Isles, North America. Vol. II. Caribbean, Africa, Asia, Australasia. Studies in Honour of Manfred Görlach*. Amsterdam, Philadelphia: John Benjamins.

Schneider, E. W. 2003. 'The dynamics of New Englishes: From identity construction to dialect birth'. *Language* 79/2: 233–81.

Schneider, E. W. 2007. *Postcolonial English: Varieties around the World*. Cambridge: Cambridge University Press.

Schneider, E. 2010. 'Developmental patterns of English. Similar or different?' in A. Kirkpatrick (ed.): *The Routledge Handbook of World Englishes*. Abingdon: Routledge.

Schön, D. A. 1983. *The Reflective Practitioner: How Professionals Think in Action*. New York: Basic Books.

Scollon, R. and S. Wong Scollon. 2001 (2nd edn.). *Intercultural Communication*. Oxford: Blackwell.

Searle, J. R. 1969. *Speech Acts*. Cambridge: Cambridge University Press.

Searle, J. R. 1995. *The Construction of Social Reality*. New York: Free Press.

Seidlhofer, B. 1999. 'Double standards: teacher education in the Expanding Circle'. *World Englishes* 18: 233–45.

Seidlhofer, B. 2001. 'Closing a conceptual gap: the case for a description of English as a lingua franca'. *International Journal of Applied Linguistics* 11: 133–58. (Available at http://www.univie.ac.at/voice/documents/seidlhofer_2001b.pdf)

Seidlhofer, B. 2002. 'The shape of things to come? Some basic questions about English as lingua franca' in K. Knapp and C. Meierkord (eds.): *Lingua Franca Communication*. Frankfurt am Main: Peter Lang. (Also available at http://www.basic-english.org/member/articles/seidlhofer.html)

Seidlhofer, B. 2003a. *A Concept of 'International English' and related issues: from 'real English' to 'realistic English'? Autour du concept «d'anglais international»: de «l'anglais authentique» à «l'anglais réaliste»?* Strasbourg: Council of Europe. (Available at http://www.coe.int)

Seidlhofer, B. (ed.). 2003b. *Controversies in Applied Linguistics*. Oxford: Oxford University Press.

Seidlhofer, B. 2004. 'Research perspectives on teaching English as a lingua franca'. *Annual Review of Applied Linguistics* 24: 209–39.

Seidlhofer, B. 2005. 'Standard future or half-baked quackery? Descriptive and pedagogic bearings on the globalisation of English' in C. Gnutzmann and F. Intemann (eds.): *The Globalisation of English and the English Language Classroom*. Tübingen: Gunter Narr.

Seidlhofer, B. 2007. 'English as a lingua franca and communities of practice' in S. Volk-Birke, and J. Lippert. (eds.): *Anglistentag 2006 Halle Proceedings*. Trier: Wissenschaftlicher Verlag Trier.

Seidlhofer, B. 2009a. 'Accommodation and the idiom principle in English as a lingua franca'. *Intercultural Pragmatics* 6/2: 195–215.

Seidlhofer, B. 2009b. 'ELF findings: form and function' in A. Mauranen and E. Ranta (eds.): *English as a Lingua Franca: Studies and Findings*. Newcastle upon Tyne: Cambridge Scholars.

Seidlhofer, B. 2009c. 'Common ground and different realities: World Englishes and English as a lingua franca'. *World Englishes* 28/2: 236–45.

Seidlhofer, B. 2010. 'Lingua franca English: the European context' in A. Kirkpatrick (ed.): *The Routledge Handbook of World Englishes*. Abingdon: Routledge.

Seidlhofer, B., A. Breiteneder, and M.-L. Pitzl. 2006. 'English as a lingua franca in Europe: challenges for applied linguistics'. *Annual Review of Applied Linguistics* 26: 1–34.

Seidlhofer, B. and H. G. Widdowson. 2007. 'Idiomatic variation and change in English. The idiom principle and its realizations' in U. Smit, S. Dollinger, J. Hüttner, G. Kaltenböck, and U. Lutzky (eds.): *Tracing English through Time. Explorations in Language Variation.* (Festschrift for Herbert Schendl, Austrian Studies in English Vol. 95) Wien: Braumüller.

Seidlhofer, B. and H. G. Widdowson. 2009. 'Conformity and creativity in ELF and learner English' in M. Albl-Mikasa, S. Braun, and S. Kalina. (eds.): *Dimensionen der Zweitsprachenforschung. Dimensions of Second Language Research.* (Festschrift for Kurt Kohn) Tübingen: Narr Verlag.

Sfard, A. 2008. *Thinking as Communicating: Human Development, the Growth of Discourses, and Mathematizing.* Cambridge: Cambridge University Press.

Sharifian, F. (ed.) 2009. *English as an International Language. Perspectives and Pedagogical Issues.* Bristol: Multilingual Matters.

Shohamy, E. 2001. *The Power of Tests: A Critical Perspective on the Uses of Language Tests.* London: Pearson.

Shohamy, E. 2007. 'The power of language tests, the power of the English language, and the role of ELT' in J. Cummins and C. Davison (eds.): *International Handbook of English Language Teaching.* Part I. New York: Springer.

Sifakis, N. C. 2007. 'The education of teachers of English as a lingua franca: a transformative perspective'. *International Journal of Applied Linguistics* 17/3: 355–75.

Sinclair, J. M. 1991. 'Shared knowledge' in J. Alatis (ed.): *Linguistics and Language Pedagogy: The State of the Art.* Washington DC: Georgetown University Press.

Sinclair, J. M. (ed.). 1995. *Collins Cobuild English Dictionary: Helping Learners with Real English.* (2nd edn.). London: Harper Collins.

Skutnabb-Kangas, T. 1984. *Bilingualism or not—The Education Of Minorities.* Clevedon: Multilingual Matters.

Skutnabb-Kangas, T. 2000. *Linguistic Genocide in Education—or Worldwide Diversity and Human Rights?* Mahwah, NJ and London: Lawrence Erlbaum Associates.

Smit, U. 2010. *English as a Lingua Franca in Higher Education. A Longitudinal Study of Classroom Discourse.* Berlin: Mouton de Gruyter.

Smith, L. (ed.). 1981. *English for Cross-cultural Communication.* London: Macmillan.

Smith, L. and M. Forman (eds.). 1997. *World Englishes 2000.* Honolulu, Hawai'i: College of Languages, Linguistics and Literature and the East-West Center.

Sobkowiak, W. 2005. 'Why Not LFC?' in K. Dziubalska-Kołaczyk and J. Przedlacka (eds.) *English Pronunciation Models: A Changing Scene.* Frankfurt: Peter Lang.

Spencer-Oatey, H. (ed.). 2000. *Culturally Speaking: Managing Rapport through Talk across Cultures.* London: Continuum.

Stewart, W. A. 1968. 'A sociolinguistic typology for describing national multilingualism' in J. Fishman (ed.): *Readings in the Sociology of Language.* The Hague: Mouton.

Strevens, P. 1980. *Teaching English as an International Language.* Oxford: Pergamon.

Strevens, P. and E. Johnson. 1983. 'SEASPEAK: A project in applied linguistics, language engineering, and eventually ESP for sailors'. *ESP Journal* Vol. 2/2: 123–9.

Swain, M. 2006. 'Languaging, agency and collaboration in advanced second language proficiency' in H. Byrnes (ed.). *Advanced Language Learning: The Contribution of Halliday and Vygotsky.* London: Continuum.

Swain, M. and P. Deters. 2007. ' "New" mainstream SLA theory: expanded and enriched'. *The Modern Language Journal* 91 (Issue supplement s1): 820–36.

Swales, J. 1990. *Genre Analysis.* Cambridge: Cambridge University Press.

Swan, M. 2009. 'Review of L. Prodromou, *English as a Lingua Franca: A Corpus-based Analysis*'. *ELT Journal* 63/1: 78–81.

Sweeney E. and H. Zhu. 2010. 'Accommodating toward your audience. Do native speakers of English know how to accommodate their communication strategies toward nonnative speakers of English?'. *Journal of Business Communication* 47/4: 477–504.

Taylor, L. 2006. 'The changing landscape of English: implications for language assessment'. *ELT Journal* 60/1: 51–60.

Templer, B. 2005. 'Towards a people's English: back to BASIC in EIL'. *Humanising Language Teaching* September 2005. (www.hltmag.co.uk/sepo5/marto5.htm, accessed 18 Sept 2010). *The Daily Telegraph, electronic edition of May 19 2011*. London: The Daily Telegraph plc, 1992. *The Observer*. 29.10.2000: 1. *The Times*. May 2000: 4.

Thije, J. D. ten and L. Zeevaert (eds.). 2007. *Receptive Multilingualism. Linguistic Analyses, Language Policies and Didactic Concepts*. Amsterdam: John Benjamins.

Thompson, A. 2006. 'English in context in an East Asian intercultural workplace'. Ph.D. thesis, Ontario Institute for Studies in Education, University of Toronto.

Thornbury, S. 1997. *About Language* Cambridge: Cambridge University Press.

Thumboo, E. 2006. 'Literary creativity in world Englishes' in B. B. Kachru, Y. Kachru, and C. Nelson (eds.): *The Handbook of World Englishes*. Malden, MA: Blackwell.

Timmis, I. 2002. 'Native speaker norms and international English: a classroom view'. *ELT Journal* 56/3: 240–49.

Todd, L. and I. Hancock. 1986. *International English Usage*. London: Croom Helm.

Todeva, E. and J. Cenoz (eds.). 2009. *The Multiple Realities of Multilingualism. Personal Narratives and Researchers' Perspectives*. Berlin: Mouton de Gruyter.

Tosi, A. 2005. 'EU translation problems and the danger of linguistic devaluation'. *International Journal of Applied Linguistics* 15/3: 384–88.

Trudgill, P. 1986. *Dialects in Contact*. Oxford: Blackwell.

Trudgill, P. 1999. 'Standard English: what it isn't' in T. Bex and R. J. Watts (eds.): *Standard English: The Widening Debate*. London: Routledge.

Trudgill, P. 2002. *Sociolinguistic Variation and Change*. Edinburgh: Edinburgh University Press.

Trudgill. P. and J. Hannah. 2008. *International English: A Guide to the Varieties of Standard English* (5th edn.). London: Hodder Education.

Tudor, I. 1996. *Learner-centredness as Language Education*. Cambridge: Cambridge University Press.

Tupas, T. R. F. 2006. 'Standard Englishes, pedagogical paradigms and their conditions of (im) possibility' in R. Rubdy and M. Saraceni (eds.): *English in the World: Global Rules, Global Roles*. London: Continuum. 169–85.

van Els, T. 2000. 'The European Union, its institutions and its languages'. Public lecture given at the University of Nijmegen, the Netherlands, 22 Sept. 2000.

van Els, T. 2005. 'Multilingualism in the European Union'. *International Journal of Applied Linguistics* 15/3: 263–81.

van Lier, L. 1995. *Introducing Language Awareness*. Harmondsworth: Penguin Books.

van Parijs, P. 2004. 'Europe's linguistic challenge'. *European Journal of Sociology* 45/1: 113–154. © Archives Européennes de Sociologie.

Vikør, L. 2004. 'Lingua franca and international language. Verkehrssprache und Internationale Sprache' in U. Ammon, N. Dittmar, K. Mattheier, and P. Trudgill. (eds.): *Sociolinguistics. Soziolinguistik. An International Handbook of the Science of Language and Society. Ein internationals Handbuch zur Wissenschaft von Sprache und Gesellschaft* (2nd edn.). Berlin and New York: Walter de Gruyter.

VOICE. 2009. *The Vienna-Oxford International Corpus of English* (version 1.0 online). http://voice.univie.ac.at/Director: Barbara Seidlhofer; Researchers: Angelika Breiteneder, Theresa Klimpfinger, Stefan Majewski, Marie-Luise Pitzl.

Walker, R. 2010. *Teaching the Pronunciation of English as a Lingua Franca*. Oxford: Oxford University Press.

Watterson, M. 2008. 'Repair of non-understanding in English in international communication'. *World Englishes* 27: 378–406.

Webster, J. (ed.). 2003. *The Collected Works of M. A. K. Halliday. Vol 3: On Language and Linguistics*. London and New York: Continuum.

Weeks, F., A. Glover, E. Johnson, and P. Strevens. 1988. *Seaspeak Training Manual: Essential English for International Maritime Use*. Oxford: Pergamon Press.

Wells, H. G. 1933. *The Shape of Things to Come*. London: Hutchinson and Co.

Wenger, E. 1998. *Communities of Practice*. Cambridge: Cambridge University Press.

West, M. P. 1934/1936. *On Learning to Speak a Foreign Language*. London: Longmans, Green, and Co.

West, M. P. 1953. *A General Service List of English Words: With Semantic Frequencies and a Supplementary Word-List for the Writing of Popular Science and Technology*. London: Longman.

West, M. P. and E. Swenson. 1934. *A Critical Examination of Basic English. Bulletin No. 2 of the Department of Educational Research*. Ontario College of Education: University of Toronto Press.

Widdowson, H. G. 1983. *Learning Purpose and Language Use*. Oxford: Oxford University Press.

Widdowson, H. G. 1990. *Aspects of Language Teaching*. Oxford: Oxford University Press.

Widdowson, H. G. 1994. 'The ownership of English'. *TESOL Quarterly* 28/2: 377–89.

Widdowson, H. G. 1997a. 'EIL, ESL, EFL: global issues and local interests'. *World Englishes* 16/1: 135–46.

Widdowson, H. G. 1997b. 'The pedagogic relevance of language awareness'. *Fremdsprachen Lehren und Lernen* (FluL) 26: 33–43

Widdowson, H. G. 1998. 'Skills, abilities, and contexts of reality'. *Annual Review of Applied Linguistics*, Vol. 18: 323–33.

Widdowson, H. G. 2003. *Defining Issues in English Language Teaching*. Oxford: Oxford University Press.

Widdowson, H. G. 2008. 'Language creativity and the poetic function. A response to Swann and Maybin (2007)'. *Applied Linguistics* 29/3: 503–08.

Widdowson, H. G. 2009. 'The linguistic perspective' in K. Knapp and B. Seidlhofer (eds.): *Handbook of Foreign Language Communication and Learning (Handbooks of Applied Linguistics, Volume 6)*. Berlin and New York: Mouton de Gruyter.

Widdowson, H. G. and B. Seidlhofer. 2003. 'The virtue of the vernacular: on intervention in linguistic affairs' in D. Britain, and J. Cheshire (eds.): *Social Dialectology. In honour of Peter Trudgill*. Amsterdam/Philadelphia: John Benjamins.

Williams, R. 1983. [1976]. *Keywords. A Vocabulary of Culture and Society*. London: Fontana.

Wittgenstein, L. 1953/2001. *Philosophical Investigations* (transl. by G. E. M. Anscombe). Oxford: Blackwell.

Wolfartsberger A. 2011. 'ELF business/business ELF: form and function in simultaneous speech' in A. Archibald, A. Cogo, and J. Jenkins (eds.) (2011): *Latest Trends in ELF Research*. Newcastle upon Tyne: Cambridge Scholars Publishing.

Wolff, D. 2009. 'Content and language integrated teaching' in K. Knapp and B. Seidlhofer. (eds.): *Handbook of Foreign Language Communication and Learning (Handbooks of Applied Linguistics, Volume 6)*. Berlin and New York: Mouton de Gruyter.

Wolff, H. 1959. 'Intelligibility and inter-ethnic attitudes'. *Anthropological Linguistics* 1/3: 34–41.

World Englishes Special Issue on ICE: Volume 23 Issue 2: 225–337 (May 2004), G. Nelson (ed.).

Wright, S. 2004. *Language Policy and Language Planning: From Nationalism to Globalisation*. London, Basingstoke: Palgrave Macmillan.

Wright, S. 2008. 'The case of the crucial and problematic lingua franca'. Paper given at AILA, Duisburg-Essen. August.

Wright, S. 2009. 'The elephant in the room'. *European Journal of Language Policy* 1.2: 93–120.

Wyss-Bühlmann, E. 2005. *Variation and Co-operative Communication Strategies in Air Traffic Control English*. Bern: Lang.

Zuengler, J. and J. Miller. 2006. 'Cognitive and sociocultural perspectives: two parallel SLA worlds?' *TESOL Quarterly* 40/I: 35–58.

Index

franchise language idea 67
free language, lingua franca defined as 81
French 3, 54
frequency, principle of 179–80
'from the house' example 135
function vs form
  in ELF 124–48
  as focus of pedagogical approaches 176,
    199–200
  in learners 195
  and variation 95–6
functional need *see also* communication,
    focus on
  code switching vs style-shifting 72–3, 104–5
  driving learning 187–90
  forms evolving to meet 126
  highly restricted languages 156
  motivation for learning 199–200
  multilingualism 68–9
  vs codified norms 73

Gal, S. 10
games, language analogized as 94, 113–14, 184
Gavioli, L. 63 n11
generative grammar 118
geography, not involved in ELF 84, 86–7
Ghanaian English 76
Giles, H. 101
Gleick, J. 114
globalization
  defined 81–2
  and ELF 7–8
  and English 81–8
  postmodern phenomenon, ELF as 73–4
globalized EIL vs localized EIL 3–4, 9
globalized English 153, 157
Globish 153, 156–8, 162, 171, 176
Gnutzmann, C. 12, 203
Gordon, E. 47
Görlach, M. 69, 192
Graddol, D. 1–2, 8, 62 n5, 64–5, 203
grammar
  focus on 112–13
  and marking social membership 128
  as sign of 'real' English 44, 58
Granger, S. 26 n18
Greenbaum, S. 21
Gricean cooperative principle 132
group membership 77–8
Guido, M. G. 49–50, 81, 121 n7, 210 n8

Hall, S. 85
Halliday, M. A. K. 86, 95, 117, 124, 125,
  148, 189, 196, 199

Hanks, J. 12
Hannah, J. 44, 58
'head and tails' example 142
headlines 145
health scares 125
hegemony 33–4, 38, 55–6, 65, 78
Held, D. 81–2
Hickey, R. 92 n2
historicity 170
Ho, M. L. 209 n4
Hoffman, C. 57
Hollett, V. 206
Holliday, A. 12, 56, 191, 200, 205
Hon, D. 157, 158
Honna, N. 122 n17
Hopper, P. 109
Hornby, A. S. 177
House, J. 7, 16, 38, 54, 68, 100
Housen, A. 184
Howatt, A. P. R. 175, 179
Huddleston, R. 20
Hülmbauer, C. vii, 10, 99, 104–5
human rights, linguistic 40, 58, 65
hybrid ways of speaking 4, 112
Hymes, D. 84, 90–1, 96, 109, 115, 132

IAWE conference 2007 76
ICE (International Corpus of English)
  21, 47
ICLE (International Corpus of Learner
  English) 21
ideal speaker–listener 72, 89, 90
ideational function 124, 125–8
identity
  and accents 128
  acts of identity 85, 97, 109, 114
  deterritorialized social identities 85–6
  and globalization 82
  and grammar 128
  group identity and linguistic
    boundaries 77–8
  identity formation 61
  indigenized varieties 83
  and language use 51–3, 85, 97
  retaining L1 identity 51
  use of L1 116
idioms and idiomatic usage
  article use 127
  as conformity/cooperative
    imperative 129–30
  corpora recording 58–9
  de-idiomatization 142
  dynamic construction of local 131
  and ELF 132–4

and English Language Teaching 190–1
and variation 74–81
  World Englishes paradigm 5
World Englishes (journal) 69
Wright, S. 55, 80, 81

Zeevaert, L. 41 n4
zero articles 127
zero morphemes 105–6, 108,
  144–5
Zhu, H. 41 n6